SPECIALIZATION, EXCHANGE, AND COMPLEX SOCIETIES

T0381985

SPECIALIZATION, EXCHANGE, AND COMPLEX SOCIETIES

EDITED BY
ELIZABETH M. BRUMFIEL
AND TIMOTHY K. EARLE

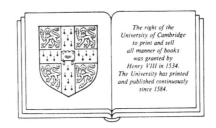

The right of the
University of Cambridge
to print and sell
all manner of books
was granted by
Henry VIII in 1534.
The University has printed
and published continuously
since 1584.

CAMBRIDGE UNIVERSITY PRESS

CAMBRIDGE

LONDON   NEW YORK   NEW ROCHELLE

MELBOURNE   SYDNEY

CAMBRIDGE UNIVERSITY PRESS
Cambridge, New York, Melbourne, Madrid, Cape Town, Singapore, São Paulo, Delhi

Cambridge University Press
The Edinburgh Building, Cambridge CB2 8RU, UK

Published in the United States of America by Cambridge University Press, New York

www.cambridge.org
Information on this title: www.cambridge.org/9780521321181

© Cambridge University Press 1987

First published 1987
This digitally printed version 2008

A catalogue record for this publication is available from the British Library

Library of Congress Cataloguing in Publication data
Specialization, exchange, and complex societies.
(New direction in archaeology)
1. Commerce, Prehistoric.   2. Social structure.
3. Social evolution.   4. Occupations – History
I. Brumfiel, Elizabeth M.   II. Earle, Timothy K.
III. Series.
GN799.C45S74 1986   305   86-6856

ISBN 978-0-521-32118-1 hardback
ISBN 978-0-521-09088-9 paperback

CONTENTS

CONTRIBUTORS

Gina L. Barnes, Department of Archaeology, University of Cambridge.

Elizabeth M. Brumfiel, Department of Anthropology and Sociology, Albion College, Albion, MI.

Timothy K. Earle, Department of Anthropology, The University of California, Los Angeles.

Kathleen F. Galvin, L.S.B. Leakey Foundation, Pasadena, California.

Antonio Gilman, Department of Anthropology, California State University, Northridge.

Kristian Kristiansen, National Agency for the Protection of Nature, Monuments and Sites, Copenhagen.

Jon Muller, Department of Anthropology, Southern Illinois University, Carbondale.

Prudence M. Rice, Department of Anthropology, University of Florida, Gainesville.

Michael Rowlands, Department of Anthropology, University College London.

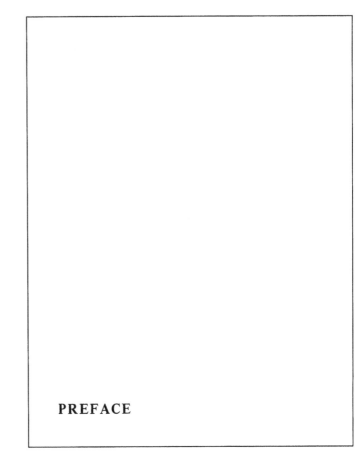

PREFACE

Both of us have shared similar intellectual histories since being graduate students together at The University of Michigan. Although this volume is our first collaboration, we have found over the years that our intellectual developments have paralleled each other. Starting in Ann Arbor, home of some of the best adaptationist theory in American archaeology, we developed independently in our dissertation research on the Aztec state and Hawaiian chiefdoms an understanding of the critical role of political manipulation in the evolution of complex society. This present volume represents another parallel step; as we read each others papers, it was difficult to continue to separate out our personal intellectual contributions. Such collaboration is certainly unusual.

The present volume began in 1980, when Tim Earle was asked by the Program Committee of the XIth International Congress of Anthropological and Ethnological Sciences to organize a symposium "Specialization and

exchange in the development of complex society: archaeological evidence." He organized nine speakers including the two co-editors of this volume, Jim Allen, Kathleen Galvin, Antonio Gilman, Kristian Kristiansen, Prudence Rice, Vincas Steponaitis, and Henry Wright. As final plans changed, Gilman, Steponaitis and Wright had to drop out and were sorely missed. The symposium took place in the Vancouver phase of the Congress, August 1983. All who participated in the session felt a common spirit and interest unusual to symposia, and we sensed the possibility of a tightly integrated treatment of the relationships between social and economic development. At this time Liz Brumfiel took over as the guiding hand of the volume. To increase the breadth of cases covered, four additional papers were solicited from Gina Barnes, Antonio Gilman, Jon Muller and Michael Rowlands. With the encouragement and support of the editorial staff of the Cambridge University Press we completed the editing of this volume in June 1985.

Chapter 1

Specialization, exchange, and complex societies: an introduction

Elizabeth M. Brumfiel and Timothy K. Earle

Most previous treatments of specialization, exchange and social complexity have followed one of three models: a commerical development model, an adaptationist model, or a political model. A review of these models, and some of the difficulties they encounter, will enable us to identify those issues concerning the relationship of specialization, exchange and complexity which need further clarification and research.

In the commercial development model, increases in specialization and exchange are seen as an integral part of the spontaneous process of economic growth. A growing economy encourages individuals to avail themselves of the efficiencies of specialization and exchange, and as the division of labor becomes more elaborate, social complexity increases. Engels (1972 [1884]) presented an early variant of this model. According to Engels, economic growth was rooted in technological improvements that made possible the production of surplus goods, their commercial exchange, and the taking of profits. Surplus production, exchange and profits generated a widening array of differentiated statuses: farmers and craftsmen, merchants and slaves, creditors and debtors, rich and poor. Finally, to maintain order in the face of burgeoning social heterogeneity, the state was born, adding its own specialized personnel to the already existing profusion of social types.

Jacobs (1969, 1984), Renfrew (1969, 1972, 1975), Parsons and Price (1971), Millon (1973), Evans (1978), and

Zeitlin (1979) might also be regarded as following a commercial development model. They envision an economic system with three definitive characteristics: first, an elaborate division of labor in both utilitarian goods and luxuries, second, an exchange system that caters to a regional population of both commoner and elite consumers, and third, an economy that is relatively free of political administration. Although elite demand for exotic goods is sometimes seen as an initial stimulus to production and exchange in the regional economy (Parsons and Price 1971, 179; Zeitlin 1979, 174), little emphasis is placed upon political elites as organizers of the economy. The intensification of specialization and exchange is regarded as an autonomous process dictated by economic efficiency and the pursuit of individual advantage. Local rulers assume no special role as economic actors.

Commercial development often does stimulate social complexity, as documented by Jacobs (1984), but it may also reduce complexity on the peripheries of commercial systems (Stavenhagen 1968; Frank 1969; Wallerstein 1974; Wolf 1982). However, cases of social complexity *originating* through commercial development must be relatively few. Sustained commercial development requires that land and labor be treated as commodities, and this seems to occur only after an extended period of political centralization and inequality (Polanyi 1944, 56–76; Wheatley 1971, 281–89; Sahlins 1972, 92–93). Further, sustained commercial development requires that sizable profits accumulate in private hands, escaping political appropriation. This would have rarely happened (Eisenstadt 1963, 318; Wallerstein 1974, 15). These considerations have favored models of specialization, exchange and social complexity where development occurs under conditions of extensive economic intervention by political elites.

The multifaceted adaptationist model is one such effort. In this model, political elites are assumed to intervene in the economy; in fact, the ability of political leaders to organize a more effective subsistence economy is considered the *raison d'être* of powerful leaders. Powerful, centralized leadership is seen as developing in environmental and demographic contexts where effective economic management is either necessary or especially beneficial.

One version of the adaptationist model sees specialization and exchange developing as a part of an economy based upon redistribution (Polanyi 1944, 48–49; Sahlins 1958; Service 1958, 1962, 1975; Fried 1960). In regions of high resource diversity (i.e., where different locales are optimally suited to producing different things), specialization and redistributive exchange would confer substantial benefits. They would enhance productivity, diversify subsistence, and provide insurance against food failures in one sector or another (Fried 1960, 710; Peebles 1971; Gall and Saxe 1977; Isbell 1978; Price 1979; Halstead and O'Shea 1982). Goods accumulating under the leader's control might also be used to sponsor craft production and public works (Sahlins 1958, 7; Service 1962, 147–50). The prestige gained by the leader's effective management of specialization and exchange would be a major support of his leadership.

The initial version of the redistributive model as articulated by Service (1962, 1975) implied the central accumulation and distribution of large amounts of subsistence goods across microenvironmental borders: coastal products to inland populations and the reverse, highland products to lowland populations and the reverse, urban craft goods to rural food producers, rural food to urban craft specialists, and so on. Accumulating evidence suggests, however, that the redistribution of significant quantities of subsistence goods across microenvironments is not a typical feature of chiefly economies and early states (Earle 1977, 1978; Peebles and Kus 1977; Muller 1978a). Current proponents of the redistributive model now emphasize redistribution as a means of managing resource perturbation (Isbell 1978; Halstead and O'Shea 1982; Muller, Chapter 2).

The benefits of specialization and exchange might also be realized by petty market exchange (Sanders 1956). A second version of the adaptationist model proposes that centralized leadership develops in regions of high resource diversity to facilitate market exchange. The government maintains peace within the market region and mediates the diverse interests of various kinds of specialists (Sanders 1965, 6; Sanders and Price 1968, 188–93). This model is supported by evidence of intensified regional exchange in the Valley of Mexico during its unification under the Aztec state, although, urban growth

rather than resource diversity may have triggered this intensification (Brumfiel 1980, n.d.).

A third version of the adaptationist model (following Wittfogel 1957) centers upon the centralized management of production rather than exchange. A complex local economy might benefit from centralized decision making, particularly in scheduling labor and land for alternative uses. It has been suggested that centrally managed economies would be especially advantageous in regions like Southern Mesopotamia where aridity forces people to devise particularly complex subsistence strategies (Hole 1966; Wright 1969; Athens 1977, 375; Redman 1978, 232–34; Galvin, Chapter 10). Johnson (1973; Wright and Johnson 1975) has suggested that economic management was needed to cope with the unpredictable stresses placed on an economy by periodic visits from pastoralists. This model is compatible with evidence of the reorganization of local production and exchange at the time of state emergence on the Susiana Plain in Southwest Iran (Johnson 1973). But it seems doubtful that such reorganization was necessitated by the appearance of full-time pastoralists in Susiana; in nearby Southern Mesopotamia, full-time pastoralism did not occur until 1500 years after the emergence of the state (Galvin, Chapter 10).

A fourth version of the adaptationist model suggests that centralized leadership develops to sponsor long-distance trade. Rathje (1971, 1972) proposed that political development among the Classic Maya resulted from their need to mount large trading expeditions and organize the production of ceremonial paraphernalia, the primary Maya export. In doing so, the Maya elite were able to provide commoners with products essential to their household economies: salt, grinding stones from igneous rock, and obsidian cutting tools. However, Marcus (1983a, 479) argues that commoners were not dependent upon elite sponsored long-distance trade; local sources of salt were available to the Classic Maya, and locally available limestone and chert could be used for grinding stones and cutting tools. Rice (Chapter 7) provides evidence that goods acquired through interregional exchange rarely circulated to commoner households outside the Classic Maya regional centers.

Flannery (1968) provides an alternative view of interregional exchange in early Mesoamerica. He proposes that long-distance trade, administered by political elites for the purpose of acquiring exotic goods to enhance their status, also enhanced the security of local populations. The exchange of 'wealth' items between elites could have created reciprocal obligations between groups so that in times of stress a more secure population would be willing to share with a less fortunate partner. Flannery distinguishes between the *purpose* of elite sponsored interregional exchange (to acquire status-enhancing symbols) and its *function* (to enhance the security of local populations). To many, Flannery's functional explanation has seemed superfluous, the purposes of elites being entirely sufficient to account for their participation in exchange. In fact, Flannary's article is transitional, presenting an adaptationist argument while opening the way for political approaches to specialization, exchange and social complexity.

Although many of the adaptationist arguments are contradicted by archaeological or ethnographic evidence, as a group, they have stimulated excellent studies of local production and resource procurement in situations of developing social complexity. Such studies indicate that increases in centralized leadership are often accompanied by significant changes in local subsistence patterns (the construction of irrigated fields, agricultural terraces, etc.) and the reorganization of local and regional exchange (Murra 1960; Johnson 1973; Palerm 1973; Matheny 1976; Earle 1978; Harrison and Turner 1978; Brumfiel 1980; Blanton *et al.* 1981, 43–109). However, in several documented cases, political intervention in the economy has had as its object financing governmental institutions and extending political power rather than enlarging or improving the resource base of local commoners (Murra 1960; Earle 1978; Brumfiel 1980). In other cases, the power of political elites has grown without any elite-sponsored improvements of the local resource base (Gilman 1981; Kristiansen, Chapter 4). Such cases contradict the premises of the adaptationist model, and they have led to the elaboration of political approaches to specialization, exchange, and social complexity, approaches that assign primary emphasis to the goals of political leaders and to the opportunities and constraints under which they labor.

In the political model, local rulers are again given an important role in organizing specialization and exchange, but they, rather than the populations they administer, are regarded as the primary beneficiaries. It is proposed that political elites consciously and strategically employ specialization and exchange to create and maintain social inequality, strengthen political coalitions, and fund new institutions of control, often in the face of substantial opposition from those whose well-being is reduced by such actions. Mobilization, the transfer of goods from producers to political elites, is seen as lying at the heart of political development, sustaining the elites and enabling them to fund new institutions and activities calculated to extend their power (Earle 1978; D'Altroy and Earle 1985). Mobilization is reflected in the changes in local production and exchange that as noted above often accompany political development; it is also reflected in changing patterns of specialization and interregional exchange, which become financed by political elites.

On the one hand, mobilization enables rulers to create new institutions of political control. These are staffed by administrative specialists who carry out critical governmental operations: tax collection, military organization and leadership, judicial decision-making, and law enforcement (Berdan 1975, 120–30; D'Altroy and Earle 1985). On the other hand, mobilization enables rulers to become patrons of certain craft specialties and sponsors of long-distance trade. In doing so, rulers achieve monopoly control over certain classes of goods, often articles of social prestige, 'wealth,' as opposed to subsistence goods, which serve as useful tools in extending political

power. Thus, this perspective includes within its analytical framework not only the subsistence economy, but also the production and exchange of wealth, a sphere of activity that commonly intensifies during periods of political development but which is often dismissed as non-essential and unimportant by those taking an adaptationist perspective (Tourtellot and Sabloff 1972; Price 1979; Sanders 1984; cf. Schneider's 1977 critique).

The political model comes in several versions, each presenting a different interpretation of how the ruler's control of certain products through the sponsorship of craft production or trade would translate into increased power. In one version, monopoly over foreign commerce is regarded primarily as a source of profit to the ruler, a source of income that can be invested in an array of mechanisms for augmenting the leader's power (Webb 1975; Kohl 1978, 472; Classen 1984; Santley 1984). In a second version, a ruler achieves coercive power over a population by monopolizing certain food crops, tools or weaponry. His ability to withhold these goods from those who oppose him establishes a base upon which to build other forms of control (Kottak 1972; Friedman and Rowlands 1978, 219; Ma 1980; Sanders 1984).

A third version of the political model suggests that the control and manipulation of wealth is a key factor in building political power. Wealth can come into play in the initial stages of social ranking. An individual may establish superior social rank by displaying the symbols associated with a foreign, already established elite (Flannery 1968, Wheatley 1975) or by monopolizing and manipulating the sacred symbols of his own population's cosmology, (Webb 1974; Friedman 1975; Drennan 1976; Earle 1978; Chang 1980; Rowlands 1980; Haselgrove 1982). Control over wealth can also be used to attract clients and allies to compete for political leadership and to cement horizontal alliances that enhance existing Power (Hicks 1981; n.d.b; Kristiansen 1981, 257; 1982, 265; Appel 1982, 31–33; Susan Shennan 1982, 31: Stephen Shennan 1982a, 38).

Wealth distribution can serve as a mechanism for integrating political power on the regional level. It can be used to maintain a nested hierarchy of political leaders exercising power at the local, district, and regional levels (Murra 1962; Ekholm 1972; Phillips and Brown 1975, 22; Schneider 1977; Earle 1978, 184–85; Frankenstein and Rowlands 1978; Friedman and Rowlands 1978, 219; Chang 1980; Hodges 1982; D'Altroy and Earle 1985). The allocation of prestige goods as a means of achieving vertical integration has received considerable attention from Mesoamericanists (Calnek 1978b; Rounds 1979; Blanton *et al.* 1981, 249; Berdan 1982, 101, 105–20; Spencer 1982, 42–62; Blanton and Feinman 1984, Brumfiel n.d.).

Finally, control over prestige goods or wealth when combined with a regional market system could provide a means of supporting administrative and craft specialists working for the state (Calnek 1978a, 101; Brumfiel 1980, 466; D'Altroy and Earle 1985). Once subsistence goods begin to circulate via market exchange, rulers can pay for specialists' services in valuables which can then be used by the specialists to purchase goods for their own maintenance. As D'Altroy and Earle (1985) point out, such systems of 'wealth finance' often replace systems of 'staple finance' in which specialists in the capital draw rations at the palace and provincial administrators are granted access to provincial land, labor, and/or tribute stores for their own support. When staple finance is replaced by wealth finance, centralized political control increases substantially.

Those who have emphasized the importance of elite-sponsored craft production and interregional exchange for political development must deal with the objection that specialized craft production, exchange, and social complexity do not always coincide. There are some instances in which social complexity has increased substantially with no corresponding increase in interregional exchange (Wright 1972; Drennan and Nowack 1984; Earle 1985a). Further investigation of these cases might yield evidence that political development was accompanied by an intensification of elite-sponsored craft production. If so, it would still be possible to argue that the ruler's control of certain products, locally produced or procured through interregional exchange, paves the way for political development. If no such evidence is found, then it will have to be recognized that mobilization through agricultural intensification alone can sometimes provide the basis for development.

There are also a number of cases in which interregional exchange occurs, sometimes on an impressive scale (e.g. Malinowski 1922), with no corresponding complexity of social structure (Sanders 1984, 278−79). These cases accentuate the need for a more refined approach to interregional exchange, sensitive to variation in its character and consequences.

Interregional exchange is not a unitary independent variable. Its character and consequences vary with context, i.e., differences in local ecology, demography, political structure, types of goods exchanged, and the organization of exchange. This has been commented upon several times in recent years (Meillassoux 1971, 86; Hammond 1973, 601; Kohl 1975, 47; Renfrew 1975, 4; Price 1977, 213; Hirth 1984, 146), but it bears repeating. Just as there is no single relationship between food production and social complexity there is no single relationship between specialization, exchange and social complexity. Meaningful statements about specialization, exchange and social complexity can only be made if the variation covered by these general terms is explicitly recognized and taken as the object of study.

Our own comprehension of specialization, exchange and social complexity has been facilitated by distinguishing between subsistence goods and wealth, independent and attached specialists, and staple and wealth finance. In the following pages, these distinctions are explained and then used to discuss the general implications of the individual studies presented in Chapters 2 through 10.

Subsistence goods and wealth

In considering specialization and exchange, it is useful to distinguish between two general classes of goods, subsistence goods and wealth. Although the classes can be seen as somewhat arbitrary divisions of what is essentially a continuum, the separation is at least heuristically valuable. *Subsistence goods* include food, drugs, and production−protection technology used to meet basic household needs. *Wealth* includes primitive valuables used in display, ritual, and exchange and special, rare and highly desired subsistence products.

In all but the simplest of complex societies, rulers must be concerned with the production and exchange of subsistence goods. After all, the basic needs of the ruler and his staff must be met. As discussed below, such needs are generally filled through systems of resource mobilization and state finance. The development of complex society, involving the elaboration of new institutions and growth in the numbers of governmental personnel, entails a corresponding elaboration of subsistence goods production and mobilization to support the growing state.

Governmental management of subsistence goods production, procurement, and distribution to the general population is, of course, a separate issue. The case studies presented in this book suggest that the extent and character of governmental management is highly variable. In a number of cases it seems non-existent; governmental intervention in the subsistence economy does not extend beyond the mobilization of resources for its own support. In at least one case, the Mesopotamian states discussed by Galvin (Chapter 10), state control of subsistence production was nearly all-encompassing.

Rulers frequently take a more active interest in the production/procurement/distribution of wealth. This is not easily explained from an adaptationist perspective, although Flannery (1968) and Sherratt (1976) have offered adaptationist accounts of it. Our own investigations have convinced us that the political importance of wealth derives from its essential role in validating social status, as suggested by Douglas' (1967) seminal essay. The production, display, and distribution of wealth are politically important activities because they are the means by which rulers define their own social statuses and the statuses of others, with all the rights and obligations adhering thereto. Because of this use value, wealth acquires an exchange value and can be used as a means of payment for services rendered the state. When wealth and subsistence goods are freely exchanged, wealth comes to serve as a true currency.

Distinguishing between subsistence goods and wealth seems nonproblematic for most of the contributors to this book. But Rice's (Chapter 7) summary of the indicators used by Maya archaeologists to establish that obsidian was an item of wealth during the Late Classic provides a very useful suggestion of how to distinguish wealth from subsistence goods in the prehistoric record. Obsidian is considered a wealth item because it is concentrated in civic–ceremonial centers as opposed to more 'rural' locales, it was manufactured into unusual, eccentric forms, and it is commonly found in special caches accompanying burials, under stelae, etc. The absence of these traits for obsidian dating to the Postclassic era suggests that obsidian was converted from an item of wealth to a utilitarian commodity by the end of the Late Classic period.

Independent and attached specialists

Specialization involves economic differentiation and interdependence: the existence of individuals who produce goods or services for a broader consumer population. Specialization is a continuum along which any economy can be gauged. At one end of this continuum is the ideal Domestic Mode of Production (Sahlins 1972) in which the division of labor (specialization) is limited to age and sex differences within the family. At the other end of the continuum is the modern industrial economy in which the division of labor is enormously complex (more than 35,000 different kinds of jobs, Lenski and Lenski 1978, 295) and outside specialists produce most of the goods and services used by domestic units. A number of anthropologists have examined specialization of whom Balfet (1965), Rowlands (1971), Trigger (1974), Van der Leeuw (1977), Evans (1978), Rice (1981), Muller (1984a), Tosi (1984), and Beaudry (1984) have provided useful insights for the present discussion.

Specialization is a complex notion that involves a number of dimensions of variation. These include: (1) the affiliation of the specialists (independent or attached); (2) the nature of the product (subsistence goods, wealth items or services); (3) the intensity of specialization (part-time or full-time); (4) the scale of the production unit (individual industry, household industry, workshop industry, village industry, or large scale industry, cf. Van der Leeuw 1977); (5) the volume of output per individual specialist.

The distinction between independent and attached specialists is central to our consideration of specialization and complex society. *Independent specialists* produce goods or services for an unspecified demand crowd that varies according to economic, social, and political conditions. In contrast, *attached specialists* produce goods or provide services to a patron, typically either a social elite or a governing institution. Attached specialists are contractually bound to the patrons for whom they work, and frequently, the patrons insure that all the specialists' basic needs are met. Because production by these two types of specialists is dictated by different principles, independent and attached specialists often differ in terms of their products, intensity, organization, and productivity even when both are members of a single society.

The products, intensity, organization, and productivity of independent specialists are guided by the principles of *efficiency and security*. Independent specialists may produce either subsistence goods or wealth items, any product in which

the gains in efficiency from specialization are relatively great. Specialization can be expected when natural resources are unevenly distributed or when the production process involves some gradually acquired skills or significant economies of scale. Pottery and obsidian blades are typical of the products manufactured by independent specialists.

The intensity of specialization is set by the size of consumer demand and by the stability of exchange institutions. Full-time specialization is practical only in the presence of a sufficiently large aggregate demand and exchange mechanisms sufficiently stable to provide reliable supplies of subsistence goods and raw materials to specialist producers. Even under conditions of a large aggregate demand, part-time specialization will persist if specialists need to be buffered against fluctuations in supply and demand (e.g., Brumfiel 1986). Aggregate demand and the intensity of specialization determine the scale of the production unit. The production unit expands until the optimal mix of efficiency and security is achieved, with less efficient units of production competitively excluded. The scale of the production unit determines the production process and consequently the volume of output per specialist.

For attached specialists, similar ties exist between demand, intensity, organizational efficiency and productivity. In the Inka empire, for example, an increase in the need for textiles used by state institutions resulted in a shift in organization from individual specialists producing for elite patrons to semi-industrial workshops producing for the military and state government (Earle, Chapter 6). Patron institutions and individuals are frequently able to insure the supply of subsistence goods and raw materials to their attached specialists, and thus full-time specialization among attached specialists is often sustained when market conditions are conductive to only part-time specialization among independent producers.

Although production by attached specialists responds to considerations of efficiency and security, it develops first and foremost in response to *needs for control* in the political economy. As described in the papers by Kristiansen (Chapter 4), Earle (Chapter 6), Barnes (Chapter 8) and Brumfiel (Chapter 9), attached specialists are involved in the manufacture of wealth items and weaponry and the provision of institutional services. Specialization arises from the explicit desire of the ruling elites to control the production and distribution of certain politically charged commodities and to direct activities of crucial political importance such as taxation, warfare, and public ritual. Simply stated, specialists develop in close association with ruling elites and institutions as a direct means of strengthening and maintaining control through economic leverage, coercive power, and legitimization.

Guided by different principles, production by independent and attached specialists follows different lines of development. As predicted by the adaptationist model, independent specialization develops in response to resource diversity and increasing population density; urbanization, market development, and stabilized levels of supply and demand are also important. Attached specialization develops largely as a function of elite coercive control and elite income, that is, according to the ability of elites to command specialist production and to attract and maintain specialist producers.

Staple and wealth finance

Political development requires new institutions of political control. These institutions have requirements for personnel, who are removed from subsistence activities, and for special paraphernalia. These requirements must be met through systems of finance that mobilize labor and goods from the general population and distribute them to state institutions and personnel. D'Altroy and Earle (1985) have discussed two major alternatives for accomplishing this, staple finance and wealth finance.

In *staple finance*, subsistence goods are collected by the state 'as a share of commoner produce, as a specified levy, or as produce from land worked with corvee labor' (D'Altroy and Earle 1985, 188). The goods are then paid out to state personnel who use them to meet basic household needs. In *wealth finance*, the state uses some form of wealth as currency; state personnel are alloted wealth which they exchange for subsistence goods, usually through some type of market transaction.

D'Altroy and Earle (1985) point out that staple finance systems are burdened with a major disadvantage; the bulk and weight of subsistence goods make their movement across distances difficult and costly. Despite this problem, staple finance systems prevail in a broad range of complex societies from fairly simple chiefdoms to early imperial states. These include the Mississippian chiefdoms (Muller, Chapter 2), the Hawaiian chiefdoms and the Inka empire (Earle, Chapter 6), the Yamato court of sixth-century Japan (Barnes, Chapter 8), the Aztec empire (Brumfiel, Chapter 9), and the early Mesopotamian states (Galvin, Chapter 10).

Staple finance systems are well suited to small, compact political units such as the Mississippian chiefdoms or the chiefdoms of Copper Age Spain discussed by Gilman (Chapter 3). When the territorial unit becomes more extensive, the collection of subsustence goods must be decentralized. Provincial administrators collect subsistence goods to support provincial government, passing only a fraction of the total on to the paramount ruler. The Hawaiian chiefdoms and Inka empire illustrate such decentralized staple finance systems. But these systems leave provincial administrators in control of an independent financial base that might fund rebellion. Earle (Chapter 6) suggests that the centralized manufacture of status-marking wealth and its distribution to provincial administrators play an important role in counter-acting the rebellious tendencies inherent in territorially extensive staple finance systems.

Another disadvantage of staple finance is that the allocation of all the varied components of household subsistence to numerous household units rapidly becomes impossibly complex

(Calnek 1978a, 101). The development of landed estates attached to specific noble families or public institutions may be one means of reducing the administrative complexities of staple finance. Estates existed in sixth-century Japan, the Aztec empire, and the early Mesopotamian states, all associated with an urban-based elite drawing its support from attached land and labor. These estates represent a potential source of monetary income as well as subsistence goods for their agricultural surpluses can be marketed. Hicks (n.d.b) argues that estate surpluses offer a much more reliable source of marketed food than peasant household surpluses; they make it possible to depend fully upon the market as a supplier of subsistence goods. Thus, the transition from staple to wealth finance is feasible.

Wealth finance systems confer stability and administrative simplicity upon territorially extensive states. The main advantage of wealth-currencies are their high value to weight ratios that permit movement across great distances. This permits a higher degree of centralization in the state economy. By moving wealth long distances and retaining it at the state's center, payment can be made to the peripheries as need arises. This greater control over the means of payment deprives peripheral areas of an independent financial base. The threat of rebellion decreases.

Specialization and exchange in subsistence goods

One of the most important conclusions to be drawn from the cases presented in this book is the lack of importance of subsistence goods specialization for political development. Either such specialization is absent, as among the Mississippian chiefdoms (Muller, Chapter 2), or it is present but carried out with little assistance or interference by political elites, as in Hawaii and the Inka empire (Earle, Chapter 6) and the Late Classic Maya (Rice, Chapter 7). A fairly efficient system of part-time specialization, in subsistence goods production and exchange operated in the Valley of Mexico without its being unified under a regional state, and when such a state did develop, it did not alter the part-time character of specialization (although it did intensify exchange, Brumfiel, Chapter 9). These cases indicate that political elites often do not function as promoters of economic efficiency through redistribution or market management as has sometimes been suggested.

On the one hand, it is probably difficult for political elites to play an important role in redistribution. The difficulties of transporting, storing, and allocating bulky subsistence goods have been mentioned in our earlier discussion of staple finance. Attempts to extend redistribution to the general population would encounter monumental problems. Markets avoid many of the administrative complexities of redistribution, but they also defy regulatory efforts. Whenever the supply of subsistence goods (particularly food) decreases, producer households provision themselves first (Wolf 1966, 16–17; Sahlins 1972, 129), and even draconian efforts by central administrators can fail to pull adequate supplies into market circulation (Gibson 1964, 355; Tilly 1975). On the other hand, peasants seem to resist dependence upon economic institutions that are under the domination of political elites. Such institutions can be more costly as leaders divert some produce for support of the political establishment. They may also be unreliable; leaders will be tempted to withhold needed goods as a tool of political coercion.

In this context, we can begin to understand why the Hawaiians and the Late Classic Maya opted for direct reciprocal exchange: it avoided elite interference and could be stabilized by personalistic obligation. Direct reciprocal exchange is practiced by contemporary Andean villagers for just such reasons (Hopkins 1984). In the Valley of Mexico, the alternative was to engage in specialization and market exchange but only on a part-time basis. Outside the Aztec capital, households maintained a basic self-sufficiency, particularly with respect to food, while augmenting their incomes with market sales and purchases.

Only in Mesopotamia, in the context of large administered estates, was a truly complex division of labor achieved (Galvin, Chapter 10). Galvin's discussion suggests that the early inhabitants of Mesopotamia found their lack of household autonomy acceptable because small household units were simply not viable economic units in the riverine microenvironment. The environment required long-range planning and capital investment which households were not able to supply on their own. Larger estates, administered as large nonegalitarian households, supplied both the economic security and the sizable population needed to support full-time specialization.

Specialization and exchange in wealth

Because of its social status defining properties, wealth must be the object of some interest for political leaders. Wealth validates the leader's right to receive payments in produce and labor from his people and to employ sanctions against them. Wealth also enables a ruler to define the status of others and to finance other people's social ambitions. Wealth frequently serves as the currency of everyday political transactions, enabling the ruler to reward allies and supporters and to monitor and manipulate political ties.

The cases presented in this volume indicate that the procurement and distribution of wealth is as an important a part of the political economy of early complex societies as the mobilization and distribution of subsistence goods to the ruler and his staff. However, no single model adequately explains how wealth operates as a political resource; at least two models are necessary. In one, specialization in the production of wealth is absent; it is the universal production and use of wealth within the population that make it a strategic resource for maintaining nonegalitarian relationships. In the second model, the production of wealth is partly or entirely in the hands of attached specialists; wealth is specifically an elite good and its circulation is restricted.

The first model is proposed to account for the wide dispersion of craft debris in the Mississippian chiefdoms (Muller, Chapter 2) and the chiefdoms of Copper Age Iberia (Gilman, Chapter 3). The dispersion of craft debris suggests the participation of many households in the production of wealth. How can wealth generate nonegalitarian relationships in the absence of elite control over its production? Douglas (1963, 1967) has described an ethnographic situation in which just such relationships prevailed. The production and exchange of raffia cloth among the Lele resulted in the formation of patron–client relationships between older and younger men. Although raffia cloth, the major item of Lele wealth, was woven by all men of the tribe:

> the demand for raffia cloths at every turn in his career and every step in status so overwhelmed a young Lele man that he could not expect to produce raffia for all his own needs. He turned for contributions to the men who were on the receiving end of the system. These old men had themselves passed through all the stages of payment and could now reckon levies of raffia cloth in large amounts. These senior men . . . did not fail to take full advantage of the patron–client opportunities of their situation [Douglas 1967, 132].

Further inequality results when the domestic system of wealth production and exchange is tied to interregional trade (Ekholm 1972; Rowlands 1979). Interacting regional elites can agree to exchange their stores of domestic wealth, each supplying the other with what becomes a stock of exotic wealth. Exotic wealth then supplements or supplants domestic wealth as the customary means of social payment (since elders control the statuses to which young men aspire, they can define the qualifying criteria as best suits them). Clients come to depend upon patrons to supply wealth which they no longer manufacture for themselves.

Among the Lele and the Kongo, hierarchy was created and maintained by the flow of wealth downward from elder to junior, patron to client, in return for deference (and labor? tribute?). Having reached the most junior level of society, the wealth flowed back upward as juniors claimed more senior statuses from their elders. As Ekholm (1972, 133–34) observes, 'the whole thing was to [the junior males'] disadvantage: it secured the position of the group in power − not only the central power, but all the chiefs all the way down the ladder.' Ekholm also points to the voluntaristic character of the hierarchy: each man subordinated himself to his senior to gain dominance over his junior.

Archaeologically, the maintenance of hierarchy through the circulation of wealth should be characterized by the widespread production of wealth items, as observed in the Mississippian chiefdoms and the chiefdoms of Copper Age Iberia. It should result in the widespread deposition of wealth in domestic refuse and in burials. Such is the case with the Mississippian burials described by Muller.

The early Bronze Age cultures of Northern Europe (Kristiansen, Chapter 4) seem to represent a fundamentally different system of translating wealth into prestige and power. Certain classes of wealth (bronze swords and daggers, bronze ornaments and drinking cups) were monopolized by a small segment of the population. These items were truly elite goods, serving to distinguish their bearers from the mass of the population and to exclude the masses from qualifying for positions of economic and political authority. Within the elite stratum, wealth, power and prestige were concentrated in a few key positions as opposed to being corporately shared among all socially qualified individuals. As a result, the key positions were the subject of intense elite rivalry.

It seems likely that successful competition required the formation of coalitions and alliances between elites and that elite wealth mediated many of these relationships. Kristiansen has described the system in the following way:

> The political system of the Nordic Bronze Age was extremely competitive and expansive in nature. The competition for rank was dependent on success in creating alliances and partnership . . . Central to the creation of alliances was, apparently, ritual and feasting, as evidenced by ritual gear, rock carvings, imported bronze vessels, golden drinking cups, etc. What circulated within such alliance systems was basically women and bronze . . . The extremely competitive nature of the system is reflected in the changing exchange networks and, more concretely, by the dominant role played by weapons in male equipment [Kristiansen 1981, 257].

Rowlands (1980) provides additional insights as to how the aristocratic, competitive wealth systems of the European Bronze Age may have operated.

Kristiansen's description of the Nordic Bronze Age would apply equally well to the pre-Aztec elites of the Valley of Mexico, the fourth- to fifth-century elites of pre-Yamato Japan (Barnes n.d.), and, perhaps, the Late Classic Maya elites as well. In these systems, inequality was not constituted by the exchange of wealth (as it was among the Lele). Inequality rested upon claims of dominion over land or over people, backed by force if necessary. But the application of coercion required personnel, and to gather and hold a warrior force, a ruler had to offer suitable rewards. The rewards consisted of exalted social position symbolized by similarly exalted items of wealth or wealth items alone by means of which a warrior might independently negotiate the advancement of his social standing.

A tendency exists among those who emphasize the coercive character of these regimes to regard wealth as an index of inequality but not as a causal factor (Gilman 1981, 5; Gamble 1982, 104; Bintliff 1982, 109). We would argue, however, that within these systems there is no priority of force over subsistence goods production, no priority of subsistence goods production over wealth and no priority of wealth over coercion. Following Rowlands' (1979) discussion of production and long-distance trade in Africa, we would argue that coercion, subsistence goods, and wealth were bound together systemically so that each was a necessary condition for the others.

Wealth was acquired through long-distance trade and patronage of skilled craft specialists. The foreign origins and high production costs of wealth maintained its scarcity and its value (Earle 1982). Exotic and highly crafted objects lent themselves well to social, as well as religious, exaltation (cf. Drennan 1976, 357). The excitement of the exotic, the pleasure of the beautiful, and the significance of the symbolic combined to make wealth items powerful statements of social status.

Rulers probably tried to monopolize all long-distance trade and elite craft production within their dominions. For example, Hawaiian chiefs controlled all steps in the production and distribution of feathered cloaks, acquiring the feathers by means of tribute payments, supporting the feather weaving specialists who manufactured the cloaks, and distributing them to subchiefs and potential allies (Earle, Chapter 6). The Bronze Age rulers of Northern Europe seem to have had similar success in monopolizing the production and distribution of bronze weapons and ornaments (Kristiansen, Chapter 4). But monopolies were not always achieved. In pre-Aztec central Mexico, efforts to establish monopolies over exotic and highly crafted goods were frustrated by highly commercialized markets and trading (Brumfiel, Chapter 9). But even in Mexico, advantages in tribute receipts and power probably enabled prudent local rulers to maintain a degree of superiority in acquiring wealth for distribution.

These aristocratic competitive societies seem to have considerable potential for political development. They appear to have contained within themselves an expansionary dynamic (Galvin, Chapter 10), and given a suitable ecological base, they were capable of generating territorially extensive, highly centralized states. In the three cases of state formation dealt with in this volume (the Inka state, the Yamato state, and the Aztec state), wealth distribution continued to play an important role in maintaining power. Not surprising, the newly formed states reorganized the production of wealth to increase the scale of production and bring wealth under tighter state control. According to Earle (Chapter 6), the Inka state removed weavers from their native communities and brought them to Cuzco and other administrative centers where they produced fine cloth for the state on a full-time basis. Earle also presents archaeological evidence of the Inka state assuming control of the manufacture and distribution of metal artifacts. The Yamato state organized the *be*, groups of attached specialists who supplied craft goods and services to the court. Barnes (Chapter 8) suggests that the *be* did not enable the Yamato state to monopolize all wealth production, but they did insure that the state would have a large supply of wealth at its disposal.

The production of wealth flourished under the Aztec state, although much of the production was undertaken by independent specialists who manufactured wealth for market sale. Nevertheless, wealth distribution served the state as an effective tool of political control. Certain wealth items were reserved for use by the ruler alone (Sahagún 1950–69 [1577], Bk. 9, p. 91). In addition, the ruler claimed a monopoly over the right to qualify individuals to display certain wealth items (although Anawalt 1980 claims this monopoly was not enforced). Moreover, the production of goods of the very highest quality under royal patronage, their distribution in public, heavily ritualized contexts, and the distribution of wealth items at no apparent cost to the recipients made wealth distribution an effective political tool even in the absence of a royal monopoly over most forms of wealth production.

Symbols, ideology and political development

The obvious importance of the production and distribution of wealth in early complex societies underscores the integral role played by symbols and ideology in processes of political change. Rowlands' (Chapter 5) discussion of native conceptual systems and political development in the pre-colonial Cameroon chiefdoms focuses upon this issue; it is also touched upon in Brumfiel's (Chapter 9) review of Aztec craft production.

Rowlands stresses that native conceptual systems are needed to understand the political consequences of specialization and exchange. The conceptual systems determine how basic resources and responsibilities are allocated; therefore, they also determine who can produce what, who needs what, who can supply what, and how different segments of society will be affected by changes in production and exchange. For example, the Cameroon chiefdoms were transformed by the new opportunities for wealth introduced by the slave trade. But the fact that the chief's men rather than the lineage elders profited most from the slave trade was a consequence of two facts: those guilty of certain social transgressions could be sold into slavery, and if they were sold, it was the chief's men who did the selling. In Cameroon culture, the chief's men were charged with exercising power in defense of the moral order; this provided a partial legitimation for participating in the slave trade. Lineage elders represented the pure moral order unsullied by coercive force; this effectively excluded their participation.

Rowlands also demonstrates that political change is accompanied by ideological transformations that acknowledge the change and evaluate it. However, innumerable transformations can be made upon any given set of symbolic components, each supplying a different commentary upon actual political behavior. For example, the slave trading that the chief's men counted as defending the moral order was construed as sorcery, a violation of the moral order, by the villagers who were preyed upon. Rowlands argues that elite appeals to moral authority to reproduce the conditions of exploitation will inevitably generate ambiguity and contradiction.

Elites can attempt to resolve ambiguity and smoothe over contradiction. One means of doing so is to employ skilled craftsmen to encode artistic products with symbolic messages that convey the elite point of view. However, it is doubtful that peasants will ever be convinced over long periods of time to accept the necessity of their own exploitation. In contrast, regional elites might be persuaded to exchange one structure of dominance for another. Ideological transformations that offer them promotions in status might be readily accepted; highly crafted items of wealth that express the new ideology would be highly appreciated. The introduction of new art styles and the reorganization of wealth-producing craft specialists are probably good indicators of change in the relationships of regional elites. As the discussions by Barnes, Brumfiel and Earle all suggest, the reorganization of elite relationships is a key task in building centralized regional states.

Chapter 2

Salt, chert, and shell: Mississippian exchange and economy

Jon Muller

Low complexity, chiefdom-level societies present special problems in understanding the development of production and exchange. Although such societies usually have not been distinguished from more complex 'chiefdoms,' they form a transition between so-called 'big-men' or 'tribal' groups and the complex, centralized systems of advanced chiefdom-level societies. The latter societies are, in fact, incipient states and may have more in common with states than with the simpler 'super-tribes' from which they develop. The question of how to best characterize these various levels of development is perplexing, but not serious. The worse mistake is to assume that terms like *chiefdom* or *tribe* (Service 1975; Fried 1967) can be used as though they indicated invariant clusters of attributes which can be checked off on a kind of society watcher's life list. If we had the methods and terminology to do so, the best solution would be simply to examine the development of social and political systems in terms of measures of control, centralization, production, distribution, and so on. This paper will first present an overview of Mississippian social, economic, and political systems, and will then return to these in more detail in order to see how data from these societies relate to the distinction between adaptationist (e.g., Service 1975) and political approaches to the development of complex social systems (e.g., Brumfiel and Earle, Chapter 1; Hodder 1980).

Overview

The Mississippian societies of southeastern North America represent the most complex aboriginal social, economic, and political systems north of Mexico. These societies evolved in the Southeast during the ninth and tenth centuries and persisted into historic times. If these developments were not 'caused' by an increase in use of Mesoamerican cultigens, maize certainly played an important part in the new Mississippian economy. Although maize is known to be present in the East before Mississippian times, there is evidence that its use was relatively unimportant in dietary terms (Bender, Baerreis, and Steventon 1981) until the ninth and tenth centuries. Even after relatively intensive use of maize began, wild foods remained very important – perhaps even exceeding domesticated plants in their contribution to the annual diet. Squash was also an important domesticate, but the domestic bean does not appear to have become common until late in Mississippian times (ca. AD 1200 or later).

Mississippian societies are best known as the latest Eastern 'Moundbuilders'; and their largest sites are truly impressive. Mississippian societies were complex by comparison to other societies in what is today the United States, but the evidence suggests that none of these societies had reached a true state-level of political organization. General population levels were low, and single political entities probably exceeded 10,000 persons in size only rarely. Historic records suggest that some of the chiefs in some areas exercised considerable political power (as discussed in Swanton 1928, 696), but it is notable that those having the most 'absolute' chiefs were those who had been in most intensive and longest direct contact with the European intruders along the coast. Since we also have our best historic documentation for these groups, there has been a possible overemphasis on the more powerful chiefs such as the Natchez Sun as opposed to the confederacies of the Creek, Chickasaw, or Choctaw. Of the existence of powerful elites in these societies, there can be no doubt; but the state-like features of some historic political systems must be examined to establish whether they are survivals of earlier complex systems, as is so often assumed, or whether they are responses to European invaders. The question really is, how complex a sociopolitical system was necessary to account for the observed complexity of the archaeological record? To this observer, at least, there seems to be no reason to suggest that most Mississippian societies were more than low-level chiefdom-level societies at best.

There is very little reason to believe that any Mississippian site, including even Cahokia, was so large as to have exceeded the carrying capacity of its nearby environment in years when local production was at normal levels. Growing appreciation for this situation has led to new discussion of the political economy of Mississippian times. The oldest 'model' of Mississippian organization was that the development of large-scale public construction and the development of elites was a natural result of surpluses accumulating through new agricultural production (specifically, maize horticulture). Later, the development of central elites and their concomitant technologies came to be seen as the result of a need for administrative control of systems of 'redistribution,' as defined by Service (1975, 75). From this view, Mississippian elites were coordinators of exchange between different localities within a society. Internal exchange – distribution of goods and services – in Mississippian societies was seen as resulting from local 'specialized' production based on differences in spatially concentrated resources (e.g. Peebles 1971). As I have discussed elsewhere (1978a, 1983, 1984a; Muller and Stephens n.d.), there is virtually no evidence for such systems of 'redistribution' in the prehistoric Southeast (or perhaps anywhere else at this level of political development, Earle 1977, 1978). Peebles and Kus (1977) argued that this model of economic distribution was unlikely, at best, for Mississippian societies.

Internal distribution has, nonetheless, been seen as important in determining the status of Mississippian elites by critics of Service's model. For example, Peebles and Kus (1977) defined the role of Mississippian elites as involving information regulation and exchange. Muller and Stephens (n.d.) have stressed the importance of risk management in the development of regional cooperation and elites. For Hawaiian

societies, Earle (1977, 1978) argued that chiefly power was dependent upon loyal retainers supported by chiefly redistribution, and his ideas might be seen as applicable to the Mississippian case.

Partly because of the Service model of chiefly production systems, it has been suggested that Mississippian producers were full-time specialists, especially in manufacture of salt and chert blanks and hoes. In part, this suggestion has followed careless use of *specialist* to refer to emphasis on local resources by some groups. As I argue elsewhere (Muller 1984a) and below, there are better ways to look at Mississippian production. At best only a few elite and their immediate household producers can be considered specialists in these societies. The question remains whether these individuals are part of a 'nonproducing sector' or not. Local production of foodstuffs and most basic commodities most certainly does not fit any useful definition of *specialization*, as we shall see.

There is plenty of evidence of long-distance exchange in many commodities in Mississippian times. Among the most common items exchanged were chert, shell, copper, fluorite, and coal. Exchange has also been treated as the activity of trading specialists. Some suggestions have been made that traders had the characteristics of Mesoamerican pochteca, but what Myer said in 1928 is still true today:

> We can find no authentic instance of immunity granted to Indians engaged in commerce who belonged to a hostile tribe unless from considerations having no relation to their occupation [Myer 1928, 740].

As we shall see, another problem in interpreting exchange in this region has been a tendency to depend too heavily on a few sources of dubious value in interpreting aboriginal exchange patterns.

Thus Mississippian societies can be characterized in general terms as at a chiefdom level, dispersed in settlement, and with an economy based in both wild and domestic resources. Internal distribution of goods has sometimes been seen as 'redistributive,' in several different usages of that term. External exchange systems of considerable scale are documented, both archaeologically and historically. There is less information on the character of these exchange systems. In the sections that follow, I will examine in turn several different aspects of the 'Mississippian Problem' – population size and 'stress'; production systems; distribution systems; and the implications of Mississippian societies for understanding the development of complex sociopolitical systems.

I will discuss Mississippian societies in a general way, and use the term more loosely than I have elsewhere (e.g., Muller 1978b, 1983). Most of the evidence relating to this society that I will draw on is from work in the lower Ohio Valley. There are a number of general and specific studies which will be useful as background for those who wish more information on these people (e.g., Smith 1974, 1978a, 1978b; Muller 1978b, 1983). Specific references to work in the lower Ohio Valley and its neighboring areas may be found in more local sources (Cole et al. 1951; Black 1967; Clay 1976; Green and Munson 1978; Lewis 1974; Muller 1978a, 1984a).

Population and 'need'

At the heart of much of the discussion of 'adaptationist' approaches is the issue of 'need.' That is, systems are thought to develop and change because the components of the system are subjected to stress or pressure from the natural and social environment. Critics have rightly emphasized a failure to clarify what kinds of stress or pressures are actually involved and how they work their effects on the system. Of course, this is a telling criticism of specific explanatory models, but not necessarily effective criticism of the adaptationist approach, *per se*. Other critics have, with equal justice, pointed to the somewhat panglossian assumption that all components of social systems serve some functions in adaptation. Obviously, this kind of reasoning can easily become circular and can confuse development with present circumstances. At the same time, it is also fair to note the equally flawed tendency to assume that particular actions are 'dysfunctional' because the observer cannot understand how they might be adaptive. Because of this kind of wrangling, any assessment of adaptation and sociopolitical factors in development has to at least warrant the presence or absence of significant pressures, needs, and stresses.

Population and public works

Much of the discussion of large population in Mississippian times has been based on overestimates of the labor forces needed to build the large public works which characterize the largest centers. There certainly is much evidence for massive public works. For example, Monks Mound at Cahokia (Fowler 1969, 1974, 1978) has a total volume of over 615,000 cubic meters and is only the largest of an immense complex of mounds. The Cahokia site ranks in the 'top ten' of New World mound construction and deserves recognition as remarkable by world standards. Most Mississippian towns were considerably smaller than Cahokia, but it is not uncommon to have mound construction totals at sites of between 30,000 to 100,000 cubic meters. Unfortunately, the scale of such sites has led to overestimates of the size of the societies who built them.

At Kincaid, in the Lower Ohio River Valley, there is something on the order of 93,000 cubic meters of earth fill in mound construction of various kinds. Lafferty (1973, 1977) has shown that the labor investment involved in this construction is likely to have exceeded any other 'costs,' if that term may be used, that had to be paid by central authority or elite in this society. If one assumes, for the sake of argument, that ancient Indian labor was neither more motivated, nor more efficient, than modern wage labor, then the number of work-hours per cubic meter of mound construction would be on the

order of two to three hours (Page 1959, 20; Erasmus 1965, 285). At these rates, providing the fill for the mounds at Kincaid would have cost between 186,000 and 279,000 work-hours or 37,200 to 55,800 person workdays of five hours. For a population of 500 workers, providing the fill (haulage and spreading do not add much to the costs on this level of construction) would have taken 74 to 112 days!

Of course, we know that mound construction at the site actually took place over a period of 500 years between AD 900 and AD 1400. Thus, very impressive sites on the scale of Kincaid (compare with other Eastern sites in Morgan 1980) show labor investment levels that are well below those of many, apparently less-organized societies (see Erasmus 1965, 280–82). All of the mound construction at Kincaid could have been put up by 500 people in 28 different four-day festivals! Monks Mound at Cahokia would have required about 370,000 work days for its fill, plus additional labor for transport and spreading — more important than in smaller, ten or fifteen meter high construction. This would imply that a work force of 2000 persons could have put up the mound in less than 200 days! It would be silly to pay too close attention to the specific labor estimates here — mound construction was sporadic and individual stages of construction would have required far more than average labor investment in a given year (see Muller 1976, 1978a). The lesson, of course, is that large-scale public works do not need to imply large populations, merely continuity of control and organization of the populations that are there.

In the past, as many as 60,000 inhabitants have been proposed for the Cahokia site, but recent work in that locality (Porter and Bareis 1984) and elsewhere (Muller 1976, 1978a, 1979b) has shown that such population density is unlikely for Mississippian communities. Most Mississippian people lived in fairly dispersed communities so that a large Mississippian site like Kincaid may have had no more than 500 people within its palisades (Muller 1978a). This level of community size is very consistent with the populations recorded for historic Southeastern towns (for one example, see the lists of peoples in Le Page du Pratz, 1972 [1758], 292ff.). Although there may have been more towns in prehistoric than in historic times, we have little reason to suppose that the size of an average prehistoric town was larger then or more complex in its political organization. In general, the size of a Mississippian central town, characterized by mounds and plazas, was closely related to the amount of alluvial floodplain surrounding it (Muller 1978a, Lafferty 1977). In frontier areas, there were larger towns, but these seem to represent nucleation of population rather than greater size of the political unit.

Thus, neither the direct archaeological evidence for the scale of settlement nor of public works in these societies forces the conclusion that the population density was very high. In absolute terms, there seems to be little argument for 'pressure' or 'stress' in terms of sheer overpopulation. In part, it was these circumstances that led Peebles and Kus (1977) to emphasize the supposedly autonomous economic capabilities of

Mississippian society. Can it be concluded that Mississippian societies were at such population levels that little or no central economic control was needed for adaptation to their environment? Well, not necessarily.

Population and risk

The catch, of course, is that so-called population pressure is not a matter of absolute population density, but rather of the amount of population relative to carrying capacity. This latter concept has come under criticism – at least partly because it is so fiendishly difficult to define in any pragmatic way. A particular animal population has reached its carrying capacity if it is K-responsive and shows the leveling off of growth characteristic of species at carrying capacity, but this can so easily be circular and does not help in defining the value of 'K' in a general way (see Pielou 1977, 20–27). To estimate the carrying capacity for such an omnivorous animal as *Homo sapiens* is nearly impossible, but we can try to see what dietary components might have been limiting factors on Mississippian population levels.

Mississippian settlers in the major river bottoms of the Gulf Coastal Plain lived in an extremely favorable environment, at its best. Their economy was based on a mixture of native wild resources and a handful of domesticated plants – particularly maize. Attempting to estimate dependence on foods from archaeological remains is an extremely chancy and unsure business. Preservation differentials and food processing practices can substantially modify the archaeological record. In the Black Bottom (Kincaid locality) botanical material, for example, maize remains account for something like 40 per cent of the non-wood botanical remains (Blakeman 1974), and the figures for various Mississippian burials reported in Bender *et al.* (1981) also support something like this ratio of maize to other foods (based on a comparison to the animal controls). Of course other cultigens such as squash were also eaten, but a substantial portion of the diet at least at times through the year would have been wild plant foods.

There is abundant archaeological and historical evidence to support the tremendous importance of nuts to the Mississippian adaptive system. The importance of game is hard to determine. Some Mississippian sites have common remains of certain game species (Smith 1974), but preservation conditions in many bottomlands, including Kincaid, usually make it impossible to determine directly how many and what kinds of species were hunted. Even though quantitative measures of hunting activities are difficult, there are some interesting indications of the Mississippian hunting pattern in the species represented. A comparison of the faunal lists from Angel and Kincaid (or from virtually any other Mississippian site) reveals that the species represented in the archaeological record are predominantly species that are major predators on maize fields (compare to the wildlife diet patterns in Martin, Zim, and Nelson, 1951). Thus, many of the animals consumed by Mississippians were those that needed to be killed in order to protect the fields. There surely were organized hunts as well,

but interpreters of historic documents on hunting should remember that a large-scale commercial trade in deerskins was established by the English which could have greatly distorted aboriginal hunting patterns. In any event, the Mississippian diet does not appear to have been high in large-animal proteins.

If horticulture (and wild plant foods?) seem to have provided the 'resources of advantage' (see Muller and Stephens n.d.), then what are the potentials for these foods in terms of population support? It is easy to see that in the best years, nuts alone could have provided enough food to feed many times more Mississippian people than were present in any given Southeastern locality. It is easy to come up with apparently ridiculously large figures for local nut production (Cremin 1978, Smith 1950); but, even taking production fluctuations and competitors into account, yields were enormous in good years. Similarly, in good years, the soils in localities like that around Kincaid were capable of producing enormous yields. Modern yields of more than 6000 kg/ha (dry weight, over 100 bushels/acre) are not uncommon, and yields are listed at over 7800 kg/ha for the soils actually occupied by Mississippians in the Black Bottom around Kincaid (Muller 1978a, Butler 1977). Nineteenth-century averages in the United States were around 1320 kg/ha (Hunt 1911) and world-wide production figures are close to this (Leonard and Martin 1963). Depending upon how one calculates food value, maize ranges from 3000 kcal/kg to nearly 3500 kcal/kg. At this rate, the slightly over 600 ha of occupied agricultural land in the Black Bottom could have produced over 2.34×10^9 kcal, not subtracting settlement area, but also without the addition of yield from double cropping or from the use of marginal zones for later, lower risk plantings. At 2200 to 2500 kcal/day/person, this yield would support roughly 2560 persons, or about double the maximum local population estimated from archaeological evidence (Muller 1976, Butler 1977, Lafferty 1977).

The 600 ha area is for land that has identifiable Mississippian remains and is above mean annual flooding. Extensive survey and testing in the Black Bottom locality (Muller 1978a) and elsewhere in the Lower Ohio Valley (e.g., Ahler, Muller, and Rabinowitz 1980) has shown that these lands were intensively utilized by Mississippian occupants of the region. Upland survey (e.g., Canouts, May, Lopinot, and Muller 1984) has shown Mississippian settlement also occurred in the upland stream valleys, but at a much reduced scale. Even the upland settlements are farmsteads rather than the supposed 'hunting stations' often discussed in the literature, but generally unsupported by site evidence (Muller 1979b).

What the foregoing means is that in good years, the Mississippian standard of living could be very good indeed. But, and this is a major concern, Mississippian societies were strongly dependent upon resources with yields that were highly variable from year to year or just plain unreliable. In addition, Mississippian farmsteads were permanently located and Mississippian farmers did not have the mobile options open to their less horticultural predecessors. Variability in yield in a locality is less serious if you can move; but if you have to 'stick it out,' it can be very risky (Muller and Stephens n.d.). As one modern farmer put it, 'You have to make it good in a good year, to tide you over the bad ones.'

Davy (1982, 96ff.) has collected data on flooding in the Black Bottom of the Ohio River. These data reveal that peak annual floods can occur as late as July, well into the growing season. On the average, all but the highest ridgetops are covered in two out of three years, and even these are flooded about every 7.7 years (Davy 1982, 99). Similar figures hold for other bottomlands occupied by Mississippian peoples. Although modern cultivation and clearing may have increased flooding to some degree, there is ample geological and archaeological evidence of regular flooding. These flood figures suggest that Mississippian bottomland horticulture would have been at risk at irregular, but not widely separated intervals. The concentration of Mississippian residence and farming on the most fertile and best drained ridgetops becomes understandable in light of the flood risks incurred on non-ridge bottomland.

Terrace soils are considerably less fertile than soils in the bottomland and are susceptible to drought, but they were also cultivated in preference to many ridgetops and other soils in the bottoms. Modern farmers in this locality explicitly recognize the benefits of having land on both the terrace and the bottom to reduce risk from drought and flood (Russell Angelly, personal communication).

Flood and drought were only two of the risks inherent in intensive cropping of a single soil zone in the Black Bottom. If, as seems possible at peak population, most ridgetops were filled with contiguous fields, conditions were ripe for the rapid and disastrous spread of plant diseases. Even without plant epidemics, repeated cropping over several centuries with the same mix of plants would have led to the build-up of weeds and pests in the fields (Greenland 1975). Soil depletion would not have been a major concern in the alluviated bottomlands, but would have been a restriction on continued settlement in upland areas and on the terraces.

Without going into more detail on the horticultural production system, it can be seen, I think, that considerable risks were entailed in the practice of maize horticulture in the bottomlands. What of other resources? There is much evidence for heavy use of nuts, especially hickory and pecan, but these too are notoriously subject to production cycles (Smith 1950; Ford 1974). If, as I said, the good years could be very good, the years when both agricultural and nut yields were minimal must have been very, very bad. Thus, any argument that Mississippian food potentials were so great as to obviate the need for central planning and coordination simply overlooks problems any farmer knows about.

Is there evidence that times were actually bad for individual Mississippians? Studies by Cook and Buikstra (1979), Cook (1979), Blakely (1971), and Milner (1982) reveal skeletal evidence of biological stress, some of it episodic or perhaps even cyclical in character. Nonetheless, it is difficult to prove that these stresses were primarily caused by household food shortages, although it certainly seems likely that dietary stress

was a part of the problems evident in Harris lines and other stress indicators.

Cooperation

Taken altogether, it seems likely that in most years the production capability of the local household unit was sufficient unto its needs. Yet it also seems likely that in at least one or two years of each decade, and sometimes more often than that, there would have been local environmental circumstances that would have meant real need for supplementary resources. Under these circumstances, the public granary described for historic Southeasterners would have been critical:

> and every man carries off the fruits of his own labor, from the part first allotted to him, which he deposits in his own granary; which is individually his own. But previous to their carrying off their crops from the field, there is a large crib or granary, erected in the plantation, which is called the king's crib; and to this each of the family carries and deposits a certain quantity, according to his ability or inclination, or none at all if he so chooses: this in appearance seems a tribute or revenue to the mico; but in fact is designed for another purpose, i.e. that of a public treasury, supplied by a few and voluntary contributions, and to which every citizen has the right of free and equal access, when his own private stores are consumed; to serve as a surplus to fly to for succour; to assist neighboring towns, whose crops may have failed; accommodate strangers, or travelers; afford provisions or supplies, when they go forth on hostile expeditions; and for all other exigencies of the state: and this treasure is at the disposal of the king or mico; which is surely a royal attribute, to have an exclusive right and ability in a community to distribute comfort and blessings to the necessitous [Bartram 1928 [1791], 401].

While Bartram described very late Muskogean patterns that were under heavy European influence, the pattern described here is one that seems to have evolved from native elements, rather than from European production systems.

In Mississippian society, one function of elites does seem to have been mitigation of risks for both communities and households. Risk reduction can be handled in several ways. Risk can be reduced by shifting to different strategies of production — such as spreading out production zones so that alternatives are there if failure occurs in one environmental zone. Risk can also be shared with other producers or reduced by stockpiling production from good years to use in poor years. Any of these approaches requires some kind of coordination, although this could have been handled by kinship ties among farmsteads, at least up to a certain scale. Larger scale cooperation within a region — 'to assist neighboring towns, whose crops may have failed' in Bartram's terms — would obviously require some kinds of linkages among these communities. There is abundant evidence on the tribal and simple chiefdom levels of organization of the value of regional cooperation (see, for example, Braun and Plog 1982; Saitta 1983;

Plog and Braun 1984). The earliest historic documents for the Southeast provide evidence of large storage facilities which seem to have been for the community (e.g. Gentleman of Elvas 1866 [1557], 43, 52, et passim). While an 'adaptationist' role for elites cannot be taken as proved by these descriptions, it clearly cannot be dismissed as improbable either. There seems to have been adaptive needs in Mississippian society that may well have been served by central coordinators. In no sense, of course, is this anything like the rationing redistribution of specialist production proposed by Service (1975) and others.

Production

The exchange in valuables is sometimes regarded as separate from production and exchange of other goods. Especially, the distribution of valuables to loyal followers is seen as a mechanism for strengthening the political power of the elite. Elite patronage of specialist producers is thought to enable elites to augment the supply of valuables available for distribution and thus to enhance elite power. Can this model be applied to low-level chiefdoms of the Mississippian sort? As we have seen, the production of foodstuffs took place on the domestic level, probably with little interference by the elite members of the society. We have also seen, however, that some warehousing by Mississippian leaders of 'surplus' production is likely. I have suggested, too, that the role of the elite in reduction of local and regional staple production inequalities cannot be ignored (above and 1984a). Then what evidence is there for specialist production in terms of valuables or other products with which a chief might reward his followers?

'Specialists'

I have elsewhere discussed the problem of 'specialization' (1984a). I argued that the term *specialist* and particularly *craft specialist* should be reserved for personnel who engage in activities full-time in order to earn their livelihood. Confusion between 'site specialization' (limited activity sites) and actual 'producer specialization' has contributed to loose assumption of 'craft' specialization in many contexts where the archaeological evidence only shows localization of production (e.g. Yerkes 1983, Tosi 1984). Localization of production does occur in specialist production, but also can occur in simpler circumstances (see Arnold 1980).

Were there any specialists in Lower Ohio Valley Mississippian? Evidence from the Lower Ohio Valley, and elsewhere, shows that it is unreasonable to describe Mississippian farmers, for example, as 'specialists' (Muller 1978a, 1984a). As far as other production systems are concerned, the evidence so far suggests that it is not necessary to invoke 'specialists' to explain the observed remains. Various kinds of materials were exploited and exchanged in the Lower Ohio, including fluorspar (fluorite) and coal. These are available in areas that were likely to have been controlled by one or both of the Angel/Kincaid centers. Both minerals were used to produce decorative objects that were exchanged into other areas of the Southeast. Whoever may

have controlled the external exchange system, there is unambiguous evidence that virtually every household in the Black Bottom engaged in processing these raw materials into beads, lip and ear plugs, and other objects. Even copper materials — most definitely not of local origin — show up in tiny fragments in very small hamlets. Similarly, galena has a wide distribution (Walthall 1981). Of all raw materials production, the best cases for Mississippian specialization rest with the production of two utilitarian materials: salt and chert.

Chert

In the case of chert, Lower Ohio Valley peoples were largely dependent upon sources that probably were outside of their direct sphere of control. The famous chert quarries of Union County, Illinois, are not far away, but seem more directly linked to Mississippi Valley Mississippian complexes. Although the chert resources of Dover, Tennessee, could have been controlled by Lower Ohio peoples, this does not seem likely from current evidence. Nonetheless, there are very substantial amounts of chert in the Lower Ohio Valley from both Union County and the Dover sources. Another possible source for chert was from quarries in Indiana, but this material is relatively rare (or still not identified?) in the southern end of the Lower Ohio. While we do not have any evidence on the quantity of exchange of perishable materials, the quantity of so-called Mill Creek (Union County) and Dover hoes is such that the exchange or transport of these chert materials represents a tremendous labor investment, easily outweighing other surviving 'exchange' materials by many times. The sharpening flakes from such hoes are found almost everywhere that we have evidence of Mississippian occupation. The hoes were clearly objects that were used in every household.

Given the quantity of material, it is possible that some degree of specialist production occurred at the main quarries. But, in the absence of more careful study, I am reluctant to accept full-time specialization even at the quarries. A more detailed study, including restudy of nineteenth-century collections, is now under way (Cobb n.d.) and should provide a better basis for assessing the intensity and organization of production system at the chert resource areas. At present, there is little evidence to support the idea that these sites were communities of specialist producers or even had resident specialists in chert production.

Salt

Salt as a dietary component is a matter of dispute. Avery (1983) has surveyed the literature and shown that the 'Bunge hypothesis' (that agriculturalists require sodium chloride as a countermeasure for increased potassium intake) has been accepted too uncritically by archaeologists concerned with salt consumption. Of one thing there can be no doubt: salt production on an increased scale did occur in Mississippian areas just at the shift to more intensive maize cultivation and just during the beginnings of Mississippian chiefdoms. It is not impossible that salt consumption does have some physiological value in moist bottomland environments, but no really convincing arguments that salt was physiologically necessary have been presented, despite the beliefs such as those expressed by the early European explorers:

> There was such a want of salt also, that often times, in many places, a sick man having nothing for his nourishment, and was wasting away to bone, . . . he would say: "Now, if I had but a slice of meat, or only a few lumps of salt, I should not die" [Gentlemen of Elvas 1866 [1557], 55].

People all over the world are utterly convinced of their need for salt, but it is less clear whether salt craving is a reflection of a need or an acquired taste. Indeed, it can be (and has been) argued that it is the rise of centralized elites that encourages the taste for salt — as a localized and easily controlled resource, salt can be used as a means of strengthening domination by the elite of the masses (as witness British attempts to control salt making in India).

The production of salt may have been an important auxiliary or even primary activity for some resident populations at the Great Salt Spring, but exploitation by visiting parties seems as likely:

> The Indians come a great way off to this place to hunt in winter and make salt. Before the French trucked coppers with them, they made upon the spot pots of earth for this operation: and they returned home with salt and dry provisions [Le Page du Pratz 1972 [1758], 153].

Further evidence for the non-specialist character of production is that production tools at the Great Salt Spring do not appear to have been standardized in the ways generally found with specialist production (Muller 1984a).

In short, the evidence for local specialization in the Mississippian economy of the Lower Ohio Valley fails to convince. Production of ornaments of fluorite and coal are seen to occur in every settlement in the Kincaid locality. The chert materials from southern Illinois and western Tennessee were widely exchanged, but the vast bulk of the chert was used in utilitarian production — mostly in the form of stone hoes. Although these may have been shaped by part-time specialists, or even full-time specialists at the quarry sites, present evidence simply is not adequate to test this hypothesis. It is, for example, equally possible that acquisition of the chert was done by work parties coming directly from other locations with subsequent exchange with even more distant groups. The historic pattern of exploitation of the pipestone quarry in Minnesota was of this kind. Note that places with salt springs were centers for salt production, places with chert outcrops, for chert production, and so on. This does not, however, imply producer specialization, although, as a society evolves, it may encourage the development of craft specialization. All in all, the production of the major classes of exchanged goods is likely to have been on a basically non-specialist level. The question of the character of exchange of these materials will be considered below; but, first, a class of non-utilitarian artifact production must be discussed — that of shell ornaments.

Shell

Because of very poor preservation conditions in the Lower Ohio Valley, we have little direct evidence there of workmanship and production of shell materials, but stylistic analysis allows some comments to be made on this problem on a regional and areal level. First, there can be no doubt that the raw materials were marine and were the result of long-distance exchange. Long-distance exchange in marine shell, often *Busycon contrarium* (or *perversum*, the Left-Handed or Lightning Whelk, see Phillips and Brown 1975, 27), is well-documented from Middle Archaic times on, although there were fluctuations in the amount of such exchange from one period to another. Thus, whelk shells were apparently of sufficient value to result in their exchange over an area from the Gulf Coast to North Dakota.

In Mississippian times proper, there is also no evidence for specialization in the acquisition of the raw materials. Some of the Florida Mississippian-like peoples no doubt profited from the collection and trade of the shells to inland groups, but shell collection along the coast, especially of the larger specimens, is an activity which seems to hold little promise for intensification of production. The Lightning Whelk is very palatable (Gibbons 1964, 125), and the initial gathering of the shells might have been a by-product of food collection (see Larson 1980, 74—75).

The bulk of trade in shell materials seems to have been in the form of whole, unworked shells. There are many indications of shell-artifact manufacturing locally throughout the Southeast. These indications include whelk shells from which shell gorget blanks were cut and the columellae which were removed from the shell in making shell cups. The major indication of local manufacture, however, is to be found in the distinctive character of the major styles in engraved shell. Each of several major regions had its own decorative themes and its own treatments of shared themes.

The question of specialization of engraved shell production is difficult to settle. In my own experiments with replication, the materials proved very difficult to work with stone tools. Cutting out a shell gorget blank or cutting out the columella would have taken a long time. Continuous cutting with chert flakes in an already established groove took hours per millimeter of depth. Using modern power tools and carbide steel drills and Carborundum cutting wheels sped up the task greatly, but it still took over 6 hours to cut out a 5.5 cm blank from a busycon shell 0.5 cm thick. Although engraving the lines used in decoration would not have been easy, the major task was preparation of the blank itself. Yet, despite the enormous time investment in a single gorget, there does not seem to be much evidence for the presence of numbers of different artists to account for the relatively large numbers of specimens.

Although a detailed analysis of the different styles remains to be done, my studies of later shell-gorget manufacturing in eastern Tennessee (1966, 1977, 1979a) do not suggest that large numbers of artists were involved at any given time. For all that, there is sufficient variation to show that creating shell gorgets was spread over a large area, and that a few shell artists, at least, existed in every region. Despite arguments about the associations of the style(s) in repoussé copper work with the styles on shell cups and gorgets (Phillips and Brown 1975, 187ff; Muller 1984b), it is clear that these styles are closely related. Links can also be pointed out between some engraved pottery styles and those of the shell gorgets, although these are not such as to suggest that the same artists were working in the different media. Such contemporary works as the drawings in the Mud Glyph Cave in eastern Tennessee, although thematically linked to the shell engravings, display no sign of having been done by a person working in the local shell art style (Muller 1984c). Thus, the creation of shell gorgets seems to have been an activity that was not engaged in by all men, for example, in a given community.

The worksmanship on the gorgets and engraved shell also suggests that those persons with access to this material were well acquainted with the medium. Few engraved shell specimens from the Southeast show signs of lack of skill of the artist in starting and executing lines or other features. Thus, it is possible that skilled shell workers may have been part-time specialists, although it is difficult to see these artisans as full-time workers in shell. Of course, these may have been like artists in some big-men level societies in Melanesia, 'artists' rather than persons with special skills in only one medium. Unfortunately, we have no really unambiguous evidence of shell gorget or cup manufacturing procedures, aside from those mentioned above.

It has been suggested that Cahokia may have engaged in 'craft specialization' in production of shell artifacts (Yerkes 1983), but this seems to overstate the case on several levels. In any case, the shell-working tools and raw materials at Cahokia are likely to have been used in shell-bead manufacture rather than shell-gorget or other shell-item manufacture; and specialization in shell-bead manufacturing does not seem likely. In the historic literature from the Atlantic Coast in the eighteenth century, there is no hint of specialization in the production of beads, despite the late historic importance of these as 'wampum' (e.g., Swanton 1946). Moreover, the distribution of the shell-drilling artifacts at Cahokia appears to be quite extensive and their level of concentration low (Yerkes 1983, 502, 511, 512) although one large cache of partly processed whelk shell was found (Dick 1949, as summarized in Larson 1980, 74). The argument for specialist production of whelk-shell beads at Cahokia also fails on the evidence from many different areas in Cahokia and the many small sites from around Cahokia. The supposed specialist tools occur in the American Bottom locality at many locations within Cahokia (e.g. Yerkes 1983, Vander Leest 1980) and from smaller farmsteads and hamlets (e.g. Milner 1983, 1984a) throughout the bottomland. Persons making shell beads were present at many different levels in the hierarchy of Mississippian life in this locality. There can be no doubt that some persons were more skilled than others at certain tasks, nor can there be any doubt that manufacture of shell beads took place somewhere; but I

cannot see that the level of production localization, the quantity of the material processed, nor the restriction in production locations were sufficient at Cahokia to justify a conclusion of 'craft specialist' shell workers who earned their living at this task.

Producers and non-producers

In a number of separate production systems, then, there is little or at best weak evidence for Mississippian production specialization. In this case, at least, the idea of low-level chiefdom elites using specialists to convert wealth does not seem appropriate. The mechanisms and personnel that could develop into organizations more like the Hawaiian case described by Earle (Chapter 6) are present, but not yet developed or promoted to the kind of production systems characteristic of high-level chiefdoms (archaic states?) and early state-level organizations. The absence or small number of full-time specialists makes it more difficult to argue the need for much staple or wealth 'finance' in order to support non-producers. Given a sexual division of labor, it is not clear that even elite families, as opposed to elite individuals, can be correctly characterized as 'non-producing.' Earle (1977, 1978) has argued that local specialization and goods redistribution cannot be supported for chiefdom and early state-level societies. The Mississippian case seems to further weaken the argument that producer specialization is a cause of political centralization. Rather, specialization is a relatively late development in the growth of a complex chiefdom, and specialization in such a society tends to be limited in scope.

In general terms, the kinds of production that can be shown to have existed in Mississippian societies in the eastern United States are only a little more complex than those proposed for earlier, Woodland Societies (e.g., Braun and Plog 1982; Braun n.d., Saitta 1983, Plog and Braun 1984). In these societies with little or no specialization there were, by definition, 'products', not 'commodities' (Marx 1975b [1865], 201–2). Without specialization ('Division of Labor') more complex than that of the sexes, classes as such do not exist; and the distinctions between exploiter and exploited are undeveloped (Engels 1975 [1891], 569–70, 571). To interpret or speak of such societies in terminology such as 'domination' obscures the true nature of political and economic development on this level. Since there seems to be little doubt that both historic and prehistoric Mississippian societies were at a chiefdom level of integration, it is probable that the elite stimulated the development of part-time specialization rather than controlled or coordinated already existing specialist producers.

Distribution and exchange

Both internal distribution and external trade are cases of exchange of goods. In developed economies, this is done by virtue of agreed-upon price, but in simpler ones, more generalized reciprocity operates. Return for 'investment' is neither immediate nor invariable. In such a domestic economy, decisions about production are not geared to external market conditions, but are measured in terms of need of the local consumer (see Chayonov 1923, 1966 [1925], 124–25).

As we have seen, production in Mississippian societies was dispersed; and local and exotic raw materials found their way into the hands of artisans who were dispersed throughout the community. From such producers, goods found their way into other communities, sometimes at considerable distance from the production locality. In the immediate locality, much of the distribution of goods was probably in the hands of the local family and other kin-based units. At the community level, the historic evidence supports a warehousing role for the leader who supported assistance to individuals and groups faced with shortages. Although intra-regional differences in production potentials existed, there is little evidence for craft specialization on the part of whole communities. The specialization-cum-redistribution proposed as an explanation for the development of chiefdoms (Service 1975) is not supported by the archaeological or historical evidence for the Southeast.

External exchange

Regional and area-wide exchange took place, but the mechanisms through which it operated are not clear. It has been suggested that most exchange was controlled and mediated by the central elites. One kind of control is that the elite provide access to exotic goods as rewards to their supporters (see Marx 1975a [1852], 177), as in the wealth finance already discussed. Under such a system, it might be expected that the densest concentrations of exotic goods would be in either central elite locations or in the locations of the subordinates being rewarded — the lesser elite.

At first glance, there is considerable concentration of 'exotic' goods in elite contexts, such as high-status burials in Mississippian cemeteries. On closer examination, the concentration of goods is not so striking. All burials with exotic goods tend to be described as 'elite burials', and centrally located, 'high-status' cemeteries have been selected disproportionately for excavation. As Milner (1984b, 475) points out, exotic goods occur in non-elite cemeteries in the American Bottom. The supposed badges of rank are probably present in greater concentration at the more centrally located sites, but access to such goods cannot be considered to be restricted to central elites. Nor are present data sufficient to demonstrate whether their greater occurrence at central sites is merely a reflection of the larger numbers of all classes of artifacts found there. In the Black Bottom, for example, fancy painted pottery appears to occur at roughly the same percentage in large and small communities, but 0.01 percent of total means a lot more sherds in a sample of 50,000 sherds than it does in a sample of 5000! This is merely to caution that glib statements about great social distance between elite and non-elite in Mississippian society must be discounted, not to deny that there was an elite/non-elite distinction nor that access to 'valuables' was an important part of elite control of their societies.

Busycon shell cups, as ritual items, are more likely to be found in quantity in ritual centers. Less is known about the 'sort of gorge worn about the neck' (Lawson 1709) in terms of its social value. It has been speculated that these are markers for membership in kinship groups and/or of elite status. Yet, shell gorgets finds are common in 'non-central' locations (Kneberg 1959; Muller 1966; Hatch and Wiley 1974). Many of the most famous finds are from small sites or even isolated graves. Some gorgets, and probably many cups as well, are found at very great distances from their probable place of manufacture.

The largest find of finished engraved shell was at a technically non-Mississippian, but closely related, site in eastern Oklahoma called the Spiro site (Phillips and Brown 1975). Although the place of origin of many of the shell cups is moot (see Muller 1984b), there can be no doubt of the ability of the Spiro leaders to acquire finished shell objects from as far away as northern Georgia and eastern Tennessee — a straight-line distance of nearly 1000 km. It is also clear that large quantities of the shell cups were engraved in the Spiro region, so that many complete whelk shells were traded into the area, far more than we have evidence for at any other site, including Cahokia. However, it should be remembered that mound construction and other evidence for public works at the Spiro site is small by eastern standards, although Craig Mound, where the shells were found, is larger than other late, conical burial mounds. There is no reason to believe that Spiro leaders were able to exact 'tribute' from other areas, but just what kinds of goods were being exchanged for these shell items is obscure (see Phillips and Brown 1975, 19–21 et passim).

Among eastern chiefdoms, the Spiro elite are the best argument for promotion through their access to external valuables (as per Fried 1967; Phillips and Brown 1975, 22) rather than through their functions in internal exchange and ritual. Nowhere else but Spiro are so many different styles representing so many different regions mixed together. For most Mississippian elites, however, shell valuables seem to be normally of local manufacture from imported raw materials. Internal distribution of the objects may have been used as rewards for subordinates (as per Brumfiel and Earle, Chapter 1; Marx 1975a [1852], 177), but the argument that shell gorgets are found mainly with elite burials is, unfortunately, largely based on the assumption that burials with shell gorgets must be elite burials. Thus even this 'non-utilitarian' class of exchange goods is not conclusively associated with 'finance' in Mississippian sociopolitical systems, although it does provide the best case for that of the known exchange systems among these societies.

There is considerable evidence to support wide-reaching exchange of more utilitarian objects. On occasion, it has been argued that stone hoes or salt were necessities for Mississippian farmers. As we have seen, there are many problems with the hypothesis that salt is physiologically necessary for maize horticulturalists beyond the levels present naturally in plant and animal foods. There is even less reason to believe that a stone hoe was an indispensable tool for a Mississippian farmer. While stone hoes are very common in most Mississippian complexes, there is no reason to believe that horticultural production would have ground to a halt without them. Non-stone hoes are well documented in many historical contexts. Both salt and chert, then, were eagerly sought after, but not truly critical to survival. Both were obtainable at many different sources, and though a few production localities provided easy access to such goods, relatively local production of substitutes was usually possible. Under such circumstances, it may be misleading to estimate price as being at or above labor value.

How exchange was carried out remains uncertain. Some later accounts suggest the existence of traders, but this question remains unanswered. Access to chert hoes could have been, but does not *need* to have been, controlled by the elite. The wide distribution of the items, occurring in even isolated Mississippian settlements, suggests that their value as rewards for subordinates must have been very low. As for salt, we have some indications of salt trade, without getting any clear indications whether this exchange was person-to-person or controlled by central authorities. Neither the sites near the Great Salt Spring nor those near various chert quarries (such as Shiloh, in Tennessee) show any clear evidence of domination of other Mississippian groups nor evidence of being dominated by larger centers such as Kincaid or Cahokia. Rather, the present evidence seems best to support the idea of relative autonomy of local production and exchange. In any case, uncertainness about control does not allow us to assume simply that there was official or professional control of distribution.

Internal exchange

There is good historic evidence for the elite storing and redistributing goods to the needy. Such centralized storage provided insurance against production risks as described above. There is, unfortunately, little evidence of centralized storage in the archaeological record. At sites like the Southwind site near the Angel site in the Lower Ohio Valley (C. Munson, personal communication), there is probable evidence for individual granaries. Some structures on the plazas, as at Kincaid (Cole *et al.* 1951, 68), may represent storage facilities. In the DeSoto and later accounts, European raiders were able to enter towns and take sufficient grain in storage to feed large parties for some time.

Given the existence of some kind of relatively centralized stores, we lack good evidence on how distribution took place. The quotation from Bartram already given suggests on-need access to centrally stored grain, but it is likely that festivals were also occasions of both chiefly and non-elite sharing of food:

> They have a third sort of Feasts and Dances, which are always when the Harvest of Corn is ended, and in the Spring.
>
> . . .
>
> At these Feasts, which are set out with all the Magnificence their Fare allows of, the Masquerades begin at

Night, and not before [Lawson 1709, 174–75].

And the feasts were also occasions for other kinds of exchange, as well:

> At these Feasts, they met from all the Towns within fifty or sixty miles round, where they buy and sell several Commodities, as we do at Fairs and Markets. Besides they game very much, and often strip one another of all they have in the World . . . [Lawson 1709, 176].

Thus, as everywhere else, public ceremonies not only gave the benefits of sharing food and other goods, but provided opportunities for establishing ties with other communities and individuals within the society (for discussion of this kind of 'redistribution', see Seeman 1979; Braun and Plog 1982; Plog and Braun 1984). Obviously, the structure of this kind of exchange is very like that of 'tribal'-level societies, except that in low-level chiefdoms, the rule of the (elite) sponsor is more institutionalized.

The power to determine the performance of rituals of public cooperation obviously gives many advantages to the sponsor No doubt the circumstances of such individuals would have encouraged their manipulation of the social system to benefit themselves. By such means, informal elites could come to dominate their systems more effectively. There were, however, alternatives open to the non-elite members of these societies. For one thing, donations to the public or chief's granary were, as seen above, not made as a result of coercive force, but as more-or-less voluntary contributions. In addition, persons who were ill-disposed towards particular leaders could easily move to other towns and communities. The historic records of the Eastern Woodlands and Plains are filled with notices of emigré members of local communities (note that DeSoto encountered such an individual at Appalachee in the early days of his entrada, Gentleman of Elvas 1866 [1557], 49). Many were, perhaps, simply refugees from abandoned spouses, but the freedom to move so freely into other communities would have severely hampered efforts of some local elites to 'intensify' their domination of their own communities.

Mississippian leaders seem to have led from the front. Their sponsorship of major ceremonies would have enhanced their prestige and given them greater influence than their less powerful supporters, but nothing we can see in historic nor prehistoric Southeastern societies suggests that a Mississippian chief would have had much luck in trying to restrict the access of his followers to only certain raw or finished goods. This leads to the question of whether access to goods was, in effect, controlled through the operation of professional traders who dealt either directly with a chief or with the consumers.

Traders?

I have purposely avoided the term *trade* precisely because it implies certain specific mechanisms of exchange. Reexamination of the historic original sources on trade, salt, chert, and other goods reveals that a top-heavy interpretative framework has been built on a very few original accounts. A complete reevaluation of this historic literature is badly needed but is beyond the scope of this paper. An example will illustrate the problems. Nuñez Cabeça de Vaca's (1871 [1542]) discussion of trading on the Texas Coast in an Archaic, hunting and gathering society has been overinterpreted as indicating the existence of a trader class. Nuñez actually describes his own initiation of trading activity, not necessarily nor even probably a pattern which existed prior to his entry into the hunting and gathering societies of the Texas area:

> Accordingly, I put myself to *contriving* how I might get over to the other Indians, . . . I set to trafficking, and strove to make my employment profitable in the ways *I could best contrive*. [Emphasis added]. [Nuñez Cabeça de Vaca 1871 [1542], 85].

Although the context, level of complexity of the native social systems, and wording of Nuñez's comments suggest that he was an innovator, the comments which he made about *his own trading activities* have been treated as though they were about a native class of traders. This might be so, but Nuñez's terminology suggests that he 'contrived' his role rather than assuming an already existing one.

Almost all of the other references to professional 'traders' in the early contacts are to Garcilaso de la Vega (1962 [1605]) rather than to the eye-witness accounts of the DeSoto expedition. The reason for this is that only the Garcilaso account mentions traders in what seems to be an unambiguous fashion. Although many unique details in this account have seemed to be validated by archaeological discoveries, it should be remembered that it was written well after the fact, largely based on interviews in Spain with an unnamed member of the expedition. Where Garcilaso mentions 'traders,' eyewitness accounts simply indicate that persons from other areas were present. As we have seen, this was common in later times without these person actually being professional traders. Later accounts mention trade, but rarely mention specific personnel engaged in trade as an occupation (see Swanton 1946, 736–42), even in economies that were becoming dependent on European traders for basic tools. Perhaps the European traders forced indigenous traders out of business, but there really is no indication that this was the case.

Conclusions

As with many other archaeologically known examples, there are too many unknown factors about Mississippian society to use it to reject conclusively either 'adaptationist' or 'political' interpretations in general. Even so, the combination of historical and archaeological evidence from the Southeast does allow some conclusions to be drawn on the relationships between elites, specialists, and exchange in the early developmental stages of chiefdom-level societies.

1. Mississippian society had production centers for some categories of raw materials which were localized geographically, but true full-time specialists do not seem to have developed at these locations, notwithstanding attempts by archaeologists to interpret limited activity sites in terms of 'specialization.' Even though limited activity production sites existed at special resource locations (such as chert quarries and salt springs), present evidence for production at these sites is consistent with non-specialist production or even exploitation by visitors on a seasonal or on-need basis. Shell gorget and other 'high-art' production may have been in the hands of a relatively small body of skilled artists, but neither historical nor archaeological evidence supports the assertion that these were 'full-time' or 'craft' specialists. Other shell manufacture such as shell beads may have been more popular at some locations than at others, but the dispersal of production is such as to suggest no more than division of labor by sex and skill, for example.

2. Lineages or similar groups within the society probably controlled most production and local distribution of goods. To the extent that the elite were leaders of these groups, they participated in this process, but their actual role cannot have been very different in this context than in earlier 'tribal' settings. The 'adaptationist model' fails because of the lack of evidence for 'rationing redistribution' and the lack of evidence of localized, specialist producers. Nonetheless, other kinds of adaptationist models that emphasize information or risk-management functions are not rejected because of the failure to identify rationing systems.

3. Long distance exchange cannot be taken as having been in the hands of specialist traders. Point-to-point exchange from neighbor to neighbor seems adequate to explain most, if not all, distributions of Mississippian exchange goods — both raw material and finished goods. By weight, the major (known) long-distance exchange item was chert. Although some 'valuables' were made from this material, the bulk of exchanged chert was used in stone hoes, and found its way into the smallest communities and settlements. Salt exchange is impossible to document with current archaeological techniques, but its movement may well have reflected long-distance foraging rather than long-distance trade in many cases. The bulk of shell seems to have been exchanged in the form of raw material, rather than finished artifacts. There was substantial movement of finished goods at several different periods within Mississippian development, however. The exchanged shell goods are concentrated at centers, but this may partly be an artifact of archaeological investigation, which has focused on these sites. Elaborate finished goods are found in modest, 'non-elite' contexts as well; and it is not clear whether these instances represent the use of valuables to reward local supporters of the central elite or simply objects that marked some general status or membership.

4. Although there is no clear evidence for craft specialization, a social hierarchy existed, even though social differences were slight. Thus, contrary to many commonly used models (e.g., Marx 1975b [1865], 201–2; Engels 1975 [1891], it is unlikely that specialization is a strong, primary cause of social differentiation. Rather, social differentiation seems to stimulate the development of specialization. In this sense, the 'first great

social division of labor' may have been the development of elites themselves out of the background of so-called 'tribal' social organization.

5. The reasons for the evolution of 'big-men'-like ritual sponsors into 'chiefs,' then, might well be found in management of 'resource perturbation' of the sort proposed by Isbell (1978), although it would be a mistake to ignore the sociopolitical circumstances that contribute to this development. Only the development of elite sociopolitical ties across a locality, and then region, could make it possible for local elites to provide staple support, not for non-producers, but for inadequate producers on irregular and unpredictable, but common, occasions. Although non-producers and even staple finance do not appear to be present to any marked degree in Mississippian society, it is clear that less-developed statuses and production systems of this sort could easily be further developed along the lines seen in the Hawaiian complex chiefdom.

Chapter 3

Unequal development in Copper Age Iberia

Antonio Gilman

Staple finance and wealth distribution (Brumfiel and Earle, Chapter 1; D'Altroy and Earle 1985) represent partly alternative, partly complementary strategies by which elites in general support their operations and life-styles. To the extent that the elite of a pre-industrial society maintains its wealth and power by staple finance, it does so by extracting a surplus from a peasantry. This inevitably and invariably involves some degree of coercion. For this reason it is difficult for a pre-industrial elite to increase its wealth and power by staple finance. To do so the elite must either obtain new peasants from which to collect rent or increase the rent collected from the peasants already within their control. To increase the size of the peasant base an elite must increase its coercion. To increase the amount of rent taken from the existing peasant base, an elite must either increase its coercion or promote greater peasant productivity (for example, by assisting in the further capital intensification of agriculture). Expanding a system of staple finance is difficult because greater coercion is necessarily risky and because measures to increase productivity involve long-delayed returns.

To the extent that an elite supports its operations through wealth distribution they do so by converting a surplus into valuables. By concentrating their surplus through craftsmanship or the procurement of scarce materials, elites obtain goods with attractive qualities that can secure support for those who control the goods' availability. Because it is the quality of the goods in which value is concentrated that is the basis of an elite's power, an elite can rapidly expand its sphere of influence, provided that an appropriate series of exchanges can be arranged. However, wealth distribution operations are vulnerable to changes in the exchange and procurement networks on which they depend. When, furthermore, the sources of surplus to be concentrated into valuables are uncertainly available, wealth distribution becomes an even more unstable long-term strategy for elite self-aggrandizement. If systems of staple finance can be characterized as protection rackets (cf. Lewthwaite in Gilman [1981]), systems of wealth distribution may be seen as Ponzi schemes.

During the third millennium BC the main centers of incipient social complexity in the Iberian Peninsula were the Tagus estuary region of central Portugal and Almería province in southeastern Spain. In both areas the emergence of social inequalities is suggested by numerous fortified settlements, an elaborate (megalithic) burial ritual with considerable wealth differentiation in grave goods, long distance procurement of exotic materials, and incipient metallurgy. The traditional explanations for the remarkable copper age florescence in these areas of Iberia have involved one or another form of diffusion from the Eastern Mediterranean, but it is apparent on chronological as well as typological grounds that the development toward greater complexity was autonomous. Recent work has emphasized the development of hydraulic agriculture, the long-distance exchange of prestige items, and the beginning of metallurgy as critical factors underlying the process of autochthonous social evolution (Chapman 1978, 1982; Gilman 1976; Gilman and Thornes 1984). Since what happened in the third millennium BC in Iberia involved, in one way or another, the incipient growth of an elite class, consideration of the two fundamental and contrasting strategies supporting elite dominance will help sharpen our understanding of the dynamics underlying the similar yet contrasting trajectories of the copper age cultures of Almería and the Tagus.

Sequences

The copper age of southeast Spain has its most spectacular manifestation at the site of Los Millares (Almagro and Arribas 1963; Arribas and Molina 1982). Five hectares of settlement at the end of a promontory were protected by at least two lines of fortifications; the base of the promontory was occupied by a cemetery of more than eighty collective tombs; contemporaneous forts overlooked the settlement and cemetery from the hills at the base of the promontory. For its period Los Millares is the most elaborate site complex in all Europe, but its elements recur at other contemporaneous sites in southeast Spain. There are many fortified settlements, several of which have been excavated recently: Cerro de la Virgen (Schüle 1980), Cerro de los Castellones (Laborcillas) (Aguayo de Hoyos 1977), El Malagón (which also has a fort on a nearby hilltop) (Arribas et al. 1978), Cabezo de la Cueva del Plomo (Muñoz Amilibia 1982). Several settlements are associated with megalithic cemeteries: Los Castillejos (Montefrío) (Arribas and Molina 1979) with the Peñas de los Gitanos tombs (Mergelina 1942); Castellones (Laborcillas) with Los Eriales (Leisner and Leisner 1943); Las Angosturas (González Gómez *et al.* 1982) with the Gor/Gorafe tombs (García Sánchez and Spahni 1959), El Tarajal (M. J. Almagro Gorbea 1976) with the El Barranquete cemetery (M. J. Almagro Gorbea 1973); Almizaraque (Almagro Basch 1965) with the Encantada tombs (M. J. Almagro Gorbea 1965).

Modern excavations in Millaran occupations have improved our understanding of the copper age in southeast Spain, but the scarcity of distinctive artifacts in settlement deposits has inhibited refinement of the copper age sequence beyond the pre-Beaker (Los Millares 1) and Beaker (Los Millares 2) phases established on typological grounds (Blance 1971 [orig. 1960]). Indeed, most of the stylistically elaborated elements (the potential type fossils) of the Millaran are concentrated in the collective tombs, which by their nature provide open contexts unsuitable for chronological seriation (cf. Walker's [1977] criticisms of Blance's [1971] attempts in that direction). The grave goods in Millaran chambered tombs are primarily items of ritual (phalange idols, baetyls) and utilitarian (ceramics, axes, points, etc.) character, some of which are made of exotic or valuable materials (such as ivory or copper). Chapman's (1981) analysis of the inventories from the Los Millares cemetery indicates substantial wealth differ-

entials with the richer tombs being located closer to the town wall. This location and the great contrasts in wealth between tomb groups are plausibly interpreted as reflecting the development of ranking both within and between communities. Calibrated radiocarbon determinations from Millaran contexts without Beakers range from the mid-fourth to the late third millennium BC; contexts with Beakers fall after 2500 BC. (Available absolute dates for later Spanish and Portuguese prehistory are listed and discussed in M. Almagro Gorbea and Fernández-Miranda [1978] and Gilman [in press].)

The main characteristics of the Millaran copper age have been well understood for a century (cf. Siret and Siret 1887), but its antecedents have been less well documented. The existence of a late neolithic 'Almería Culture' of pre-metallurgical, open-air settlements and simple megalithic tombs has often been proposed (see, for example, Savory [1968: 79–81, 90–96]), but the contexts of the sites assigned to such a phase are problematical and not replicated in modern excavations. Indeed, the lack of a clear predecessor to the Millaran has supported the diffusionist account of copper age development in the southeast. At Castillejos (Montefrío) the stratigraphic succession from a late Impressed Ware neolithic to a late copper age (with some Beaker fragments) occurs without obvious cultural breaks, however. Even if continuities between neolithic and copper age can be documented, any evolutionary account of Millaran origins must be prepared to explain profound transformations in all aspects of the materials' cultural record.

If the late neolithic antecedents of the Millaran copper age are poorly known, its bronze age successor in southeast Spain, the El Argar culture of the period 2250 to 1500 BC, is well documented. The transition from Millaran to Argaric is marked by changes in settlement patterns (villages are typically placed on easily defended hilltops) and house forms (rectangular structures replace the round huts of the Millaran). The practice of collective burial is not entirely abandoned (Argaric types are sometimes found in megaliths), but the prevailing burial rite involves individual interments under house floors. Grave goods tend to be more standardized than in the Millaran (Mathers 1984) and consist, not of ritual and utilitarian items, but of the personal finery of the dead: weapons of copper or bronze, bronze and silver jewelry, special pottery like the characteristic chalices, and so on. The shift to an "individualizing" ritual (cf. Renfrew 1976), the sumptuary standardization, and the increased wealth differentials between grave lots may all be interpreted as reflections of strengthened class divisions (cf. Gilman 1976).

In its large lines the copper age of the Tagus estuary region — the Vila Nova de São Pedro (VNSP) culture — is similar to its contemporary, the Los Millares culture. As in southeast Spain, there is an abundance of fortified settlements, but of the twenty VNSP villages noted by Spindler (1981) only three — the type site of Vila Nova (Paço and Sangmeister 1956, Savory 1972), Zambujal (Sangmeister and Schubart 1981), and Rotura (Silva 1971) — have received modern excavations. These sites make it clear that one is dealing with long-term occupations of round houses with complicated histories of defensive construction. Stratigraphies from the sites permit a division between an earlier copper age (VNSP 1) with a distinctive slipped, burnished, and channeled fine ware (the so-called *Importkeramik* of Paço and Sangmeister [1956]) and a later copper age (VNSP 2) with Beakers as the luxury ware. This sequence can also be observed in the stratigraphically excavated collective tomb of Pai Mogo 1 (Spindler and Gallay 1973). As Harrison's (1977, 1980) fundamental work on Beaker associations and distribution has shown, the VNSP 2 phase can be subdivided on associational and typological grounds into two subphases, the earlier with Maritime Beakers, the later with Palmela Beakers, and this is confirmed by preliminary analysis of ceramics from the Zambujal stratigraphy (Sangmeister 1976, 432).

As in the Millaran, collective burials in chambered tombs are characteristic of the VNSP copper age, and the grave goods recovered from the tombs consist of a similar range of ritual and utilitarian items. The VNSP complex differs from its Millaran counterpart in many matters of detail (ceramic styles, tomb design, types of ritualia, and so on) and in some matters of substance (notably the greater density of VNSP settlements and the absence of megalithic cemeteries associated with those settlements), but these contrasts are more than compensated for by the broad similarities between the two complexes in settlement types, burial rituals, and metallurgy (Harrison 1974). The many specific stylistic resemblances in their respective inventories make it clear that the VNSP and the Millaran developed conjointly in a process involving exchange and mutual emulation. It is the strength of their similarities that has made the hypothesis of their common Eastern Mediterranean origin plausible.

As in the Millaran case, the diffusionist account of VNSP origins has been furthered by the lack of a clear neolithic antecedent for the copper age in the Tagus estuary region. Largely on typological grounds Spindler (1976) has isolated a 'Parede group' attributable to a later, post-Impressed Ware neolithic, but its nature is difficult to assess adequately in the absence of well-documented contexts. In the interior of southern Portugal the neolithic is represented by the 'Alentejo Culture' of collective megalithic tombs (Leisner and Leisner 1951, 1956, 1959; Leisner 1965). In the Orientalist view these would have been contemporaneous to the copper age centers of the Tagus and made by natives under their influence, but radiocarbon and thermoluminescent determinations now date some Alentejo tombs to the fifth and fourth millennia BC (Whittle and Arnaud 1975; Kalb 1981), so that the copper age elements present among the grave goods of some tombs must be attributed to the longevity of the Alentejo tradition. There are reports of settlement sites contemporaneous to the Alentejo megaliths (Arnaud 1971), but documentation of their character is inadequate. The lack of balanced information on the Portuguese neolithic is no doubt partly caused by the state of research, but it should be noted that the settlement component

of the VNSP complex was known prior to modern investigations (cf. Åberg 1921). '. . . *Ein mehr küstegebundenes Pendant der binnenländischen Alentejo-kultur.* [An aspect of the inland Alentejo culture more attached to the coast]' (Spindler 1981, 36), such as the Parede group, may be ancestral to the VNSP copper age, but as in southeast Spain any autochthonous account of VNSP origins must be prepared to explain very substantial changes in the archaeological record, namely the establishment of long-term fortified villages, the development of metallurgy, and the elaboration of the collective burial rite.

Although the VNSP resembles the Millaran in the problematical character of its neolithic antecedents, it differs strikingly from the Millaran in that it has no well documented, distinctive bronze age successor. Harrison (1977) suggests that Beaker styles (the Palmela variant) continued into the second millennium BC, and some radiocarbon dates (from the Praia das Maças tholos and from Penha Verde [cf. Kalb 1981]) are consistent with this. Spindler (1981) assembles various poorly controlled contexts into a 'VNSP 3' phase in which materials of copper age character are supplemented by bronze age types such as riveted daggers, but without '*zweifelsfreie Datierungs-möglichkeiten*' [with no probability of dating them without doubt](p. 200). These hypotheses of a copper age survival into bronze age times in the Tagus area are partly the result of an absence of reliable, well documented contexts permitting adequate description of the differences between the cultural inventories of the third and second millennia. More importantly, however, it is the result of an absence of components from the second millennium sufficiently massive and distinctive to permit their identification by the relatively rudimentary techniques that until recently have been the rule in Iberian archaeology. After all, in southeast Spain such techniques immediately identified the Argaric (Siret and Siret 1887).

In both southeast Spain and the Tagus estuary the archaeological record reveals approximately contemporaneous shifts from a poorly documented neolithic to a copper age with fortified villages and elaborate collective burials in chambered tombs. In southeast Spain the Millaran complex is replaced by the distinctive Argaric bronze age. In the Tagus estuary, however, the second millennium sees, apparently, a continuation (possibly in attenuated form) of copper age lifestyles. It is this contrast, in particular, that can be elucidated by the differing implications of wealth distribution and staple finance.

Subsistence

Palaeoeconomic evidence from the Tagus estuary region is limited, but what there is suggests that copper age settlements were supported by a relatively intensive agriculture. Palaeobotanical remains from older excavations include broad beans, wheat, barley, and linseed (Spindler 1981, 128–30). The more systematic recovery of samples from Zambujal (Hopf 1981) indicates that the wheats and barleys were mainly naked, hexaploid varieties (*Triticum aestivum, Hordeum vulgare* var. *nudum*) and that olive stones were abundant and possibly from cultivated trees. Faunal collections from older excavations of VNSP settlements indicate the presence of the modern range of domesticates (horses, cattle, sheep/goats, pigs) (Spindler 1981, 130–32). At Zambujal the dominant species (by weight) in the massive faunal collections is cattle, followed by pigs and sheep/goats (Driesch and Boessneck 1981; cf. Fig. 3.1). Some two-thirds of the cattle survived to adulthood and among the adults the ratio of males to females was 3:5; this and the strong size differentiation between adult males and females suggests that the former were exploited for their traction (Driesch and Boessneck 1981, 305). Clearly, the 'secondary products revolution' of Sherratt (1983) is well under way in the VNSP complex.

The available evidence from copper age sites in southeast Spain suggests similar farming patterns. Published palaeobotanical reports are mainly from older excavations, notably the work at Almizaraque by Louis Siret (1948). They include the same range of cultivars as those from VNSP sites (Arribas 1968). Recent excavations from several sites have made possible quantitative analyses of faunal collections (cf. Fig. 3.1). At all but one of the copper age sites cattle were the dominant domesticated animal, followed by sheep/goat and pig.

Palaeoeconomic evidence from neolithic sites in southeast Spain (none is available from Portuguese neolithic settlements) contrasts with that from the copper age. Palaeobotanical samples are available from the fifth millennium Cueva de los Murcielagos (Zuheros) (Hopf and Muñoz 1974) and from a fourth millennium silo at Cueva de Nerja (Hopf and Pellicer Catalán 1970). The barley from both sites is *Hordeum vulgare*, but the wheat is mainly emmer (*Triticum dicoccum*). The scanty faunal remains from Nerja and from the basal levels of Montefrio show a predominance of sheep/goat among the economically significant species (cf. Fig. 3.1). The increased importance of cattle during the copper age reinforces the notion that they were used for traction as well as for food (Harrison 1984; cf. Sherratt 1983). What little information there is suggests a less intensive pattern of cultivation than in the copper age. This is consistent, of course, with the scarcity of open-air neolithic settlements from the Iberian Peninsula in general: a relatively mobile settlement pattern based on long-fallow cultivation would have left neither sizeable architectural remains nor thick habitation deposits; occupation sites would, accordingly, have passed unnoticed except in caves and rockshelters, where archaeologists have sought them out. In the copper age a more intensive pattern of cultivation involving a greater variety of more productive annual crops, tree crops, and the plow (drawn by the cattle that are so abundant in the faunal assemblages) would have permitted longer-term, more substantial, and archaeologically salient occupations.

	Species					
Sites	Horse (*Equus caballus*)	Cattle (*Bos taurus, B. primigenius*)	Sheep/goat (*Ovis aries, Capra hircus, C. pyrenaica*)	Pig (*Sus scrofa, S. domestica*)	Red deer (*Cervus elaphus*)	N (kg)
Nerja, Early Neolithic (EN)	0.0	33.5	48.6	14.8	3.2	5.26
Late Neolithic (LN)	0.0	31.1	58.6	9.1	1.2	1.67
Montefrio, LN	6.2	30.2	30.3	13.9	19.4	3.13
Copper Age (CA)	0.0	40.6	16.4	21.1	22.0	3.41
Laborcillas, CA	0.0	42.3	38.9	11.7	7.0	9.95
Virgen 1, CA	1.9	32.4	27.3	36.1	2.4	51.26
2, CA	15.9	35.0	25.9	18.0	4.3	259.41
Terrera ventura, CA	0.6	30.5	33.7	17.7	17.5	32.42
Zambujal 1-2, CA	1.8	57.9	13.9	21.0	5.5	402.11
3, CA	2.6	53.9	14.1	23.1	6.3	121.89
4, CA	1.6	52.8	15.3	23.9	6.4	70.62

References: Boessneck and Driesch (1980), Driesch (1972), Driesch and Boessneck (1981), Driesch and Kokabi (1977), Driesch and Morales (1977), Uerpmann (1979).

Fig. 3.1. Percentage by weight of economically significant species from Neolithic and Copper Age sites in southeast Spain and Portugal.

Contrasts

To this point we have emphasized the common features of the Millaran and VNSP copper ages. The establishment of long-term settlements, the incipient development of wealth differentials, and the importance of warfare, all prominent features in both central Portugal and southeast Spain, can be seen as consequences of the establishment of a relatively intensive agriculture which would open up possibilities for the concentration of surplus (by some form of incipient staple finance) (cf. Gilman 1976, 1981). The contrast in the trajectories of the Millaran and VNSP complexes – the development of a full bronze age with heightened class divisions in the former and not the latter – cannot be explained by their common denominators. Chapman (1982, 50) has proposed that the development of the Iberian copper age must be understood in terms of 'three critical resources, water supply, copper, and other interregionally traded prestige items.' Following this suggestion, we may ask what contrasts existed in VNSP and Millaran metallurgy, trade, and agriculture which could have led to the differences in their second-millennium successors.

Metallurgy

The numerous spectrographic analyses of the SAM program (Junghans et al. 1960, 1968–74) form the basis of our understanding of copper age metalworking in Iberia. As Harrison's (1974) careful study of the SAM results has shown, the earliest metallurgical industries of southeast Spain and the Tagus estuary region are very similar to one another. Finished artifacts, which share a common typology, are made of copper which either is relatively pure or contains a substantial proportion (up to 2.5%) of arsenic. Just as the outcomes of VNSP and Millaran metallurgy are similar, so are their respective production practices. In both complexes metalworking is documented at many sites. The three Millaran settlements most extensively investigated by Louis Siret – Campos, Parazuelos (Siret and Siret 1887), and Almizaraque – all produced casting droplets and slag. Similar evidence of on-site metalworking has been uncovered by the recent excavations at El Malagón and Virgen. In the Tagus estuary region evidence of on-site smelting and casting of ores have been found at Vila Nova, Zambujal, and several other VNSP sites (Spindler 1981, 106). The available evidence suggests metalworking was a commonplace activity requiring no special facilities and carried out at both larger and smaller sites. Rowlands' (1971) admonition that metalworking and full-time craft specialization need not go hand in hand seems appropriate to the Iberian case.

There is also no evidence for the frequent hypothesis (e.g., Walker 1981, 177) that copper age settlements were located in the vicinity of ore bodies the better to exploit them and to control access to them. In southeast Spain the mean distance of better-known copper age settlements to the known copper source nearest them is greater than the corresponding distance of an equal number of randomly selected points (Gilman and Thornes 1984). In the Tagus estuary region copper sources are not unknown (Harrison 1977, 35), but their scarcity is in such contrast to the abundance of settlements that it seems unlikely that habitation sites were situated to facilitate access to copper ore. Occasional exploitation of small ore sources, many of which might fall beneath modern commercial attention, would have sufficed to supply the small amounts of metal being put into circulation at any given time during the third millennium (cf. M. Almagro Gorbea and Collado Villalba 1981). To place metalworking at the root of the development of the bronze age is a temptation to which prehistorians still succumb, but it is clear that no difference existed between Millaran and VNSP metallurgy which could possibly account for the divergence in their culture-historical trajectories.

Trade

We can compare VNSP and Millaran trade by considering the exotic goods found in central Portugal and southeast Spain, on the one hand, and the distinctive VNSP and Millaran products found outside their primary areas of distribution, on the other hand. The first approach has the difficulty that the lack of control over contexts and the lack of a systematic coverage of sources make contrasts difficult to assess. Thus, ivory of undoubted North African provenience has been found at some twelve VNSP and nine Millaran localities (Harrison and Gilman 1977), but the openness of most of these contexts makes even a comparative assessment of the amounts imported problematical. Amber is found in VNSP, but not Millaran, contexts,

but the possibility of a Portuguese source for them (Ferreira 1966) would obviate a commercial explanation of their differential presence. Callais, a turquoise-like blue stone, is found much more abundantly in VNSP than in Millaran contexts; its source may be in Brittany, but this is not certain (Harrison 1977, 36–39). Clearly, exotic valuables were prized in both areas, but with the possible exception of callais it is hard to assess the relative amounts imported.

The question of trade in metal presents similar problems. Harrison (1977, 35) has argued that all copper at VNSP sites must have been imported because prehistoric exploitation of the few known Tagus estuary sources has not been documented. The evidence for ore reduction at several VNSP sites argues against this propostion, since presumably imported copper would already have been smelted. The scarcity of known ore deposits from central Portugal in comparison to southeast Spain contrasts with the broadly equal abundance of copper artifacts from third millennium contexts. This may indicate that VNSP centers needed to import some metal. Both the Millaran and the VNSP were engaged in trade for a variety of exotic valuables. It is difficult to assess the relative volume of such imports, but the available evidence suggests that more may have been coming into the Tagus estuary region than into Almería.

Materials of Millaran and VNSP typology are found well beyond their primary areas of distribution in southeast Spain and central Portugal. The mechanisms underlying this broader distribution cannot be specified with precision. No doubt some items were direct exports from the primary copper age centers. This clearly is the situation in North Africa, where Beaker pottery is completely different from the indigenous ceramics and thus presumably intrusive (Gilman 1975). Elsewhere some combination of exportation and emulation may account for the presence of Millaran and VNSP items abroad. Be that as it may, the nature of the items distributed and the patterns of their distribution indicate clear differences in the external relations of the two centers.

Elements characteristic of the VNSP 1 phase of the Tagus estuary sequence, such as the *Importkeramik* luxury ware or the decorated bone cases, are largely restricted to the Tagus estuary region itself (Spindler 1981, Tables 45, 47). A few pieces of the fine ware are found further afield (e.g., at Castelo de Santa Justa in the Algarve: Gonçalves 1980), and the bone (and ivory) combs which are characteristic of VNSP 1 are found as far as Almería (in Los Millares tomb 12, for example [Leisner and Leisner 1943]). These are the exceptions to the generally local distribution of distinctive VNSP artifacts.

During VNSP 2 times this localism changes completely. Maritime Beakers and associated elements such as Palmela points are found in all regions of Iberia, as well as in Morocco, France, and beyond (Harrison 1977, 12, 40). This international distribution has been the basis for the idea that the Beaker complex is a separate 'culture' from the VNSP and, thus, intrusive in central Portugal. Harrison's (1977, 1980) clear and thorough contextual survey of Beakers has disproved the notion of a *Glockenbecherkultur* once and for all. As he has shown, the much greater concentration of Maritime Beakers along the Tagus shows that that region is the origin of the 'culture', and the continuity from earlier times in settlements and burials shows that the 'culture' is simply the second phase of the VNSP sequence. Outside central Portugal Maritime Beakers are found in small quantities in funerary contexts (where they are often accompanied by Palmela points and gold trinkets) or as stray sherds in settlement deposits. These thinly but broadly dispersed finds attest to the extent of VNSP connections during the later copper age. The Palmela Beaker style is also clearly indigenous to the Tagus estuary region, where it is much more abundant than anywhere else and where it is found in the same kinds of contexts as earlier VNSP 1 and 2 materials. Outside central Portugal the distribution of Palmela Beakers is much more restricted than that of its Maritime predecessor, however. A few finds have been made in Atlantic Morocco (Jodin 1959), and there is an important concentration of material at El Acebuchal on the lower Guadalquivir (Harrison *et al*. 1976), but that is the entire extent of Palmela Beaker distribution outside the Tagus estuary region (Harrison 1977, 17). It would appear that during the final phases of the copper age the development of local Beaker styles elsewhere in Iberia — the Ciempozuelos Beakers on the Meseta, the Salamo and Pyrenaean Beakers in Catalonia — impeded the continued penetration of the Peninsula by the ceramic style preferred in central Portugal.

Studying Millaran exchange networks is problematical because there are few classes of copper age artifacts which are typologically characteristic and whose distribution is concentrated in southeast Spain. Millaran ceramics mostly consist of non-descript plain wares. The rare incised pottery, the so-called *Symbolkeramik* often decorated with eye motifs, is mostly found in open funerary contexts. The ceramic periodization of the Millaran uses as type fossils exotic pottery (Maritime and Ciempozuelos Beakers) because distinctive local wares from good contexts are too scarce to provide reliable chronological markers. This same circumstance makes it difficult to identify pottery types which, when found outside southeast Spain, could be said to be of Millaran derivation. The painted pottery from Gar Cahal in northern Morocco has some Millaran parallels (Tarradell Mateu 1955), but painted pottery is so scarce in southeast Spain that it is hard to be sure of the attribution. As noted above, Millaran and VNSP metalwork shares a common typology. Thus, when one finds metal artifacts of copper age type outside the primary centers, it is difficult to say whether they are of Millaran or VNSP derivation/inspiration. (The exception is the Palmela point, which is clearly part of the Maritime Beaker VNSP 2 complex.) Copper age lithic industries from Iberia contain distinctive elements, such as the bifacially flaked points of various kinds, but their typological distribution has not been studied in detail; so the attribution of particular types to particular regions is not possible.

Thus, in considering the distribution of Millaran items outside southeast Spain, one is left with a series of ritual fetishes — the *Symbolkeramik* and its associated eye motif, flat anthropomorphic figurines, phalange idols — as the main candidates for determinable Millaran exports. These are regular elements of collective grave lots in the Millaran heartland and are occasionally found in copper age contexts throughout southern Iberia. These items of ritualia have the variability which, as Mathers (1984) has correctly emphasized, is typical of copper age funerary materials. Thus, it seems as reasonable to interpret their broad distribution as the result of a common ritual complex (of which collective burials and chambered tombs would be other aspects) as to suppose that the distribution reflects specifically Millaran prestations. From the available evidence one cannot say whether those items of copper age ritualia that are more abundant in southeast Spain than in other parts of the Peninsula originated in the Southeast or simply were more popular there. In VNSP 2 times the Tagus estuary supplied the Peninsula (and much of southwestern Europe) with the materials or the inspiration for a distinctive elite sumptuary assemblage. Nothing of comparable interregional impact can be said to originate with the Millaran.

Agriculture

The main points of similarity between VNSP and Millaran subsistence practices have been outlined above. Both complexes seem to have depended on a similar range of domesticates husbanded by techniques more intensive than those of the preceding neolithic.

However, while the farming strategies of VNSP and Millaran villagers may have been similar in their archaeological outcomes, they were carried out in sharply differing environments. The Tagus estuary region is one of the richer agricultural provinces of the Peninsula (cf. Lautensach 1964, 488–503). The annual rainfall is generally more than 600 mm/yr and does not vary greatly from year to year; the summer dry season lasts some three months. The oak forest climax vegetation both generates and retains thick soils. In southeast Spain the environmental possibilities for agriculture are much less favorable (Chapman 1978; Geiger 1973; Vilá Valentí 1961). Upland regions to windward of the various chains of the Betic mountain system have an annual rainfall as high as central Portugal (although the dry season is longer and rainfall varies more from year to year), while the intermontane basins and the coastal lowlands are in the rainshadow of the *sierras* and receive low, variable rainfall. In the arid sector of the southeast (the 'Níjar Desert' of Meigs [1966]) mean rainfall totals can be lower than 200 mm/yr, with medians generally lower than means; temperatures are high even in winter so that there is a soil water deficit for all but two or three months of the year. The arid zone's climax plant communities of chaparral and thorny scrub form soils slowly and retain them poorly. Dry farming in the arid zones will yield a crop of barley once every three or four years, crops of wheat even less frequently. Productive agriculture is largely restricted to irrigated plots on alluvium or on terraces with anthropogenic soils. The Tagus estuary region and the arid coastal zone of southeast Spain represent the extremes of potential agricultural productivity within a Mediterranean climate. Since they are the result of relief and general atmospheric circulation patterns, the contrasts between the major zones of copper age florescence in Iberia are permanent ones, unlikely to have been affected by minor post-Pleistocene climatic fluctuations.

Millaran and VNSP farming worked toward similar goals in spite of substantial environmental differences. It is true that in southeast Spain faunal assemblages vary with aridity to some extent: cattle are more abundant at Castillejos (Monte-frío) and Castellones (Laborcillas) (precipitation over 500 mm/yr) than at Virgen (300 mm/yr) or Terrera Ventura (250 mm/yr). Even in the most arid zones, however, cattle and pigs, both relatively water-demanding, are important and, indeed, recognized as such in ritual: the fauna from the chambered tombs at El Barranquete (220 mm/yr) consists over-whelmingly of cattle (Driesch 1973). It seems reasonable to hypothesize that the copper age inhabitants of the arid south-east made up for insufficient rainfall by controlling and diverting water sources. Evidence for this is the presence of water-demanding cultigens (such as linseed) at Almizaraque (235 mm/yr), the irrigation ditch excavated at Virgen (Schüle 1967), and the systematic orientation of sites toward hydraulic resources in the arid zones, but not in the moist uplands (Gilman and Thornes 1984). The introduction of irrigation where it was required is another of the intensifications which characterize the farming of the centers of copper age flores-cence in Iberia.

The point of contrast to be emphasized here is that, to achieve those similar goals, irrigation was necessary in the Millaran heartland. Irrigation involves a substantial preliminary investment of labor in the land, an investment whose return is over the long term. It can be fairly said, therefore, that Millaran farming involved a higher level of intensification than its VNSP counterpart. Furthermore, once irrigation systems are initiated, they provide suitable opportunities for progressive increases in the level of investment. It is significant that hydraulic agricul-ture in southeast Spain continues to develop during the Argaric bronze age, when the practice spreads from the arid zone to the moist uplands of the interior (Gilman and Thornes 1984). In southeast Spain irrigation provided opportunities for the expansion of a system of staple finance, opportunities which were absent in central Portugal.

Conclusions

The main changes in the Millaran–Argaric sequence in southeast Spain are straightforwardly interpreted as the material cultural expressions of increasing agricultural intensi-fication, warfare, and class differentiation. As I have argued elsewhere (Gilman 1976; Gilman and Thornes 1984), the increased investment in the land which primary producers had made over the course of the copper age made it possible for

their leaders to use the exaction of rent instead of (or in addition to) the provision of services as a means for maintaining power. 'Capital intensification of subsistence transfers the problem of security from the material to the social field. The investments of labor to ensure future production would have to be defended, but the value of these same assets would dampen the potential for social fission, so that it would be difficult to check the aspirations of those to whom the defense had been entrusted' (Gilman 1981, 7). In short, intensified agriculture permits protection rackets. In terms of the frame-work within which this article is set, Millaran and Argaric elite operations were based on an expanding system of staple finance. The potential for expansion of hydraulic systems would have permitted elites to expand and consolidate their power by extracting more agricultural produce from their subjects. Within such a strategy wealth distribution would be of secondary importance: valuables, whether obtained from abroad (like ivory) or produced locally (like metal), would serve to concen-trate, store, and display wealth, but would not be essential to the acquisition of wealth. This would account for the relatively passive participation of the Millaran centers in the long-distance exchange networks of their time.

The VNSP 1 complex of the Tagus estuary is similar in many respects to the Millaran. An agricultural base with some elements of capital intensification supports long-term fortified settlements and an elaborated communal burial rite.[*] The distribution of VNSP 1 type fossils outside central Portugal suggests a limited involvement in long-distance trade. After 2500 BC the culture histories of central Portugal and south-east Spain diverge, however. Maritime Beaker pottery, the fine ware of the second phase of the VNSP sequence, is distributed over all Iberia and beyond as part of an elite sumptuary package of luxury drinking vessels, weapons, and jewelery. Harrison (1977) has shown that this distribution is part of an intensification of the procurement networks already established in VNSP 1 times.

It appears, then, that the incipient elites of the mid third millennium in central Portugal chose to aggrandize their power by a strategy of wealth distribution. What combination of cir-cumstances led to this choice is hard to specify on the available evidence. It is at least possible that in a relatively fertile and well-watered area it was difficult to establish the degree of control over peasant cultivators required for a successful expansion of power by staple finance. This is a level of process in which, as Adams (1974) has stressed, the goals of individual entrepreneurs can make a significant difference. Be that as it may, the Maritime Beaker network of prestation and emulation was short lived, lasting as little as a century or two. In the final phases of the copper age there arose several regional styles of Beakers within Iberia, and the central Portuguese variant, the Palmela style, is much restricted in its distribution. The absence of a distinctive bronze age along the Tagus in the second millennium BC is the final manifestation of an involu-tion which had started in the final copper age. The florescence permitted by the expanded elite prestations of the Maritime

Beaker phase fell victim to the changes of fashion and the vulnerability to import substitution which characteristically beset wealth distribution.

Cyclical florescences of the kind which occurred in central Portugal during the third quarter of the third millennium are common in various regions of Europe during the final prehistoric periods. The Hallstatt D phenomenon in southern Germany and eastern France is one particularly well-documented example (Wells 1980). Consideration of the interplay between staple finance and wealth distribution may be helpful in the explanation of all these relatively brief expansions of elite fortunes. The general establishment of elite classes in later prehistoric Europe may be explained in terms of economic developments permitting the reliable operation of systems of staple finance (cf. Gilman 1981). The particular trajectories of elite success and failure may, however, be better explained by the more variable successes of systems of wealth distribution.

Note

*As Stephen Shennan (1982b) and Gilman (1976) have pointed out, the intensification of copper age collective burial rites, compared to their neolithic antecedents, is meant to mediate the incipient social differentiation of the third millennium. The effort to maintain a communal rite in the face of increasing intra-community cleavages is reflected in the manufacture of utilitarian and ritual grave goods from valuable materials (copper, ivory) instead of the stone and bone of earlier, simpler times. The if anything greater ritual complexity of the Millaran cemeteries can, in this light, be seen as a compensation for the greater level of exploitation involved in the expansion of staple finance in the arid lowlands of southeast Spain.

Chapter 4

**From stone to bronze – the evolution of
social complexity in Northern Europe,
2300–1200 BC**

Kristian Kristiansen

Introduction

The introduction of bronze in Northern Europe in the
late third millennium and the subsequent development of
bronze technology in the beginning of the second millennium
raises a basic question: was bronze channelled into already
existing social and economic networks, primarily replacing
existing tools and status symbols made of flint, stone and
other materials – or did it lead to the formation of more
elaborate social and economic hierarchies? We are thus dealing
with the implications of technological change. Earlier scholars,
like Gordon Childe, regarded the introduction of bronze as
one of the most decisive steps in the evolution of European
society, allowing an upper class of metallurgists and chiefs to
separate themselves from daily subsistence production, while
trade in bronze transmitted new cultural information from the
Near East to Northern Europe (Childe 1957; also Coles 1982a).

Others, like Colin Renfrew and Andrew Sherratt, have
stressed that neither bronze nor copper imply such a significant
change. Metal tools were only slightly more effective and tech
nically more demanding than Neolithic skills of flint, pottery
and stone working, whose distribution already linked wide
areas of Europe by primitive exchange networks (Renfrew
1973; Sherratt 1977).

But perhaps even more intriguing than this is the problem
of explaining why bronze was adopted, especially in areas
without copper and tin. Was it primarily for social or economic

reasons? And if some developments really occurred with
respect to social stratification and international exchange, was
this actually caused by bronze alone, or should it rather be
explained by internal demographic or economic factors? Such
an internal framework has recently been given first priority as
a precondition for the adoption and development of metallurg.
(Renfrew 1973), in opposition to earlier scholars stressing
external factors as the driving force (Childe 1957). We are thus
dealing with the preconditions of technological change and the
old question of internal versus external influence/the primacy
of the social versus the economic. But before we confront
these basic issues let us first present the cultural and chronological framework of our research area.

Chronological and cultural framework

The temporal sequence we shall be dealing with spans
the period 2300–1200 BC. Culturally and chronologically it is
made up of three main periods – the Late Neolithic or
dagger period (2300–1900 BC), the first period of the Bronze
Age, EBA 1 (1900–1500 BC) and the second period of the
Bronze Age, EBA 2 (1500–1200 BC) (Fig. 4.1).[1]

The dagger period represents both continuation and
innovation compared to the preceding period of the Single
Grave or Battle Axe Culture, which after the initial Pan-
European expansion had developed still more local cultural

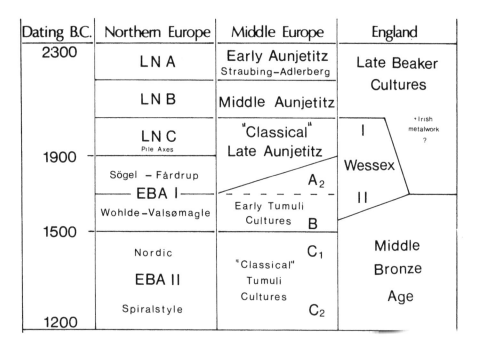

Dating B.C.	Northern Europe	Middle Europe	England
2300	LN A	Early Aunjetitz Straubing–Adlerberg	Late Beaker
	LN B	Middle Aunjetitz	Cultures
1900	LN C Pile Axes	"Classical" Late Aunjetitz	I Wessex II +Irish metalwork ?
	Sögel – Fårdrup —— EBA I ——	A₂	
	Wohlde-Valsømagle	Early Tumuli Cultures B	
1500	Nordic EBA II Spiralstyle	"Classical" Tumuli Cultures C₁ C₂	Middle Bronze Age
1200			

Fig. 4.1. Table showing the major cultural and chronological sequences discussed (based on Lomborg 1973, Fig. 87)

groups. However, a new expansion in Central and Western Europe of bell-shaped beakers accompanied by the first metallurgy, simple copper daggers and highly specialized bow and arrow techniques, initiated a new and lasting period of international information exchange. Gradually, this new metallurgic tradition developed into highly stratified chiefdoms in certain nodal areas, based on the control of production and exchange in metal work. The driving force in this development was the Unetice culture in Central Europe (East Germany, Austria and Western Czechoslovakia) with Adlerberg and Straubing cultures in Southern Germany as small local centers. In England the beaker tradition lived on, and in the Wessex culture, it developed similar stratified chiefdoms at a later date. It was not until approximately 1700–1600 BC that these early metallurgic centers were replaced by a Pan-European tradition of metal work based on abundant and widespread supplies of bronze (see Fig. 4.1).

In Northern Europe the concomitant adoption of the dagger as the dominant prestige object (instead of the battle axe) and the development of a new elaborate flint technology characterizes the beginning of the *Late Neolithic Period* around 2400–2300 BC. However, while the dagger was employed as prestige object, the old flint smiths took over its production by adopting a new technique. Through mass production flint daggers were spread all over Northern Europe from a few source areas. The primary area of distribution was Southern Scandinavia/Northern Germany, but daggers were also distributed to the remote areas of Northern Scandinavia, just as a few of them also occur in the Unetice Culture of Central Europe. Five main types characterize the Late Neolithic Period (Fig. 4.2), while a late type continued into the Early Bronze Age. The major types are imitations of metal daggers. Thus

flint technology succeeded in competing with metallurgy throughout most of the Late Neolithic in Northern Europe. When bronze prestige objects gradually took over this resulted in some last outstanding efforts from the flint smiths.

During the latest phase of the LN, bronze imports, especially of axes, became numerous and the first crude local imitations were produced, however, with a very low alloying of tin (approximately 2 per cent). These imports originated from the two dominant centers of metal production: the Late Unetice Culture and the Anglo-Irish Bronze Age Culture. The Unetice products which dominate are mainly found in the central parts of Southern Scandinavia, while the Anglo-Irish products are mainly found in the western parts. All finds are from hoards, some of them impressive trading hoards (as Fig. 4.3).

With respect to burial rites, however, there is no uniformity. In Western Scandinavia, especially Jutland, the barrow tradition of the Single Grave Culture continued, while in Zealand and Southern Sweden big stone cists for collective burials dominated, under influence from Western Europe. But also graves below ground-level without barrows or stone cists were common, just as were secondary burials in the old megaliths. Thus a variety of burial traditions were employed throughout the LN and EBA 1. The standard burial equipment was naturally the dagger, but also arrowheads and small bone pins imitating Unetice pins are common. In addition individual hoarding of flint daggers was widespread.

During the *first period of the Bronze Age* from 1900–1500 BC the importation of bronzes increased, just as local production became more widespread. A stable alloying of tin around 8–10 per cent was achieved. During the early phase (the Søgel-Fårdrup phase) both importation and local

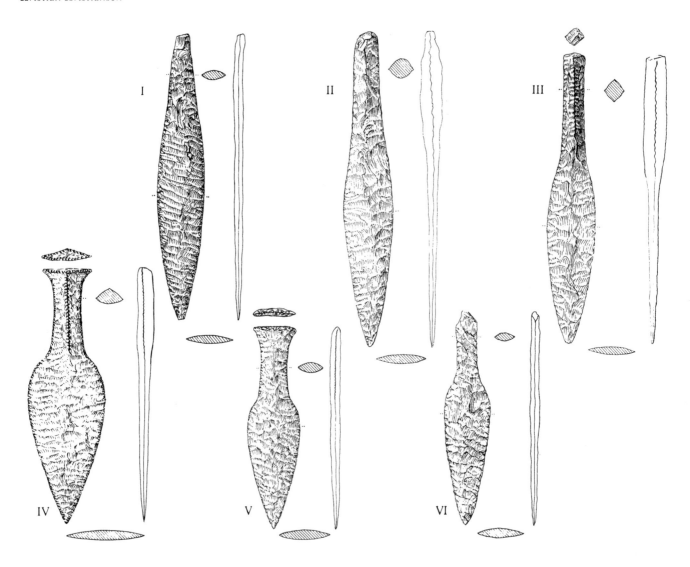

Fig. 4.2. The six major types of flint daggers of the Late Neolithic in Southern Scandinavia (after Lomborg 1973)

production was confined to a small number of types, mainly daggers and axes. The bronze spearhead represented a new dominant weapon together with the short sword. Local production was dominated by massive shafthole axes, imitating the local working axes of stone and a few primitive daggers. Such axes, weighing up to 5 kgs, represented a big investment of bronze. Quite clearly a stock of bronze was built up, which is reflected in the hoarding of such objects throughout EBA 1. Burial consumption was still too costly, just as the irregular supplies did not allow the development and maintenance of more skilled metallurgical craftsmanship.

In the later 'Wohlde-Valsømagle' phase the variety of bronze types increased somewhat. Long swords were imported for the first time just as local production was steadily developing. However, most objects were still hoarded and burial equipment confined to flint daggers or small objects of bronze. In the 'Søgel-Wohlde' group, however, bronzes were employed as burial equipment for the first time.

Throughout EBA 1 new centers of metal production developed and Northern Europe was culturally divided between two international influence zones – that of the Carpathian Siebenburger Cultures of South-East Europe (Fig. 4.4) and that of the Søgel-Wohlde Culture of North-Western Europe (Fig. 4.5). However, imports from South-Western Europe still reached Scandinavia, especially axes.

By the end of EBA 1 these various cultural influences were moulded in the development of the original Nordic Bronze Age that signalled the beginning of EBA 2.

From *Period 2* (1500–1200 BC) Southern Scandinavia was culturally integrated in a common Nordic tradition of metallurgy based on rich supplies of bronze in combination with the development of an elaborate Nordic tradition in metalwork of unsurpassed mastery and beauty. A stock of bronze that allowed the maintenance of highly specialized metallurgic skills and regular depositions of metals in burials had been built up and big trade hoards were rare. A wide variety of metal objects were now produced, some of them formerly made of organic materials, and others completely new. The sword becomes the standard male weapon, just as elaborate female bronze ornaments appear for the first time.

Fig. 4.3. A hoard from Gallemose with ring ingots and local pile axes. The function of the three other objects is unknown (photo the National Museum).

Monumental barrows are now employed all over Scandinavia as a common burial type, as in the Pan-European Tumuli Culture, and prestige objects of bronze become standard burial equipment.

This represents a period of cultural integration and acculturation of wide areas in Europe, normally labelled the Tumuli culture. It was based on a highly increased production and distribution of copper, tin and bronze from many dispersed source areas which supported an extensive supply area. International alliances of exchange ranged thousands of kilometers transmitting ideological and cultural influences between the Mycenean area, Central Europe and Scandinavia.

Processual framework

In the following I shall analyze the various social, economic and ideological components of the cultural and temporal sequence outlined above as a basis for interpretations and explanations.

Let us first consider the implications of bronze. If bronze led to the formation of new social and economic hierarchies we should expect that

– specialization became more differentiated and eventually linked to new status positions;
– exchange systems became more differentiated and far reaching;
– warfare became more efficient and organized;
– new social positions are reflected in burials;
– ritual and religious organization become more complex;
– settlement structure is differentiated.

Specialization

Since specialization is relative to the organization of society, I shall define it as any exclusive activity which a person or small group perform for long periods demanding economic support for their living from one or several settlements. Such activities might comprise anything from textile manufacturing, boat and house building to metallurgy. The decisive factor is not always the actual degree of specialization but the range and impact of such activities on economic and social organization. Thus specialization is defined by social rather than technical means.

Since the Early Neolithic, flint technology had involved a number of specialist skills – flints were extracted by mining and worked and polished in a time-consuming process. The same is true of the Late Neolithic, which saw a new flourishing in flint mining and superior technology combining polishing and flattening. On the other hand, this was no exclusive skill, and raw materials were available everywhere, although the flint-rich chalk layers in South-Eastern and North-Western Denmark clearly were the primary extracting areas. Settlement finds indicate that flint technology was generally mastered although probably not everywhere at the level of the most exclusive pieces. Thus although mining areas probably manufactured the masterpieces and held a favourable position in the exchange network, no monopoly of skills could really be achieved except by ritual or other means unknown to us.

Compared to flint, bronze technology was both more demanding and exclusive. First of all, access to bronze was limited and prevented most people from gaining knowledge of bronze working. In order to develop and maintain professional skills, it would actually be necessary to put the work in the hands of as few people as possible as long as supplies were scarce. And after all bronze never really became abundant. Thus from late Period 1 and early Period 2, the explosive development of local metallurgy in Southern Scandinavia can only be explained by highly developed specialist skills in combination with increased supplies. The repertoire and the technological mastery of Nordic metal work indicate this, showing the employment and fitting of different techniques, e.g. modelling, casting, hammering, chiselling of ornamentation, fitting of gold and amber, etc. This is supported by the fact that we do not find evidence of bronze casting on most settlement sites. But it has also to be admitted that very few settlement sites are excavated. However, analysis of prestige weapons and ornaments have made it possible to single out regional production centers and some times even the same hand in pieces widely distributed (Fig. 4.6). In comparison the products of

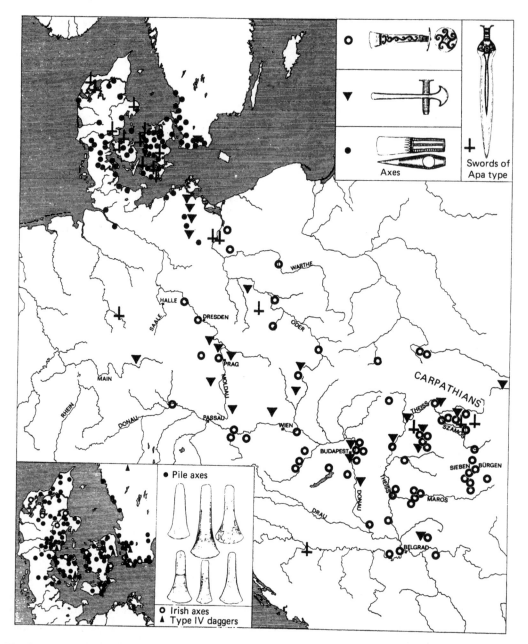

Fig. 4.4. The distribution of Southeast European bronzes and local Nordic bronzes in period 1 (after Struve 1971, Table 2)

less specialized centers, e.g. local Swedish and Norwegian imitations, are easily recognizable. This is supported by a rare hoard from Smørumovre of a fresh production of 200 axes and spears evidently intended for distribution to a larger area. Thus the Bronze Age of Northern Europe gives no support to the ethnographic models of metal work (Rowlands 1971). They would apply better to iron technology (Nicolaisen 1962) or to local areas where simple bronze tools were commonly produced, at least in the Late Bronze Age.

Other areas of specialist skills were wood working. Here the wooden cups, the elegantly shaped folding stools (and war chariots?), carvings on dagger sheets, etc. reveal a mastery not seen in the evidence of the Late Neolithic, although the material from this period is very scarce compared to the Bronze Age. At the same time pottery degenerates into astonishing primitivity, losing its former ritual and social functions.

Also textile manufacture developed a very high professional level and a variety of dressings in EBA 2, but here we lack comparative evidence from the earlier periods. Areas of possible specialist skills unknown to us would be ship building, so vitally important for trading expeditions as reflected in rock carvings.

We may conclude then, that a certain development in specialist skills from LN to EBA 2 can be observed, especially with respect to metallurgy and wood working.[2]

Exchange

'Exchange is the code through which status information is communicated' as stated by Goldman (1970). With this as our premise we shall concentrate on the intensity and extent of exchange rather than its organization, as the archaeological evidence is dominated by status items.

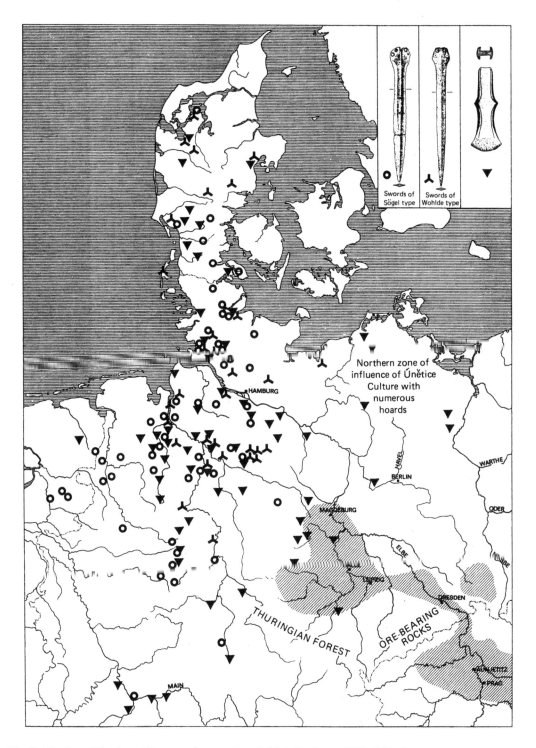

Fig. 4.5. The distribution of Northwest European bronzes in period 1 (after Struve 1971, Table 5)

In terms of exchange the Late Neolithic marks a significant change compared to the previous period, which was dominated by closed regional cycles of exchange. Inter-regional exchange in daggers and other flint tools now integrated most of Scandinavia into a common cultural tradition of identical weapons (daggers, spears) and tools (sickles, axes). Daggers were circulating along the Norwegian coast to the most remote areas, and in the Baltic we even find trader hoards in Northern Sweden, several hundred kilometers north of the nearest agricultural settlement.

By overlaying a map of the flint-rich chalk layers in Denmark with the distribution of hoards and of daggers in general (Fig. 4.7) it becomes clear that they were produced and distributed from two major areas. The rapidly falling frequency with distance from resource areas indicated the reciprocal nature of exchange. Daggers probably circulated within the local alliance areas of common ritual and religious beliefs as reflected in local regional groups of burials. Early types were mainly distributed from North-Western Jutland and they have their greatest density in Western Scandinavia, whereas later

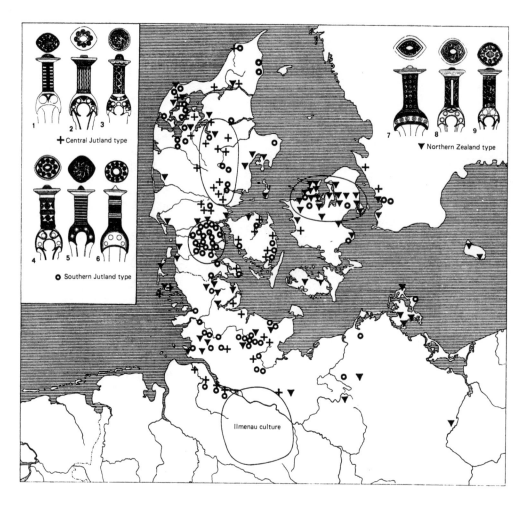

Fig. 4.6. Workshops of full hilted swords from period 2, as defined by Ottenjahn (1969)

types were mainly distributed from the South-East Danish area with greatest density in Southern Scandinavia. However, trading expeditions took place over sea – to Norway, Northern Germany and also up along the East Swedish coast. The intensive consumption in burials and hoards and the widespread distribution of daggers suggest both a high production and strong status competition with little chance of obtaining a monopoly. It also suggests the spread of common status systems.

There is no reason to believe that the earliest imported bronzes could not have been channelled through the same local networks as flint daggers. The same may even be true of the Anglo-Irish axes. The fact that the northern border of Aunjetitz hoards coincides with the southern border of Nordic flint daggers would seem to indicate different and partly incompatible exchange systems. As long as importation remained at the level of finished products for restricted prestige circulation, this situation need not change.

Exchange, however, had to be organized in different ways if larger quantities were to be more constantly supplied – a precondition for local metallurgy. Stable alliances had to be established that linked Northern Europe to the circulation of bronze and this might imply the gradual adoption of new social and ideological ideas and beliefs. Secondly, part of the

return was amber and fur which had to be exchanged from its source areas along the west coast of Jutland and Central and Northern Scandinavia,[3] and this demanded efficient interregional exchange (in the previous periods amber was mainly found in burials in Jutland with no further distribution).

The development stated above seems to have characterized LNC/EBA 1, and by EBA 2 Southern Scandinavia had been linked to the common European bronze network, just as a common Nordic tradition of bronze production had developed. I doubt, however, if this new exchange system was substantially different from earlier ones. Probably, it was both more competitive and vulnerable as participation in the dominant alliance networks determined the potential for controlling the distribution of bronze, in opposition to flint that could be more widely obtained. We should consequently expect more conflict. Also a certain diversification of alliance networks can be observed, the dominant alliances taking place over longer distances. Marriage alliances were established between Zealand and Northern Germany (Lüneburg, an important center of metal production), cross-cutting several settlement areas and chiefdoms, in distance more than 200 kilometers. This is for example reflected in a complete female Lüneburg burial in South-Eastern Zealand (Aner and Kersten

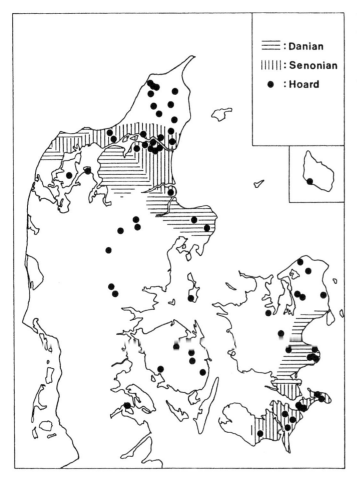

: Danian

: Senonian

● : Hoard

Fig. 4.7. The flint-rich chalk layers of Danian and Senonian types and the distribution of hoards with flint daggers (after Jensen 1982 and Lomborg 1973)

1970 no. 1269A), and later in a heavy Lüneburg impact on the development of female ornaments on Zealand. Such exchange networks imply a degree of organization above the level of local settlement units (Fig. 4.8).

Thus with respect to exchange systems, we see an increase in scale. However, the implications of this new situation were rather to be found in social organization and in warfare.

Warfare

As long as no separate or permanent military organization has developed, warfare and its organization are intrinsically linked to social organization in such a way that no distinction can be drawn between social, political or military behaviour. This is also reflected in the dominant position of certain weapons as status symbols in burials and hoards throughout the whole period. Consequently, I shall consider both warfare and social organization.[4]

The effectiveness of weapons and the military organization of their use determine the potential for exercising control, with organization as the most decisive factor. Although one should distinguish between symbolic and actual control, we

take as our point of departure that the actual military potential of control is decisive for the impact of indirect control – whether sustained by religious means, war games or other symbolic ways of directing social behaviour to conform to certain organizational principles. Our attention should therefore in the first place be directed towards the use of weapons and their technical development, spheres of control by force and finally the social organization of warfare.

The LN is characterized by 3 weapons – bow and arrow, the spear and the dagger. Bow and arrow seem to have reached a high level of perfection, employing wrist protection and new efficient types of arrow heads. Probably the most efficient weapon in close combat was the spear, as today the bayonet. However, spear heads of flint were most probably for throwing, giving weight to the spear, whereas it would break in hand to hand fighting. The flint dagger could only have had little practical importance.

Axes were apparently not employed in fighting, but served primarily practical purposes for cutting trees and wood working, although they still retained some of their symbolic functions in ritual.

EBA 1 sees two important innovations: the bronze lance and the bronze sword. The bronze lance increased the danger and the efficiency of close combat considerably, just as the sword introduced a new type of efficient hand to hand fighting. Thus lance and long sword soon became the dominant weapons.

Functionally, bow and arrow serve other purposes than lance and sword. They represent action at a distance together with the throwing spear. This could then be followed up by lance and sword in close combat if necessary. War axes were also employed, but their prime function was ritual. Thus we witness a technical development in the performance of military close combat, also reflected in the development of personal defense weapons such as shield and war helmet (although not evidenced until the late Bronze Age). Although war chariots are pictured on rock carvings, they would probably not have had any significance, just as riding is not testified either. But they reflect a new aristocratic warrior ideology linked to the spread of the long sword.

The actual use of weapons and the organization of warfare is naturally a difficult question. A regular occurrence of one or two arrowheads in burials throughout the period would seem to indicate killing in warfare in opposition to 5 or 10 arrowheads reflecting a quiver. However, from period 1 we have the possibility of observing actual traces of sharpening of spears and swords of bronze due to their use in warfare. This shows that most swords in period EBA 2 bear clear evidence of actual use – points are sharpened and the upper part of the sword blade below the hilt is normally heavily sharpened to repair injuries caused by warding off (Fig. 4.9). Thus warfare and war games were consistent features of the mature Bronze Age.

If we examine the dominant weapons used in burial equipment we get a further idea of the symbolic importance

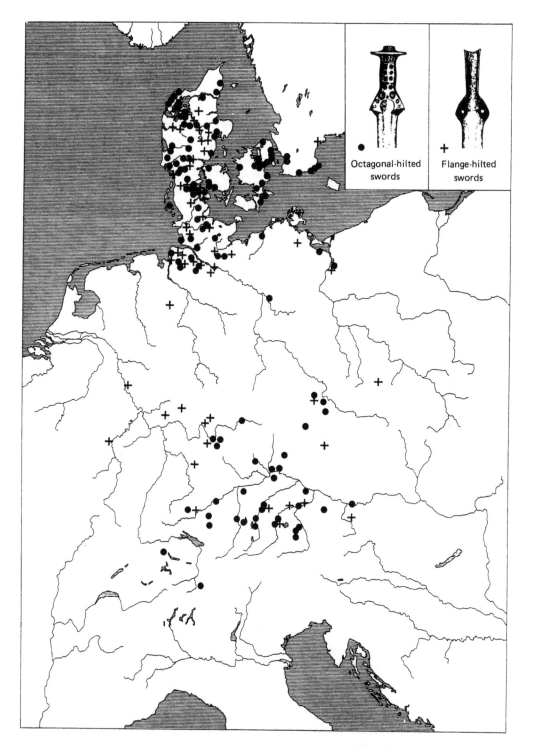

Fig. 4.8. The distribution of full hilted octagonal swords and flange-hilted swords of Central European/Aegean influence (after Struve 1971, Table 26)

attached to the various aspects of warfare. Thus during the LN bow and arrow often accompanied the dead. In period 1, however, the spear becomes the most important weapon in burials in some areas, together with short daggers and war axes. But from period 2 spears disappear and the long sword is dominant, often in combination with mostly ritual war axes.

Naturally, regional variations can be found, but in general this development seems to reflect a temporal sequence of military innovations, and the social and ritual importance attached to them. In actual close combat, spear and lance were probably the most important, but prestige was clearly attached to sword fighting. Thus it seems that warfare was determined not only

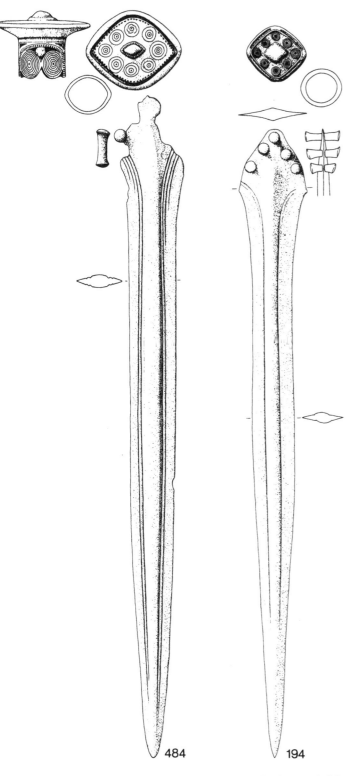

484   194

Fig. 4.9. Example of sharpening of sword blades from period 2. Sharpening is most distinctive at the point (attack) and under the hilt (defense), where the profileration may disappear and the blade become asymmetrical (after Aner and Kersten, 1970 ff.)

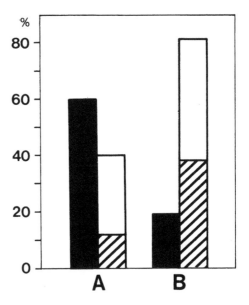

A   full hilted swords & swords with pommel
B   flange hilted sword

■ 1 NO SHARPENING

□ 2 MODERATE SHARPENING

▨ 3 HEAVY SHARPENING

Fig. 4.10. A quantitative analysis of degrees of sharpening of period 2 sword blades according to type. A full hilted chiefly swords and B flange hilted warrior swords (modified after Kristiansen 1984b)

Military efficiency is primarily determined by organization and tactics (and attack of course), but the archaeological evidence only gives slight hints of this. Was combat performed by small or big war parties or by selected sword fighters? Probably a combination depending on the context. Some weapon hoards give an indication that a group of sword fighters of 6–7 was maximum, and the same is true of spear fighters. However, the number of men without prestige weapons, equipped with bow and arrow and a lance with a bone spear head cannot be estimated. As defense works do not occur, we must think in terms of rather small warbands raiding trading expeditions or settlements beyond their own alliance network, capturing slaves, cattle, etc. Territorial control of larger areas extending beyond alliance networks is unlikely. The prime function of raids is to increase one's own wealth and productive basis (e.g. more cattle and manpower). However, internal control and influence was rather determined by alliances and supported by prestige gained in warfare with neighbouring chiefdoms and on trading expeditions. This secured access to bronze and the support of other settlements which could be furthered by

by military considerations but also by social and ritual rules of combat – a sword fight representing the most important element in period 2 and onwards.

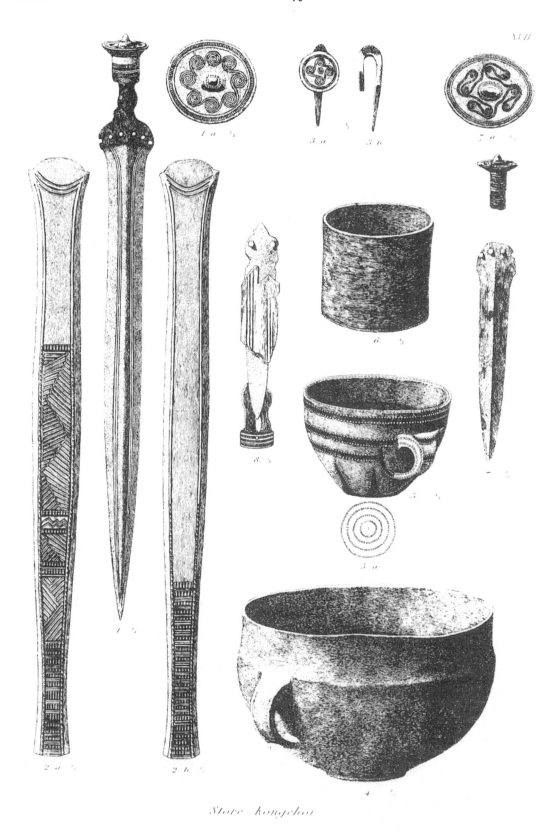

Fig. 4.11a. Chiefly sword and daggers from a period 2 burial 'Store Kongehøj' in Jutland (after Boye 1896)

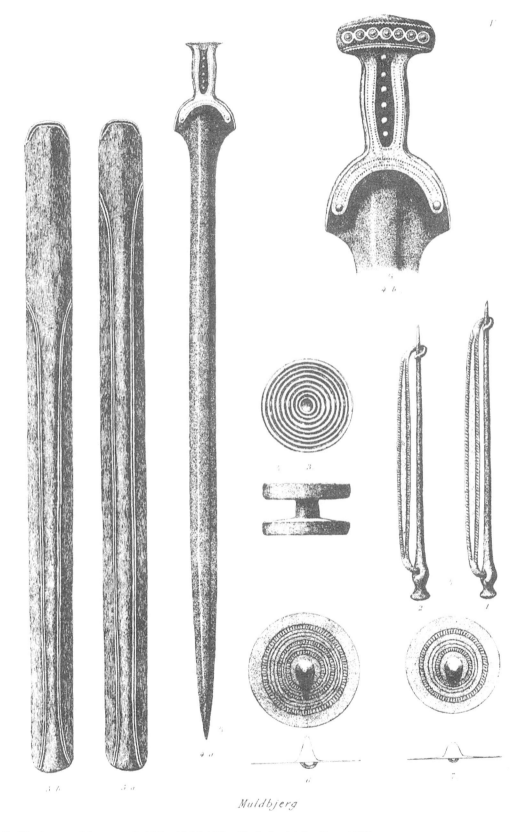

Muldbjerg

Fig. 4.11b. Warrior sword from a period 2 burial 'Muldbjerg' in Jutland (after Boye 1896)

military threat and oppression. Thus alliances and warfare, raid and trade were intermingled in the attempt to extend the sphere of influence of dominant chiefly settlements, thereby increasing their share of prestige and bronze.

What we see then is a trend towards increased military efficiency, especially in close combat, based on the employment of the bronze sword and the lance. This is reflected in a heavy symbolic display of such weapons in burial equipment or hoards and the absence of female ornaments of bronze until EBA 2. Bronze was a scarce material and access to bronze weapons was restricted compared to traditional weapons of flint, bone and wood. The dominant role played by warfare in Bronze Age society is also testified on hundreds of sword blades showing heavy traces of actual fighting. It can further be proposed that this was the outcome of a process towards increasing political control and the concomitant rise of new ruling elites – a warrior aristocracy – in period 2 and onwards. If that is so, we should also expect it to be reflected in grave goods diversification.

Burials

Grave goods represent a selective categorization of the dead by the living and are one among many ritual dimensions of burials. Thus grave goods are not a passive, or one-to-one reflection of social structure, but a dynamic way of enforcing, by ritual means, dominant trends in social organization. This can be done either by masking, repressing or displaying certain elements or items (see articles in Hodder 1982; Hedeager and Kristiansen 1981; Kristiansen 1984a). Thus, in some regions and periods, the display of individual grave goods was regarded as less important than the collective ritual framework of burials (Shennan 1982). However, throughout the period in question individual grave goods depositions seem to have been constantly performed despite various regional burial and hoarding customs in the LN and EBA 1 that will be considered later.

In the LN burial equipment was rather standardized with few distinctions. We see a trend towards increased diversification in burial equipment from EBA 1, reaching a climax in EBA 2. Thus in the LN the dagger was standard male equipment, but it was also extensively hoarded until LNC, when bronze tools took over this function. From EBA 1 grave goods became extremely rare and the most valuable bronzes, swords, spears and axes, are generally hoarded. However, in North-Western Europe we see the first male burials with a more complex equipment of weapons, and from EBA 2 both males and females were buried with grave goods of bronze and gold. As in the LN those who received a burial represent but an upper segment of society, but from period 2 we are presented with significant grave goods stratification even within this group (Randsborg 1974). Among the weapon burials a division between chiefs and warriors can be demonstrated (Kristiansen 1984b).

Chiefly swords are highly artistic (full-hilted) while warrior swords are plain and functional (flange-hilted swords). Chiefly swords only rarely reveal traces of fighting and heavy sharpening – many of them are not even sharp – whereas all warrior swords bear heavy witness of fighting (Fig. 4.10).

To these distinctions we can also add that chiefly burials often symbolize ritual and other occupational specializations. Ritual equipment such as a special shaman bag with amulets, in a few graves a golden sun disc, and more often a ritual axe is found. Also tools for specialized wood working or metal working occur (saw, chisel and hammer). To this should be added the universal chiefly symbols: the golden armring and the stool (a folding stool of wood preserved in a few burials). But also big drinking cups of wood with tin sprags or in rare cases an imported metal vessel belong to this group. Such equipment is never or very rarely associated with warrior sword burials. What they may have in common as high-ranking males are the symbols of special body care: tweezers and razors of bronze, and naturally, the chiefly burial in a monumental barrow (Fig. 4.11).

Thus by period 2 a differentiated warrior aristocracy is fully established. On top are chiefly and ritual leaders that only rarely performed actual warfare, and below them a group of high-ranking warriors without ritual and specialist functions. We are a long way from the standardized equipment of petty chieftains in the Late Neolithic, each hamlet having its own chief or big man.

A similar development characterizes female equipment. By EBA 2 we meet a clearly defined group of high-ranking females with ritual functions, with the big sun disc, shaped belt plate, and a bronze collar as diagnostic ornaments. Also golden earrings seem to have indicated a special function going back to the LN. Ritual functions and the sun disc ornament also seem to be associated with the special corded skirt, just as elaborate hair arrangements were part of the outfit of high-ranking women (Fig. 4.12).

This diversification among high-ranking chiefly families is also demonstrated by the construction of barrows. An analysis of the size of more than 3000 preserved barrows in Schleswig-Holstein revealed a very significant diversification with only a rather small group of truly monumental size (Fig. 4.13). Although this variation is also determined by the frequency and period of use, new burials adding to the barrow, it is well known that the most outstanding chiefly burials, such as Skallerup on Zealand, also were covered by some of the biggest barrows in the entire region (Jensen 1984). It is also demonstrable that some barrows reveal rather poor burials throughout their period of use, while others mainly contain rich burials, thereby demonstrating differences of wealth among high-ranking families over long periods of time.

Thus the pattern of social hierarchy and wealth differentiation that manifests itself from EBA 2 onwards seems to be one of permanency. Although EBA 2 is based on traditions rooted in the LN, this differentation is interpreted as reflecting a real development in social stratification and complexity linked to the introduction and employment of bronze in prestige building. The heavy display of weapons among high-ranking males is taken as an indication of the importance of warfare in

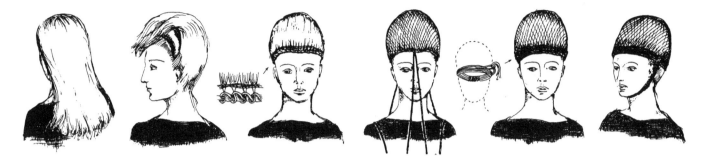

Fig. 4.12. Example of the arrangement of complex hair style on a high-ranking Early Bronze Age woman from Skrydstrup (after Lomborg 1964)

the process of establishing new social hierarchies. Not until EBA 2 did bronze become so common that it was employed in the production of female ornaments.

Ritual and religion

Ritual and religion are closely linked to ideological legitimation of dominant trends in social organization. By institutionalizing certain practices and beliefs (song, dances, myths etc.) their cyclical repetition makes the world seem without beginning and end. What has once become ritualized cannot be questioned, 'belief' does not exist in primitive social organization. But, perhaps more important, ritual tends to be exclusive — it can only be performed by those who are, in some way or another, qualified. The nature of these qualifications is the crucial point. In tribal social organization they are often linked to certain social prerogatives, such as direct descent from mythical forefathers or 'kinship' relations with powerful chiefs and gods from outside. Control of and access to ritual is therefore an important precondition of power. However, the relationship is a complex one, as demonstrated in several recent papers (Shennan 1982; Kristiansen 1984a). Ideology may both mask and demask, hide and emphasize. An analysis of ideological change is therefore basic to any social analysis in order to understand the relationship between social organization and ideological representation.

With respect to burials the tradition of single graves under barrows, which had prevailed in North-Western Europe, came to dominate all over Scandinavia in late EBA 1/EBA 2 and onwards, in a monumental version selecting the highest and most impressive locations in the landscape. Thus in Southern Scandinavia the LN/EBA 1 tradition of collective burials in stone cists, heavily inspired from Western Europe, but rooted in Megalithic tradition, was given up. This burial tradition, however, was also linked to old traditions of ritual hoarding and communal ritual that continued throughout the Bronze Age. These two traditions — a North-West European one of single burials in monumental barrows and a South Scandinavia one of ritual hoarding and communal ritual — were moulded into a single Nordic tradition in EBA 2 and onwards.

To this synthesis of Scandinavian traditions was added

new religious mythology in Late Period 1 and onwards, especially Aegean mythology. The spiral style and the new warrior swords are examples of diffusion from Central Europe/the Aegean, but in mythology this was accompanied by the idea of double axes with representations of warrior gods, the horse-drawn sun on a chariot, war chariots, bull and horse games, etc.[5]

All in all, the whole mythology of a warrior aristocracy is seen to have accompanied the employment of the bronze sword in Northern Europe. To this should be added the idea of demonstrating and conserving ritual sceneries (Fig. 4.14) soon

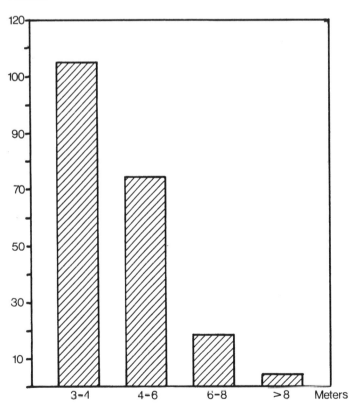

Fig. 4.13. Large Early Bronze Age barrows from Schleswig-Holstein classified according to height (based on Struve 1971)

Fig. 4.14. The eight decorated stone slabs from the Kivik grave (wash drawing by H. Faith-Ell, after Malmer 1981, Fig. 6)

leading to a widespread tradition of rock carvings – an invaluable source of ritual and religious knowledge.

Some of this religious mythology, so completely separated from traditional communal and tribal ritual, quite evidently was rooted in local traditions. The ritual importance of the war axe and the whole symbolism of pairing is also found in the Single Grave Culture (e.g. double male burials, which now became widespread throughout the whole of Northern Europe). Also sun fertility is universal. However, the ritual framework was new – the idea of drawing the sun on a chariot and the mythology of chiefly warriors (war chariots, stools). In fact the pictures of war chariots have their closest parallels among Egyptian war chariots, just as the few preserved folding stools are of similar dimensions to Egyptian stools. It remains an astonishing phenomenon that Egyptian/Mycenean mythology and prestige equipment could be transmitted over such distances. The pictorial stone slabs in Kivik are impossible without Mycenean/Mediterranean prototypes, e.g., pictorial rugs and the grave stelae at Mycenae, just as are folding stools and war chariots without their Mediterranean/Egyptian prototypes.[6] From the Scandinavian centers of foreign influence this new ritual/religious complex spread, and in more remote areas as in Southern Norway the elegant war chariots with 4-spoked wheels from Southern Sweden turned into rather clumsy local imitations with solid wheels and drawn by oxen (Fig. 4.15).

From late EBA 1 there developed a whole ritual equipment of big paired double axes and spears, probably early lures and drinking vessels, making possible a complete correlation between the impressive ritual sceneries on rock carvings and the actual archaeological evidence of ritual hoards and grave finds (see Kristiansen 1984a, Figs. 10–11). To this is added the widespread employment of animal and bird masks in ritual and on the bows of ships, as evidenced in rock carvings and bronze figurines. We can thus distinguish between a sphere of personal status items as seen in burials and one of communal ritual equipment, only rarely found in burials but sometimes in hoards. The evidence allows us to link the performance of the extensive communal rituals with the ritual warrior chiefs. In this way they legitimized and demonstrated their social and political privileges by ritual means. Thus chiefs combined religious and political monopolies. Access to ritual and new religious ideas was channeled through the same lines of chiefly alliances as bronze.

This specific combination of extensive communal ritual and the demonstration of personal wealth and prestige (social inequality) in burials and barrows is the ideological basis for the development of warrior aristocracies in Northern Europe from approximately 1500 BC onwards, and it further explains the richness of the archaeological evidence. Thus old traditions of communal ritual were linked to a new external ideology of warrior aristocracies in combination with a prestige-goods economy based on long-distance exchange of bronze and gold that lasted throughout the next millennium.

The strength of this new political/ideological system is demonstrated by the fact that at least part of it was adopted in Central and Northern Scandinavia in areas with little access to bronze and a mixed economy of hunting and agriculture. Thus along the Northern coasts of Finland, Sweden and Norway – 800 kms from Southern Scandinavia – we find

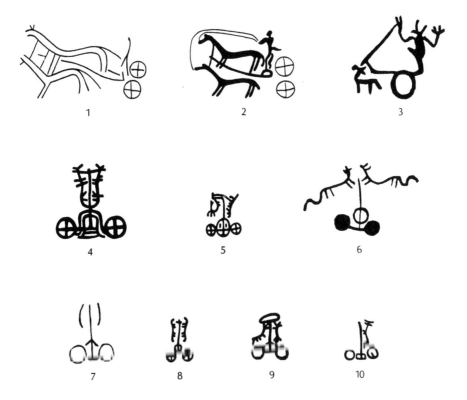

Fig. 4.15. A selection of rock carvings of chariots from the Early Bronze Age (after Schousbo 1983)

thousands of monumental barrows situated at dominant locations, dating from around 1500 BC (Broadbent 1983, Fig. 2; Kristiansen in press). Once again this exemplifies that exchange is the code through which status information is communicated. And it further exemplifies that it was not the employment of bronze in itself, but rather its social and ritual framework, that was significant. The full-scale development, as seen in Southern Scandinavia, however, would not have been possible, and could not survive, without the prestige goods of bronze and gold. That is clearly exemplified by the decline of the Bronze Age and the beginning of the Iron Age around 600–500 BC. But this is quite a different story (Kristiansen 1980, 24 ff.).

Settlement structure

With respect to house types[7] the LN and EBA 1 represent a continuum, characterized by the rectangular two-aisled type. In Western Denmark (Jutland) hamlets apparently consisted of a group of rather small houses of individual households, while in Eastern Denmark/Southern Sweden we find a few rather large houses of extended families/communal houses (some up to 40 metres long).

The evidence of settlements thus conforms with other evidence (ritual), suggesting different principles of social organization in Eastern and Western Scandinavia, originating respectively in the Single Grave Culture and the Megalithic Culture. By period 2 the rectangular three-aisled type apparently replaced the two-aisled type in a rather big version all over Scandinavia. This corresponds to other observed changes,

and the evidence of the LBA suggests that the communal type of household organization (extended families) of the Megalithic Culture came to dominate throughout the Bronze Age.

With respect to settlement differentiation the evidence does not allow any safe conclusions. However, the only extensively excavated settlement of period 2 seems to be both larger and more diversified than those from the previous periods. Generally, the preliminary nature of the above suggestions should be stressed, since at present there are rather few totally excavated settlement sites from the periods in question. Analysis of metalwork, grave goods and pottery are thus both quantitatively and qualitatively much more informative and reliable with respect to spatial dimensions of differentiation.

Explanatory framework

Our expectations set out in the beginning of the previous section have to a large degree been fulfilled. Diversification could be observed in most cases, however, accompanied by increased cultural homogeneity. It seems that we are dealing with a rather complicated process of interaction between technological, social and ideological change – a kind of 'cluster interaction' (Price 1977; Shennan 1982). This was interpreted as a development towards more complex social hierarchies amplified by a new ideology of warrior aristocracies and sustained by more efficient military organization of political and economic control. It gives strength to our hypothesis that these processes could be observed independently both with respect to specialization, military techniques, grave goods diversification and religious organization. Thus the importance attached to developments in specialization, e.g., metallurgy and wood working, was reflected in grave goods. From EBA 2 status was attached to crafts specialization, indicating the interlocked development of status systems and craft specialization (for comparative evidence see Goldman 1970, 491 ff).

What we witness then is a development both in social organization (hierarchization) and in scale (political control of larger areas/long-distance alliances). It has to be admitted, however, that this development is most clearly evidenced when contrasting the LN and the EBA 2. The intermediate stage EBA 1 is more diffuse.

The evolutionary potential of this development was apparently rooted in the individualizing segmentary tribes of the Single Grave Culture with its strong emphasis on personal status display, demonstrating social inequality rather than hiding it (Shennan 1982; Kristiansen 1984a). When linked to the ceremonial traditions of the old Megalithic regions in Southern Scandinavia, a strong theocratic synthesis emerged ideal for legitimizing a new social order of a tribal warrior aristocracy. Its actual power basis was the monopoly offered by the control of bronze and the elite exchange of prestige goods. This gave access to both religious power (new rituals, etc.) and military power (weapons).

However, we have not yet faced the difficult question of what triggered this development. What are the determining factors? It has been suggested that the status ideology linked to the spread of bronze weapons was a decisive factor. Also the potential of establishing a monopoly of certain prestige goods — that is a potential of creating and protecting new social and political privileges reflected in new status positions — has been emphasized. And to this was added the evolutionary readiness or potential of the pre-existing social and religious order. However, was bronze the cause or the effect? Did its application lead to an economic development in subsistence creating a basis for converting increased surplus into exchange of more bronze, etc., or was bronze primarily a social phenomenon with only little direct importance for subsistence?

And secondly, was this technological–ideological complex a driving force in itself or were developments rather determined by factors rooted more deeply in economic, ecological and demographic conditions, following their own internal trajectories?

To answer these questions we must briefly discuss demographic and economic factors as reflected in the exploitation of landscape, settlement and subsistence systems.

First it should be stressed that the effect of bronze technology on subsistence might be caused both by social dynamics (stronger competition and need for surplus leading to economic intensification) and by more efficient bronze tools. It can be observed that bronze axes gradually take over the role of stone and to some extent flint axes from LNC/EBA

1, whereas flint dominates all other tool production. As bronze axes are not significantly more efficient than flint and stone axes, and as the major settlement and economic expansion occurred before the introduction of bronze (see below) its main importance is not within the sphere of subsistence production. Right from the onset bronze belonged primarily to the sphere of prestige goods.

Having stated this, we may now turn to our second question — the impact of internal economic and demographic conditions.[8]

In general the overall settlement structure throughout the period in question is a continuation from the Battle Axe Culture, and the same is true of subsistence (Kristiansen 1982). However, in several areas the LN marks an expansion of settlement, especially in Sweden and Norway where agriculture now for the first time becomes dominant in marginal areas or supplements hunting and fishing. Pollen diagrams reveal a heavy expansion of open land, and archaeology, the spread of daggers, sickles and stone axes — the latter an efficient multi-purpose tool for both cutting of forest and preparing the ground. Thus when analyzing archaeological settlement densities the LN represents either expansion or clustering in most areas of Scandinavia, which is supported by pollen diagrams. There can hardly be any doubt that this was due to a combination of new subsistence strategies and population increase. Also pollen diagrams indicate an extensive land use based on cattle and sheep grazing. This is reflected in low frequencies for cereals and the first increase of fagus, the only tree not eaten by grazing animals. Thus most of Northern Europe is characterized by open grass land, shrubby woods with hazel and secondary oak-mixed forest. As coastal settlement densities increased in many areas, it may also be suggested that fishing played an important role supplementing the diet.

In conclusion the LN represents a boom period in terms of settlement expansion and expansion of open land in many areas, a development which had already begun in the preceding period. The intensive exploitation of the landscape continued during the EBA 1 and 2 with some regional displacements. Thus in most areas of Northern Europe, the period LN/EBA 1 represents the formation of the open cultural landscape — although with regional expansion and regression phases dependent on local trajectories.[9]

We may thus conclude that bronze was introduced after a rather long period of settlement expansion and increased exploitation of the landscape. It may be suggested that this inherent trend of settlement expansion and population increase held a potential for developing more hierarchical structures if contradictions arose between economic potential and population densities. This, however, was apparently not the case until the Middle and Late Bronze Age (Kristiansen 1980, 1984a). I am, therefore, inclined to believe that the introduction of bronze triggered a development towards a more stratified social order, at least in Southern Scandinavia, due to its potential for monopolizing wealth, prestige and power. It should be stressed, however, that the pre-existing social and economic order of the LN with its competitive individualizing ideology of social inequality represented a necessary background — unable to release its inherent evolutionary potential until triggered by prestige goods exchange. Social dynamics were consequently the driving force.

Thus the social organization of EBA 2 was founded upon the structural principles of the preceding periods and does not represent another stage on the evolutionary ladder, but rather the ultimate development of a segmentary tribal system. With this as our explanatory structural basis, let us finally consider Scandinavian developments in a wider European perspective.

Basing itself on imported prestige goods, the new social order of the mature Bronze Age was vulnerable to fluctuations in the supplies of bronze or in the rate of exchange. Unfavorable exchange rates might lead to increasing exploitation and eventually overexploitation to secure a larger surplus. It seems, however, that during the EBA 1 the rate of exchange developed in favor of the recipient areas, bronze becoming more abundant and cheaper, which was a precondition for development in EBA 2 and onwards.

However, there is more to it than rates of exchange. It seems that the resistence to developing a full bronze technology at an earlier stage was also due to a structural incompatability between Scandinavia and the highly stratified bronze producing areas in Central Europe. We may speak of a kind of center/periphery relationship between these areas, the rather few centers trying to monopolize production and know-how. During this phase the periphery was primarily supplied with rather simple tools (e.g., axes).

From approximately 1600 BC a new widespread chiefdom structure emerged without paramount centers of production and know-how but instead dominated by numerous smaller chiefdoms linked by extensive alliance systems. The international spread of the Tumuli Culture and the incorporation of Northern Europe into this new framework was based on a structural compatibility ranging from the Baltic to the Danube.[10] In opposition to the preceding period it was characterized by widespread production and exchange of personal prestige goods and the employment of a new ideology of warrior aristocracies, linking Northern Europe, Central Europe and the Mediterranean to a common ideological framework. Within this perspective we may regard the spread of bronze technology as a decisive step in the evolution of European society which for a rather short period until 1200 BC unified large areas of Europe within a common structural framework that was never to reappear and which represents the climax of European tribal evolution.

Acknowledgement

I want to thank Søren Dietz, the National Museum in Copenhagen, for information about the most recent Mycenean chronology. He is of course responsible for neither my interpretations nor my lack of familiarity with Mycenean archaeology. I also wish to thank Helle Vandkilde for references to literature on Mycenean archaeology.

Notes

1. The absolute chronology applied in Fig. 1 is mainly based on calibrated C-14 dates. I have, with some modifications, followed Klaus Goldmann's reinterpretation of the sword typology and of Mycenean influences in Europe, whose implications for cultural interrelations and chronology I find convincing in most aspects (Goldmann 1980/81). Unpublished C-14 dates of oak coffins from Montelius period 2 burials in Jutland span the period 1500–1200 BC (calibrated after Clark). These datings tend to support the above chronology and the traditional historical cross-datings. The datings are significant since they are from outer rings, and thus very precise. They are furthermore mostly supported by preliminary dendrochronological datings, although they tend to narrow the time span a bit. Of 21 datings the majority fall in the first half of the fourteenth century. I want to thank the First Department of the National Museum in Copenhagen for permission to refer to these preliminary datings that are part of a joint project with the Munich laboratory and Professor H. Schwabedissen.

   The above datings imply that several of the calibrated datings from the European Middle Bronze Age, extending back to 17– 1800 BC, are to be questioned. Such internal contradictions, however, were already pointed out in 1975 by Snodgrass. We should, naturally, be open to the possibility that the Danish dates do not cover the initial phase of period 2, although some of the burials on archaeological grounds belong to the earlier part of the period. Its termination, on the other hand, cannot be later than 1200, and we should probably expect an overlap with the beginning of the period III during the second half of the thirteenth century, according to a few recent datings.

   For the Unetice and Wessex Cultures I have followed the calibrated C-14 dates (Coles and Harding 1979, 67 ff). The late dates of the final Wessex Culture imply that it runs parallel with the Latest Unetice and Early Tumuli phase (A2/B1)(Hawkes 1977; Burgess 1980, 106 ff). This makes sense archaeologically and in terms of cultural interrelations (for Europe see Kubach 1977).

   While it seems that local series of controlled C-14 dates of the later phases of the Early Bronze Age (late Wessex/Tumuli Culture/ Nordic) in connection with more precise calibration curves are beginning to correspond to the archaeological/historical crossdatings, there are still unsolved problems with respect to the Earlier Bronze Age. This implies that the calibration curve needs further adjustment for that period, that too many C-14 samples are too unspecific (no control of the sample's own age, e.g., by outer rings, the archaeological context of the sample is not safe) or that historical dates are wrong. As the latter at present is regarded improbable (Hankey and Warren 1974; also Hänsel 1982) we are left with the two first alternatives. Thus there can be no doubt the Shaft graves, which are now thought to cover the period 1650 (1700)–1450, and Bush Barrow graves with uncalibrated C-14 dates from 1700–1450 BC belong to the same sequence. As Bush Barrows are considered to be late within Wessex (Burgess 1980, 108 ff.) they may overlap with the Shaft graves with some good will. But the situation is not at all satisfying. What we need at present then is a critical reexamination of the existing C-14 datings and their context. However, C-14 samples are to be regarded as typological elements and we should therefore apply the same methodological criteria with respect to probability as for typological dating. In that respect relative typological dating is still in most areas more precise and reliable in archaeological terms (I am not referring to archaeological/historical cross-datings).

With respect to the *cultural sequences* the reader is generally referred to Gimbutas (1965), Coles and Harding (1979) and Müller-Karpe (1980). A recent summary of research of the Bronze Age in Western Europe is given by Coles (1982b) and in Eastern and Central Europe by Harding (1983). With respect to *regional publications* Lomborg is still the standard work for the Late Neolithic in Denmark (1973). For England Burgess (1980) gives an outline of the whole period in question, while the Pan-European Bell Beaker Culture is synthesized by Harrison (1980). The period 1900–1500 BC is still best covered by Hachmann (1957), with Buttler (1963) on the Western connections. The period 1600–1200 BC is rich in publications, none, however, dealing with the whole period and region, except the old work on the Tumuli Culture by Holste (1953). Mention should be made, however, of the monographical series "Prähistorische Bronzefunde," covering a large number of selected objects, such as pins, swords, axes etc. Fully illustrated catalogues of all copper and bronze finds in selected regions are found for Denmark in Aner and Kersten, Volumes 1–7 (1970 ff) and for Sweden in Oldeberg (1974). For Schleswig-Holstein a useful outline of the Early Bronze Age is given by Struve (1971).

The sequence treated in this article is traditionally divided between the Late Neolithic or Copper Age and the Early Bronze Age. The implications and limitations of this old technological division for understanding and explaining the social evolution during the transition and during the subsequent Bronze Age, has recently been illuminated by Rowlands (1984).

2. With respect to metallurgy a major publication is still that of Oldeberg (1942–43). Textiles in Broholm and Hald (1940); Munksgård (1974) and recent articles by Jørgensen, Bender, *et al.* (1982). Rock carvings are classified and quantified in Malmer (1981).

3. The question of inter-Scandinavian exchange and of fur-hunting will be treated in a forthcoming article (Kristiansen in press) but see also Malmer (1981, 105 ff.) and Johansen (1983). The impact of Lüneburg on Eastern Denmark was originally analyzed by Sprockhoff (1940). Evidence of regional and interregional alliances, however, is testified in many specialist works, some of them referred in Kristiansen (1981, 248 ff.). The objective in most of these works is classification and chronology. Thus we need a reanalysis of such patterns in terms of alliances and exchange for which the evidence holds a great potential.

4. An outline of prehistoric warfare in Denmark is given in Hedeager and Kristiansen (1985), and is analyzed for the Bronze Age in Kristiansen (1984b). Basic principles of primitive warfare are described in Turney-High (1949, second ed. 1971).

5. In this section the so-called *Mycenean influences* in Central and Northern Europe are put into an ideological framework of tribal social organization and evolution. However, the whole notion of Mycenean influences has been much disputed on archaeological grounds. It is therefore necessary to comment briefly on this debate. Some of the implications for the Nordic area are treated in note 6.

The situation is characterized by a group of proponents, mainly Central European scholars, and a smaller group of opponents, mainly English scholars. However, the discussion has been hampered by methodological problems: proponents have tended to rely on rather loose typological critieria without due respect to the prescribed procedures of typology (Malmer 1963, 27 ff.). Opponents, on the other hand, have chosen the easy way of relying primarily on C-14 dates and demonstrate little familiarity with – or simply disregard – the methodological principles of typology that are basic to any archaeological solution of the problem. Thus, as each side applies different criteria, a balanced

view based on a systematic analysis is not possible at present.

Recently Goldmann (proponent) has tried to reinterpret some of the archaeological evidence in a way that corresponds to the C-14 dates. This is in some aspects convincing, especially with the most recent datings of Montelius period II and the Shaft graves. This implies that they may cover both Later Wessex/East Europe A2–3 and B/early C. (Goldmann 1980/81).

In a new book Harding (opponent) has summarized the evidence (Harding 1984). It is an extremely valuable synthesis from a critical or rather sceptical point of view, although also problematic. A detailed and balanced assessment of the evidence is given with respect to amber and faience beads and with respect to genuine Mycenean objects and pottery. Thus, Harding concludes that direct contact was responsible for the occurrence of similar amber spacer plates in Wessex and the Shaft graves. It is therefore indeed strange that he tries any argument to explain other, expectable, similarities in Wessex as accidental or insignificant. This reflects a weakness of the book: the discussion of each group of evidence is carried out in isolation. The significance of the cultural context is therefore overlooked or perhaps more precisely only a local (archaeological) type of context is accepted. We are thus sometimes presented with rather surprising arguments to explain away cultural connections of undisreputable significance, such as the zig-zag mounts in Wessex, Bush Barrow, and the Shaft grave Iota (Harding 1984, Fig. 31), where not only form, but also construction and number of mounts are identical. Not to mention the exclusive symbolic significance of such an object. It is also quite clear that when stylistic and symbolic similarities *a priori* are considered subjective and insignificant, then there is little justification in discussing such evidence at all.

A counterweight to Harding's scepticism is found in Bouzek (1966), Vladar (1973), and in a number of articles in *Jahresberichte des Instituts für Vorgeschichte der Universität Frankfurt a.M.* 1977 and *Prähistorische Archäologie in Südosteuropa* 1982. They make it clear that the so-called Mycenean influences were part of a much larger cultural and ideological complex, some of it Eurasian (Hüttel 1977 and 1982), some of it Mediterranean or Near Eastern, including Asia Minor (Pingel 1982, Schauer 1984). Some of these traditions, especially that of metal toreutic, were well established centuries before the Shaft graves (Müller-Karpe 1977) and exercised influence also on the Early European Bronze Age. Also the Shaft graves themselves bear witness to diverse traditions, demonstrating trading expeditions and far-reaching alliances of adventurous chiefs or kings (especially the later LH I – the A-circle). The 'nouveau riche' display is a typical example of the founding phase of a dynasty (for discussion Dickinson 1977).

Thus when discussing this kind of evidence, reflecting trade and alliance systems not only between centers, but also between centers and 'peripheries' in several links, we are often dealing with a combination of a few genuine imported finds and local imitations or inspiration. And as genuine finds often occur isolated in a foreign context or in exceptional contexts such as Wessex and the Shaft graves, it is extremely difficult to assess the significance of the data both in archaeological and cultural-historical terms. It demands rigorous methodological analyses of both local, regional and international cultural and chronological contexts. But without a theoretical idea about the nature of the structural framework within which these historical processes were operating, the significance of the material evidence can never be properly interpreted and explained, as stressed by Müller-Karpe (1977), also Bouzek (1982). To this author there can be no doubt that the rise of the Shaft graves rested on the capacity to explore and exploit a position on the fringe of the 'civilized' world of the Eastern Mediterranean and the 'barbarian' hinterlands of the West Mediterranean and Central and Eastern Europe.

These hinterlands, however, were probably much less barbarian and more organized than we have tended to believe. And the capacity to establish far-reaching trading links with remote areas, cross-cutting areas of different political systems is testified in the Near East and Asia Minor. But also in the hinterlands, such as Scandinavia, trading expeditions crossed the open sea of the Baltic and sometimes extended 500–600 kms northwards along the coast.

While trading contracts with Wessex were given up, those with the Western Mediterranean and Europe were strengthened and developed until climax and decline around 1200 BC. The fourteenth century especially was a period of expansion in trade (LM IIIA).

After the completion of this chapter, Bouzek's recent book (Bouzek 1985) (proponent) on the interrelations between the Aegean and Europe in the second millennium, appeared. It contains a detailed listing and discussion of all relevant finds. Together with Harding it will be a standard work for years to come.

6. For the last 100 years it has puzzled archaeologists that the development of the original Nordic Bronze Age Culture shows a 'Mycenean' impact. And especially the fact that the Central European area does not display similar features, as one would expect of a transient zone. A number of Mycenean cultural influences were apparently transformed into a genuine Nordic style. However, many elements bear witness to the original prototypes. This has most recently been pointed out by Goldmann, but deserves a systematic study since it can be supported by much more evidence. What is considered important here, however, is not only the actual influence, but rather the ideological and ritual context within which it was transmitted. One such context is the ideology of warrior aristocracies as reflected in the concommitant occurrence of images of war chariots, long sword and a number of other symbols of elites. This group of evidence will therefore be discussed in more detail.

With respect to *swords* there is a general agreement that developments were highly international, e.g., the shift from dagger to sword, or the development of the flange-hilted sword. Thus the flange-hilted sword of Sprockhoff's type 1b is related to Sandars' type D1 swords, and a sword from Ørskovhede in Jutland bridges this connection (Randsborg 1967). Although Harding (1984, appendix 4) in a detailed critique has pointed out, rightly, that in its major features it belongs to the European group, it stands out from the majority of 1b swords by a number of details, whose inspiration is the Aegean type. I agree with Harding that the rounded point at the shoulder is most significant. The angle of the sword at 130°, however, is, to my knowledge, only found on a few other swords, which distinguishes them from the majority of 1b swords that have more hanging shoulders (140–150°). Thus, it must still be concluded that Ørskovhede, more than other 1b swords, reflects a rather specific Aegean influence, despite Harding's critique. It belongs to an early phase of the Montelius period 2 (see a related, but heavily sharpened sword from Southern Jutland with an early period 2 pommel, Aner and Kersten no. 3559D). In accordance with Randsborg (1967) and Schauer (1972), and in opposition to Hänsel (1982, 12), we ought to be in the fifteenth century BC, perhaps its later part.

Other traits that link developments in sword types between the Nordic and Aegean area are the pommel and the big rivets preserved on another sword from Southern Jutland (Aner and Kersten no. 2538B). Given the nearly unlimited variety in sword pommels, such features are significant. Another small feature which may support an early date for the beginning of period 2, is the 'Mycenean' dagger from Ahhoteps grave from Thebes (Helck 1977, Abb. 2.3., p. 12 ff.), dating from the mid sixteenth century

BC. The long hanging shoulders and the oval-shaped termination of hilt/shoulder with pointed ends is a combination of traits that is commonly found in the early phase of Montelius period 2 (and not in earlier or later periods). Given the variation known throughout the Bronze Age of the termination of the hilt against the blade, and considering the many other Egyptian/Aegean influences in the early period 2, this parallelism is hardly accidental.

The introduction of the full-hilted long sword in late period I and the flange-hilted warrior sword in period II was followed by a number of other international features linked to warrior aristocracies that spread in the sixteenth century. The significance of the *war chariot* in the Near East and Asia Minor in this respect has been documented from written sources by Zaccagnini (1977) and its spread in Eurasia is documented by Hüttel (1977 and 1982) on archaeological grounds. The employment of war chariots demanded not only a complex technology, but also specialized dressage and fighting techniques, which could only be mobilized in the empires around the Eastern Mediterranean and the Near East.

What could be transmitted was the ideology and part of the technology. Thus Egyptian chariots demanded the importation of different sorts of wood from temperate regions (Littauer and Crouwell 1979, p. 81). It is therefore a relevant question to ask if such chariots actually existed in equal numbers in the Nordic area. To answer that, we have to look at the evidence of carpentry, wagon models, rock carvings and the Kivik grave.

The preserved evidence of specialized carpentry is mainly restricted to folding stools that are simple but quite advanced constructions. The numerous rock carvings of ships, however, teach us that the technology for more complex constructions (including the bending of wood) must have been available. This is not to say that it was employed for war chariots. The four-spoked wheel especially is a complicated construction that is not testified in wood until the Iron Age in the Northern region. However, it was known already from Montelius period 2, as the bronze model of the sun chariot from Trundholm in Northern Zealand shows, together with a few other early examples of cast four-spoked wheels of bronze (Thrane 1962). Also rock carvings regularly show four-spoked wheels. Prototypes could be imported models of chariots in bronze, real chariots or pictorial blankets or rugs. None of the possible foreign prototypes have been found. We therefore have to deduce which is most likely. To do so we must turn to the evidence of rock carvings. Here the Kivik burial is important, together with other carvings of war chariots from the neighboring areas.

The decorated slabs from the Kivik grave (Fig. 14) are just as exceptional and unique in the Nordic Bronze age as the Trundholm sun chariot. We can therefore also expect them to be the result of extraordinary achievements and events. They are designed with frames and decorated divisions, e.g., like the Shaft grave steles, or as one would expect from pictorial rugs. Their background is evidently not Nordic, but most probably Mediterranean/Aegean. This is supported by a few of the motives. Although some of the ritual scenes may be said to conform to known Nordic traditions (the lur blowers), others are unique, just as the occurrence of altar and war chariot (together with some objects or constructions with no parallels, e.g., the two open circles that could be the grave circle). What we see is most probably the ritual sceneries of the burial, and the employment of a war chariot indicates its relationship both with tribal elites and with ritual.

On the slabs without sceneries are depicted a number of objects, perhaps the grave goods and/or the most important belongings of the buried chief. The four horses (2 × 2) correspond to the wheels of two chariots, also depicted. To this are added his ships, lances and ritual axes. Finally there are two axe-like objects with open curved endings. They are paralleled in gold in the Shaft grave Omincrom that is rather late within the B-circle, probably after 1550 (Mylomas 1972, plate 181).

According to the above there ought to have been two genuine war chariots in the possession of this extraordinary chief. This has been challenged by suggesting that the ritual scenes were idealized and replaced the real thing (Malmer 1981). Rituals, however, are performed by specialists and demand performance and participation in order to survive and retain their function. They cannot be replaced by carvings or figurines. It is therefore not probable that rituals could be illustrated without an intimate knowledge of their mythology and performance. The only thing that can be replaced, is the ritual depositions of the objects themselves, e.g., by drawing them or by using miniatures. The war chariot is both participating in the rituals and is also depicted in isolation (wheels and horses) together with other archaeologically known objects. From this follows that a real chariot, not a model, took part in the ritual, and that its deposition was substituted by drawing it together with other ritual objects (axes and lancebeads) that are normally not found in burials, but only (rarely) as votive or hoard depositions, and normally in pairs. This is supported by other evidence.

North of Kivik we find the most detailed carvings of war chariots, those from Fränarp (Fig. 14, no. 4). Depicted from above they show a completely realistic war chariot of the simple type, as preserved from Egyptian burials (Littauer and Crouwell 1979). The perspective and the realism of the carvings could not possibly have been derived from pictures, only from the model or a real chariot. The location of Kivik on the southeast coast of Scania is also perfect as an entry point for trade with the south coast of the Baltic, from the mouth of both Oder and Weichsel and down to Southeast Europe (Thrane 1977 and Fig. 4.).

Taking the evidence of Kivik and Fränarp together, I am inclined to conclude that in this area real chariots existed in the Early Bronze Age, probably imports from the Mediterranean/Aegean (in the Late Bronze Age imported prestigious wagons from Central Europe are documented archaeologically, e.g., Skjerne and Egemose [Jacob-Friesen 1970]). This naturally does not exclude the possibility that miniatures in bronze also were produced from the original prototypes. This was apparently the case in Denmark. A closer comparison of the Trundholm wheel from Northern Zealand and the wheel from Storehøj in Southern Jutland with Aegean/Egyptian prototypes and drawings on pottery reveals that the differences between the two Danish wheels (Thrane 1962, Figs. 11–18) correspond closely to similar differences among the prototypes. The Trundholm type has thin spokes and hub (Crouwell 1981, Plates 85, 76–77, 60, 136–137 and Fig. 5). The Storehøj type has more solid spokes, hub and felloe (Crouwell 1981, Plates. 32A, 135). Part of its ornamentation reflects constructive details on the original wheels. The Storehøj type corresponds to the more solid four-spoked type, which occurs both early and late. It differs, however, from the later even more solid type, as seen in Skallerup and Ystad (Thrane 1962, Fig. 19). The Trundholm type with its lighter construction corresponds rather to the later six-spoked type from the later fifteenth century onwards. (Crouwell 1981, 81 ff.).

Thus the Danish bronze wheels were not simple imitations of a general four-spoked type as depicted on the primitive models of clay or bronze in the Aegean and Central Europe (examples also in Crouwell 1981). They are precise imitations of a specific type of wheel most probably a real wheel and they reflect technological developments in the Mediterranean, just as later Urnfield and Hallstatt bronze wheels (Piggot 1983, Littauer and Crouwell 1979). As Storehøj is dated to the earlier part of period 2 by an imported pin of Zargenkopf type (and also contained a

British jet bead!), an early dating for the introduction of two-wheeled chariots – or at least their type of wheel – is suggested.

That we are dealing with something very exclusive, but also very real, is indicated by the more primitive imitations in areas further away, such as Bohuslän in Sweden and Østfold in Southeastern Norway. Also the exceptional pictorial stone slabs were imitated on the inner kerb of sandstone slabs round a barrow in Sagaholm (Malmer 1981, Figs. 14 and 15). The exclusive nature of war chariots is also demonstrated by their restricted distribution in South Scandinavia, their restricted number on rock carvings (19 in all) and short duration (Early Bronze Age) (Malmer 1981, 43 ff.).

This import of two-wheeled war chariots took place during period II, from its early part, as already mentioned. Kivik, however, has traditionally been dated to Montelius period 3 (eventually, late 2) based on the form of the axes and a few pieces of hammered bronze in the plundered burial. Hammered vessels, however, already occur in period 2, and the axes are then the only indication of a dating in period 3 (the wide and curved blade). The two axe symbols, on the other hand, might indicate an earlier dating. In that case Kivik could be the original source of inspiration of the employment of ritual sceneries on rock carvings in Scandinavia. This would also be in better accordance with the ship motive that belongs to the early type (Rørby), which begins in late period 1 (Malmer 1981, 31 ff.).

Accompanying the new ideology of warrior aristocracies was also the universal symbol of dignity: *the stool*. In the Bronze Age a folding stool that has been fully preserved in a few burials from Jutland, dating to Montelius period 2 (the calibrated C-14 dating of outer ring of one of them, Guldhøj, is 1480). The form and construction of this folding stool, however, is not local. Based on comparative studies of the Egyptian and Danish pieces, the architect Wanscher has convincingly demonstrated, also in precise drawings, that the Danish pieces conform to the constructive principles of the Egyptian type, just as dimensions are very much the same. There seems to be little doubt that they are the result of direct imitation of original Egyptian or Mediterranean pieces (Wanscher 1980).

Other symbols of exclusive social positions transmitted from the Mediterranean/Aegean area to Central and Northern Europe at the same time were razors and tweezers. However, European symbols of high rank from this time are also found in the shaft graves: not only amber necklaces, but also an old symbol of specific rank, such as the small rectangular pendant, normally of slate or the like, but in the Early Bronze Age sometimes also of amber. Such small things that had no value without knowledge of their specific social context tend to support the hypothesis that the shaft grave kings maintained alliances with, and were familiar with, the European hinterland (see also Davies 1985).

Taken together the group of evidence presented above leaves no doubt about the origin of warrior swords, war chariots and folding stools. This technological and ideological complex most probably reached the Nordic area during the final period 1/early period 2 in the late sixteenth and fifteenth centuries BC. Mycenean/Mediterranean influences continued to be transmitted to the Nordic area also in the subsequent centuries, and a later date for other 'Mycenean' influences is therefore highly probable. How the objects came to the Nordic area is a difficult question to answer at present, except in very general terms. Two possibilities seem at hand: 1) one or a few expeditions organized from the Mycenean area, or from one of their trading posts, reached the Nordic area in search of amber. It could either be from Western Europe (the sea route) or from the major river systems of Central Europe. 2) Areas in Europe with Aegean/Mediterranean contacts traded such objects to several areas in Northern Europe as part of prestige chain exchange.

The second hypothesis is the more probable, since the ideological context could not have been transmitted to the whole Nordic area by one or a few trading expeditions. This is perhaps the significant difference between developments in Wessex and South Scandinavia. Due to specific historical events the ornamental style of the Aegean/East European area was adopted in metalwork, and due to the ritualized theocratic nature of the Nordic Bronze Age, and exceptional conditions of preservation, much more of the original evidence was deposited and preserved archaeologically than in Central Europe.

7. Most of the evidence on settlements is very recent. For the LN/EBA 1 articles by Simonsen (1983), Nielsen and Nielsen (in press) and Boas (1983). For EBA 2 and the Later BA articles by Boysen and Andersen (1983) and Becker (1982).

8. The standard symmary on the development of the cultural landscape is still Berglund (1969) and for Denmark Andersen, Aaby and Odgaard (1983). The relationship between settlement/regression and climatic trends is summarized by Gräslund (1980).

9. To this should be added the important evidence of physical anthropology. In the LN population is markedly taller on average than the old Megalithic population. In Denmark males increase on average from 165.4 cm to 171.1 cm, and females from 151 cm to 159.5 cm (Brøste and Balslev 1956). A single stone cist in Central Sweden with at least thirty individuals also revealed a very tall population. If we consider life expectancy it is also higher during the LN (50% maturis/senilis compared to 35% in the MN), although all burials also show quite a few children and juveniles. As we have no skeleton data from the intermediate period of the Single Grave Culture, we do not know if these changes were rooted in this period or if migrations may have played a role. However, it may be assumed that the expansion of settlement and the subsequent intensification in subsistence, at least to some extent, may be responsible for this development due to an improved diet. The rather homogeneous evidence of tall, healthy people strongly suggests that we are dealing with a rather small upper selection of the population during the LN (from the EBA the evidence is unfortunately too scarce to infer anything).

10. This structural and technological change in Eastern and Central Europe is summarized in articles by Hänsel, Kubach, Primas and Vulpe in *Jahresbericht*, Frankfurt 1977.

Chapter 5

Power and moral order in precolonial West-Central Africa

Michael Rowlands

Introduction

Rulers of precapitalist states and empires rarely imposed their will in the absence of divine aid. Religious legitimation is at the centre of any complexly organised precapitalist society. The classic statement on this theme was made by Frankfort in *Kingship and the Gods* where he argued that at the heart of the matter is a denial that human polities can be seen as things in themselves. Rather they exist only to the extent that embedded in the life of the cosmos, they are themselves sustained through maintaining the harmony of its integration (Frankfort 1948, 25). Following a useful distinction made by Merquior, authority in this view is less a 'power over' than a 'power from' (Merquior 1979, 25). It emanates from sacred tradition, origin and the very essence of things. Understandably, there has been a consistent reaction to this ideal since it conflicts with the experience of the often brutal realities of 'power over'. Religious legitimation is interpreted instead as a form of holistic ideology which serves to conceal sectional interest through the projection of beliefs, invested with universal validity, onto other groups whose interests are not well served. It matters little whether the bearers of sectional interests realise this or not; it is sufficient to demonstrate that their interests are served whilst those of others are not. Opposed in this manner, these two views generate a debate which must necessarily veer to either emphasising the validity of the subjective experience of the former or the underlying reality of interests of the latter.

Moreover very different material effects stem from which of these views is emphasised. If the glitter of a cosmological centre often appears to blind the observer to the role of coercion then equally too narrow a view of exploitation denies the very real consensus which can bind ruler and ruled in a shared 'moral community'.

Studies of the history of African leadership exemplify this dichotomy of view. Some of the most subtle studies of divine kingship have been produced in this context (Evans-Pritchard 1948; Young 1966; Adler 1982). Most of these writers have had difficulties in reconciling two aspects of the ethnographic and historical data available. One of these aspects is the apparent ritual nature of precolonial African kingship, so defined that power is subordinated to hierarchy and hierarchy is a manifestation of the sacred. The other aspect is that this subordinated power is in reality founded on control of resources. These controls have been variously interpreted as controls over means of production and reproduction (Meillassoux 1981); over means of destruction (Goody 1971); the control of slaves (Terray 1974) and monopoly access to long-distance trade (Coquery-Vidrovitch 1978; Meillassoux 1971). In most interpretations one of these aspects inevitably becomes an epiphenomenon of the other, depending on the perspective adopted. Due to the efforts of some of the French Marxist anthropologists working in West Africa, attempts to bridge the two interpretations have been made in recent years. In several

Central and West African contexts, e.g., it has been recognised that the passion for circulating rare wealth items, whose overt economic significance was minimal, was the crucial link in the articulation of social reproduction with the definition and legitimation of authority (Meillassoux 1960; Ekholm 1977). The link between symbolic value and production and exchange was, in consequence, sought and found in social structure and, in particular, in matrimonial alliance and idioms of descent. The objective of this chapter is to develop further these attempts at 'bridging' through a study of a group of societies of varying degrees of political complexity inhabiting the southern and western parts of Cameroon in the nineteenth century. In a situation where archaeology is the equivalent elsewhere of modern history, the aim is to establish an historical baseline at the end of the nineteenth century which may then be used elsewhere to help interpret certain aspects of the fragmentary and uneven archaeological record of earlier periods. The approach will demonstrate a more general analytic point. The difficulties which have been encountered in interpretation are largely due to the uncritical acceptance of concepts such as authority, legitimation and the 'economic' which are too specific to the experience of modern state formation in Europe. This is not to deny human universals but it does raise the question whether an analysis should start with the implicit assumption that techno-economic, social and cultural levels exist which subsequently have to be articulated with each other. If social anthropology and sociology can no longer be sure of the autonomy of culture, politics and economics then, as I hope to show, archaeologists may find that in their traditional holistic practices, they have avoided already some of the puzzlements of their colleagues in the social sciences.

The Cameroon Grassfields

The Grassfields is a high-altitude savanna area of west Cameroon which from the early colonial period was recognised to possess a distinctive unity and was given its name by German colonisers after the nature of its dominant vegetation (Fig. 5.1). The geological region coincides remarkably with three closely related language groups called Mbam-Nkam, Ring and Momo and with a type of society which can be briefly summarised in the following manner. They are composite groups resulting from what Horton called 'disjunctive migrations' so that members of non-related descent groups are found in the same residential unit (Horton 1971). Political organisation covers the range from acephalous group, or a group with a chief or *fon*, to 'state' in traditional terminology and yet these share a common basis in lineage organisation, council of notables and a chief or *fon*. The latter, in modern times, has acquired important administrative powers but still symbolises the unity of the chiefdom through alliances between descent groups of different origins and the resolution of social conflicts by ritual means. At the end of the nineteenth century, these societies were involved in systematic trading relations with populations occupying lowland tropical forest environ-

ments to the south. In a superficial sense, the range of specialisations illustrate the differences of ecology and labour organisation: the highland areas were a source of grains, small livestock, slaves and craft products for which palm oil, salt, brass rods and European trade goods were gained in return. The Grassfields was never in direct trading contact with European entrepots on the southern coast and throughout the eighteenth and nineteenth centuries were suppliers of slaves to intermediate populations in return for guns, gunpowder, cloth, brass rods and beads. The role of supplier of labour power did not change appreciably in the early colonial period when the area became a major source of forced labour for road and rail construction and of wage labour for the coastal plantations until the present day. The niche that these populations have occupied in recent history is therefore a consistently marginal one in relation to the larger regional system and this consideration has to be borne in mind when considering local political development.

Since Greenberg first formulated the thesis, it has been known that the zone of origin of the Bantu languages lay in the area between the Cross and Benue Rivers which includes the Grassfields (Greenberg 1966). The massive spread of the Bantu languages, starting by at least 2000 BC, is assumed to be a function of the settlement of the subcontinent by food producing populations. From a point of origin in the Benue-Cross River area, these populations are supposed to have migrated south and eastwards to Central and parts of Southern Africa by the end of the first millennium BC. The speakers of Western and Eastern Bantu are now known to have had the same origin, but to have diverged at such an early date in these migrations, that no trace exists of Eastern Bantu languages west of the Interlacustrine region (Vansina 1984, 131). The spread of western Bantu from Cameroon into Central Africa occurred in three waves with initially a tendency to keep to savanna/forest ecotones and subsequently a diversification to more specialised environments. The modern distribution of western Bantu in an area from southern Cameroon to northern Namibia, the Zambezi and the Great Lakes appears to have been achieved by the late first millennium BC. The Mbam-Nkam and western Bantu languages diverged from a common stock and hence it is of significance that the settlement of the Grassfields appears to have been stable for at least three millennia or more. Shum Laka, a rock shelter site in the Grassfields, has evidence of food production and ground stone tools and dates from the beginning of the seventh to the end of the fourth millennium BC (De Maret 1980, 10). A continuous series of corrected radiocarbon dates for iron-working sites in the Grassfields are spread over a period from the third to the seventeenth centuries AD (Warnier, personal communication). The linguistic evidence shows that Grassfields Bantoid speakers share 55 per cent basic vocabulary with linguistic diversity and density falling off rapidly outside this region. We can assume therefore the presence of a set of fairly stable populations that are often described in the ethnographic literature as culturally homogenous and yet display a significant diversity of political culture and differences in the resources required to sustain this diversity.

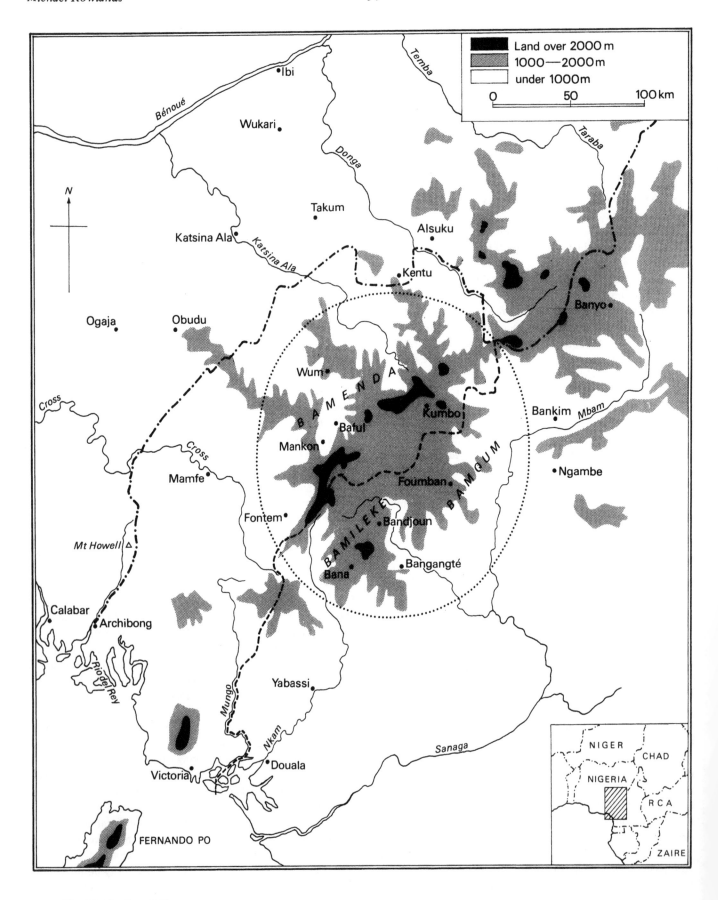

Fig. 5.1. The Grassfields

Power and hierarchy

Over a large area of southern Cameroon, Gabon and Equatorial Guinea, people believe that men and women who acquire riches and influence do so because of their possession of an *evu*. There is no unique and authorised version of the myth of *evu*, so I will take one version well described by Mallart Guimara for the Evuzok of South Cameroon.

Evu was originally a being of the forest, neither male nor female, having neither back nor front. A woman approached it one day and agreed to carry it back into the village. *Evu* demanded that it should be brought back in her womb because it could not stand bright light. Once arrived in the village, *evu* refused to come out and demanded food. The woman brought it chickens, then goats and having exhausted everything, was constrained finally to bring it her own children. Since that day, *evu* (and death) has remained in the village. The Evuzok, in addition, believe that *evu* is transmitted through the mother to her children (Mallart Guimera 1981).

This summary brings out certain pertinent features which are found in all variants of the myth. Evu is a being of the forest and is introduced as a foreign body into human society. Evu is a phenomenon of living society. The ideal society, that of dead ancestors, is without *evu* since it dies with the host and must be transmitted to future generations in order to assure its survival in living society. It is a being which settles in people's stomachs in the shape of an organ which can be detected through autopsy. It gives power to its owner which, if socialised, and reinforced by appropriate rituals, is used for the good of the individual and the community. But, if the person's intentions are bad, such powers lead the person to practise sorcery and to kill people for personal gain. In most of these societies, such beliefs also assume a close association between women and the introduction of *evu* as ambiguous power into human society and the transmission by them of this imaginary power to their children.

The point I wish to stress is that power in this ideology is viewed as a direct consequence of persons using this inherited capacity for either good or bad purposes. Such power is deeply ambiguous since it depends on the person's intentions. In nature, the power of these imaginary beings is invariably malevolent and is equally so in society if used in an individualistic and selfish manner. Such uses would invariably attract accusations of sorcery resulting in ostracism and, in the past, the poison ordeal and execution. Yet it is improbable that anyone in authority should not be thought to have this power and a 'chief' would be expected to use it to harm enemies and to protect his people from their ill-will.

However, being a chief or an elder would not depend on simply possessing a power superior to that of other persons. The socialisation of power for morally correct purposes is an achievement of ritual practices which encode ancestral order. Hierarchy is distinct from power in the sense that it is a representation of moral order sustained by ancestors as distinct from the possession of *evu* by the living. A dead person loses all power of the *evu* type and occasionally there are appropriate

funerary rituals to ensure this. Dead elders are out of power although its possible that their ill will may continue if they were so inclined. As dead elders devoid of power, they embody pure legitimacy and together with living elders they form a category of their own. Living elders are the embodiments of ancestral purity and their behaviour should express the appropriate qualities of honesty, generosity, knowledge and the ability to resolve conflicts among their followers. Moreover, they are the principal officiants in rituals which invoke ancestral support for the fertility of crops, animals and women and defense against such external threats as disease and enemies. Continuity between living and dead elders is expressed by use of the same word for both and by the fact that society is believed to extend beyond death.

The main features of this ideology can be briefly summarised. Moral order as an ideal type of pure legitimacy is a projection on the living of the ideal world of dead ancestors. This is contrasted to the natural order as the source of power which no society can be without yet exists as an alien substance of external origin. Power in its unsocialised form is always a reification of the pathologies of moral order. Evil, practised as sorcery, is the antithesis of the ideal society of dead elders. However, it is recognised that socialised power is necessary for all form of human endeavour and success. Power, which in its 'raw' state would lead to sorcery, can be domesticated for socially good uses through rituals which invoke ancestral protection of the person, the descent group and the village. Personal and group boundaries are literally seen to be 'armour plated' by ritual means against uncontrolled acts of power from outside and any weakening of these defences requires immediate attention. Social conflict is seen as the most serious and pervasive act which weakens these defences since aggrieved parties are likely to resort to sorcery or to collude with outside enemies to bring misfortune to the village. Much effort is spent by persons and groups to detect the sources of envy, jealousy and ill-will which disrupt ideal order and expose the victims to misfortune, illness and possibly death.

We can now see why a concept such as authority with its modernist implications of a single source of legitimate and coercive power is inappropriate in this context. There are at least three forms of hierarchy generated by this political ideology. There is a hierarchy of socialised power which is widely diffused amongst both men and women. There is a hierarchy of sorcery which is evil and nocturnal and into which people with bad intentions are born or those with socialised power may lapse due to greed, envy or grievance. Finally, there is the hierarchy of pure legitimacy expressed in the behaviour of living elders as officiants of the rituals which cleanse polluting acts and manage the social effects of disordering events. Their capacity to do this depends on their relations with dead elders to whose title they are successors, and who can withdraw their 'blessing', causing people and the land to 'dry up'. Each of these hierarchies had a different basis in material resources, which it could manage and control and each operated within distinct spheres of social action which generated conflicting interests. Yet the notion of 'centralisation' of these functions into a more unified form of authority is not entirely inappropriate. As we shall see, the form this takes depends upon the conditions promoting the dominance of one form of hierarchy over the others and the combination of the first and third in order to combat the socially disruptive effects of the second.

The limits of political centralisation

So far we have only considered some general principles of a broadly defined societal type. An ambiguous conception of power in which a capacity for sorcery plays a dominant role is so widespread that it suggests that we are dealing with a pervasive and historically deeply rooted feature of the ideological systems of western and central Africa. The notion that power for either good or evil stems from possession of an inherited substance is described as *tsav* for the Tiv (Nigeria) by Bohannan (1958); as *dua* for the Gbaya and Maka of east Cameroon by Burnham (1980) and Geschiere (1981); as *mangu* for the Azande (CAR) by Evans-Pritchard (1937) and as *kindoki* for the Bakongo (Zaire) by MacGaffey (1970). The group of societies in southern Cameroon and Gabon are more closely linked and this is reflected in the use of lexically similar terms (the Fang of Gabon call the imaginary being *evus*, Bureau 1972; the Evuzok, Beti, Bulu of south Cameroon call it *evu*, Mallart Guimera 1981; the Basaa of south west Cameroon call it *Hu*, Bayiga 1966; and the Duala call it *ewusu*.)

The societies of the Grassfields are a particular segment of this range which have been consistently described as 'centralised' (Chilver and Kaberry 1967). By this is meant the presence of hereditary chiefship, palaces, retainers and titled officials attached to the palace and regulatory societies specialising in pollution removal and social control. Mankon is a small chiefdom in the northern Grassfields which had a population of approximately 8000 at the end of the nineteenth century. What outsiders erroneously call a chief is indigenously called a *fon*. The distinction is important. In European thought 'chiefs' are less secure versions of kings who retain attributes of authority and power to command, to punish, to reward and to exploit; all of which are quite foreign to the Mankon notion of *fon*. Warnier describes this person appropriately as the incarnation of cultural order: when asked to describe a *fon* his informants would never use the language of discipline and punishment but rather the language of generosity, redistribution and fertility. (Warnier 1983, 474). This is no longer a particularly original point in archaeological or anthropological investigations of chiefship (cf. Sahlins 1982; Bott 1981; De Heusch 1975). The distinction between ritual and political chiefs, for example, is a well-known feature of descriptions of both African and Polynesian chiefly authority; the cleavage appropriately relocates the concepts of redistribution in ideology rather than in stratification. The case of Mankon is somewhat purer since there are no 'political chiefs' acting as real leaders. The *fon* is the embodiment of hierarchy as previously defined and represents the essence of ancestral substance for the 'chief-dom' as a whole. He maintains a hierarchy of moral order by being head of the royal clan and is superordinate in the hierarchy of household, lineage and clan heads and by his actions denotes a model form of purity which others cannot hope to emulate. The quintessence of being *fon* is realised in the annual dry season festival at the end of the agricultural cycle when the *fon* returns to the graves of his ancestors to make offerings which, if accepted, initiates several days of feasting and dancing. In the glow of shared moral unity and harmony, the palace distributes large quantities of food and drink and ritual substances such as camwood, a red powder which when rubbed on people's bodies gives off a healthy sheen as a visible representation of harmony, incorporation and ancestral blessing. A few weeks after the dance, the palace conducts the rituals of protection of persons, groups and boundaries against sorcery and natural disasters prior to the beginning of the next agricultural cycle. Now this is not to argue that lineage and clan heads and the *fon* were purely ritual figures. They were owners of land, had numerous dependents and accumulated large numbers of wives. Unlike the more acephalous forest groups already mentioned, a *fon* was believed to possess a socialised power; otherwise how else would he be able to combat the anti-social behaviour of witches? The difference is that legitimacy and power are fused in the person of the *fon* as long as his actions are directed to the public good. There have been cases in the past where *fons* have behaved anti-socially (i.e. in their own interests) and have been deposed and even killed. Hence hierarchy embodies the values of descent and ancestors and, as a pure form of legitimacy, is associated with the earth and agriculture, with truth and the power of speech, with the avoidance of polluting acts and with rituals of cleansing and protection. In the language of Dumont (1970) these are the highest values in Mankon culture (or as Marx said, the ether which lends its colour to all things). The maintenance of hierarchy depends on subordinating its contrariety, the imaginary being engendering power, in order to neutralise the challenge of a different vision of how society should be ordered (see Rowlands 1985 for the objectification of these principles in material culture).

But there is a logical contradiction in the ordering of this political culture. How can it be that a *fon* who epitomises purity and goodness is involved in the repressive and subordinating processes which preserve moral hierarchy? The answer, in the case of Mankon and other neighbouring chiefdoms, is that he cannot. There are, on the contrary, strict rules of avoidance separating the *fon* and lineage/clan heads from the repressive aspects of social control which, in the precolonial past, included the execution of criminals. Such functions were handled instead by the members of a regulatory association, now widely referred to by the term *kwi'fo*. In Mankon, its members were a group of men drawn from a number of different clans. None of them were clan heads i.e., mediators with ancestors and all were believed to possess special powers and instruments which permitted them to purify the pollution resulting from odious acts. As masters of pollution they were thus able to inflict on members of society what would otherwise be considered as abominations. The repressive and coercive aspects of power were thus controlled by a group of men (viz., members of the royal clan of Mankon could not belong to *kwi'fo*) whose actions were seen by all as deeply ambiguous, polluting and barely tolerable. To consider such persons as 'political chiefs' would thus give them undue honour although this is not to deny the power they wielded nor what they were to achieve in the colonial period when the Germans and the British were looking for 'real chiefs'.

Mankon political culture can thus be interpreted in terms of a dualism of legitimacy and power and diagrammed as follows:

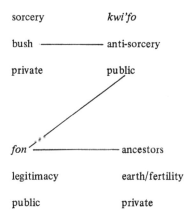

Chiefdoms of the southern Grassfields, now grouped together as the Bamileke, an ethnic title acquired during the colonial period, provide us with instances of a different kind. Bamileke chiefs could be safely described as 'real chiefs' and, as in our cultural experience of such persons, were regarded as wielding deeply ambiguous and threatening powers. In the area of Dschang, 60 km, to the south of Mankon, the ambivalence of political power of a Bamileke *fon* is recorded by Miaffo in the following manner:

> Bon, grand, puissant, certes, mais méchant et mauvais
> à souhait, capable de tous les mauvais sorts. On le définit
> souvent par des tours de ce genre: 'Tuez-vouz sa mère, il
> la mange; la vendez-vous, il en consomme l'argent'.
> Good, illustrious, powerful certainly, but dangerous and
> arbitrary, capable of every kind of bad act. He is often
> discussed using a turn of phrase like 'if you kill his
> mother he eats her, sell her and he will take the money'.
> (my translation, Miaffo; 1977, 99)

The foundation legends of a number of Bamileke chiefdoms exemplify the contrast. They share very similar motifs. The dynastic founding ancestor is always an immigrant who has left another established chiefdom after a quarrel over succession. He is an accomplished hunter (note the associations with the forest and sorcery) who comes to a place where the indigenous population are farmers and their chiefs own the land and ensure agricultural success (the founder of the Mankon dynasty was a farmer). The immigrant hunter establishes himself through gifts of wild game and takes local

women as wives in counter-gifts. He attracts people to him through his generosity and finally, by a ruse, drives out the indigenous chiefs or converts them into sub-chief status. We do not need to assume real history here; the point being that the origin myths charter the transformation of a dualism of legitimacy and power into an ambiguous form of political authority which may be legitimate or illegitimate according to personal motivation and intention. A Bamileke *fon* cannot be the embodiment of purity because he belongs to *kwi'fo* and is deeply involved in the repressive and coercive actions of that institution. However, the extent to which a *fon* combines legitimacy and power for the public good rather than despotism and exploitative personal gain still defines political authority. Ambiguity lies in the fact that what is unified in Bamileke chiefship are two contradictory principles that ideally should be kept separate in a just and moral order. In the Bamileke chiefdoms, it is the patrilineage and patriclan heads (the 'notables') that retain purity through avoidance of *kwi'fo* and hence it is not surprising to learn that the line of major conflict in one of these chiefdoms was between the notables and the *fon* supported by members of *kwi'fo* (Pradelles, personal communication). Nevertheless a Bamileke *fon* is a higher order authority than either notables or *kwi'fo* because he constitutes a synthesis of both of these structures, and it is this that gives content to the description that Bamileke chiefdoms were politically centralised. The transformation can be represented as follows:

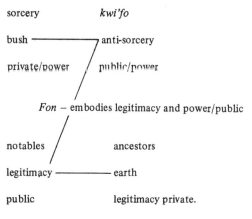

(after Pradelles, personal communication)

If we compare our three cases and their cultural properties, we can decontextualise a simple acephalous to centralise continuum to show that a set of common principles are manipulated in the following sequence of reversals and transformations:

where $>$ ranks higher than:

1. ancestors : pure ligitimacy $>$ power : Evuzok
2. ancestors : legitimacy : socialised power for public protection $>$ socialised power for repression and punishment $>$ sorcery : Mankon
3. ancestors : legitimacy : socialised power for public protec-

tion, repression and punishment > ancestors : pure legitimacy > sorcery : Bamileke

Political centralisation is therefore only possible by fusing the
ambiguous nature of power with the pure legitimacy of ancestral order in the institution of chiefship. Yet the result is full
of contradictions and it is not surprising to learn that Bamileke
chiefs were frequently accused of abuse of power and the
exploitation of their subjects.

Sorcery, alliance and exchange

As an ideological representation, 'centralisation' thus
glosses two processes: one is incorporation requiring that the
legitimacy of moral order and the coercive aspects of power
should be combined in the same institution and only with
great ambiguity in the same person; the other is inversion,
since this combination requires legitimacy to dominate power
and yet be superior to the value of moral order without power.
Since linked ideas and values do not of themselves transform
in this way, we have to investigate their setting in the concrete
political conditions promoting such transformations.

The myths of origin of the Bamileke chiefdoms and the
parallel structuring of symbolic codes both suggest that what is
also inverted is the value of descent over alliance. This inverted
value is projected as a 'conquest myth' in the Bamileke case, in
which 'immigrant hunters' take wives (alliance) and subsequently subordinate indigenous populations rooted in land,
fertility and ancestors (descent). The association between
sorcery and marriage is also brought out in the myths of the
origin of sorcery since it is a woman who brings the imaginary
being (*evu*) from the bush (nature) into the village (culture).
Moreover, as we have seen, witchcraft substance is thought to
be transmitted through women to their children (who will
belong to the father's patrilineage); hence it is the act of
marrying women from other lineages and clans as a consequence of the incest and exogamy rules which brought sorcery
into a descent group. It is not surprising to learn therefore that
Bamileke chiefs would favour marrying endogamously within
their descent group via patri-lateral parallel-cousin marriage
or would marry their daughters to other chiefs for bridewealth
or to slaves rather than to their own commoners. (Pradelles,
personal communication).

The point I wish to stress is that a belief in sorcery and
the politics of marriage alliance were part of the same inter-
connected structure. Marriage implies formalised exchange, for
what was given was a woman whose value to her natal descent
group was never completely alienated. For this reason, it was
contextualised within formalised rules of reciprocity between
the heads of separate descent groups and the morality of the
transaction ensured through the threat of retribution of ancestral anger. This was no idle threat since a woman could trans-
mit her *evu* to her children which could be activated by the
anger of the wife's father if the obligations to him by the
husband and his agnates were not honoured. Marriage as an act
of formalised exchange, literally made 'society' possible only

through the role of ancestral order in sustaining the morality
of the transaction. If such obligations were breached, the anger
of the wife's father was capable of unleashing fearsome anti-
social forces within the husband's descent group and could
cause illnesses to or the death of his daughter's children. Needless to say some men's speech was more powerful than others
in this respect; the fear engendered through offending a
Bamileke marriage lord for instance was frequently cited as a
threat that could cause misfortune for many future generations. When the obligations of affines were not honoured,
marriage alliance degenerated into a kind of transaction without social responsibility akin to trading for profit where
individual self-gain takes precedence over the morality of
social relations. Persons who had been responsible for placing
society at risk by such actions were caught in the conceptual
link made between sorcery, anti-social behaviour and the
pursuit of personal gain. Sorcery (which, if committed by a
woman leads to the death of her children; if by a man, to the
death of kinsmen) is anti-alliance and anti-exchange. A woman
accused of sorcery would leave her husband's compound and
have to return to her father's whilst a man would be driven
from his kin group and out of 'society'. It is perhaps worth
stressing at this point that the same interpretative scheme
would be applied to many other, apparently unrelated acts, if
they offended the general principle that moral order, embedded
in a hierarchy of ancestral titles, should constrain unregulated
acquisition of power. In the late nineteenth century, for
example, the trade in slaves was part of sorcery since it was an
act which colluded in taking people out of society and selling
them for gain and, in consequence, inverted the legitimacy of
formalised exchange. It was part of the ambiguous role of
kwi'fo that they were entitled to dispose of social miscreants
in this manner and could act in an overtly antisocial manner
(with great potential for abuse) by claiming to do so for the
good of all. The notion that anti-social acts could sustain moral
order was a claim so full of ambiguities and contradictions that
it was tantamount to accusing someone of sorcery to denounce
them for being a trader in slaves. Consequently it was a secret
affair carried out at night by men belonging to special associations. One of the commonest accusations made against chiefs
and notables was that they secretly belonged to such associations and were 'eating their people' rather than protecting and
feeding them. Needless to say, there is a close link between the
development of the slave trade, its offence against moral order
and the belief in a hierarchy of sorcerers who were evil and
killed people at night.

We can now see that the ideological structure which
asserts that legitimacy should act to constrain the worst excesses
of power is part of a practice which upheld the obligations of
marriage alliance as well as reproducing the asymmetries which
uneven access to marriageable women would tend to produce.
Moreover the fact that marriage was a part of a wider system
of formalised exchange opposed it to the other modes of
exchange where personal gain was the primary rationality.
Marriage alliance and formalised exchange were thus embedded

in legitimacy since ideally they served to expand descent groups and to ensure the succession of ancestral titles. It was/is the neglect of ancestors and the anger they feel which causes illness and disease, barrenness in women and poor crops; events which reverse an ideal moral order in which well disposed ancestors should take care of their living descendants. Yet the ideal function of the marriage system as support to descent, was strongly distorted by the expansion of the slave trade following European contact in the seventeenth century. The supply of captive women, brought as 'alienated products' meant that their owners were free of any threat of supernatural sanctions from their kin. Control over the circulation of female slaves and that of their female offspring provided a source of power over their husbands' patri-groups since the sanction of ancestral anger now became a monopoly of the original owner of the 'slave woman' given as a wife, and his male descendants. Effectively, marriage alliance became embedded in power and utilised an idiom of descent as an unrestrained ideological buttress for the pursuit of personal gain. The moral order had been reversed and the combination of alliance and power acted to subvert the principles of descent and legitimacy for ideological purposes.

I can illustrate this by examining the conditions which promoted this transformation in three Grassfields chiefdoms, two of which I have already mentioned, Mankon and the Bamileke, and including as a transitional form Bafut, a near neighbour to Mankon. Mankon is a case in which the descent idiom was dominant (Warnier 1975 and 1983). At the end of the nineteenth century, there were nine exogamous clans subdivided into thirty-two lineages of which the royal clan was the largest, estimated to include 50 per cent of the population. Clans were non-fissioning patri-groups of often diverse origin, which competed with each other in the acquisition of titles and positions in the various palace-defined ritual associations. Making claims to titles depended on the ability to make payments and thus upon wealth, which was largely defined in terms of the productivity of household and supra-household economies. Marriage alliances were directed towards increasing the size of household, lineage and clan, and other practices such as pawning, clientage and the incorporation of war captives and slaves as lineage members were directed towards the same end. Bridewealth payments were made for wives so that the debt to wife-giver groups was nominal and cut after birth of the first child, although minor payments and help to the mother's father and his descendants would be expected to continue. Mankon political culture was thus organized around the core principle of agnatic descent, and internal conflict was largely a product of the fluidity of this structure. As we have seen, this is consistent with a clear separation of a hierarchy of pure legitimacy vested in lineage/clan notables from the polluting activities (anti-sorcery) of the main regulatory association, *takoengoe*, and the ambiguous role of the *fon* in mediating between these two principles (Warnier 1983).

Bafut was and still is one of the largest chiefdoms in the northern Grassfields. It shares with its neighbour Mankon, a similar emphasis on descent and recruitment to large non-fissioning descent groups organised and cross-cut by ritual ward associations (Ritzenthaler 1962). A major difference is that new royal lineages were and still are created after the second successor to a deceased *fon* has been installed. Members of such lineages revert to commoner status once all the first born children of that *fon* are also dead. Commoner lineages or clans of separate origin were therefore constrained from segmenting in order to maintain their demographic coherence in the face of the rapid and systematic creation of new lineages by the palace. Segmentation on this scale was not possible under normal demographic conditions: it was possible because a Bafut *fon* was able to take wives from commoner lineages without payment of bridewealth whom he then distributed to his sons and palace retainers. Perhaps it is more significant that Bafut was an expanding conquest state by the 1880s and warfare was directed to taking war captives who were either exported or, more often, absorbed into royal lineages, particularly if they were women and children. Through the acquisition of a regular supply of captive women who could be redistributed without payment of bridewealth, claims could be made on the disposal of their female offspring. This marriage system worked in favour of the expansion of the royal clan and against commoner clans, which were forced to rely on normal demographic reproduction. Yet, acquiring excess wives from 'slave traders' or by capture was to connive in 'illegitimate' trade or to deflect actions designed to protect the chiefdom as a whole (warfare) to serve particular interests. Hierarchy as pure legitimacy was always in danger of being exposed as the use of power for personal ends. This is reflected politically in the practice of avoidance by commoner clan heads of the palace institutions concerned with discipline and punishment: the *fon* on the other hand was and is an active participant in their decisions. The Bafut also share with the Bamileke 'an immigrant hunter' origin myth in contrast to the Mankon foundations legend which stresses that the first *fon* was a farmer (Warnier 1983, 406–7).

The Bamileke represent a more extreme case of the dominance of alliance over descent. Bamileke chiefs and the heads of large polygynous households used to practise what is generally called a 'marriage lordship' or *ta-nkap* marriage system. Preferably, such men would give daughters and marriage wards to sons, servants and impecunious subjects without payment of bridewealth so that they and their successors could claim the right to dispose of the female offspring of these women *in perpetuum*. Moreover, since bridewealth had not been paid, the husbands were in perpetual debt to the original marriage lord who thus controlled a vast pawnship system. Before the suppression of this institution by the French, it is estimated that 80 per cent of Bamileke women were married in this way; Hurault estimates that in one case, a chief had 1500 such marriage wards and was linked in asymmetrical debt relations with the majority of his subjects (Hurault 1962). Chiefs, on the other hand, either married endogamously within the royal patri-group, or married the daughters of other chiefs for bridewealth, thus insuring their independence. It is debatable whether agnatic descent groups were still a feature of Bamileke social organisation by the end of the nineteenth century. Hurault, for instance, denies that they were (Hurault 1962, 35). Probably they were more like small patri-groups formed around the inheritance of titles, property and rights in marriage wards rather than true lineages. The fissioning of descent groups and the creation of new descent lines was constantly generated by inheritance rules, encouraging the creation of shallow patri-groups as the only route open to non-inheriting sons to establish a separate patrimony and make claims to increased status.

The Bamileke conception of power is based on the link between marriage alliance and sorcery. They have an explicit notion of sorcery as an inherited substance (*atok*) transmitted through the matriline (Pradelles, personal communication). The control of marriage wards and their offspring is, to a certain extent, encouraged by and kept in check by the fact that this is seen as the way in which sorcery is distributed through a chiefdom. It is not surprising to learn that the majority of sorcery accusations are made by wife-takers against wife-givers. Marriage lords possessed deeply ambiguous and unchallengeable powers since to offend them or to break the conditions of indebtedness of alliance, would unleash fearsome anti-social forces in local patri-groups. Moreover, as we have seen, the separation of moral order from repressive control is dissolved in the figure of the Bamileke chief. Instead, we see the development of single hereditary chiefs based on the ambiguous unification of legitimacy and power which other notables were unable to challenge.

The dominance of the marriage wardship system in the Bamileke chiefdoms is linked to the important role they played as middlemen in the slave trade. Situated on the southern edge of the Grassfields and linked to European entrepots in Douala and Calabar in the eighteenth and nineteenth centuries, chiefs and notables gained access to large numbers of female slaves whom they retained whilst selling male slaves for European trade goods. When these female slaves were given in marriage, rights over their children were restricted and continued to be the property of the descendants of the original owners even though the memory of the slave status of the original ancestress would have been suppressed. Ultimately therefore, it was an unusual set of externally derived conditions which promoted the dominance of alliance and exchange and subverted the principle of descent in the internal organisation of these chiefdoms.

Production and exchange in a 'moral community'

The analysis so far has detailed the antithesis between an ideal society of ancestral order, land, production and autochthony and a subversive reality of an ambivalent and threatening notion of power and its connections with marriage alliance, formalised exchange and the slave trade. The ideal of a closed and involuted society, spatially represented in dense settlements behind massive defense works, on fuller examina-

tion revealed a 'reality' of external dependency and exchange with power itself as a foreign substance which could serve to tear society asunder. The evidence of chiefdom fragmentation and the movement of numerous splinter groups from chiefdom to chiefdom in the nineteenth century is perhaps the best indicator of the inherent instability and fluidity of chiefdom composition, growth and decline which the ideal representation sought constantly to deny. Even so, the principle that an ideal order should always dominate and neutralise the worst excesses of this 'reality' was no simple mystification or 'false consciousness'. Both the ideal and the real have to be conceived as dual principles of a single reality generated by continuous attempts to reconcile the irreconcilable in this political culture.

If the 'outside' is the source of all evil, then logically it was this external arena which had to be brought within the bounds of moral order. Warfare, formal alliances, gift exchange, inter-marriage and the diffusion of royal regalia were all elements of a single strategy to achieve this end. The capacity of a *fon* to keep the respect and following of his population depended a great deal on the influence he wielded in the regional political hierarchy. Alliances between *fons* were most cogently expressed as a belief in common ancestral origin and expressed in terms of an idiom of common descent. In the Grassfields, the *fons* of the largest centralised polities, Bamoum and Nso, as well as some of the smaller chiefdoms of the Bamenda plateau (e.g. Bafut, Nkwen, Bambwi and Bambili) claimed a common origin from a prestigious centre in the Tikar region of the Upper Mbam valley. The founding ancestors of these polities are said to have migrated together in a mythical past and after various travails come to settle in their present locations. Each living *fon* recognised (and still does) common descent and relative rank with his 'brothers' expressed in terms of genealogical distance and the details of the migration myth. A regional hierarchy of polities of different size and status was seen as the product of a shared common ancestral substance, embodied in the acquisition by *fons* of common elements of regalia, masquerades, music and dance as well as rituals for pollution removal and the paraphernalia of a distinctive form of regulatory association. It was access to the legitimacy of origin which defined a *fon* from an ordinary clan or lineage head in his chiefdom and set him apart in terms of access to superior ancestral blessing. In essence, personal security lay in living in a large chiefdom possessing a prestigious *fon*. Moreover titled *fons* had a vested interest in extending a network of dependencies through gifts of regalia to prominent notables in neighbouring populations so that they could claim superiority over their competitors by achieving an inferior position in the regional hierarchy.

Rank was both modified and reinforced through ritualised gift exchange between *fons*. Moreover the relative rank of a *fon* was clearly defined by the kind of gifts that he might ask for as well as those that he might be willing to give. Yet 'gifts' were not simply wealth items intended for elite consumption. They were made meaningful by encoding the role they played in sustaining moral order, in particular, their capacity to contradict the efforts of sorcery. For example, all human artifacts were seen literally to be the embodiment of ancestral substance. To deliberately break a pot or to damage a domesticated plant was an abomination which polluted the compound where it occurred until an appropriate ritual was performed. This rite could be performed only by household heads, lineage or clan elders depending on the gravity of the offence and the range of kin involved. Yet where such acts affected the chiefdom as a whole (e.g. stealing, spilling blood, suicide, arson), only the *fon* had the ritual means to cleanse the community. A *fon's* claim to possessing superior ritual means of pollution removal emanated from his access to a more potent ancestral substance which he shared with *fons* of similar descent originating from the same remote yet prestigious origin. What is meant by such terms as regalia in this context is therefore the symbols and materials which embodied this ancestrally defined potency. What constituted a gift was defined by a set of codes which relates a disparate range of artefacts and materials as representations of the legitimate power of a *fon* to seek out the causes of misfortune, to protect his population and to rebalance a disturbed moral order (see Rowlands 1985 for a fuller discussion of these codes).

Formalised gift exchange characterised all other levels in a chiefdom hierarchy. For example, camwood, palm oil and water or palm wine were the minimal requirements for a lineage elder to perform ancestral rites. Camwood is a hard redwood which, ground into powder, was smeared on the body to give it a healthy sheen indicative of ancestral blessing and group harmony. Yet camwood could only be obtained from the forest zone some 50–100 kms to the south and whilst no restriction was exercised over its acquisition, conditions of insecurity meant that only those with far flung exchange partners were likely to receive it and were able to redistribute it to their dependents. Sasswood was another important exchange item: it is a poison and was used in an ordeal undergone by those suspected of sorcery. It also came from the forest zone and members of *kwi'fo* were responsible for obtaining it. Yet all members of a chiefdom recognised that without it, sorcery would go undetected and unpunished and 'society' would no longer be possible. The interregional hierarchy of *fons* was crucial therefore both for facilitating profitable trading and for acquiring the symbolic materials necessary to maintain social order. A similar emphasis on formalised exchange determined the acquisition of European trade goods which until the end of the nineteenth century were obtained through trade partnerships. Moreover, certain trade goods were selected and valued because they were a visible demonstration of the power of ancestral order to incorporate an alien and potentially hostile world and subvert it to serve its own purpose. A hidden contradiction lay in the fact that what had to be given in return was slaves and this quite blatantly invalidated this claim since the sale of persons as alienated objects, except under very exceptional conditions, was a polluting act. The demands of European trade thus introduced the amorality of power into the process of expanding legitimate authority and made exploitation of persons for sale as slaves its principal determinant.

At all levels in a nineteenth century 'Grassfields' chiefdom, formalised and ritualised exchange characterised social relations and underpinned the unity of moral community. Moreover it made possible a unified sphere of production and exchange since 'gifts' were inalienable. They embodied both a particular and a shared ancestral substance and the separation entailed in satisfying a request was acknowledged in the incorporation of a gift received. A *fon* would have a special storehouse of foodstuffs, palm oil and salt, and if produced in his chiefdom, they were the product of special plots and of labour on special days. Woodcarvers, potters, and smiths might produce for the palace on special days and recognise that their labour was of a different quality from normal. The important point is that the inappropriateness of distinguishing production and exchange in the ritual sphere was in stark contrast to trading for gain.

Precolonial trade in the Grassfields was mercantilist in the sense that the circuit $m^1 - c - m^2$ operated so that wealth acquired in a variety of transactional modes was ultimately realisable in a single monetary form. Currencies varied by area from brass manillas to cowries to trade beads with well defined conversion rates operating in the major regional markets. The Grassfields formed a complex precolonial regional economy with different chiefdoms specialising in the production of commodities for exchange (Rowlands 1979; Warnier 1983). There is no reason to assume this to have been a recent development. The oil palm had been an important source of protein for millennia and yet grows poorly if at all in the Grassfields and palm oil had to be gained through trade with peoples in the tropical forest zone. Some of the earliest descriptions of the area by Europeans in the seventeenth century mention the Grassfields as a source of iron exported as far as the Atlantic ports of Calabar and Rio del Rey (Ardener 1968, 87). Before the appearance of European trade goods, it seems that salt was the major commodity given in return by coastal populations and iron hoes and salt are recorded as local currencies at this time. This would imply, but cannot confirm, that Pre-European trading was for profit as well as to obtain scarce objects. This certainly was the case by the later nineteenth century. By then, most household heads would engage in local inter-chiefdom trade and made profits through taking advantage of different measures used in different markets and by using a smaller set of measures for retailing at home. Specialist longer distance trading was more profitable still and was in the hands of 'merchant houses' whose members could raise the necessary finance and had the personal contacts needed to ensure security for themselves and their goods. Personal relations between merchant houses of widely separated chiefdoms were cemented through formal oaths and intermarriage. Of 60–70 genealogies collected from a number of Grassfields chiefdoms, an average of 30 per cent of wives at the end of the nineteenth century came from chiefdoms other than their husbands'. The importance of marriage alliances in facilitating profitable long-distance trading was already well established by this period. In ideal terms, trading for gain was a function of and dependent on formalised exchange for its very existence. Yet, in contrast to formalised gift exchange, profitable trading required alienation of the product from its producers. In this case, the latter were either women who produced all the agricultural surplus or male dependent labor who raised livestock and made craft products. In both cases, a household head could appropriate their product at will as long as he fulfilled certain obligations; that wives retained sufficient foodstuffs for themselves and their children and were provided with hoes, palm oil, salt and cloth and that bridewealth was paid for a son's first wife.

Precolonial regional exchange in the Grassfields was organized into two major spheres: one formalised and ritualised in which the prime concern was the establishment of a regional moral unity of social relations, and the other directed to personal wealth accumulation through trading for profit. Formalised exchange purported to circulate goods for the satisfaction of needs whilst avoiding the socially disruptive effects of trading for gain. It retained the unity of production and exchange through the non-alienating properties of the 'gift', cemented rather than antagonised social relations, and maintained the principle of reciprocity as essential to moral order. Trading for gain had the opposite effect of alienating the products of labour through exchange, introducing exploitation into social relations and emphasing wealth differences in the acquisition of power. In certain respects, formalised exchange served to dominate and constrain the affects of trading for gain. Moreover there were very few goods that were limited in circulation to one or other of these modes of exchange. Palm oil, salt, iron, cloth and gunpowder, for example, could be acquired as 'gifts' and the practitioners of specialist skills such as diviners or smiths were unlikely to have to buy from traders to satisfy their basic needs. In principle it was also the moral duty of elders, notables and *fons* to satisfy requests for help from poorer dependents. Palace retainers and officials were also sent to regulate the affairs of the market, to exclude from it traders with bad reputations and to sanction exorbitant rates of exchange. However, were the effects of formalised exchange contingent upon the power relations which it served to maintain? In this sense it is part of the wider ideology of hierarchy and served to channel wealth acquired through different transactional modes into the established order of inherited titles and roles. Many cases are still remembered of the palace sending masked retainers to destroy the possessions of an arrogant man made rich through successful trading who chose not to expend his wealth in this way. The accumulation of wealth for personal gain was (and still is) interpreted as counter to moral order and likely to promote envy and sorcery attacks, and the acquisition of influence in a chiefdom through the possession of wealth alone was (and still is) fiercely denied.

Formalised exchange was therefore part of the wider ideology used by dominant interests as a direct means of preserving and legitimising power asymmetry. In this instance, ritualised exchange (hierarchy) dominated commerce (power) although the principles by which this was done may not of themselves have been exploitative but seen rather to satisfy the interests of all sections of the community. Yet when examined more closely, a *fon*, notable or elder, whilst not parti-

cipating directly in trade, was often the major supplier of finance and personal contacts to a trader and would benefit directly from the proceeds. Moreover by ensuring that the resources of others were channelled into various wealth-distributing activities consistent with acquiring titles, they located themselves at the centre of wealth accumulation in the chiefdom as a whole. The effects of the constraint that hierarchy and ritualised exchange placed on 'trade' and production for exchange were clearly exploitative. Yet the effectiveness of the system derives from the fact that it was not seen to be so by those whose actions it constrained. The fear that unrestrained trading would introduce disruptive effects into society, produced the contrary belief that whilst rapacious *fons* or notables might abuse their positions, in essence their role was non-exploitative and served the interests of all. This belief was sustained by the link established earlier in this paper between trading for gain and the marriage system. If wealth were not distributed, it could be diverted directly back into production through payment of bridewealth for more wives and offspring. This, of course, was done by prominent title holders and the hidden effects were highly exploitative, particularly in terms of their ability to control the circulation of marriageable women as seen in the case of the Bamileke chiefdoms. Yet the absence of overt competition outside the order of hierarchy and title sustained the belief that 'wealth' was a product of achieving high status rather than the outcome of entrepreneurial success in appropriating the product of others and trading for gain.

The possibilities that this allowed for the almost complete control by *fons* and notables of all forms of wealth accumulation to sustain fully centralised authority have their most extreme expression in the kingdom of Bamoum. By the 1870s, this 'state' had established an almost continuous cycle of warfare with its neighbours which produced large numbers of captive women for marriage and men for external sale (Tardits 1980). Tardits has demonstrated that the whole population was affinally linked to the royal clan and all other previously autonomous descent groups had been absorbed into it. The palace populated conquered land by sending princes to settle in border areas and by giving wives and land to trusted commoners to found new patrilineages. All external trade was a monopoly of the palace, as was the disposal of slaves and war captives, and was administered by specialist traders under the patronage of the king and clan elders. What we have only seen so far as general tendencies are thus fully realised in this case. In the 1890s, King Njoya of Bamoun converted to Islam as did many of the royal notables, and we may surmise that the ideological role of ancestrally defined moral order was no longer a major source of legitimacy.

Conclusion

In the introduction, I argued that central to the analysis of this chapter would be the problem of how an holistic ideology, claiming the authority of sacred origin and tradition, could be articulated with a reality of power stemming from control over people and resources. Moreover I claimed that there were good reasons for being unhappy with theories that treat these ideologies as a mere screen for exploitation and that they needed to be treated with more respect.

It would indeed be difficult to summarise this chapter as an illustration of how ideology conceals and mystifies the secret workings of the political economy. Precolonial society in the Grassfields was structured on a dual principle which created a unity of a set of cultural, political and economic practices and opposed it to and claimed to dominate the functioning of another set. Hence we are presented with the difficulty that we cannot proceed with a simple homogenised notion of ideology, politics and economics which function at different levels of dominance and determination. Instead we are drawn to recognising the dominance of a collectivist vision which united a moral definition of authority with ritual practices ensuring group harmony and conflict resolution and claimed that it should be sustained through agricultural pro- duction and formalised exchange. In a sense this served to unify a selected set of material, political and cultural practices in order to foster social cohesion and guide collective action and to define negatively another set of practices condemned as antithetical to this ordering. Such a 'strategy of containment' allows what can be thought of as internally coherent while repressing and fragmenting the unthinkable which lies beyond its boundaries. What is subsumed and made incoherent under the general gloss of sorcery is the unconstrained pursuit of power over others, the use of coercion and violence, the acquisition of wealth for personal gain and all forms of indi- vidualistic and selfish behaviour. The recognition of the unlikelihood of such an idealised moral society being con- stituted in reality is reflected in the projection of this ideal

on the world of dead ancestors (who alone live out these practices in their pure form) and its role as a means of socially containing individual action in everyday life. There existed (and still exists) a subordinate reality of coercive power and exploitation which is acknowledged as necessary for the functioning and reproduction of society and yet is viewed with considerable mistrust and aversion. The domestication of such negative social actions for approved purposes and their condemnation if used outside these limits was central to social identity although, in the contemporary setting, this is seen as a hindrance to development.

There is considerable evidence to suggest that this basic dualism has been a long-term tendency in Grassfields culture but there is little doubt that contact with an expanding sphere of European-dominated trade severely distorted the capacity of this sphere of formalised social relations to cope with increasing opportunities for gaining wealth and power. In effect, the dominant ideology of moral order and the cultural, political and economic practices that it sustained were increas- ingly abused by its officiants, who were at the same time actively engaged in more negatively defined activities, both to further their ambition and as a means of defeating their rivals. As we have seen, political centralisation in the nineteenth century had the ambiguous tendency to concentrate and expand the symbolism of moral order whilst at the same time subverting it for increasingly superstructural and mystifying ends.

Acknowledgements

Fieldwork was funded by the Social Science Research Council (UK) and the Hayter and Central Research Funds of the University of London. I am grateful to Liz Brumfiel, Phil Burnham, Sally Chilver, Danny Miller and Jean-Pièrre Warnier for their comments on this article.

Chapter 6

**Specialization and the production of
wealth: Hawaiian chiefdoms and the
Inka empire**

Timothy K. Earle

Introduction

Specialization is the economic essence of complex
society. Economic efficiency, interdependence, and control
are various outcomes of specialization that have been linked to
the evolution of chiefdoms and states (Brumfiel and Earle,
Chapter 1). Economic efficiency permits both higher population densities and the production of a surplus to support a non-
subsistence sector of the population. Economic interdependence resulting from specialized production and distribution
of food and crafts is both the cause and the effect of larger
societies, which become economically intertwined by food
exchange as real energetic systems. Economic control derived
from proprietorship and management is the necessary element
of finance, the channeling of resources differentially to support
the elaboration of institutions of government, stratification
and legitimization.

Specialization is undeniably important in any explanation
of complex societies, but its highly variable role in evolutionary
processes needs to be specified and investigated. In our introduction we lay out the different kinds of specialization,
independent and attached, and the economic conditions under
which they have become important. The two general perspectives
on the role of specialization have been discussed — the
adaptationist explanations involving independent specialists
for markets and the political explanations involving attached
specialists for elite/institutional patrons. We do not claim that
one perspective is right and the other necessarily wrong, but
they both play a role that varies according to specific environmental, social, and economic conditions. We need to specify
those conditions under which different kinds of specialization
arise and how they are linked to evolutionary processes.

To do this, I will evaluate the role of specialization in
two critical cases of complex society — the Hawaiian chiefdoms
and the Inka empire. Explicitly I disclaim any general application to the evolution of *all* complex societies. Quite to the
contrary, the Hawaiian and Inka cases together represent
variants of one type of society, similar in their control of
surplus staple production, but different in their scale and complexity. Staple finance underlies many, but not all, early
complex societies. The main point of the Hawaiian and Inka
cases is that specialization in complex societies may be quite
limited and related closely to political finance and control.

The Cases

The Hawaiian islands at the time of first western contact
(1778) were occupied by Polynesians organized as complex
chiefdoms (Malo 1951 [1898]; Sahlins 1958, 13–22; Earle
1978). Characteristically, following violent wars of succession
and conquest, a paramount chief ruled a major island (Hawai'i,
Maui, O'ahu, or Kaua'i) and nearby smaller islands (such as
Moloka'i or Ni'ihau). Repeatedly the paramounts attempted to

extend political control through marriage and conquest, but limits imposed by sea transport caused these attempts to fail or to be quite fragile. Within any Hawaiian chiefdom, there was a hierarchy of chiefs tracing their relationships to the senior ruling line. These chiefs received community land grants, *ahupua'a*, according to their status and their support for the paramount in his wars of succession and conquest. A hierarchy of priests, chiefs in their own right, was also involved in elaborate rituals of legitimization, demonstrating the sanctity of the ruling chiefs and their significance for the fertility, stability and livelihood of the commoner population.

The economic basis of the Hawaiian chiefdoms was control of subsistence production. Primary subsistence came from irrigated agriculture and intensive shifting cultivation. All land was owned by the paramount chief who granted community land to loyal, ranking chiefs. These community chiefs, through their appointed land manager (*konohiki*), allocated subsistence land parcels to commoners in return for their labor on the chief's land. Produce from the chief's land went to the community chief who retained part for his own support and the support of his retainers such as the land manager. A portion then was given over to the ruling paramount, as rent for the initial land grant. Rights to use land were thus distributed down the social hierarchy and produce from the land was mobilized up through the hierarchy.

As discussed in a moment, the *ahupua'a* community was largely the social segment within which production was managed and controlled. Importantly this community was economically self-sufficient and more generally isolated by endogamy from other local communities (Earle 1978).

The Andes at time of first western contact (1532) was dominated by the mighty Inka empire (Cobo 1956 [1653]; Rowe 1946; Moore 1958; Murra 1980 [1956]; Schaedel 1978). The empire began as a chiefdom in Peru's southern highlands and expanded rapidly during the 1400s to control at contact perhaps 980,000 km^2 and 8 to 14 million people. The empire was structured as an administrative hierarchy with vertically arranged offices. The empire was partitioned into four quarters, each subdivided into provinces and districts (*saya*) based on existing ethnic distinctions. Administration at these highest levels was handled by ethnic Inka. The *saya* were then divided into local land holding units (*ayllu*). Administration of the *ayllu* was handled indirectly through its own ethnic leaders. The overriding principle of administration was to emphasize vertical ties of dependence through the state hierarchy (Schaedel 1978, 308). This control depended on the independence of units such as the *ayllu* community from other similar units, and their ultimate dependence on the state for basic rights to land (Earle 1985a).

Very similar to the Hawaiian island chiefdoms, the Inka empire was based on the control of subsistence production. Primary subsistence depended on massive irrigation complexes in the coastal and some intermontane valleys and on intensive shifting cultivation cycles throughout the rolling highlands. All land was owned by the state based on rights of conquest and

allocated to commoner communities in return for their *mit'a* labor on state lands and in other productive activities. A local chief (*kuraka*) served the double function of local leader and state representative. He was responsible for managing local production to support the community and to generate a surplus to finance the state.

Throughout the empire were administrative centers spaced along the major road network. At these centers were large warehouse complexes (Morris 1967; D'Altroy 1981; Earle and D'Altroy 1982) where the staples collected from the local communities were stored to support state administrative and religious personnel and the mobile army.

In the next two sections, I examine the role of specialization and exchange in subsistence goods and wealth. In both Hawai'i and the Andes, specialist production and exchange in subsistence objects were remarkably limited. This point demonstrates the inapplicability of the adaptational model of specialization in these early complex societies based on staple finance. Rather, economic specialists developed in these and similar cases to produce a highly stable and exchangeable wealth used to strengthen and centralize political control.

The adaptationist approach to specialization

The adaptationist approach characterizes the work by cultural ecologists (Steward 1955; Service 1962; Harris 1979) and by the 'New Archaeologists' (Binford 1964; Sanders and Price 1968; Hill 1977). In general terms, cultural evolution is seen as adaptation. New cultural forms, such as the complex governing institutions of the state, are seen as developments to solve specific environmental and economic problems. As population grows in a region, problems are created that require management to guarantee that the needs of the population are adequately met. The specific requirements for management vary according to particular environmental conditions – management of irrigation in dry environments, management of warfare in circumscribed regions, the management of exchange in regions of resource diversity. It is of course the causal linkage between environmental diversity, specialization, exchange, and complex social forms that concerns us here.

The adaptationist position with regard to specialization has been articulated clearly by Sanders (1956) and Service (1962, 1975). In areas of high environmental diversity (i.e., where different locales are optimally suited to produce different things), local communities become specialized in their optimal production strategies, and then the communities become economically interdependent as they exchange specialized products. Local community specialization can involve food production (for example, one locale specializing in grain agriculture and exchanging for meat produced by pastoralists or fishermen) or craft production (one locale, impoverished agriculturally, may specialize in crafts that are traded for food [Arnold 1975]). What actually causes the increased specialization is population growth. As production increases to support a growing population, declining yields (increasing costs) will not be uniform in a diverse environment but will be highly localized according to particular conditions of elevation, rainfall, soils, and the like. To compensate for these differences, local populations should emphasize production in their best local strategy.

The resulting community specialization then leads to a regional exchange in subsistence products (food and procurement tools). Communities that had formerly been at war find themselves dependent on each other for their very livelihood. A new level of regional integration is necessary to mediate the conflicting interests over resource access which if unchecked break out in conflict. The chief and eventually the state government evolve to regulate these regional relationships and keep the peace of the market.

This scenario is certainly appealing; it combines a formalist economic theory of decision making to the biological motor of population growth in environmentally constrained circumstances. In the past two decades, anthropologists have come almost to assume that it must be true. But is it? Perhaps in some circumstances, but in both Hawai'i and the Andes where all conditions seem to be met, actual outcomes of development were very different.

In the Hawaiian islands, environmental diversity is very high. Resource availability and productivity change radically as one moves inland from the coastal fisheries and lowland irrigation complexes to the upland forests and as one moves from the rainy windward side of the islands to the near desert leeward side. Major environmental contrasts, as between leeward and windward, certainly determined major differences in subsistence production. Leeward communities emphasized sweet-potato cultivation, and windward areas emphasized taro.

Population density at contact was moderate (39/mi^2), but locally much higher where productive lowland alluvium was concentrated. Recent research (see Kirch 1982) has documented a leveling off of population growth after AD 1600, a pattern suggesting a density-dependent mechanism.

Despite both environmental diversity and comparatively high population density, regional exchange in subsistence products was remarkably limited in prehistoric Hawaiian chiefdoms (Earle 1977, 1978). Because of the high environmental diversity, community territories could be laid out as a strip from the coast to the mountains that contained within their boundaries a range of necessary resources. In many communities, individual households were within several hours walk of all elevations. What specialization existed, as between fisherman and farmer, was contained within the social bounds of the community. Where community resources differed, the result was not large-scale exchange; rather productivities in crops simply resulted in different local diets and community sizes.

Exchange in Hawaii consisted of two forms. First and most important was 'redistribution' used to mobilize subsistence products and certain raw materials as a means to finance the chiefly institutions (Earle 1977). Quite explicitly this exchange did not distribute goods among specialized commoner communities; rather it provided for the elites and their retainers. Second was reciprocal exchange apparently on a small-scale,

unregulated by the chiefs. Some stone materials with unusual properties, fine grain basalt for polished axes and basaltic glass for cutting flakes, were limited in their availability to specific geological sources. Production, possibly involving independent specialists, concentrated at quarries such as the basalt source at Mauna Kea where a considerable volume of adze blanks were manufactured presumably for exchange (McCoy 1977).

In the Andes, environmental diversity is also very high. In the central highlands of Peru, for example, a number of distinct ecological zones are found at different elevations: on the intermontane valley floors below 3400 m were the maize-producing lands which were often irrigated; between 3400 and 3900 m were the rolling uplands and hill slopes farmed in rotation to produce potatoes and other indigenous tuber and grain crops; above 3900 m were the grasslands where herds of llama and alpaca grazed.

Recent archaeological surveys (Parsons 1976a; Parsons and Hastings 1977; LeBlanc 1981) have documented a long-term and consistent growth in settlements and human population in the central highlands of Peru. Prior to the rapid expansion of the Inka empire, population density reached high levels and intensive systems of production included drained fields, elaborate terracing, and irrigation (Earle et al. 1980).

With high environmental diversity and high population densities, the adaptationist theories would argue for the evolution of community specialization and a regional market system. One would expect either major exchange developing prior to state formation or at least expanding after state formation as regional peace was established.

Ethnohistorical work, however, has claimed that the Central Andes under the Inka empire was a marketless society (Murra 1980 [1956]; La Lone 1982). The Inka empire itself was financed by the mobilization, local storage, and disbursement of staple goods (D'Altroy and Earle 1985). This aspect of the economy was centrally managed by the state. It did not involve movement of goods between specialized producers, but involved the local mobilization of subsistence goods used to support state personnel. Movement of goods was thus limited to state finance.

Instead of developing markets, local communities extended their territories across the landscape to incorporate within their boundaries colonies isolated several days walk from the main settlement in remote areas where special products, such as coca, were procured (Murra 1972). Was this possible and, if so, why?

Recent archaeological work in the Mantaro valley (Earle et al. 1980; Earle and D'Altroy 1982; Hastorf 1983; Earle 1985a) unambiguously supports the limited nature of exchange. We have been conducting extensive excavation to contrast economic production and exchange in the periods immediately before Inka conquest (Wanka II; AD 1300–1460) and during Inka domination (Wanka III; AD 1460–1532). Evidence from basic commodities, namely food and household utensils and tools, shows considerable localism with limited specialized production and intercommunity exchange.

Foods are being studied from systematic flotation sampling of all proveniences and from $\frac{1}{4}''$ screening of excavated soils. Plant remains are unexpectedly well preserved with consistent recovery of seeds and plant parts from domesticated and wild species. Virtually all domesticated plant remains derive from species such as maize, quinoa and various tubers, that are produced in the area immediately (< 10 km) surrounding the sites. Out of 611 flotation samples already analyzed for the Mantaro region, only three (0.5%) contained traded plant products (Hastorf 1983). Settlements located at different elevations practiced different agricultural strategies, as seen in the stone tools (Russell and Hastorf 1984), but this resulted simply in different diets without exchange (Hastorf 1983). Although analysis of faunal remains is at present more limited, all species identified were clearly from local highland species, such as the camelids, guinea pig, dog, and deer (Earle *et al.* 1985). A handfull of mussels (*Aulacomya alter* and *Choromytilus chorus*) indicates possible trade in food with the coast, but mussel occurrence is very low (1.4% of proveniences) and would not have been significant. No other tropical or coastal species have been identified.

Household utensils and tools included an extensive inventory of domestic ceramics and lithics. For ceramics, sherds have been identified as local (probably manufactured within 10 km of the target site), regional (within 10–15 km), and interregional (beyond 50 km). The majority (82%) of ceramics were locally produced (Earle 1985a). This percentage dropped from 89% in Wanka II to 75% in Wanka III because of the introduction of Inka ceramics (18%) that were apparently state produced and regionally distributed. Definite regional ceramics were not common (decreasing from 6% in Wanka II to 5% in Wanka III). Ceramic types from outside the region were rare (0.4% of the ceramics); they decreased slightly in abundance (0.5–0.3%) following Inka conquest.

For lithics, the majority (83%) were locally (< 10 km) procured (Earle 1985a). The percentage of local materials actually increased from pre-Inka (79%) to Inka times (86%). The regionally traded materials (a chert and phyllite) were not traded broadly (less than 20 km), but there is good evidence for their specialized production similar to the Hawaiian case. The one traded chert was procured from a large quarry to the west of our main research area; it was then removed as prepared cores to settlements where blades were produced for exchange. At the Wanka II site at Umpamalca, large quantities of manufacturing debris (exhausted cores, substandard blades, and shatter) were recovered in all households excavated; this contrasted with other sites, such as the nearby Wanka II site of Tunanmarca, where used blades were recovered but without manufacturing debris. Evidence for limited village-level specialization in lithic manufacture is clear, but this never represented a large-scale or long-distance operation. Long-distance exchange was very limited. Such a desirable material as obsidian, which is available from the productive Quispisisa source in Huancavelica only 130 km to the south, is represented by only a handful of scattered flakes (0.2% of the lithic assemblage).

To summarize, despite the prerequisite conditions (environmental diversity and high population density) and despite the evolution of social complexity, specialization in subsistence products was of limited importance. Rather the opposite was true. Levels of community self-sufficiency were high in both Hawai'i and the Andes, and if anything increased with the establishment of regional peace. Food commodities were apparently not exchanged between communities except as a system of political finance. Local environmental differences resulted in differences in production but not exchange and symbiosis; the simple outcome was differences in diet. Exchange in household goods was more common (perhaps 20% of the inventory) but it was limited to certain unusual goods with properties not locally replaceable – such as the fine-grain basalt and basaltic glass for Hawai'i, and the chert for the Andes. Long-distance exchange was negligible. Although some exchange undoubtedly existed for both Hawai'i and the Inka empire, it was remarkably restricted in range of goods and considerably less than some egalitarian societies, such as California hunter-gatherers (Ericson 1977) and Italian horticulturalists (Ammerman 1979). Evidently the adaptationist hypothesis linking environmental diversity and population growth to community specialization and regional symbiosis to the evolution of complex societies does not apply well to the Hawaiian and Inka cases.

The political approach to specialization and exchange in complex societies

If the adaptationist approach to cultural evolution is inadequate, can the evolution of complex society still be linked to specialization by drawing on the alternative political approach? Obviously, I think it can.

In essence the political approach reverses the primary direction of causality in the model. Specialization, induced by environmental and demographic conditions, is not seen as causing political complexity; quite the opposite, political complexity causes the elaboration of specialization as a means to strengthen political and economic control. Some might say that this is simply a 'chicken-and the egg' dilemma common in the feedback relationships of cultural evolution. In part this may be true, but the *kind* of specialization and the way it articulates to the broader social and economic system is quite different in the two models. In the adaptationist model, specialists produce for a general market of commoners; specialist producers exist because of gains in *efficiency* resulting from underlying economic conditions. In the political model, specialists are attached to elite patrons or governing institutions for whom they produce special products or provide special services; attached specialists exist because of gains in *control* that they provide to the ruling segments of society.

For the political approach, primary is the evolution of social stratification. As argued elsewhere (Johnson and Earle n.d.), the evolution of social stratification is based on economic control arising characteristically from dominion over resources (land). Status rivalry then involves intense competition among elites for dominion and results in a distinctive growth-oriented political economy (Earle 1978). Elites are under constant competitive pressure and must search out opportunities to maximize economic control through prudent investment and management. (The parallels to the capitalist entrepreneur are obvious). Institutional elaboration as related to attempts to maintain and extend economic and political control underlies the increasing scale of complex societies (cf. Johnson 1978). It is in this context that we must understand specialization as linked to explicit strategies to extend control.

In the Hawaiian and Inka cases, I will examine how specialization is linked to the financial base of expanding governing institutions. Two major alternative forms of finance can be recognized — staple finance and wealth finance (D'Altroy and Earle 1985). It is in the operation of these systems of finance that specialists played such an important role in early complex societies (Brumfiel and Earle, Chapter 1).

Staple finance is the simpler tribute system whereby subsistence goods, needed by all, are mobilized from the commoner producers and distributed to support the ruling elite, their retainers, and other institutional personnel. The basic logic is that resources are held by the ruling elites and access to these is granted in return for labor or goods. Considerable variation existed in the centralization of the staple finance system from feudal systems to fully fledged state bureaucracies. Taking an explicitly sociopolitical view of these societies, specialists (retainers of the ruling elites) work to maintain, extend, and legitimize elite economic control.

In the Hawaiian chiefdoms, a proliferation of specialists provided at least five basic roles in the operation of the system of social stratification. First and perhaps most prominently the ruling paramount chief and other chiefs were surrounded by retainers who provided special goods and services to support a sumptuous lifestyle. The paramount moved, surrounded by retainers entrusted with particular jobs such as carrying his feather flyswatter or his elaborate spit bowl. Second were those specialists involved in information processing and administration. Particularly important were the district administrators who established specific personnel and product quotas in order to meet general chiefdom requirements for upcoming wars or ceremonies. Genealogists retained through memory the very lengthy and often complicated pedigrees of chiefs necessary to establish their rank and potential rights. Third were the land managers, who were responsible for guaranteeing the smooth operation of the subsistence economy so as to generate the necessary staple surplus used in finance. They allocated lands to the commoners and supervised work on chiefly lands and on special projects, such as the construction of irrigation systems. Fourth were the military specialists, chiefs trained in the art of war and responsible for combat in battles. Directly associated with the paramount chief and military men were specialists who manufactured the equipment of war, that included special clothing such as wicker helmets, wooden spears, and the large double hulled sailing canoes used for seabased invasions. Fifth were the religious specialists who conducted annual and special ceremonies related to warfare and legitimization. Most important were the annual Makahiki ceremonies in which the paramount chief representing the god

Lono proceeded around the island accompanied by his priests. As Lono he received annual gifts, as part of his staple finance, and performed ceremonies to ensure the fertility of the communities' land and people. The list of specialists in the Hawaiian chiefdom was long indeed and most were involved directly in the ruling operation of the chiefs.

In the Inka empire, the general list of specialists included the same five basic functions described above. With the much greater scale of the empire, the number and specific jobs of the specialists were expanded. This can be illustrated in two areas of particular importance for state integration — information handling and military support. Information handling in the Inka empire involved several kinds of specialists including administrators at the different levels of the hierarchy, inspectors sent out from the capital at Cuzco, record keepers, and message carriers. The record keepers, using a mnemonic device of knotted strings (*khipu*), monitored the payment and disbursement of staple goods through the warehousing system. The message carriers (*chaski*) were runners stationed along the roads who would carry messages rapidly in relay throughout the vast empire. Military support was greatly expanded because of the size of the army involved in external conquest and in suppression of internal rebellion. The amount of equipment, such as clothing, sandals, shields and maces, must have been staggering. Semi-industrial production of clothing for the army may have become quite common (see later discussion of weavers on Lake Titicaca).

The new institutions of chiefdom and state were always associated with such diverse specialists as we have described for the Hawaiian and Inka cases. A few general points should be emphasized about these specialists. Their involvement with a general population was limited to situations where the chiefdom or state was directly involved. The specialists rather served the social elite and newly developed institutions involved in finance and control. The number and specificity of specialists proliferated with increasing scale of the chiefdom and state institutions.

As I have indicated, staple finance was the simplest, and I believe most common, basis for early complex society. It, however, has a major liability, namely decentralization. Because of the bulkiness and weight of staple products, transportation of the goods is prohibitively expensive over long distances (D'Altroy and Earle 1985). Staple finance is therefore suitable only for regionally compact societies, such as Hawaiian island chiefdom, or a decentralized state, such as the Inka. In the Inka case, for example, each region had its own administrative center and maintained its own, separate storage system for support. Local staples were collected to pay for local state activities and, because of the cost of moving staples long distances (cf. Drennan 1984), little was moved through the empire

This decentralization created severe problems of control for the developing state. The locally produced and stored staples, in addition to creating local finance, created opportunities for local revolt. Rebels could seize the stores and use them to fund their revolt against the central government. In order to solve this problem, most developing complex societies used some elements of wealth finance in which attached specialists played a central role.

Wealth finance consists of the procurement and use of exchange valuables to pay personnel (D'Altroy and Earle 1985). The use of exchange valuables (wealth) as payment exists in all societies (Earle 1982); however, the elaboration of its use, eventually with true currency, plays a critical role in the development of finance in states. The main advantage of wealth as a basis for finance is its high value to weight ratio; this of course minimizes the cost of transportation and permits movement across great distances. In the evolution of the state, a shift to wealth finance permits an expansion in the regional scale of the polity while retaining centralized control. Wealth collected from incorporated populations can be moved into the state's center, where it is held until used as payment. The central storage of the wealth gives central control over finance which deprives peripheral areas of financial independence and a base to fund rebellion. The central control of wealth strengthens vertical ties of dependence and inhibits the growth of opposition coalitions (cf. Brumfiel, Chapter 9). Storable wealth used as a fund for payment and as a display of eliteness becomes monopolized.

Now it is essential to consider the significance of wealth in the societies under consideration. Personnel working for the chiefdom or state must have a means to obtain necessary subsistence goods. In the elemental staple finance system, the needed subsistence goods are collected by the ruling government and distributed directly to its support personnel. But what role does wealth play in the operation of a staple finance system? No matter how valued are metals and cloth they cannot be eaten. In a system of wealth finance, the solution is to have the wealth convertible to subsistence goods in a market exchange; this is the apparent solution for the Aztec state (Brumfiel 1980). In the Hawaiian and Inka cases, and I suspect in most early stratified societies, wealth was *not* easily convertible into subsistence goods because it circulated in a separate sphere of exchange (cf. Earle 1982). Although not directly convertible into subsistence goods, wealth was inextricably linked to access to subsistence goods. To be specific, as I will try to show, wealth acted as a highly visible symbol of status, meant not as abstract prestige but as a status position the holder of which had explicit rights to income in the staple finance system. Without written contracts, the physical demonstration of status is essential to define one's rights in the sociopolitical hierarchy, especially the rights of subsistence support (Earle 1985b).

At this point, specialization in craft manufacture as it relates to state development takes on a different significance. Wealth objects must be scarce; this limited availability can reflect the natural rarity of the raw material used, as in the case of the Hawaiian feather cloaks and the Inka metal, but it also reflects the amount of skilled labor required in manufacture. Wealth, made by specialists, can be controlled by controlling the production process.

The Hawaiian and Inka cases illustrate the control of wealth production in the development of complex societies with similar staple finance bases. Hawaiian and pre-Inka (Wanka) societies were similar chiefdoms organizing polities in the tens of thousands. The Inka were an imperial state organizing an overall population in the millions. Production of wealth in the chiefdoms was handled by specialists attached to elite patrons who distributed the wealth as symbols of authority along with direct right to land. In the imperial state, some production continued in this manner but much changed. The use of wealth in status display and legitimization remained unaltered, but the control over the production and distribution was centralized as a direct means for strengthening political control over the decentralized empire. Production shifted from the many attached specialists of local elites to semi-industrial workshops under direct state management.

In the Hawaiian chiefdoms, staples were not stored or moved over distances; staple finance was highly decentralized such that the paramount chief and his large retinue of advisors and functionaries moved through the chiefdom living in turn on the staple products of dependent communities. This 'moveable feast', as it was called in fuedal Europe, was necessary as the large retinue quickly devoured locally available surpluses. Obviously this decentralized staple base was fraught with problems of control that resulted in a repeated pattern of local rebellion against the paramount chief. It is my argument that the wealth, as symbols of legitimacy and explicit rights of economic access, helped to overcome this weakness. Wealth objects, that included cloaks, helmets, standards (*kahili*), and necklaces, were crafted of rare raw materials, feathers and whale ivory, by skilled specialists. Wealth was scarce because of its natural rarity (especially of certain feathers) and the skill required in its manufacture. The Hawaiian case illustrates both the symbolic importance of wealth and the role of attached specialists in controlling its availability.

The most important objects of wealth and symbols of power were the feathered cloaks, *'ahu'ula* (Malo 1951 [1898], 76–7; Brigham 1899, 1903, 1918; Buck 1957, 215–31; Cummins 1984; Earle 1985b). The finest cloaks were full length and brilliant yellow with contrasting red designs. They were made with a fine fibre net base onto which were attached small bundles of feathers. On a single cloak, hundreds of thousands of these feathers created a shining, velvet finish of incomparable beauty.

Access to and control over such wealth items illustrates well the linkage between craft specialization, wealth, and symbolic representation in complex polities (see also Brumfiel, Chapter 9). In Hawai'i, feathered cloaks could only be worn by high ranking, male chiefs 'as an insignia in time of war and when they went into battle' (Malo 1951 [1898], 77). They were also worn on special ceremonial encounters between high chiefs to demonstrate potential power and thus intimidate a potential foe and/or attract a valuable ally. In full dress, Kalani'opu'u, ruling chief of Hawai'i, and his supporting chiefs came out to meet Captain Cook, the first westerner to contact the islands:

> The next day, about noon, the king, in a large canoe, attended by two others, set out from the village, and

paddled toward the ships in great state. Their appearance was grand and magnificent. In the first canoe was Terree-oboo [Kalani'opu'u] and his chiefs, dressed in feathered cloaks and helmets, and armed with spears and daggers; in the second, came the venerable Kaoo, the chief of the priests, and his brethren, with their idols displayed on red cloth. These idols were busts of a gigantic size, made of wicker-work, and curiously covered with small feathers of various colors, wrought in the same manner with their cloaks [King 1784, 16–7].

The accompanying illustration by Webber (Fig. 6.1) shows a large double-hulled sailing canoe with about twenty paddlers and forty people standing on the platform between the hulls. At least seven of these, including Kalani'opu'u, were wearing feathered cloaks. In a very similar meeting Kamehameha I, the new paramount of Hawai'i, dressed in a full length yellow cloak, came out in his large canoe to greet Vancouver (1798, 126). Vancouver, as representative of the British crown, was obviously an important potential ally for Kamehameha. Other occasions when cloaks were worn included the confrontation when Captain Cook was killed by the Hawaiians and later when his bones were returned to the British (King 1784, 137).

Cloaks varied considerably in size, shape, and color (type of feathers used) which denoted the relative status of the high chiefs and distinguished warriors who wore them. For example, the brilliant large circular cloaks of *mamo* feathers were battle regalia for an island's paramount (Malo 1951 [1898], 77). The smaller rectangular cloaks with tropic bird and man-of-war feathers were worn by lower ranked chiefs (King 1784, 136–37).

Cloaks were physical representatives of status with its system of rights to position and land title. *'Ahu'ula* means literally red (*'ula*) garment (*'ahu*), red being the symbolic color of the gods and chiefs through Polynesia (Buck 1957, 216; Cummins 1984). In fact, the finest cloaks in the Hawaiian islands were not red but yellow, because the yellow feathers from the *mamo* and *'o'o* were exceedingly scarce and highly valued. Each bird had only a small tuft of yellow feathers (most of the bird being black) such that ten thousand birds might be caught to make a single magnificent cape. The natural rarity of the feathers created the limited availability necessary to establish and maintain value. This rarity was also coupled to a control over the production process that was necessary to the political manipulation of their distribution.

The control was manifest at all steps in the system – initial procurement of the feathers, their fabrication into cloaks, and presentation. The feathers themselves were procured by professional bird hunters (*po'e hahai manu*) who used sticky bird lines and nets (Buck 1957, 217). The bird skins or feather bunches were then valuables apparently used in exchange but especially used as tribute payments. When Captain Cook first landed on the island of Kaua'i, he was

Fig. 6.1. Kalani'opu'u, paramount of Hawai'i, coming out to greet Captain James Cook (Webber engraving in King 1784)

offered 'great numbers of skins of small red birds for sale, which were often tied up in bunches of twenty or more, or had a small wooden skewer run through their nostrils' (Cook 1784, 207). Later, on the island of Hawai'i, when Cook first visited the paramount chief Kalani'opu'u, Cook observed an abundance of tributary gifts to the chief that included 'a vast quantity of red and yellow feathers, tied to the fibres of cocoa-nut husks' (King 1784, 28).

Feathers were an important annual tributary payment made to the paramount chief by communities where birds were found. As described by Malo (1951 [1898], 77),

> The lands that produced feathers were heavily taxed at the Makahiki time, feathers being the most acceptable offering to the Makahiki idol. If any land failed to furnish the full tale of feathers due for the tax, the landlord was turned off (*hemo*).

The paramount chief, as the earthly manifestation of the Makahiki god Lono, received the feathers directly. The staple finance system was thus extended to require payment in a rare raw material from which his valuables (the cloaks and other feathered objects) were to be fabricated.

Little is known about the actual organization of production for the valuables, but it seems highly probable that this was done by specialists attached directly to the paramount and perhaps other high ranking chiefs. Kepelino (Beckwith 1932, 134) states that the cloaks were 'woven by persons skilled in the art into fine nets.' Kepelino's description is found in a general account of chiefs and attached specialists (military guards, genealogists, land experts, and personal attendants). The implication by context is that the feather weavers were also part of a high-ranking chiefly household.

The paramount chief by controlling the surplus flow of staple goods was in the best position to support attached specialists including feather weavers. In this situation, the craft specialist functioned as a converter. He was personally supported by staples mobilized by the chiefly hierarchy for which he manufactured a highly visible and storable wealth. The craft specialist in this role was the main link between the mobilization of food and raw material production and the creation of wealth for distribution (cf. D'Altroy and Earle 1985).

The distribution of the feather cloaks by the paramount chief is a clear indication of their use in the definition of political statuses. In his inventory of the feather cloaks, Brigham (1899, 1903, 1918) records the history of all capes known at that time. The history of transfer is recorded for fifteen capes: one by inheritance and fourteen by gift from a paramount chief. The majority of these were given by Kamehameha III to western dignitaries or others in his service. Recipients included William Lee (first Chief Justice of the Hawaiian Islands), William Miller (British representative), Fredrick Byny (who attended Liholiho on his visit to London), Samuel Whitney (first missionary to Kaua'i), J. H. Aulick (Commander, USN), and L. Kearny (Commander, USN on diplomatic errand). Two dramatic examples of cloak gifts were recorded in early explorer accounts. When Captain Cook was first visited by the Hawaiian paramount, he was given several cloaks:

> they [Kalani'opu'u and Captain Cook] had scarcely been seated, when the king [paramount chief] rose up, and in a very graceful manner threw over the Captain's shoulders, the cloak he himself wore, put a feathered helmet on his head, and a curious fan [feathered *kahili*] into his hand. He also spread at his feet five or six other cloaks, all exceedingly beautiful, and of the greatest value [King 1784, 17].

Similarly, Vancouver received a fine cloak from the new paramount Kamehameha I:

> Kamehameha conceiving this might be his last visit, presented me with a handsome cloak formed of red and yellow feathers, with a small collection of other native curiosities; and at the same time delivered into my charge the superb cloak that he had worn on his formal visit on our arrival. This cloak was very neatly made of yellow feathers; after he had displayed its beauty and had shown me the two holes made in different parts of it by the enemy's spears the first day he wore it, in his last battle for the sovereignty of this island, he very carefully folded it up, and desired that on my arrival in England, I would present it in his name to H.M. King George; and as it had never been worn by any person but himself, he strictly enjoined me not to permit any person whatever to throw it over their shoulders, saying it was the most valuable in the island of Hawaii, and for that reason he had sent it to so great a monarch, and so good a friend, as he considered the King of England [Vancouver 1789, 271].

These two formal presentations show clearly the importance of the cloaks as gift exchanges between highest ranking individuals. Almost surely the exchanges were meant as a ceremony of formal alliance. (See Brumfiel's Chapter 9 for additional discussion of wealth exchange as a means of validating political relationships).

The other main context for transfer involved warfare. Cloaks, worn in battle, were given to great warriors in recognition of their valor and were seized from those defeated in battle.

> The *ahu-ula* was also conferred upon warriors, but only upon those who had distinguished themselves and had merit, and it was an object of plunder in every battle.
>
> Unless one were a warrior in something more than name he would not succeed in capturing his prisoner nor in getting possession of his *ahu-ula*. [Malo 1951 [1898], 77].

Although it is implied that a successful warrior received a cloak directly in plunder, this appears not to be strictly the case. The only historically documented case of such seizure is one cape in the Bishop Museum (number 2 in Brigham's [1899] inventory); this cape was seized by Kamehameha I when he slew Kiwala'o, rightful heir to the paramountcy of Hawai'i. The large number of cloaks listed by Brigham as given by the Hawaiian rulers early in the historic period strongly suggests that the cloaks captured in the rapid expansion of the newly formed Hawaiian state went not to the victorious warriors but to the victorious paramount who then distributed the cloaks to his supporters and allies.

Ownership and distribution of the cloaks were thus very similar to the system of land tenure and in fact may have been linked to it. All lands were the property of the paramount chief, and, on his victories in wars of succession and conquest, the lands were then distributed by the paramount to his high ranking relatives and close military supporters. Access to land through conquest and central distribution was apparently identical to that for the cloaks. Based partly on this clear parallel it seems reasonable to suggest that the elite regalia including the cloak was a declaration of right to a landed estate on which the chiefs depended for their income.

What I am arguing is that the Hawaiian cloaks, a highly visible and limited wealth, were symbolic of a system of status and resource access on which the Hawaiian chiefdoms depended. Control over the raw material and fabrication of the cloaks translated into a control of the symbolism of power and its religious legitimization.

In the Inka empire, the role of specialist-manufactured wealth is similarly apparent, especially in cloth and metals. These wealth objects served primarily to define visually the status divisions within society, and the objects were important commodities of exchange. In clothing, status was marked not by tailoring but by different grades of cloth and kinds of ornamentation (especially of metal and shell) (Murra 1962, 711). Access to this visual wealth was thus essential to demonstrate one's position with its concomitant economic and political rights.

Cloth was of particular importance in the Andes because of its symbolism and exchange value (see especially Murra 1962 for a summary of the ethnohistoric evidence). Often a simple distinction is drawn between rough, domestic cloth used in everyday contexts and the fine *kumpi* cloth used for elite clothing, to wrap the idols, in sacrifice, and in similar special contexts. The *kumpi* was smooth and tightly woven, and it was often decorated with shells and feathers.

The major life crises and marriage ceremonies were marked in the Andes by exchanges that frequently involved cloth. At birth, puberty, marriage and death cloth was displayed, ceremonially worn, and exchanged. After death the Inka mummies were annually taken out and paraded around dressed in sumptuous cloth (Guaman Poma 1936 [1613], 256). In order to function in society — to define one's status, to obtain a wife, and to create and maintain social relations — access to cloth and other valuables was essential. This was not a creation of the state, as identical conditions characterized stateless societies generally (Earle 1982); however, it created an opportunity for control that was enhanced by the state through its central management of production, storage, and distribution of the wealth.

Production of cloth was organized in at least three ways that illustrate the nature of state involvement in this critical process. First, thread was spun and cloth was woven at the household level. Presumably much of this was used for family consumption, but the household was also required to produce a certain quota of cloth, perhaps one blanket a year, for the state. As described by Murra (1962, 715), the household was obligated to produce cloth for the state in return for access to community herds residually owned by the state through rights of conquest. Cloth production at the household level therefore fitted into the broader pattern of mobilization in the staple finance system. The cloth derived would have been of common quality and would have served the daily uses of state personnel.

Second, specialists involved in weaving of the fine cloth that represented wealth were attached to elite households for which they produced objects for elite use and exchange. Generally, the high quality of Andean textiles argues convincingly for specialized manufacture predating the Inka empire by at least a thousand years. Examples of such fine textiles include the technically elaborate Necropolis textiles decorated with embroidery that date to about 200 BC (Lumbreras 1974). In its simplest form, multiple wives of local leaders may have been specially involved in weaving. Cock (1977), in his analysis of Collagua *kuraka*, mentions that artisans, especially weavers and smiths, belonged to local elites for whom they produced goods for distribution. In the Mantaro Valley excavations, spindle whorls and needles were recovered characteristically from all households but were more abundant in elite households for both the Inka and pre-Inka period (Costin 1984). Following conquest, the products of these attached specialists became gifts to the Inka.

Third, and as far as the argument goes most important, specialist weavers, who were attached formerly to elite households, became involved in semi-industrial large-scale production directly for the Inka state. Weavers, recruited from local communities, were brought together to form specialist villages like Millerea on the northern shore of Lake Titicaca. There, 'one thousand' Aymara weavers manufactured cloth for the heavy demands of the military which used cloth both to differentiate status and to reward participation (Murra and Morris 1976; Murra 1982). *Aqllacuna* were a singular group of 'chosen women' recruited from the local communities but removed to the regional administrative centers where they were involved in a number of functions but most importantly in the manufacture of the fine *kumpi* cloth. Cieza (1862 [1551], 432) mentioned the presence of *aqllacuna* at Hatun Xauca in the Mantaro valley. At the administrative center of Huánuco Pampa, Morris (1974) has identified a large, enclosed compound that he believed housed *aqllacuna*. The compound contained forty-five large, regular structures, spacious plazas and corridors, and a distinctive concentration of spindle whorls and weaving instruments. At present, we do not know the kind of cloth being manufactured, whether *kumpi* or domestic, but the semi-industrial scale of production is well documented. LeVine (1985) has identified a similarly organized compound at the nearby center of Pumpu where large-scale production may also have taken place.

The state received cloth through all forms of production —

as part of corvée labor obligation, as gifts from regional chiefs, and as production from institutional specialists. The large amounts of cloth received filled many of the state warehouses through the empire. The extent of the cloth stores must have been impressive even to the conquistadors whose interests were more in the precious metals:

> Among the eyewitnesses of the invasion, Xerez reports that in Caxamarca there were houses filled to the ceiling with clothes tied into bundles. Even after 'the Christians took all they wanted,' no dent was made in the pile. 'There was so much cloth of wool and cotton that it seemed to me that many ships could have been filled with them.' As Pizarro's army progressed across the Inka realm, similar stores were found at Xauxa and in Cuzco. In the capital, it was 'incredible' to see the number of separate warehouses filled with wool, rope, cloth both fine and rough, garments of many kinds, feathers, and sandals. Pedro Pizarro mused some 40 years later about what he had seen as a youth: 'I could not say about the warehouses I saw, of cloth and all kinds of garments which were made and used in this kingdom, as there was no time to it, nor sense to understand so many things' [Murra 1962, 717].

The state used these massive stores of cloth as a means of payment. Cloth was paid for state services such as carrying tribute or a regional idol to Cuzco. Particularly important were the payments from the ruling Inka to local chiefs in return for their special services. Cloth, with its symbolic definition of status and its exchange value, was given over to the local leaders who could use the cloth directly in ceremonial display of his status or exchange it for desired goods and services.

The Inka state centralized the distribution of cloth by establishing payment in cloth both from commoners and elites. More revolutionary, it established large-scale production of the cloth by specialists which provided a large volume of wealth for distribution similar to the feathered cloaks of the Hawaiians.

The manufacture and use of metal in the Inka state illustrates a pattern of production and distribution similar to the cloth. The Andes witnessed the independent development of complex metallurgical technology involving smelting and fabrication of gold, silver, copper, lead, and a number of alloys (Lechtman 1979, 1984). Metal working was quite sophisticated involving such techniques as smelting sulfide ores (Lechtman 1979), plating (Lechtman 1979, 1984), and lost-wax casting. Simpler procedures using native metals and oxide ores, and fabrication with sheet-metal hammering and cutting were common through the region. Uses for the metal were quite varied including institutional decoration (gold and silver sheet covered walls, of the Inka), personal ornamentation (pins, discs, head bands, ear spools, and the like) and simple technology (needles, axes, bola weights).

Metal was highly valued for its symbolic identification and exchange value. From at least Chavin times (800 BC), gold and silver were symbols of rank, power and religious force (Lechtman 1984). In Inka cosmology, gold was the sweat of the sun and silver, the tears of the moon, two central high gods. Helms (1981) has argued that Inka nobility used metals in their lives to identify themselves with the celestial realm, symbolized by the colors of metal. Lothrop's (1938) description of the sumptuous metal wealth of the Inka is remarkable. Included were elaborate symbols of the high gods (golden suns, silver moons), lifesize golden statues of ancestors, and great vessels of gold and silver. The use of metals in status and political display was central to the legitimization of relationships within the Andean world. Annual ceremonies featured public displays of metal wealth as with the parading of the ancestral idols; artificial golden gardens of maize and other plants were probably aspects of fertility rites (Lothrop 1938). Status and wordly or spiritual power were conveyed by restricting the wearing of certain metal objects, such as the beautiful ear spools, to the Inka rulers (Lechtman 1984). The wearing of the ear spools, along with special cloths, was a visual statement of status and associated position. Along with cloth, metal was also a standard gift at life-crisis ceremonies (Murra 1962). During the marriage ceremony, the woman gave the man metal and a wool tunic (Rowe 1946, 286). Morúa (1946 [1590], 64–65; referenced in Murra 1962, 719) described the gift by an Inka ruler to his bride of a fine cloth and a metal pin. Metal was also frequently included as part of the burial offering.

The conquering Spanish were of course first and foremost in search of precious metals, and it was in the Andes where their dreams were realized. The famous ransom of the Inka Atawalpa is said to have been 238,000 oz. of gold, filling the ruler's cell higher than a man could reach (Lothrop 1938). Certainly the Empire was manufacturing and stockpiling massive amounts of metal, but why? Partly the metals displayed at ceremonies of legitimization were the critical prop of defining the distinctiveness and sanctity of the ruling Inka. In addition, however, metal may have come to be an important means of payment.

Some of the best information on the uses of metal and how these uses changed with Inka conquest come from the recent excavation of twenty-nine domestic patio groups in the Mantaro Valley (Earle *et al.* 1985). Although it has long been recognized that metal was an important component of burial offerings, its uses in domestic context have not been systematically studied. Metal products, including pieces of silver, copper, and lead were recovered from 120 of 2168 nonburial proveniences excavated (total ubiquity = 5.5%). Forms included ornaments (silver and copper pins, discs, and pendants), various copper and tin bronze tools (needles, axes, chisels, and weights), and lead tools (possible spindle whorls or weights) and ceramic mends or plugs. In all, metal increased somewhat in overall occurrence from pre-Inka (3.8% of proveniences) to Inka (7.0% of proveniences).

More dramatic were certain shifts in the types of metals recovered. During the pre-Inka period, the most common metal recovered was silver used in ornamentation. As seen in Fig. 6.2, silver was concentrated in elite households and probably

Ubiquity of metal artifacts

	Ag	Cu	Pb	Other	Total	Ubiquity of production byproducts	Number of proveniences
Wanka II							
elite	3.0	2.2	0.2	0.2	5.2	0.5	594
commoner	0.8	0.5	0	0.3	1.5	0.3	389
Wanka III							
elite	1.6	8.1	0.7	0.3	10.3	2.2	669
commoner	0.2	2.3	0.4	0	2.7	0.6	516
Total	1.5	3.7	0.4	0.2	5.5	1.0	2168

Fig. 6.2. Ubiquity of prehistoric metals: percentage of excavated proveniences containing metal for pre-Inka (Wanka II) and Inka (Wanka III) contexts.

denoted high status. During Inka domination, silver became significantly rarer. Although it is possible that silver production decreased, it seems more likely that the silver produced locally in Mantaro Valley was expropriated by the Inka and used as display and payment primarily among the highest levels. Silversmiths worked at the Mantaro administrative center of Hatun Xauxa (Cieza 1862 [1551], 432). The increase in frequency of lead (0.1% of proveniences in pre-Inka to 0.6% of provenience in Inka) probably indicates silver smelting from galena with lead as a byproduct. If the silver were won from galena, lead oxide would have been produced. Since the lead would have to have been smelted from the galena, a complex process, it would seem unjustified by the very simple and mundane uses of lead documented and more likely to have been derived from a silver smelting byproduct.

Copper increased dramatically in overall occurrence (1.5% of provenience in pre-Inka to 5.6% in Inka). In part, copper replaced some ornamental uses of silver. For the first time, copper discs were found, as silver discs became quite rare. Small pins of both silver and copper were made in identical forms during the Inka period.

Importantly, the Inka state may well have been directly involved in the manufacture and distribution of these copper objects. Prior to Inka conquest of the Mantaro, coppers were an arsenic bronze, most probably derived from smelting local sulphide ores (Howe 1983; Lechtman 1976). During the Inka period, the coppers contained significant amounts of tin that must have come through long-distance exchange with the southern highlands. As Lechtman (1976) has discussed, tin bronze became a uniform metal throughout the Inka empire. Although a major study of this point is wanting, I would argue that the manufacture of the coppers had become centralized and under direct state supervision.

Direct evidence for the organization of metal production under the Inka is quite limited. Mining is said to have been done as part of the annual labor tax (*mit'a*) (Rowe 1946). Moore (1958, 39) suggests, based on her analysis of the ethnohistoric documents, that mines were the property of the Inka state, similar to agricultural and pastoral resources, but that ore production and metal fabrication were under the control of local leaders who delivered the wealth objects as gifts to the Inka. Specialists, miners and craftsmen, were then exempted from regular labor tax. At least in part, therefore, the production of metals was closely tied to the more general system of mobilization through staple finance. Attached specialists working for local leaders were supported by local elites who then delivered up the finished goods as gifts to the state. This is *not* state controlled production; rather it was a continuation of the pre-Inka pattern redesigned by the Inka.

In the Mantaro Valley, ore, slag, casting spill and other manufacturing debris is quite rare in domestic contexts (ubiquity = 1.0%), suggesting that the level of production at the household was very low (Fig. 6.2). What evidence we did recover was concentrated in elite household contexts, especially during Wanka III. This pattern fits Moore's suggestion of local production by specialists, attached to local elites; however, the evidence for production is really very limited. In our survey of the settlements, no debris of metal production was noted. Smelting was probably not practiced locally and metal fabrication was probably on a limited scale. Metal production off the settlements investigated may have been handled at other local settlements, but it is plausible that metal production, like cloth, had come under direct state control.

Murra (1980 [1956]) has brought together ample evidence for full-time specialist smiths attached to the state. These individuals, such as the highly skilled smiths of the Chimor state, were moved to the capital at Cuzco and to other administrative centers where they produced goods for the state, its direct institutional use, and distribution to local leaders. Cieza (1862 [1551]) mentioned smiths located in all the Inka administrative settlements. These smiths were most probably *yanacona*, individuals removed from their community association and working full time for the state (Rowe 1946, 268).

To summarize briefly, prior to Inka expansion in the central Andes, the production, distribution and use of wealth was very similar to the pattern seen in the Hawaiian chiefdoms. Production appears to have been mainly by specialists attached to elite households and the metal goods were distributed over relatively short distance to be used as status markers. With the Inka expansion, the local production at elite households continued and became part of the more general mobilization of goods to support the state. Dramatically, the state appears to have taken charge of production in key wealth objects, especially the metal and cloth, and to have created large-scale systems of manufacture, warehousing, and long-distance movement. At this point, production had taken on a semi-industrial scale with direct state involvement.

Murra (1980 [1956]) develops a most interesting argument for a possible economic transformation under Inka domination. At first production of cloth and metals appears to have been handled indirectly; a requirement of each community was to provide goods (cloth and metal) as part of the broader labor assessment. The Inka shifted emphasis to production of key wealth items by specialists removed from their local community contexts. The implication is that wealth, used in ceremonies of legitimization, as status markers, and as exchange valuables, was being produced by full-time specialists working for Inka state institutions.

The reasons for this significant change in the nature of production appear to be two. First the larger volume of production surely had certain economies of scale. Second, and probably more important, the centralization of production brought it under direct state control. This would have strengthened the economic basis of the empire and helped counterbalance the centrifugal forces inherent in a staple finance system (D'Altroy and Earle 1985). The development of specialized production of course underlay this critical move.

Conclusion

To return to the initial question, what is the relationship between specialization and the evolution of complex societies? In complex societies such as the Hawaiian chiefdoms and the Inka empire, the economic basis of stratification was control over staple production. Ownership of productive resources, especially land, was most basic. In these situations regional exchange, linking local communities, was remarkably little developed except in certain raw materials and craft goods. In this context, where regional exchange was limited and on a small scale, the independent specialists working for a general market were comparatively unimportant. In at least these cases, local specialization and intercommunity interdependence were neither the preconditions for nor the outcome of complex society.

Rather, specialization appears to have developed as an outcome of the development of social stratification and large political and religious institutions. These attached specialists performed a variety of functions that included monopoly of force, economic management, and ceremonial legitimization. In terms of craft production, the manufacture of special wealth (feathered cloaks, cloth, and metal) served strategically to control the society economically and symbolically. The items of wealth served as means of payment, as symbols of legitimate power, and as evidence of sanctity. To understand the evolution of attached specialists from the retainers of complex chiefdoms to the semi-industrial workshop of states is to understand the role of their products, i.e., the society's wealth, in the developing system of stratification.

Acknowledgements

This paper was first presented at XIth International Congress of Anthropological and Ethnological Sciences, Vancouver (1982). I am grateful for discussions with the audience and symposium panel. Cathy Costin, Glenn Russell, and Bruce Owen have helped critically evaluate the paper's ideas, and have made available their own data on ceramic (Costin) and lithic (Russell) production and exchange. Elizabeth Brumfiel's work as seen in this volume and earlier papers has influenced my consideration of the linked economic and symbolic aspects of wealth. The Mantaro Valley research was supported by a grant from National Science Foundation (BNS82 03723).

Chapter 7

Economic change in the lowland Maya Late Classic period

Prudence M. Rice

In this paper I synthesize available data on the production and exchange of two important goods in ancient Maya society, pottery and obsidian. In treating these goods, I address not the parts they played in the development of complex society, but rather their structural roles in a society that had already achieved complex levels of organization: southern lowland Maya civilization in the Late Classic period.

This focus has several advantages for understanding the particular relationships between commodity production and exchange in Maya society, as well as more general interactions of economic, political, social, and technological changes. Pottery and obsidian are useful because — aside from their ubiquity — these materials represent, respectively, non-elite versus elite, or 'subsistence' and 'wealth' goods (Brumfiel and Earle, Chapter 1) among the Classic Maya. Comparisons and contrasts between these two categories of commodities thus permit relatively broad-based insights into economic behavior. In addition, the Late Classic period of the southern Maya lowlands is the pinnacle of that civilization, followed by what is traditionally viewed as an abrupt 'collapse'. It is increasingly clear, however, that the 'collapse' was largely a failure of the economic role or power base of elites; it was felt to varying degrees in different parts of the area; and rather than being a sudden disaster at the end of the Late Classic, it was instead a socioeconomic transition observable through changes in commodity production and distribution evident *during* the Late

Classic. This transition provides the backdrop for the investigation of the relationship between declining elite political power and economic organization. A look at pottery and obsidian among the Late Classic lowland Maya is thus instructive for understanding the changing roles in a complex society of different kinds of goods, produced and distributed by different means, in periods of political, economic, and social transformation.

The period of interest here, the Late Classic, is customarily divided into three parts: the early Late Classic, or Tepeu 1 (AD 600–700); the late Late Classic, or Tepeu 2 (AD 700–830); and the Terminal Classic, or Tepeu 3 (AD 830–950). The spatial context for the Late Classic lowland Maya political and settlement organization appears to be the *region*, a territorial expanse surrounding a civic–ceremonial center. Epigraphic (Marcus 1976) and settlement (Adams and Jones 1981; Bove 1981) data suggest that after AD 534 the southern lowlands can be divided into four major divisions, each dominated by a 'capital' or 'primary' civic–ceremonial center. Beneath these capitals exists a hierarchy of several subsidiary administrative levels of secondary and tertiary (or 'major' and 'minor') centers, and relatively dispersed populations of individual or extended households.

Despite decades of research into Late Classic Maya history at these large civic–ceremonial centers, however, there is distressingly little that is securely known about the relationship of Maya sociopolitical organization to economic production, either agricultural or commodity (see Marcus 1983a). The lack of real understanding of the economic system is all the more ironic given the prominence of trade theories in explaining both the rise and the fall of southern lowland Maya society (Rathje 1972; Webb 1973). Well-known among these is the argument linking the rise of elites in 'core' versus 'buffer' zones of the lowlands to the long-distance procurement of so-called 'basic resources,' such as obsidian, salt (Andrews 1983), and basalt, supposedly necessary for tropical lowland agrarian societies (Rathje 1972, 1973).

Lowland Maya economies in the Classic period were integrated on the local and regional (rather than interregional) levels (Adams 1977a, 147). The foci of these regional economies are generally thought to be the large civic–ceremonial centers: it has been hypothesized that the centers 'functioned largely... [in] economic networks that dealt heavily in both subsistence goods and utilitarian craft products' (Culbert 1977, 512; also Folan, Kintz, and Fletcher 1983, 149). Little evidence exists, however, to support a strong directive role for Classic centers in regional economies, at least in terms of traditional archaeological indicators of centralized systems of production and exchange. That is, the Classic lowland civic–ceremonial centers have no structures clearly identifiable as storehouses or markets, although the open plazas have been suggested to be areas for fairs or markets (Coe 1967, 73; Folan *et al.* 1983, 49–64; Freidel 1981, 378, and n.d.). Nothing suggests that the writing system was used to record transactions, yields, tribute, or other economic affairs. Nor have workshops been found in concentrations in the centers that would indicate barrio-like organization (cf. Folan *et al.* 1983, 149–60), administrative control of production (i.e., taxation), and/or a desire on the part of artisans to establish themselves in proximity to a market. Instead, the pattern is one of non-urban, geographically dispersed lowland craft-production locales, a pattern which has parallels with the village specialization found in highland Maya groups today (Smith 1976, 341–42) as well as in ancient highland Mexico (see Marcus 1983b, 216–18; Freidel 1981, 376–78; and Brumfiel, Chapter 9).

The evidence (albeit mostly negative) suggests that the Classic Maya had neither a hierarchically organized market economy nor an economy based on centrally administered production and exchange on a large scale. Instead, they relied primarily on low-level specialization and redistributive mechanism(s), probably based on kin relations. 'Certain goods and services are given the head of kin groups, who in turn redistribute these items in return for still other goods and services' (Adams 1977a, 147), 'with goods controlled by the upper classes exchanged for services by lower classes' (Adams 1977a, 155). The situation is thus similar to the 'staple finance' system proposed for the Hawaiian chiefdoms (Earle 1978), in which direct exchange rather than strict marketing principles was a primary feature of maintenance of relationships of producers to non-producers.

Pottery production and distribution

Occupational specialization in the Maya lowlands is a matter of no little interest to archaeologists (Adams 1970; Becker 1973, 1983; Haviland 1974; Shafer and Hester 1983). A variety of different specialties has been proposed, and in some cases even specific residence compounds and lineage type social organization have been suggested for certain occupations (Haviland 1974). Most attention has been directed toward pottery production (see Fry 1981 for a review). Elaborate human-figure polychrome vases associated with sumptuous tombs are the most widely appreciated examples of the Classic Maya potters' skilled artistry. These would have functioned as 'wealth' goods, being circulated – sometimes between regions (Adams 1977b) – by gift-giving at the time of elite funerals or other ceremonial occasions. Yet simpler polychrome and monochrome slipped serving vessels, together with vast quantities of unslipped utilitarian jars, were manufactured and used in large quantities throughout the Maya realm.

It is the production and exchange of these goods, rather than the burial vases, that have been most intensively investigated by Mayanists. These studies are limited to inferring economic processes primarily on the basis of differential spatial occurrence of the artifacts, but it should be noted that locations of recovery reflect the patterns of use or 'consumption' of the pottery, rather than the actual economic processes by which it circulates. More precise studies of production, which are a necessary prelude to study of commodity distribution, are not yet possible because actual manufacturing loci (kilns) have not been located in the lowlands (see P. Rice 1986a).

The data base for most of what is known about pottery production in the Classic period in the southern Maya lowlands proceeds from technological and physicochemical studies of pottery, principally from two sites (Fig. 7.1). These sites are Palenque, in Chiapas, Mexico, and Tikal in Peten, Guatemala; to these might also be added data from a third site, Lubaantun, in southern Belize. It should be noted here that Tikal and Palenque are two of the four Late Classic Maya political capitals or 'super-centers' (Marcus 1976; 1983a, 465), while Lubaantun is a small center lacking carved monuments (Hammond 1975) and is thus below the fourth order in the lowland site hierarchy. All three sites have smaller minor or 'satellite' centers within their domains.

At Palenque, the analyses focused on the distribution (in an area with a radius of approximately 50 km from the center) of utilitarian vessels, serving wares, and special purpose pottery, characterized by inclusions and trace elemental composition (Rands and Bishop 1980; Bishop 1980; Bishop and Rands 1982; Bishop, Rands, and Harbottle 1979). At Tikal, frequency/distance graphs of technological and stylistic characteristics of formal/functional pottery classes were used to study pottery distribution within a transect extending 12 km north and south from the site center (Fry 1979, 1980; Fry and Cox 1974; see also Becker 1983, 40). The transect sampled a 'sustaining area' of 123 sq km (Haviland 1970, 190). A possible locus of

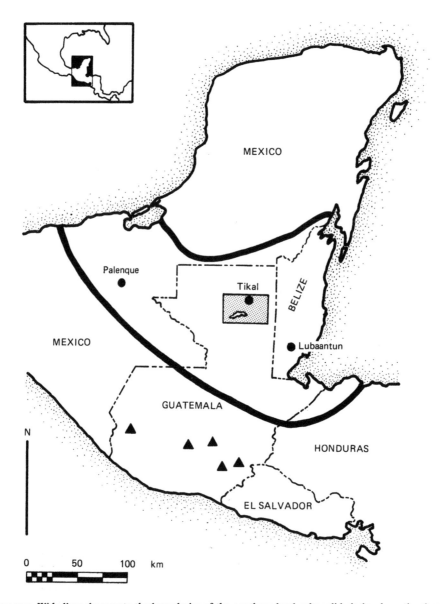

Fig. 7.1. The Maya area. Wide lines demarcate the boundaries of the southern lowlands; solid circles show the three sites discussed in terms of pottery production; triangles indicate known obsidian sources in the volcanic highlands region of Guatemala and El Salvador.

serving-ware pottery production north of the site was hypothesized on the basis of the distribution of muscovite pastes along the transect. At Lubaantun, trace elemental analyses were performed on pottery from the center and on local clays in order to identify resources and examine production (Hammond 1982, 228; Hammond, Harbottle, and Gazard 1976).

On the basis of these studies, it can be suggested that production of pottery vessels seems to have been in the hands of multiple sub-regional and local specialists residing in the peripheries of the centers or at some distance from them. At Palenque, for example, most of the Late Classic utilitarian pottery (jars and basins) was made within the Sierras and Plains zones, up to 20 km to the north of the center. At Tikal, the hypothesized location for production of serving wares of micaceous pastes was approximately 8 km north of the site center. At Lubaantun most vessels were produced within 6 km

of the site. No definite workshops have been located at these sites, and there is no indication of participation at the level of full-time, barrio-like craft organization. The non-center locations and the lack of capital investment suggest that potters combined their part-time craft activities with involvement in agricultural production (see Brumfiel, Chapter 9).

The products of the potters (at least within non-elite wares) were diverse form classes. For example, the producers using micaceous pastes at Tikal manufactured serving vessels but not wide mouthed jars (Fry 1979); at Palenque, the phytolith-bearing clays of the Plains were used for figurines and utilitarian jars, while the micaceous clays of the Sierras were used for serving vessels (Rands and Bishop 1980, 34, 42). Thus these data support ethnographic models drawn from the Maya highlands (McBryde 1947; Reina and Hill 1978) of community specialization by vessel forms.

The Classic civic—ceremonial centers were largely consumers rather than producers of pottery, particularly of utilitarian or serving wares. The centers themselves produced and distributed only small quantities of pottery, and that was principally 'non-utilitarian' or 'elite'. For example, the potters who are suggested to have resided at Group 4H-1 in the Tikal center produced 'censers, simple polychrome vessels, whistles and figurines, and probably . . . ceramic masks' (Becker 1983, 40). At Palenque, the paste group associated with the center itself was used primarily for incensario supports, cache vessels, figurines, and some serving wares (Rands and Bishop 1980, 43). At Lubaantun figurines seem to have been the principal products of manufacture within the center (Hammond 1975, 371—74). Hammond suggests the possibility of a workshop for making or painting polychrome pottery within the Lubaantun ceremonial precinct, mentioning the likelihood that here as at other small provincial centers the painting might have been done by traveling artists who decorated locally made vessels (Hammond 1982, 227). Distinctive 'Codex Style' polychrome vases probably were produced only at the largest Peten centers (see Robicsek and Hales 1981). Prestigious ceramic items produced within the centers may have been manufactured under direct elite administration, commission, or patronage.

The areas of distribution of the vessel shape categories produced in the different manufacturing loci are highly variable, reflecting both demand (including rates of breakage and replacement) and the existence of competing producers. In general, however, the areas are rather small. For example, at Tikal slipped bowls of the micaceous paste were apparently circulated primarily within 15 km of their hypothesized source (Fry 1981, 161); unslipped widemouthed jars were made of a large variety of pastes and were rarely distributed in areas more than 4—5 km from their presumed source. These jars may have been produced by individual households (Fry 1979, 495).

These data can be used to evaluate two alternative models of pottery exchange proposed on the basis of general reconstructions of Maya settlement and sociopolitical relations (Rands 1967). One model is 'inward-looking,' and postulates similar ceramic assemblages occurring at sites throughout the sustaining area of a major center (such as Palenque or Tikal) by virtue of that site acting as an economic central place for local exchange (analogous with 'solar' marketing systems, for example). Outside the sustaining area the sites would have individually differentiated assemblages. The alternative 'outward-looking' model hypothesizes great variability among the ceramic assemblages of local communities resulting from independent exchange relationships and individual patterns of non-center oriented economic ties. Evaluations of these models, as well as other observations on the nature of lowland Maya pottery manufacture drawn from the studies at the three sites, are revealing as to the nature of production and distribution of utilitarian goods in general in the Late Classic period.

Available data concerning the exchange and distribution of ceramic goods conform more closely to the 'outward-looking'

model than to the 'inward-looking' model (cf. Marcus 1983a, 477), and it cannot be clearly demonstrated that political centers exerted any region-wide influence in the production or distribution of most classes of pottery. Graphs of frequency of utilitarian vessel classes against distance from the civic—ceremonial centers do not indicate true 'supply-zone' behavior. Elite (or 'wealth') items seem to be the single exception, showing distribution curves interpreted as typical of centralized exchange (Rands and Bishop 1980, 33; Fry 1980, 12). Recent studies (Hodder 1974; Hodder and Orton 1976; Renfrew 1977) caution, however, that reciprocity versus redistribution, and redistribution versus market exchange, may not be distinguishable on the basis of fall-off curves alone. The multimodality of the Maya pottery distribution graphs — and particularly the differences in occurrence of micaceous wares in comparing North Tikal with Central Tikal (Fry 1979, 509) — tends to suggest that 'non-economic' or non-centralized and unmeasured factors were operating to control the circulation of these wares. One such factor is kinship; another — status differences — was controlled in Fry's studies.

The spatial patterns of occurrence of pottery from different locations of manufacture within a region could be explained in theory by market models or by redistribution. Rands and Bishop, however, declined to accept either the 'inward' or the 'outward' models of ceramic exchange on the basis of their Palenque data. They concluded that the pottery produced at the center itself does not 'enter a regional exchange system; sharp decrement occurs at a short distance from the site, a pattern which fails to conform well to either of the models unless the 'sustaining area' is defined in severely circumscribed terms ' (Rands and Bishop 1980, 43). The same is true at Tikal, where not only the presence of markets but the operation of a money economy has been claimed (Becker 1983, 42). Despite advocating a complex market system at Maya centers, Fry (1980, 16) concluded from his examination of ceramic data at Tikal that 'even the largest Classic Maya sites, such as Tikal, were apparently not the major nodes of redistribution of craft items as many had anticipated.'

In addition to these difficulties in assessing the role of the large centers in Late Classic ceramic production and distribution, other factors complicate the picture. Although the non-center spatial location of production of utilitarian and serving ware pottery seems to have been stable during the course of the Late Classic period, changes are evident in production organization. Evidence from Tikal suggests that the number of producers increased and the pottery assemblage became more varied (in both technological and stylistic attributes) between the early and late Late Classic periods (Fry 1979, 509, especially Figs. 3 and 4). At Palenque, this same tendency is also apparent in the increased ceramic diversity in four paste/form combinations in the late Late Classic Murcielagos complex (Rands and Bishop 1980, Figs. 12—16) There is also a tendency toward production of increasingly regionalized lowland polychrome styles from the early to the late part of the Late Classic period. Variability and regionalization are particularly evident in the succeeding Terminal Classic Period, when highly localized ceramic assemblages characterize the largely 'rural' lakes area of central Peten (P. Rice 1986b). Stylistic sharing is conspicuous only between the largest central Peten sites, such as Tikal, Yaxha (center), and Uaxactun; for example, the distinctive feather or 'dress shirt' motif is common on Terminal Classic polychromes at these large centers, but this motif was not found in rural assemblages in the lakes area.

Obsidian procurement and distribution

Although pottery provides little evidence of an integrated market system existing on regional or extra-regional levels in the lowlands, the fact remains that a tremendous variety of non-local or exotic goods is spread throughout the area, at sites which appear to have been composed of all socioeconomic statuses. Obsidian is one category of exotica that is not only ubiquitous in the lowlands, but is particularly useful as a vehicle for studying long-distance exchange processes (see Nelson in press). The stone occurs naturally only in the volcanic highlands of Guatemala and Mexico some 350 or more miles (500 km) to the south and west (Fig. 1), and probably traveled much of the distance to the southern lowlands by overland human transport. Its widespread occurrence in the lowlands bespeaks some organized procurement system for non-local goods.

Despite the analytical advantages of obsidian's ubiquity and the ability to identify its specific highland sources through provenience analyses (Stross, Hester, Heizer, and Jack 1976; Stross, Sheets, Asaro, and Michel 1983; Nelson in press; Nelson, Sidrys, and Holmes 1978; P. Rice, Michel, Asaro, and Stross 1985), there are some unanswered questions in Maya obsidian exchange studies. An important one concerns the locus of control of the exchange: did it reside with lowland polities or in the highlands? Most lowland archaeologists ignore the latter, and accept a major role for the large lowland centers in both the organization of its procurement (i.e., its 'production') and the control of its local distribution.

It is generally posited that obsidian, like other exotic goods, was acquired by lowland 'central places,' i.e., the large civic–ceremonial centers such as Tikal, Uaxactun, Palenque, and Yaxha, from which it circulated to smaller and/or less influential areas (Sidrys 1976, 1977; Nelson in press). The stone was probably brought in from the highlands in the form of large polyhedral cores rather than fragile finished blades, because of the ease and efficiency of bulk transport. It is not known, however, if cores then were moved from the large centers out into the hinterland, with blades being produced at individual smaller centers, or if blades were manufactured only at the importing centers themselves and exchanged, the cores never leaving the immediate area of the procuring site. (As with pottery, few if any obsidian workshops are known in the lowlands, and processes of exchange have to be inferred from spatial disposition, which more directly reflects patterns of 'consumption' and use.) Whatever the mechanism or form of

movement, it is generally thought that the spatial occurrence of obsidian in the lowlands reflects central place redistribution. Provenience analyses of obsidians from several lowland sites have revealed that the centers seem to have exploited multiple highland sources simultaneously; the reason for this may be to ensure a steady supply of the stone in case of trade disruptions (Stross et al. 1983), or to acquire different stone for different kinds of tools and uses (Moholy-Nagy, Asaro, and Stross 1984, 116).

Obsidian is a paradoxical commodity in the Maya low-lands if one compares theories concerning its procurement against the realities of its spatial occurrence. On the one hand, it has been regarded as a 'basic' resource essential for the efficient practice of the maize subsistence economy in the lowland rainforest environment (Rathje 1972). This hypothesis is founded on the ubiquity of obsidian, its sharp cutting edges (presumably necessary for cutting trees and/or harvesting the grain), and the inferred unavailability of local chippable stone that could serve as a substitute. If the hypothesis were indeed true, it would be expected that greater quantities of obsidian would be found in rural residential and non-elite contexts outside the limits of the ceremonial centers, in the areas of primary agricultural production (see Stoltman 1978, 20, 27).

This expectation is not at all fulfilled, however. Considerably greater quantities of obsidian are found in and around large centers than at more peripheral locations, as much as five times more per capita (Sidrys 1976, 458–60; see also Moholy-Nagy et al. 1984). As a consequence, obsidian is usually identified as an elite 'wealth' commodity by its manufacture into special unusual flaked forms, such as animals or human profiles, called 'eccentrics'; also, incised obsidians appear to be a peculiar elite item manufactured only at Tikal and are found virtually nowhere else in the lowlands (Moholy-Nagy et al. 1984, 109). Not only are most obsidians recovered from large centers, but most of them come from special deposits as opposed to general midden or fill. Their use in special ritual, such as bloodletting, or extravagant caching on special ceremonial occasions (for example burials or dedications of stelae or temples; see Moholy-Nagy et al. 1984, Table 1), or 'pot-latching' (Sidrys 1976, 461), further supports obsidian's primarily elite, ceremonial, and 'wealth' status.

All of these features argue for centralized procurement and control of the material by elites. As wealth, obsidian procurement and distribution may have been a narrowly guarded perquisite of high status, the stone being obtained for purposes of making offerings on ceremonial occasions. Local movement of obsidian into rural areas surrounding the centers would have been through redistribution by means of a patronage system and/or kin relations. It is significant that long-distance trade activities are thought to have been controlled and/or led by elites in the Late Classic period (Thompson 1964), as they were at the time of contact. It has been hypothesized additionally that in the Classic period the material served as a 'currency,' or exchange equivalent, in international 'cartel-like' highland–lowland trade systems in Mesoamerica (Freidel 1986).

A wider perspective on the role of this wealth commodity in Maya society can be gleaned from an obsidian data base that represents a broader geographical, temporal, and socioeconomic range of Maya society than those previously available. Such a context is provided by the obsidians from the Central Peten Historical Ecology Project (CPHEP), an archaeological survey project in the lakes area of Peten, Guatemala (Deevey, Rice, Rice, Vaughan, Brenner, and Flannery 1979; D. Rice and P. Rice 1980, 1982, 1984). Although in comparison with work at the large civic–ceremonial centers, the CPHEP excavations yielded miniscule quantities of obsidian, the sampling of 'rural' residential structures through a long period of time in these six lake basins (Fig. 7.2) results in a broad context for investigating and interpreting changes in obsidian distribution (P. Rice 1984; P. Rice *et al.* 1985).

The occurrence of obsidian around two lakes, Yaxha and Sacnab, conforms to patterns found in other areas of the Maya lowlands: it is heavily concentrated near centers. Nearly three-quarters of the total obsidian recovered from all periods in this pair of lakes comes from excavations in a single survey transect, the one immediately west of the center of Yaxha (D. Rice 1976, 323). Yaxha, a large, thriving site on the north shore of the lake, was a secondary-level ceremonial locus in the Late Classic lowland hierarchy (Marcus 1983, 465, Table 1) with architectual ties to Tikal. The same transect adjacent to the center also accounts for all obsidian cores recovered from pre-Late Classic contexts, suggesting heavy elite involvement in the importation, use, and distribution of obsidian in the area prior to the Late Classic period.

The CPHEP excavations suggest, however, that the role of obsidian in the Maya economy was changing in Late Classic times. First, it was becoming more available to rural residents. In the Late Classic, obsidian was less concentrated in the single transect west of the Yaxha center, and was correspondingly more equitably distributed around the basin (Fig. 7.3). Second, its absolute availability in the lake basins actually diminished, a situation which was paralleled at Central Tikal, where the ratio of obsidian to flint declined from 52:1 in Tepeu 1 to 13:1 in Tepeu 2 (Moholy-Nagy 1975, 517). Third, only in the Late Classic are fragments of exhausted prismatic cores or core fragments of obsidian recovered from transects other than the one adjacent to the Yaxha center. This suggests that during this time the cores themselves may have circulated, in addition to the finished blades (P. Rice 1984).

Further evidence for a changed role of (or access to) obsidian in the Late Classic comes from elsewhere in the southern lowlands. For example, at Becan, a fortified center in Campeche, Mexico, 130 of 147 obsidian blades come from

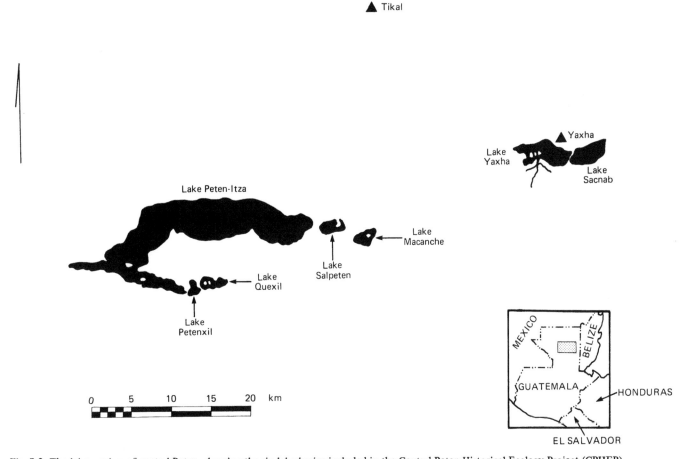

Fig. 7.2. The lakes region of central Peten, showing the six lake basins included in the Central Peten Historical Ecology Project (CPHEP) archaeological and ecological studies, and some of the centers in or near the basins. Lake Peten-Itza, the largest of the lakes in the area, was not included in the survey project.

Fig. 7.3. Ratio of obsidian to occupation in the Yaxha–Sacnab lake basins.

	Preclassic		Early Classic		Late Classic[†]	
	Obs	Occ[*]	Obs	Occ[*]	Obs	Occ[*]
Lake Yaxha	9	16	19	27	36	71
Yaxha Op. 2	87	18	54	11	69	24
Lake Sacnab	6	15	19	18	9	27
TOTAL	102	49	92	56	114	122
% Yaxha obs. in Op. 2	90.6%		73.9%		65.7%	
Ratio of obs. per occ.	2.08		1.64		0.93	

[†]Late Classic figures do not include the Terminal Classic period, A.D. 830–950.
[*]'Occ.' refers to the number of excavated occupational or constructional episodes dated to that period. Data from D. Rice and P. Rice 1980, Table 1.

within the site center; of the other thirteen phased obsidians recovered outside the site walls, twelve are from Late Classic or Terminal Classic contexts and only a single blade was found outside the center prior to that time (Stoltman 1978, Table 5). Additional insights come from Rathje's (1973, Table 30 and Fig. 57) analysis of 1009 burials from thirteen southern lowland sites. These burials evidenced a significant drop in the use of obsidian as a grave offering between the early (Tepeu 1) and late (Tepeu 2) portions of the Late Classic period (Fig. 7.4). At Central Tikal, although obsidian appears *more* frequently in Tepeu 2 tombs, it declines in use in special deposits, such as structure or stelae caches (Moholy-Nagy 1975, 515).

These data draw attention to the fact that the social and economic status of this commodity alters during the Late Classic. The possibility exists that models of centralized obsidian importation and exchange, focusing on the large political centers as administrators of this activity, may not be appropriate for the Late Classic period. Either direct access to (or distribution of) cores rather than solely to blades was newly manifest in these areas, or non-center or rural locations were able to import this material. In other words, the traditional status of obsidian as an elite-controlled 'wealth' commodity seems to be changing during the Late Classic.

Table 7.4. Percentage of grave goods in 1009 southern lowland burials (after Rathje 1973, Table 30).

	Preclassic	Early Classic	Tepeu 1	Tepeu 2
Exotics				
Obsidian	5.8	14.7	20.5	3.8
Shell	24.0	23.3	22.2	14.1
Jade	23.1	22.1	18.1	15.4
Local				
Pottery	51.9	51.6	56.7	65.4

Discussion

This summary of data on the economics of obsidian and pottery in the southern Maya lowlands in the Late Classic period provides a useful basis for comparing production and distribution of utilitarian and prestige (or 'subsistence' and 'wealth') goods, and for looking at changes in economic organization in the context of a sociopolitical system in transition. The Classic Maya economy seems to show parallels with that suggested for Hawaii (Earle 1978, Chapter 6) in being a decentralized system based on 'staple finance' and redistribution of locally produced and stored commodities. 'Wealth' in the Maya system – like Hawaiian feather cloaks – existed in several forms, only one of which, obsidian, is investigated here. The organization of production and distribution of pottery and obsidian underwent some transformations between the early and late parts of the Late Classic period. This shift signifies broader changes in lowland Maya political economies, and these changes demand some explanation. The questions are all the more compelling because the Late Classic period preceded the 'collapse' of Classic civilization in the southern lowlands.

In the southern Maya lowlands in the Late Classic, observed changes in the production and distribution of pottery and obsidian include: an increased number of producers of pottery from the early (Tepeu 1) to the late (Tepeu 2) period; increasing regional and local variability in technological and stylistic (including formal) attributes of pottery from the early to the late period; broader spectrum availability of obsidian, a prestige good; and a decline in the absolute availability of obsidian during the Late Classic as opposed to earlier periods. The first three changes suggest wider participation in a more commercialized economy. Increased variability in technological and stylistic attributes of pottery has been linked with heightened competition between producers, and decreased administrative control of ceramic production (Feinman 1982). The more even distribution of obsidian cores and artifacts also suggests diminished administrative control over its procurement and distribution.

It is useful to probe further into why these changes in production occurred in the Maya Late Classic period, in terms of the general dynamics between social and political change, and economic organization. Smith (1976, 334), for example, notes that relaxed administration and free competition between producers are associated with stable and secure political systems that are not threatened by local economic independence. The other side of the coin is described by Feinman (1982), who observes in Oaxaca a correlation of political interference and increased administration of large-scale ceramic production industries with population nucleation and periods of probable localized food shortages that may have caused social stresses.

The Late Classic in the southern Maya lowlands was a period of instability and transition, with evidence of demographic shifts (D. Rice and P. Rice 1982), political conflict, and warfare (indicated on inscriptions; Marcus 1976). The elite class expanded in size (Willey and Shimkin 1973, 483–84), moving to establish new centers and erecting more and more carved monuments at these sites. Household residential plans were increasingly variable, suggesting broad differences in labor investment in their establishment and in the activities carried out therein (see Wilk and Rathje 1982, 632). Polychrome pottery styles became increasingly localized, perhaps as a result of favored artisans having been moved as part of the retinue of elite households. The growth of elites doubtless placed tremendous burdens of production on the non-elites in order to support the attendant ceremonial activities.

Climaxing the social, political, and demographic instability was the so-called 'Maya collapse,' the ninth- and tenth-century cessation of patterns of conspicuous consumption among the elite. The traditional catastrophist view of sudden 'collapse' and depopulation is strictly applicable only to the elites and the largest centers, however. The CPHEP data from the rural lakes area show that in this peripheral region the events were much less dramatic, and there is greater evidence for population and craft continuity (D. Rice 1986; P. Rice 1986b). Thus, if the Late Classic period is viewed not as the *peak* of the civilization prior to its collapse, but simply as a phase of a complex society preceding a transformation of the system, some of the data on commodity production and distribution can be seen in a broader framework.

It is plausible to suggest that the increased numbers of people moving into ceramic manufacture in the Late Classic were exercising one option for coping with social and economic (especially agricultural) insecurity: diversification. There is no evidence to suggest that pottery production had ever been a tightly controlled full-time specialization; thus there was probably a certain fluidity of membership in producing groups over time. It is particularly likely that in times of economic stress, manufacture of low-value/high-consumption goods (such as utilitarian pottery vessels) would become an attractive way of augmenting one's livelihood. The need for these goods

would be relatively continuous, in contrast to the probably fluctuating demand for splendid polychromes on the part of the stressed elites, thus making it a comparatively secure occupation to adopt. Furthermore, pottery-making might have been especially opportune in highly populated areas suffering some degradation in agricultural productivity as a result of heavy farming in earlier periods.

The greater numbers of producers in Tepeu 2 times would contribute to increased variability of the products (see P. Rice 1981, 226), and the marked regionalization of pottery styles and compositions in the late Late Classic and Terminal Classic periods bears this out. Diversification in pottery production was not limited solely to utilitarian pottery, however. During the Terminal Classic in the lakes area, a widespread 'tradeware', Pabellon Modeled-Carved type of Fine Orange Ware (see Bishop and Rands 1982), was imitated in at least four distinct pastes at Yaxha (P. Rice 1986b), suggesting that innovations in production extended to localized copying of exotic prestige materials.

With respect to obsidian, changes in spatial distribution are significant in light of the long-recognized phenomenon that after the Late Classic period, obsidian became more widely available to the inhabitants of the lowlands in the Postclassic period. Sidrys (1976, 1977) sees this as 'devaluation' resulting from the ease of Postclassic waterborne trade; Freidel (n.d.) feels that obsidian ceased to serve as a currency in the Postclassic (being replaced by lowland products such as cacao and cotton cloth; see also Piña Chan 1978, 43–4).

Although obsidian is found in far greater quantities in large centers such as Tikal in the Late Classic than in rural or non-elite regions, there is an overall decline in absolute availability from Tepeu 1 to Tepeu 2 times. This decline suggests the early stages of failure of the organization of procurement (see also Rathje, Gregory, and Wiseman 1978, 168). Such failure may be a consequence of the elites having to cope with increasingly frequent political or economic crises (warfare, crop failures, etc.) within their territories by the end of the Late Classic, and a forced retrenchment policy with respect to far-flung long-distance exchange. In addition, it may reflect changes in the economies of polities in the highlands near the obsidian sources (see, for example, Zeitlin 1982).

A look at the distribution of several categories of exotics in lowland burials (Fig. 7.4) suggests that both factors were involved. Shell, jade, and obsidian, for example, all decreased in Tepeu 2 burials as compared to Tepeu 1, being supplanted by locally made polychrome pottery (Rathje 1973, 448–49). These three commodities are all highland materials (much shell is from the Pacific coast; Tourtellot 1978, 80–81), and their decline in the Late Classic may be a function of problems internal to the highlands rather than a deterioration of the economic power or international standing of lowland elites. At the same time, the reduction in obsidian is more dramatic than that in shell or jade. This reduction must also be considered in light of the fact that in the Tepeu 2 or Terminal Classic period a new obsidian source, Ixtepeque, in eastern Guatemala, began to be used again after a long hiatus, and continued as the major source through the Postclassic (P. Rice *et al.* 1985).

Another non-local item of interest in Late Classic Peten is a distinctive fine-grained brown chert from northern Belize, over 150 km distant. Only very small quantities (fifty-nine pieces) of this distinctive brown chert were recovered in CPHEP excavations in the lakes area (M. Aldenderfer n.d., and personal communication), so it was never a very abundant commodity in the region. Nonetheless, three observations are significant with respect to the occurrence of this commodity in the early and late Late Classic periods. First, of the seventeen pieces of brown chert that can be phased within the Late Classic, only two were from Tepeu 1 deposits, while fifteen were from the late Late Classic or Tepeu 2 period (an additional seventeen were from 'general' Late Classic deposits that could not be further subphased). Brown cherts continued to occur in Postclassic deposits in the lakes, with twenty-one pieces being recovered. Second, brown chert showed no tendency to be concentrated around the Yaxha center, as did obsidian, suggesting that it was not a prestige good. The greater quantity of this non-local chert in the late Late Classic period is evidence that exotic goods continued to circulate in the lowlands, even in the rural lakes area, and the major change in commodities concerns the role of obsidian as a 'wealth' item. Third, the investigators of Colha, Belize, the area of specialized production of artifacts from this chert, note that during the Late Classic period the number of workshop sites increased, although there may have been diminished per capita participation in lithic production (Shafer and Hester 1983, 540). This observation parallels the patterns of economic diversification hypothesized here for Peten during the Late Classic.

These changes in the distribution of ceramic and exotic lithic (obsidian and chert) materials in the lowlands are significant in light of the strong likelihood that in the Postclassic period both the organization of long-distance coastal trade and production of important cacao and cotton cloth commodities were controlled by lowland elites. Together, they suggest the first steps of a general restructuring of the procurement system for non-local goods in the southern lowlands during the late Late Classic. The wider distribution of obsidian in late Late Classic[1] and Postclassic times, I would argue, reflects one element of this reorganization: the conversion of obsidian from a 'wealth' good to a utilitarian good. Its new status is evident in the changed patterns of procurement and distribution in the 'rural' lakes area, and in the decline of its use in burials and caches in a geographically broader sample of centers. Such a conversion may have been necessitated by the increasing size of the Maya elite class and the consequent difficulties in establishing rights of inheritance to land and titles. Under less stressful conditions, the procurement, distribution, and use of obsidian in elite rituals such as bloodletting, in offerings to the gods, and on ceremonial occasions such as stela dedications, played an important role in demonstrating access to these privileges. With the strain on elites during the Late Classic period, however, the right to engage in such ritual, the nature of the ritual itself, and/or the rights and abilities to acquire the material, may have been transformed.

It is doubtful that the changed status of obsidian was a complete 'devaluation'. It was used in increasing quantities in Tepeu 2 tombs at Central Tikal (Moholy-Nagy 1975, 515), which suggests that elites at this large center may have maintained its status as a prestige good. Not totally devalued or democratized, obsidian in the late Late Classic may have undergone a process of gradual decontrol that culminated in the Postclassic period, at which time the stone had lost its status as 'wealth,' ritual offering, and 'currency.' At the same time, its commerce drew broader participation (though still within the elite sector), perhaps among 'petty elites' who were not inheriting land or rule. These individuals, lacking other alternatives, could have constituted an additional (and potentially disruptive) burden at the upper echelons of an already stressed economic system. Broader access to obsidian and its commerce may have been an outgrowth of patronage or gift-giving relationships, and institutionalized as means of accommodating a burgeoning secondary elite social segment.

Conclusions

Economic pressures within southern lowland societies in the late Late Classic (or Tepeu 2) period are reflected most dramatically in the decontrol of obsidian, a former item of 'wealth,' and its possible redefinition as a utilitarian commodity in the Postclassic period. But what are more interesting are the parallels between the changes in production of both pottery and obsidian at this time in response to the changes in the social system. Production and distribution of both goods appears to have become more widespread and decentralized, involving more individuals who were presumably seeking to increase their economic well-being by taking on new or additional productive pursuits. This transition may be viewed as a harbinger of the later commercialization of Mesoamerican economies, highland and lowland, evident in the succeeding Postclassic period. It is probably safe to say, however, that the two activities, obsidian trade and pottery production, were not alternatives effectively open to everyone. That is, rural non-elites would not have been able to enter into long-distance obsidian commerce, while elites at the large centers were unlikely to adopt utilitarian pot-making in order to fill the family coffers.

Finally, it remains to explain why the Mayas' economic response to political instability was decreased rather than increased control of production and distribution, contrary to expectations discussed above. Maya rulers at the large centers seem to have had no tradition of tight control of utilitarian commodity production underlying their power base in the Late Classic. Power rested in the genealogies of the rulers, not in their administration of production and distribution of utilitarian goods within their realms. For this reason, arguments linking the rise of southern lowland elites to trafficking in exotic but supposedly 'basic' commodities such as salt, obsidian, and volcanic stone metates (Rathje 1972, 1973) call attention to an empirical correlation, but do not constitute a satisfactory explanation of the phenomenon.

This leads to broader questions of lowland Maya economic organization. It was observed recently that 'The economic implications of regional centers have been particularly neglected, and one can only conclude that most Mayanists consider such centers to have functioned almost entirely in the political realm' (Culbert 1977, 512). On the basis of the political and settlement hierarchies, Mayanists have tried valiantly to force their artifactual data into an idealized central place economic model, for example a hierarchical solar or dendritic model typical of the Chiapas and Guatemalan highlands today (Smith 1976, 339–48). Although the characteristics of the organization of production seem to fit such systems in the lowland Maya Classic period, the degree of commercialization of the distribution system does not.

Yet Mayanists have been slow to acknowledge the implications of their findings. The distribution of pottery, taken together with the absence of clear archaeological evidence for marketplaces or 'supply zone' behavior at these centers, provides little support for commercialized exchange in the Classic period. Noncentralized marketing, reciprocal exchange, 'outward-looking' models, or 'basically autonomous localized marketing' (Fry 1981, 149) may be more appropriate explanatory constructs for Classic lowland Maya economic systems. Because hierarchization is only one of three structural attributes of distribution systems, Mayanists may find it more profitable to focus on the others – networks and inclusiveness (Smith 1976, 314). As has been remarked recently (Marcus 1983a, 466; see also 1983b, 209–10), 'political, religious, and economic hierarchies may not be coextensive' among the Maya.

Note

1. This wider spatial distribution may be more apparent than real, however. It could result in part from the growth and dispersion of elites into more of the area between the large centers, as is registered in the distribution of elite 'dower house' residences (Haviland 1981), the growing prominence of new satellite centers (Marcus 1976), and the large numbers of stelae erected between AD 751 and 771 (Willey and Shimkin 1973, 461). Nevertheless, these late Late Classic elites apparently did not have access to the same quantities of obsidian and did not dispose of it in the same conspicuous manner as did their predecessors.

   Furthermore, whether or not the decline of obsidian in burials indicates a decline in real *availability* of the good is another question; it may simply signal changing mortuary customs. The entire issue of the procurement and distribution of exotics in the Late Classic is extremely complex (see Tourtellot and Sabloff 1972; Rathje, Gregory, and Wiseman 1978, 168), particularly as they relate to highland–lowland interactions.

Chapter 8

The role of the *be* in the formation of the Yamato State

Gina L. Barnes

Introduction:

The *be* system has long been recognized by historians of Japan as the economic basis of the protohistoric Yamato State: it provided the craft goods, foodstuffs and supplies necessary to sustain the Yamato Court and Imperial family. Furthermore, it has been identified as the means by which the Yamato Court exercised and consolidated its authority over local areas by breaking down traditional community and kinship ties, and appropriating people and land for its own direct use (Kiley 1983; Vargo 1979).

In this chapter, I will also make a case for regarding the institutionalization of the *be* (pronounced 'bay') occupational groups as one of the crucial mechanisms by which the Yamato State was actually brought into being. Prior to the initiation of the *be* system in the late fifth century, the Yamato Court presided over a highly stratified society and hierarchically organized territory. In the ordering of relationships, however, it was the social aspects of status which were probably most important, and all economic transfers were determined by social obligations linked to the nature of stratified society. An organized decision-making administration with responsive and responsible local agents did not yet exist. A coherent system of administration first emerged in the late fifth century, resulting from several innovations including the institution of the *be*, the appointment of *be* overseers, the incorporation of territorial lords into the court, and the establishment of imperial estates. These were the elements that comprised the Yamato State; they were assembled during the late fifth century, and the state itself was extant by the early sixth century.

The institution of the *be* is the concrete embodiment of those qualitative changes believed to occur during the evolution of social organization. It represents a restructuring and reordering of the basic political, social and economic relationships in protohistoric Japan through the direct appropriation of land and labor resources. The consequent administrative organization, developed around the *be*, entailed:

(1) the establishment of a continuous political hierarchy with direct access to the individual commoner, a hallmark in state structure as regards taxation methods, litigation, etc. This hierarchy replaced the earlier discontinuous or chiefly hierarchy where most territories were locally controlled and relations between levels were of an allegiance nature, the higher level having access only to the representatives of the local areas but not to the individuals under the latter's jurisdiction;

(2) the breaking up of the cellular areas of local autonomy by (*a*) co-opting land and people in those territories and (*b*) by entrusting local elites with administrative duties over blocks of land and people that did not form part of their local power base;

(3) and the creation of a highly integrated and interdependent local administrative structure that militated against the re-emergence of autonomous local units.

The administrative system of the early Yamato State had a life span of only 150 years, until reforms in the mid seventh century instituted a Chinese style of government referred to as Ritsuryo. In investigating the state's formation and development from the late fourth to the early seventh centuries, much information can be gleaned from Japan's earliest extant chronicles, the *Kojiki* and *Nihon Shoki* which were finalized in AD 712 and 720 respectively (Philippi 1969; Aston 1896). Because these narratives were written to provide historical precedent for the politically powerful groups of the eighth century, the history and legends they contain have been subjected to wilful misrepresentation including chronological distortion, conscious omission, and reordering of relationships both genealogical and political. In addition, they postdate the early Yamato State by three-quarters of a century. Thus much of the research on the early period must be carried out on remnants of history embedded in the political documents, often using etymological analysis — especially on personal names, which frequently incorporate early occupational and court functions.

In the first section below, I give a résumé* of the historical research concerning the development of the Yamato Court. Each element discussed is the product of separate analysis, and most reconstructions are to some extent controversial. The various reconstructions have been synthesized here with reference to those points that are know anthropologically to be important in early state systems. Following this discussion, the nature of the *be* is described in some detail in order to evaluate the archaeological evidence for craft reorganization in fifth-century Nara, the locus of state formation.

The Yamato Court

Pre-Ritsuryo Yamato (Fig. 8.1) was headed by a Great King (*okimi*). This title is attested in sword inscriptions from the fifth century and was used until approximately AD 600, when the title of Emperor/Empress (*tenno*) was adopted. The Great King of Yamato was "simply a *primus inter pares* vis-a-vis the other nobles" in the early fifth century and "held a vague hegemony over similar kingships elsewhere" (Kiley 1973). Kiley states that by the late fifth century a court structure began to develop which was based on a non-royal service nobility and on certain court assets such as craft and service groups (*be*) and royal estates (*miyake*).

Some of the earliest court officials were functionaries called *tomo* or *tomo-no-o* (with the male suffix added; female *tomo* are also referred to in the chronicles). These functionaries appear to have been in charge of various tasks: there were *tomo* who bore the quivers or carried the swords, groups of palace guards (*tonomori*), scribes (*fubito*), and palace custodians (*kanimori*). References to the 80 *tomo-no-o* possibly predate the later fifth centry when the *tomo* were reorganized

into the 180 *tomo*, each with an overseer (*tomo-no-miyatsuko*). These numbers of *tomo* are almost certainly nominal, and it is unclear whether the word *tomo* refers to individuals or groups of individuals, which would change the scale of the court structure quite considerably.

It is significant that one of the groups of court functionaries in the early fifth century was the scribes. These skilled persons were immigrants from the state of Paekche on the southwestern Korean peninsula. They served to keep the records at the fifth-century Yamato Court, and fragments of the Paekche chronicles (called *Kudara Ki* in Japanese) which they brought with them to Japan were later used in the compilation of the eighth-century Japanese chronicles. The scribes were part of the first historically known wave of Korean immigrants to the Yamato area of Japan; other skills introduced by the immigrants were brocade weaving, horse breeding, saddle making, gold working and Sue ware production, all of which became important to the Yamato Court.

The reorganization of *tomo* in the later fifth century was probably undertaken partially to incorporate these new groups of immigrant craftspeople into the court structure. This reorganization was apparently carried out under the influence of the administrative system of the Paekche state, whence came many of the skilled immigrants. It was at this time that the word *be* was adopted from Korean, where it had referred to a social or administrative unit, perhaps territorial in nature. In Japan, however, it was applied, probably by the Paekche scribes, to the native Japanese system of organizing service groups (Hirano 1962, 98). As in the case of the word *tomo*, it is not always clear whether the word *be* refers to individuals or groups; and the two words seem to be used in combination or interchangeably in many cases.

By the end of the fifth century, the managers (*tomo-no-miyatsuko*) of the various courtly *tomo* and *be* were divided into two status groups: *muraji* or service nobility and *miyatsuko* or service functionaries. The most powerful of the *muraji* headed the Otomo ('great attendant'), Mononobe ('goods specialists'), Imbe ('ritual specialists') and Nakatomi ('intermediary nobles') families. The Otomo-no-Muraji and Mononobe-no-Muraji were responsible for the military functions of the Yamato Court as hereditary warriors, palace guards, and military commanders. The imbe and Nakatomi-no-Muraji were in charge of religious affairs at the court.

The *muraji* were second in status at court to the *omi* — nobles of the highest status who performed generalized ministerial roles at court. In contrast to the *tomo-no-miyatsuko* managers, whose names reflected their occupations, the names of the *omi* nobles specified location of residence. In this sense they were the local nobility; most of the *omi* families were located in the Kinai region surrounding Yamato and traced their ancestry to former kings. The *omi* differed from the *muraji*, who had also come to be treated as high-ranking nobility at court, both in the derivation of their names and in the fact that the *omi* were allowed to provide consorts to the Yamato kings whereas the *muraji* were not.

Parallel to the *tomo/be* system, which supplied craft

*This overview is based on summary material presented in the *Kodansha Encyclopedia of Japan*, the *Nohon Rekishi Daijiten*, the *Jidaibetsu Kokugo Daijiten*, *Kokushi Daijiten*, and especially Kiley (1973, 1977, 1983).

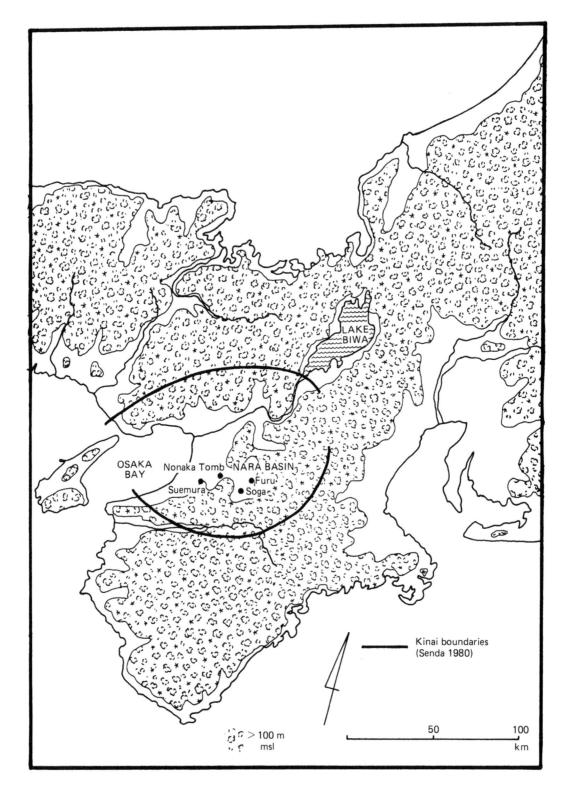

Fig. 8.1. The Kinai region of west-central Japan, locus of the Yamato State

goods and services to the court, the *miyake* system was developed to ensure the supply of foodstuffs. The word *miyake* is commonly translated as 'granary' (cf. Aston 1896; Senda 1980) for keeping the produce of the *mita* ('honorable fields'). But contextual analysis suggests that *yake* does not apply simply to a building with a roof, and the word *miyake* was usually written with two characters respectively meaning 'quarters' and 'storehouse'. Moreover, it is important to recognize that the *yake* element of *miyake* was a common word for housestead. In this early period, then, 'estate' may be a better approximation of the meaning of *miyake* than 'granary'. That individual agricultural hamlets may have been designated as part of imperial *miyake* is supported by Senda's (1980) identification of historical villages that are associated with *miyake* placenames and surrounded by fields that do not conform to the geometrical layout of the seventh-century *jori* land divisioning system. These fields thus pre-date the *jori* field system and presumably formed the substance of the earlier *miyake* system.

In addition to the *tomo-no-miyatsuko* managers, a second set of functionaries designated by the Yamato Court in the late fifth century were the *kuni-no-miyatsuko*, indigenous governors of outlying territories (*kuni*). The *kuni* are first described in the *Wei Zhi* chronicles of China, referring to the chiefly polities of the Japanese Islands in the third century (cf. Tsunoda and Goodrich 1951). In the seventh century a system of provinces was established under the Ritsuryo government, and these were also termed *kuni*, as in Yamato-no-Kuni. From these two examples, it can be seen that size and complexity were variable attributes of *kuni* through time, and in the fifth and sixth centuries it is unclear exactly what size territorial unit was being referred to.

Senda (1980) has identified two types of *kuni* which existed in the sixth century: 'one was a relatively large territory governed by the Greater *Kuni no Miyatsuko*, which became the *kuni* [province] in the *ritsuryo* period, and the other was a smaller unit governed by the Lesser *Kuni no Miyatsuko* which became the *gun* [county] in the *ritsuryo* period.' The governors of the smaller territories were once independent chiefs of their own autonomous territories. During the fifth and sixth centuries, however, they one by one submitted to the Yamato Court. They were incorporated into the court hierarchy by being given the title of *Kuni-no-miyatsuko* (governor); and their territories, once independent, were gradually agglomerated to the regional administrative structure of the court.

It is significant that many of the *kuni-no-miyatsuko* governors held the title of *kimi* (lord). This title parallels the usage of *okimi* for the Great King of Yamato, the hegemon. The territories of the *kimi*, therefore, probably represent the scale of autonomous cellular political organization before the formation of the fifth-century Yamato hegemony; this is supported by the *Wei Zhi* recordings mentioned above of 100 or so *kuni* existing in the third century. But it must be noted that the *kimi/kuni* combination in the fifth century represented

territories *outside* the central Yamato area, and the units of territorial administration internal to the Yamato area are currently unknown.

Some historians and historical geographers (e.g Senda 1980) view the *agata* also as a unit of regional administration. The word refers specifically to arable land and the units were governed by *agata-nushi* ('*agata*-masters'). The *agata* may have existed by the fifth century, but very little is known about them even during the succeeding sixth and seventh centuries when one might have expected elaboration of the local political structure. References to *agata* in the chronicles place them throughout Japan. There does not seem to be a hierarchical relationship between *agata* and *kuni* with respect to size, nestedness or importance − until, that is, just before the institution of the Chinese-style Ritsuryo government; then a clear reference indicates the spatial congruity of *agata* with the counties (*gun*) that were established in the Nara Basin (Fig. 8.2) when the Chinese system of districts, provinces, and counties was adopted in the seventh century (Senda 1980).

All the nobles and higher officials, in addition to serving at court, came to be heads of corporate families called *uji* developing under their nurturance. Japanese scholars once thought that *uji* were the primeval units of social organization in Japan, similar to 'clans' as known elsewhere. Recent scholarship, however, identifies them as specifically political products within the elite class only, resulting from the institution of *be* in the late fifth century (Vargo 1979; Kiley 1977, 1983).

The *uji* are thought to have been supported by their own *be* called *kakibe*, which have been distinguished from the *tomobe* and *shinabe* owned by the court (Inoue 1970). *Uji* members apparently lived fairly close to their *kakibe* producers (cf. Borgen 1975, 411), and in one sense, the *uji* were fairly localized: many of them bore placenames as their *uji* names, and reconstructions have shown that at least in Nara, the different *uji* were spatially distributed around the basin's perimeter (Date 1963)(Fig. 8.2). However, many *uji* developed several branches that lived in widely separated regions: witness the Haji family (Borgen 1975). The Haji no Muraji apparently had villages or producers under his private control in a set of widely spaced regions.

It is apparent from all aspects of the Yamato Court system that the important resource to be organized and administered was people, not land. Even in the case of estates, households and field labor (*tabe*) seem to have been the significant units. All produce for the court was collected from the producers generically (by category) through specially designated managers, the *tomo-no-miyatsuko*, rather than through territorial governors. This system is in clear contrast to the Chinese-style government instituted in the seventh century and consisting of hierarchically nested territorial administrators, among whom the county heads were responsible for the collection of taxes within their territories.

By the mid sixth century, then, the Yamato state was firmly established, its court consisting of the *omi* nobles, the *muraji* service nobility, the *miyatsuko* functionaries, and the

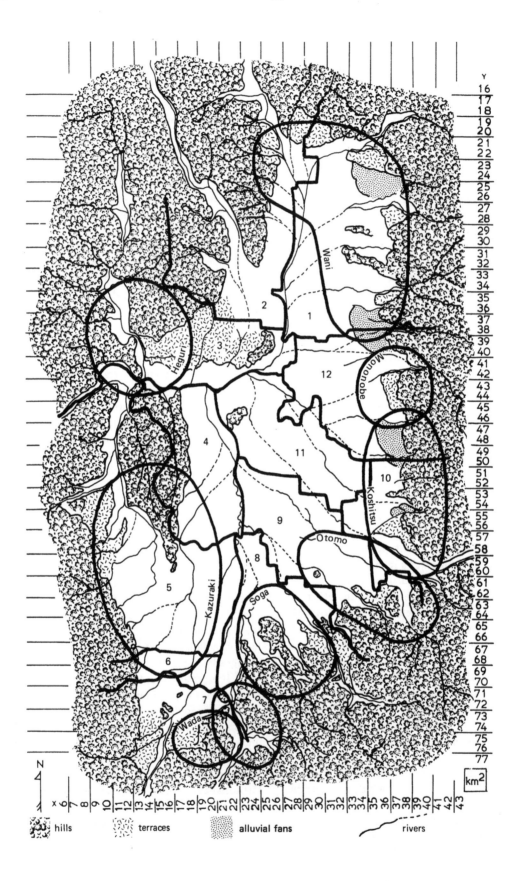

Fig. 8.2. Distribution of historic clans in the Nara Basin, Yamato

kuni-no-miyatsuko governors. As *tomo-no-miyatsuko* managers, men of *muraji* and *miyatsuko* rank were both in charge of the court's producer and service groups. Finally, with the incorporation of ever more governors into the regional structure, it became a custom for them to present groups of *be* workers for service at the court. Other officials or *uji* heads also occasionally presented *be*, thus providing for the elaboration and increasing integration of the central and regional administrative structure.

The be

In the previous section, we examined the structure of the Yamato Court during its development and the functional position of the *be* and their managers, the *tomo-no-miyatsuko*, during that time. In examining the *be* in more detail, it is first necessary to understand that there are several methods for classifying them. The currently accepted scheme, developed by Inoue (1970), is based on ownership of the three kinds of production and service *be* mentioned above, the attendant *tomobe* and craft *shinabe* were owned directly by the Yamato Court, while the commoner *kakibe* were owned by the different aristocratic *uji* families. Furthermore, there were two types that were owned by the imperial family: *koshiro* and *nashiro*. These latter were usually named after a particular person for whom the produce or service was rendered – thus the generic designation of *ko* ('child') + *shiro* ('substitute') and *na* ('name') + *shiro* ('substitute'). Ota (1955) identifies a final group of *be* (unnamed) that belonged to the shrines. This system of classification accords well with the generic names for most of the *be* groupings; however, other schemes have been developed for different analyses.

Ota (1955, 140–141) presents several classifications based on content and derivation of the names of individual *be* or on whether the members were called *be* or *hito*. His preferred system is to divide them into the following categories: occupational *be*; the *koshiro* and *nashiro*; those that bear the names of aristocratic families; *be* whose members were of ethnic derivation but excluding occupational *be*; and finally, *be* bearing regional names not belonging to royalty or aristocratic families. Such categories might not have been mutually exclusive.

Hirano (1983) also presents what he calls a 'functional classification' of *be*, but closer inspection reveals that his categories are really based on the source of the *be* individuals: immigrant craft specialists; *be* donated to the Yamato Court by the regional governors; and producers who were native residents of their local areas. A purely functional classification would perhaps consist of craft *be* (whether of native or immigrant craftspeople, and whether owned by the court, a royal or aristocratic family); subsistence goods producers (including charcoalers, shellfish collectors, tillers etc.); and attendant or service *be* (scribes, guards, stablers, etc.). Even then these categories would not be mutually exclusive, for example in the case of subsistence *be* providing firewood for kiln works, or soldiers who made their own gear, or craftspeople such as saddlers who serviced their products after manufacture. Finally, Kleinberg (1970), in undertaking a functional analysis of the *be*, specified the following as important groupings for study:

1. general groups of farmers
2. non-agricultural suppliers of food
3. groups regularly involved in the military system
4. domestic servants at court
5. groups of skilled craftsmen
6. groups constituting part of the administrative bureaucracy

Of all these various possibilities, the most pertinent for the purposes of this paper is the category designated by Ota as the occupational *be*. This category contains 162 types of *be* whose occupations are known from their names. Among these, Ota identifies 16 types of *be* with ritual functions, 7 literary or artistic types, 67 craft types, 12 agricultural types, 7 fishing types, 5 hunting types, 4 forest types, 3 husbandry types, 5 transportation types, and one miscellaneous type of *be*, etc. The 67 craft-related types of *be* are subcategorized into 4 makers of ritual objects, 9 makers of military objects, 13 kinds of weavers, 6 kinds of dyers, 3 kinds of distillers, 6 kinds of metal-workers, 6 kinds of ceramicists, 3 kinds of stoneworkers, 14 makers of architectural tools or builders, and one each of lacquerers, salt-makers and scale manufacturers.

In the above classification, the specified numbers refer to the *types* of *be*; they give no indication, however, of how many actual *be* groups existed in each category. It is very likely that there were many more than 162 operating groups of occupational *be*, but on the other hand, these probably did not all exist simultaneously. Certainly, new *be* were established as the Yamato Court gained power and the administrative system matured. Some of the *be* listed by Ota could have been early types which were superseded later as emphases changed or as groups merged or split.

The development or institutionalization of the *be* system is very difficult to investigate using the existing historical sources. The early chronicles do not give a clear account of the temporal development of the *be*. For example, even the earliest imperial records, such as the chronicle of the second emperor, Suizei, ostensibly referring to events of the first century AD (revised chronology, Kidder 1966, 209), imply the existence of the *be* at that time:

> they caused Yumi Be no Wakahito* to make a bow, and Yamato no Kanuchi Ama-tsu-ma-ura** to make a true-deer arrow-point, and the Ya Be*** to prepare arrows [Aston 1896, I, 139].

*   Young Man (Wakahito) of the Bow (Yumi) *be*
**   Ama-tsu-ma-ura, blacksmith (Kanuchi) of Yamato
*** Ya (Arrow) *be*

And records supposedly referring to the fourth century, such as those of the eleventh emperor, Suinin, provide instances of the establishment of specific be:

> there was further established the Be of bird-catchers, the Be of bird-feeders, and the Homu-tsu Be [Aston 1896, I, 175].

If, in fact, the word be is a fifth-century loanword as mentioned above, and if it was applied to producer and service groups only after its adoption from the peninsula, then these early records clearly consist of later interpolations. It is generally recognized that the chronology of the Nihon Shoki is not reliable until the events recorded for the fifth century, and certainly no faith can be placed in reference to be groups and their establishment in the earlier centuries.

What is difficult to assess from these chronicles, because of their projection of the be system backwards in time, is the nature of the economic system before its incorporation into the be system and how the institutionalization of the be system conditioned further economic development. It was indicated above that in the late fourth and early fifth centuries, there seems to have been an incipient court system dependent on specialized service groups (tomo), and certainly craft specialization as an economic phenomenon existed in various manifestations at least from the beginning of agricultural society in the archipelago (ca. 400 BC) (cf. Kanaseki and Sahara 1978; Hitchins 1978).

The question here, however, is how to distinguish adequately between the elaboration of craft specialization as an economic phenomenon and the establishment and extension of administrative control over production. Following the line of reasoning given above, the social and spatial units of craft production, as they occurred within the native system or as they were established by the immigrant craftspeople, were not originally tied to concepts of an administrative unit such as the tomo before the adoption of the word be. In other words, the production unit existed in its own right before it was designated as an administrative unit (be). This is an important point, for it provides the hypothesis that the elaboration of craft production in the fifth century was the result of spontaneous development at the local level and was not imposed from above or through central planning. It is within this framework that the flood of immigrant craftspeople into the Yamato area during the fifth century is conceived to have been the stimulus for the court to extend administrative control over craft and agricultural production in general. The be thus represent, as it were, an administrative reaction to an economic reality.

The development of craft specialization as a purely economic phenomenon can be investigated archaeologically for many common crafts which leave abundant material remains. Moreover, we should in theory be able to assess what changes occurred when administration was extended over existing production and what organizational forms resulted

from it. However, the point in time at which administration was extended over any particular realm of production may be quite difficult to pinpoint unless obvious administrative artifacts are associated with craft materials.

To my knowledge, there are no such administrative artifacts identified with the be system; indeed, the first such artifacts do not appear until the late sixth century, in the form of inked wood tablets serving as tax labels, office schedules, practice writing tablets etc. (cf. Loewe 1980). It is therefore questionable whether one can ever bring together the written documentation for the institutionalization of the be system and the archaeological evidence for craft production. Nevertheless, as a beginning inquiry, one can at least investigate the development of craft production according to the material remains and construct various hypotheses concerning the relationship of the craft group as a unit of production to the be as a unit of administration. Some of the difficulties in relating these two aspects of the problem will be indicated below.

Archaeology of craft organization

In this section, we will look at three different crafts — stone coffin production, Sue stoneware manufacture and bead-making — which have been the subject of considerable archaeological research by Wada (1976, 1983, in press), Tanabe (1966, 1981), and Teramura (1966, 1980) respectively. Aspects of production of these crafts, moreover, are known from actual workshop data or raw material source utilization rather than just from an examination of the finished products as with several other crafts of note. The following descriptions of these crafts are synthesized from the works of the above investigators.

Sue ware manufacture

Sue ware is an unglazed, grey stoneware derived from a ceramic tradition of the southern Korean peninsula. After a very brief period of importation of the Korean stoneware into Japan in the early fifth century, production of these vessels was initiated by Korean ceramicists in the hills of southern Osaka in the mid to late fifth century (Fig. 8.3). Since the imported wares — such as those Korean vessels found in the Nonaka Tomb in Osaka (Fig. 8.4) — are most similar to the ceramics found in the Nakdong River valley of the southern peninsula, it is thought that the craftspeople who immigrated to Japan to initiate Sue ware production were from that region, which at that time was organized into the Kaya federation of small polities. The kilns established at Suemura in Osaka (over 500 out of an estimated 1000 have been identified and many excavated) are assessed by Tanabe to have been the major suppliers of Sue ware (Fig. 8.5) throughout the Kinai region as well as adjacent areas, even though three other early kilns which produced initial Sue varieties have recently been discovered in Aichi, Kagawa and Miyagi Prefectures (Tanabe 1981, 45–52).

In the early sixth century, independent kilns were established in all the different regions supplied by Suemura

Fig. 8.3. Location of initial Sue ware kilns in Japan and the extent of distribution of fifth-century Suemura products

and beyond. Tanabe postulates that the increase in kiln sites was due to the broadening of the social stratum that demanded Sue vessels for their tombs. The change in funerary customs of the Late Kofun period (sixth and seventh centuries) which stimulated this demand involved the proliferation of small round mounded tombs with passage chambers. These were used as family tombs for successive interments; incorporating food offerings in Sue vessels, such passage tombs were built in large clusters in hilly areas, forming virtual cemeteries for the elite clans.

The *Nihon Shoki* chronicles imply that Sue ware production was begun under the direct auspices of Emperor Yuryaku (r. 457–79):

> the Emperor commanded Muruya, Ohotomo no Ohomuraji, to instruct Tsukami, Yamato no Aya no Atahe to remove Ko-kwi, of the Potters' Be, Kyon-kwi, of the Saddlers' Be, In-sa-ra-ka, of the Painters' Be, Chong-an-na, of the Brocade-weavers' Be, and Myo-an-na, the Interpreter, all belonging to the New Aya, to other

residences at the following three places, viz., Upper Momohara, Lower Momohara, and Magami no Hara [Aston 1896, I, 350].

Momohara, in fact, is recorded as a place in the southern Osaka hills (Sakamoto 1965, I, 476, note 22) approximately where the Suemura kilns are located. Moreover, near the kiln site are a tomb and shrine bearing the name of the brocade-weavers' *be* (Osaka Bunkazai Senta 1977). Thus, there seems to be some congruence in both time and space between this document and the archaeological record.

It should be noted that the names of the craft specialists in the above passage are all rendered in Korean pronunciation, but it is not clear where they are being removed from. The Yamato no Aya and New Aya were, respectively, older, naturalized Korean craftspeople and newer (as of Yuryaku's reign), immigrant Korean craftspeople. It is thought that the Yamato no Aya were located in the Takechi region of the southern Nara Basin while the New Aya settled along the Soga River in the south-central basin; thus, it could be that members

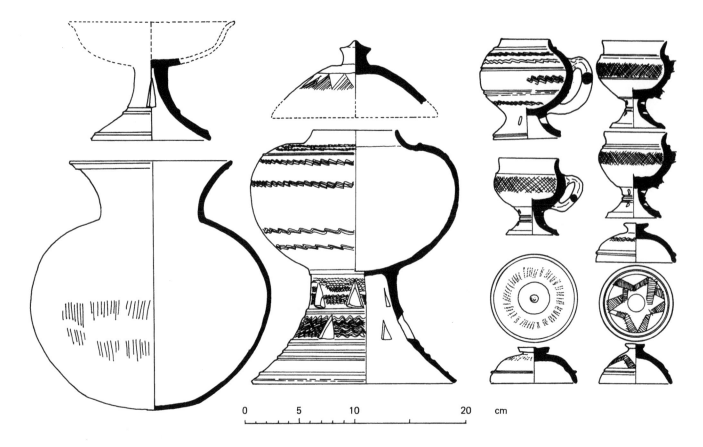

0 5 10 20 cm

Fig. 8.4. Korean stoneware in the Nonaka tomb, Osaka (Kitano 1976)

of the New Aya were being moved from southern Nara to the southern Osaka hills at imperial request. Moreover, another source records that "Otokimi, Kibi no Omi, returned from Paekche, and presented a Be of Aya workmen, a Be of tailors, and a Be of fleshers" (Aston 1896, I, 351), indicating that these craftspeople at least did not immigrate freely to a new country and establish their crafts anonymously.

Archaeologists, however, are more likely to downplay the overt political possibilities for the institution of Sue ware manufacture in Japan and emphasize pure economic considerations. Tanabe offers, as reasons for Sue production to have been established in the southern Osaka hills, 'the natural conditions of clay, fuel and topography and the political conditions of being close to the Yamato homeland of imperial authority' (1981, 46). He is reluctant, however, to attach too much significance to political intervention, saying that if it played a part in the initial establishment of Sue ware manufacture then it also must have played an important role in the decentralization of its production — which he apparently doubts.

Tanabe's position can perhaps be fairly represented by the notion of 'patronage', in the sense that it was the supply-and-demand relationship that regulated production rather than its being administered through formal political machinery. Under this system of patronage, the craft expanded from a single center of production in the fifth century to multiple centers of production in the sixth century. This situation compares well with what is known of the developments regarding stone-coffin manufacture in the same time span.

Stone-coffin manufacture

During the fifth century (Middle Kofun period), almost all the large keyhole-shaped mounded tombs in the Kinai region, which are assumed to belong to the uppermost regional elite, were equipped with stone coffins resembling storage chests and assembled from slabs of stone. These assembled-chest coffins were manufactured from Tatsuyama tuff, a rhyolite tuff quarried in southern Hyogo Prefecture (Fig. 8.6). The coffins, therefore, were issued from one source and were highly standardized in form. One can hypothesize that a single group of stone masons was responsible for their manufacture, probably located close to the source of the stone.

These stonemasons derived their craft from the Korean peninsula, whence techniques for working large blocks of stone were introduced into Japan sometime in the late fourth century (Wada, in press). Whether they were invited or transplanted by imperial agency is not known, but as with Sue ware, it is obvious that their craft was patronized by the fifth-century elite. Not only did the stonemasons supply stone coffins to the Kinai elite, but Wada further postulates that the

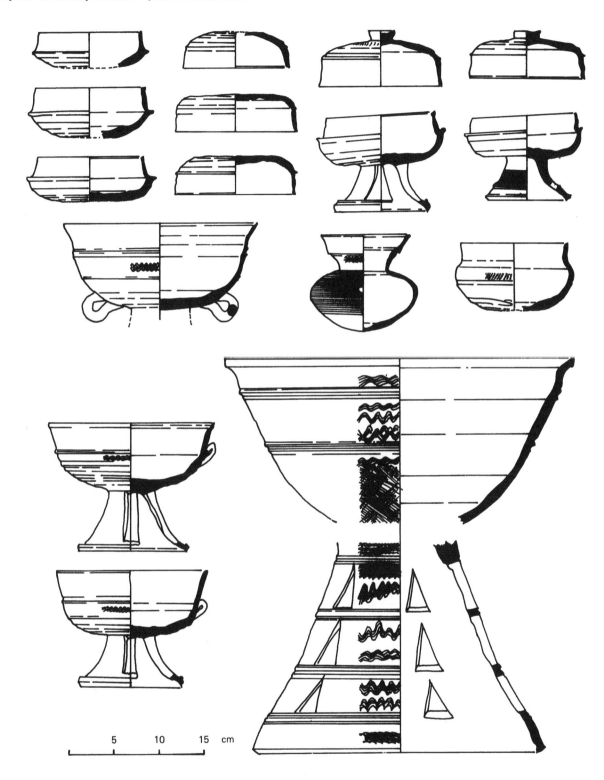

Fig. 8.5. Sue ware excavated from kiln TK208 at Suemura (Tanabe 1966)

stonemasons accompanied their half-finished products, both sarcophagi and ceiling rocks for tomb chambers, to the site of tomb construction and finished them there (1983, 520). Consequently, the masons were an indispensable element in mounded tomb building and are conceived to have worked in close contact with the central elite.

However, the end of the Middle Kofun period, in the late fifth century, witnessed a decline in the size of keyhole-

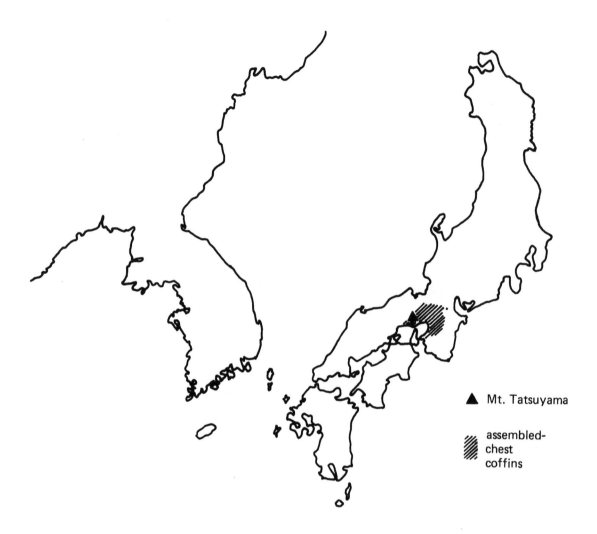

▲ Mt. Tatsuyama

/// assembled-
chest
coffins

Fig. 8.6. The Tatsuyama quarry and distribution of assembled-chest coffins in fifth-century mounded tombs

shaped tombs and a concomitant disappearance of assembled-chest coffins. In the latter's place arose the house-shaped stone coffin, so called because of its pitched roof (Fig. 8.7). Its manufacture was initiated in a small corner of the Nara Basin and subsequently spread to five different locations throughout the Kinai where multiple groups of stone masons are thought to have had exclusive quarrying rights to specific stone sources (Wada, in press). In contrast to the earlier assembled-chest coffins, which were homogeneous in form and material, the house-shaped coffins occurred in at least ten major temporal and regional variations involving both style and material.

Clearly, production decentralization from a single focus of stone utilization to multiple foci of quarrying and production is apparent in the transition from fifth- to sixth-century stone-working. To account for the five new production centers of house-shaped coffins in the Kinai and the stylistic variation of their products, Wada postulates that 'each powerful family in the Kinai district organized its own group of masons which began to produce the house-shaped coffins in unique shapes' (Wada, in press). Particularly, he cites the Kazuraki-type coffin as having been manufactured under the auspices of the Kazuraki family in the southwestern Nara Basin (Wada 1983,

note 4). The terminology Wada uses for the relationship between the sixth-century elite families and the stonemason groups is specifically political. The masons were 'ruled' (*shihai*) by their patron families. Unless by this term he is only casually analogizing the stratified relationship between elites and commoners to one between the rulers and ruled, Wada is postulating a more complex intervention in the organization and decision-making of production than mere demand and supply.

One is struck by the parallels between Sue ware and stone coffins in terms of craft importation and in the expansion from single-focus to multi-focus production. At first glance, the third craft to be examined — bead-making — does not seem to follow these trends, perhaps because it was an indigenous rather than an imported craft; but closer inspection reveals the same trajectory of regionalized production within a wide elite trading network leading into localized production for a restricted group of consumers.

Bead production

Teramura (1980) has distinguished three phases in the production of beadstone objects, corresponding roughly with the three divisions of the Kofun period. In Phase I or the

Upper

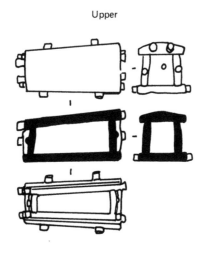

Middle

Lower

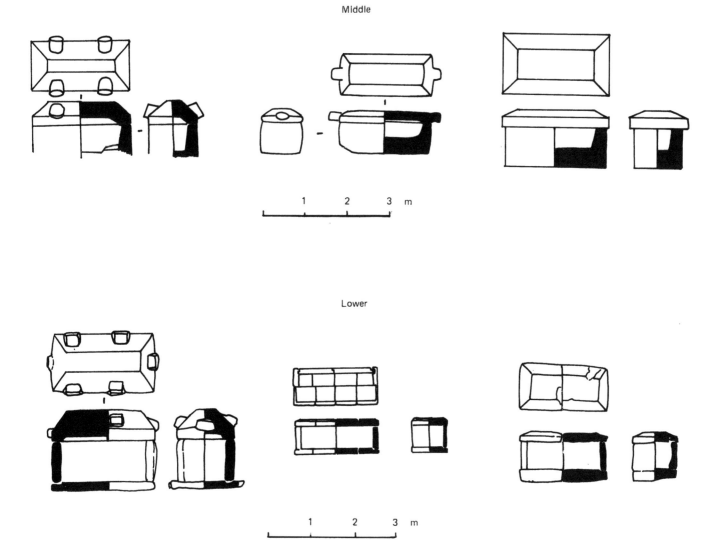

Fig. 8.7. Stone coffin varieties: top: Kinai assembled-chest coffins, fifth century Ostuka and Kobayashi 1982 bottom: Kinai house-shaped coffins, late fifth to sixth centuries (Wada 1976)

Early Kofun period (fourth century), the major products were stone objects for burial in the mounded tombs, including three kinds of stone bracelet and several types of beads made of green tuff or jasper-like stone (Fig. 8.8b, d). The main areas of beadstone working in this phase were Hokuriku (especially the Katayamazu and Nigozuka sites) and Kanto (the Odake, Hongo, Uenodai and Toriyama sites) (Fig. 8.9). These sites exploited local sources of beadstone, and it is important to note that all existed outside the sphere of Early Kofun mounded tomb distribution, bespeaking a long-distance trading network which served to supply central elite needs for beadstone products from these peripheral manufacturing sites. The organization of production at all of these sites but Katayamazu involved specialist craftspeople operating within a generalized village context. Katayamazu alone can be conceived of as a specialist village.

In Phase II, corresponding with the Middle Kofun period (fifth century), there is a complete reorganization of beadstone crafts with the establishment of an entirely different set of sites, the replacement of stone object production by the manufacture of stone imitations, and the introduction of a new flaking technique of manufacture. Sites are clustered in three regions – Hokuriku, San'in and Kanto – but they are organized as specialist production sites and are accompanied by mounded keyhole tombs of the central Kinai style.

Teramura interprets these as evidence of the extension of Yamato authority into these regions, while I prefer to see them as evidence of the integration of these beadstone-working regions into the elite cultural realm as a result of their participation in the Early Kofun trade network (Barnes, n.d.). The stone imitations produced at these sites are furthermore conceived of by Teramura as special ceremonial or ritual products which were produced for ritual specialists other than the rulers themselves. The hiving-off of military and ritual functions from the person of the leader, giving rise to rulers with true political power supported by military and ritual specialists, is thought by Teramura to be a fifth-century phenomenon and one *raison d'être* of the stone imitation manufacturing sites.

Finally, Teramura points out that there is another massive extinction of bead-working sites in the early sixth century at the beginning of Phase III; most of the Phase II sites thus either did not survive very long or underwent reorganization in the sixth century. In fact, the focus of beadstone production in Phase III shifts almost entirely to the site of Izumo in the San'in region.

A point touched on but underemphasized by Teramura, partially because sufficient data were not yet available, was the significance of bead-working sites established in the Kinai region during Phase II. He mentions three sites in the Nara and Osaka areas (Takamiya, Furu and the Yao site cluster) which had appeared in the fifth century, but the extensive discoveries at Soga and Furu in Nara had not yet been made. The new evidence from these sites is very significant for our investigation of craft specialization and the *be*.

The Soga Tamazukuri site was discovered during preconstruction excavation of a roadway in 1982 in the south-central Nara Basin (Kashiwara 1983). The northeastern end of the site contained five pillared buildings, separated by a 15–20 meter-wide streambed from the ditches and pits associated with bead-making in the central area. Most of these features belonged to the late fifth and early sixth centuries. The surprising aspect of this discovery was that no previous knowledge – place-name data or direct historical reference – existed to indicate bead-working at this particular spot in the basin.

At Furu also, workshops for bead-making and possibly iron-working were excavated in 1977 (Okita 1980). These consisted of pillared buildings with central pits from which jasper flakes, talc beads and iron slag were recovered. Several other locations in the area have also yielded bead-making debris and products, and unfinished hilts and scabbards were recovered from riverbed deposits. All of this material is dated to the second half of the fifth century, and it indicates the newly localized production of several crafts in this area of the basin.

Thus, in Phase I, the regional manufacture of beadstone objects in areas of their source materials is comparable, for example, to the production of coffins at Tatsuyama and Sue ware at Suemura where the necessary resources were close at hand. The differences would have been that the stonemasons and potters probably had direct relations with their elite patrons whereas the beadmakers were likely represented to the central elite via local chiefs through whom trade was funneled. In Phase II it can be seen from the Nara data that beadworkers were brought into central Yamato at some distance from the beadstone sources to set up production close to their patron consumers, as indeed happened later in the proliferation of stone quarry and kiln sites in the coffin and ceramic industries. The collapse of these local bead-producing sites and recentralization of bead production in Izumo in Phase III was peculiar to bead-making and not characteristic of the two other crafts under consideration.

These variations in the organization of craft production between the fifth and sixth centuries raise the question of the *be* unit and exactly which organizational form it applied to. Some possible interpretations are discussed below.

Discussion

It is clear from the data presented above that the period designated historically as the time of *be* establishment coincided with a trend towards multiple foci of craft production: the individual kilnworks succeeding Suemura, stone quarries succeeding Tatsuyama, and bead workshops in the Kinai. However, it cannot be concluded that these production units were established through the direct intervention of the Yamato Court. An equally likely stimulus in the elaboration of production could have been the increasing power of the aristocratic families to attract and patronize specialists to supply their sumptuary needs.

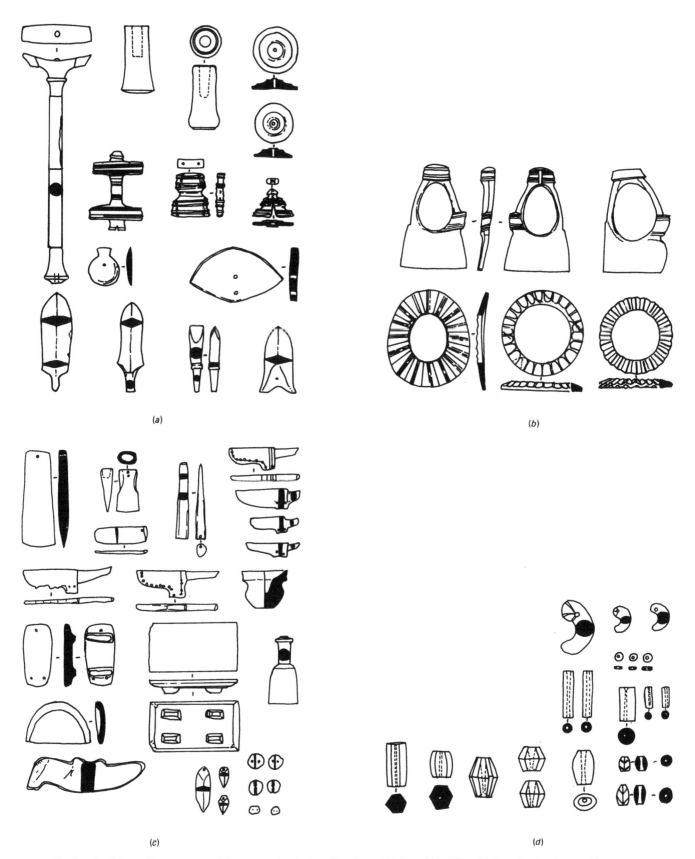

(a)

(b)

(c)

(d)

Fig. 8.8. Beadstone objects recovered from mounded tombs. (Otsuka and Kobayashi 1982) a. High quality beadstone objects including staff and ferrules, arrowpoint and chisel blade replicas b: Beadstone bracelets in hoe, wheel and radial shapes c: Low quality talc imitations of sheathed knives, tool blades, perforated discs, arrowpoints, household objects, and a horse image d: High quality beads of curved, cylindrical, faceted and incised shapes

Fig. 8.9. Beadstone source locations and manufacturing areas

The proliferation of production sites within the Kinai region presumably resulted in the scaling-down of the distance factor in the exchange network, with regions becoming more self-providing. It was thus the designation of *be* as producers for the court which counteracted increasing self-sufficiency at the local level. For example, *Suebe* and *Suehito* are terms known from the chronicles within the *be* system, referring to the potters who were designated to supply a set number of vessels to the court every year. But given the nature of the levy, these *be* cannot be considered full-time specialists attached direct to the court: many may also have been simultaneously serving aristocratic families.

Recognition of this dual nature of the producers' obligations has led to a re-examination and rejection of Inoue's strict categorization of *be* by ownership (Kamada 1984). Kamada proposes that most producer groups were both *shinabe* as regards their obligations to the court and *kakibe* in terms of their attachment to specific clans. If this interpretation is accepted, then the issue of exclusive 'ownership' becomes a moot question; of more importance are the separate questions of access rights to products and the form of subsistence support available to producers.

The Yamato Court established access rights to produce by designating groups which remained settled throughout the various regions as *be*. These taxes were levied directly on the producers rather than on intermediaries such as the territorial lords; this drove wedges of imperial authority, represented by the *tomo-no-miyatsuko*, into the outlying regions. These *be* acted as units of taxation which drew no support from the

central court but were obligated to supply the court with goods and could be manipulated by the court against their territorial overlords. The designation of *be* gave the state direct access to individual commoners and crosscut previously existing territorial divisions. Thus *be* designation acted as the precise mechanism that weakened cellular territorial organization and allowed the formation of a continuous hierarchy, establishing organic interdependence within the Yamato State. In anthropology, this step in state formation is recognized as the crucial distinction between chiefly and stately organization, whereby the complex political structure is no longer able to fragment back into independent, replicative components.

Separate from these taxation *be*, the court also seems to have supplied the support for the direct employment of specialists. These are usually conceived of as the naturalized Koreans who comprised *be* of blacksmiths, brocade-weavers, stablers, saddlers, and goldsmiths (Hirano 1962, 100). Note the absence of bead-makers from this list. The issue of support becomes crucial when trying to understand the initiation of bead-working in the Kinai region in contrast to the foreign craft *be* or more utilitarian crafts.

Beads and beadstone products were not merely items of personal adornment but objects with specifically political connotations. Teramura (1980) hypothesizes that the fifth-century manufacture of stone imitations were intimately related to the military expansion of the Yamato Court both into eastern Japan and north Kyushu. He postulates that the talc talismans (of sheathed knives, button-like perforated discs and disc beads) were somehow important to the rituals accompanying military expansion. Thus the sudden appearance of bead-making activities in the Nara Basin could be interpreted as having been instituted as a palace activity under direct supervision of the court.

For this interpretation, it is important to note that the chronicles record that four successive fifth-century emperors — Hanzei (r. 433–38), Ingyo (r. 438–53), Anko (r. 454–56), and Yuryaku (r. 457–79) — made their respective palaces at Shibagaki in Kawachi, and at Asuka, Anaho and Asakura in the Nara Basin. These palace locations correspond generally with the four Kinai locations that have yielded bead-manufacture remains: Yao, Soga, Furu and Takamiya. It is possible that each emperor established a bead workshop at his residence which then continued (at Soga and Furu) or died out (at Yao and Takamiya?) with the removal of the palace. This scenario would be consistent with anthropological models of early state society which emphasize the installment of full-time specialists as an important step in the development of internally differentiated settlements and state administration. In this case, support of the specialists is assumed to have come directly from court revenues.

However, one might ask why the fifth-century emperors established their palaces in these locations in the first place, and why did some of these locations continue with bead production — at least until the mid-sixth century — even after the palaces were removed? Archaeologically, the Furu and Soga site areas can be demonstrated to have been densely and continuously occupied long prior to the establishment of the imperial residences (Barnes 1983). Moreover, the Furu site falls within what is historically recognized as the territory of the Mononobe clan,* while the Soga site is situated near a shrine to the Imbe clan, which is known to have had lands in the Asuka region of southern Nara. It is possible, therefore, that the initial bead-working at these sites was carried out under the early manifestations of the Mononobe and Imbe clans: the *mono-no-be* and *imu-be*, although it is unlikely that these *be* were established merely for the production of beads.

The Mononobe and Imbe *uji*, two of the most powerful clans serving the Yamato Court, are historically known to have been responsible for military and guard duties and ritual activities at court. These were service rather than production groups; although it is conceivable — given Teramura's thesis concerning the importance of talc talismans to the military and their role in fifth-century ritual — that bead-making was a necessary but subordinate aspect of their responsibilities. If the beads (and weapons at Furu) were produced for internal consumption within the Mononobe and Imbe clans in order to conduct their court duties, however, the nature of administration over bead-making would have necessarily differed from the direct court supervision and support of the *be* of foreign

craftspeople, whose products were presumably consumed by people other than themselves.

If bead-making was initiated spontaneously by the local elite in the Furu and Soga areas, then these sites represent some of the earliest examples of localization in the Kinai of formerly distant productive activities, foreshadowing the trend toward multiplication of production sites in other crafts. Moreover, the institution of bead-making and weapons production at Furu contributed to the process of urbanization, as defined by intrasite economic differentiation. This trend is further evidence of Yamato state formation in the latter half of the fifth century AD.

This prolegomenon concerning the problems surrounding the investigation of the *be* system sufficiently illustrates that much of the system was instituted in an *ad hoc* manner through a reasonably long period of time. Many of the details we may think important for understanding the role of the *be* in Yamato state formation may never be accessible; yet the data are sufficiently rich to illustrate aspects of general processes of state formation that have not been elucidated in other case studies. Conversely, research on other economic systems of early state societies suggests that what is needed in future investigations of the *be* is a clearer explication of the actual circulation of goods and the finance system of the court.

Glossary

Agata: units of regional administration?
Agata-nushi: *agata*-master
Be: administrative units of production and service groups
Fubito: scribes
Gun: county division under the Ritsuryo system
Hito: person
Jori: eighth-century field system
Kakibe: production and service groups serving the *uji* families
Kanimori: palace custodians
Kimi: chief (fourth c.); lord (fifth c.)
Koshiro: 'child-substitute' *be* owned by imperial family
Kuni: countries (fourth c.); territories (fifth c.); provinces (sixth c.)
Kuni-no-miyatsuko: territorial governors
Mita: imperial rice fields
Miyake: imperial estate
Miyatsuko: service functionaries
Muraji: service nobility
Nashiro: 'name-substitute' *be* owned by imperial family
Okimi: Great king of Yamato (= paramount chief)
Omi: court ministers; highest-ranking nobles
Ritsuryo: Chinese-style administrative system based on codified laws
     instituted in the mid seventh century
Shinabe: production *be* supplying goods to the court
Tabe: rice-field cultivators
Tamazukuri: bead-making
Tenno: emperor/empress
Tomo: court functionary
Tomobe: service *be* serving the court
Tomo-no-miyatsuko: managers of the *tomo* and *be*
Tomo-no-o: male court functionary
Tonomori: palace guards
Uji: corporate families developing around the Yamato Court officials

---

* The excavator of the Furu site, M. Okita (pers. comm.), declines to link the Furu bead-making with the Mononobe clan; thus this interpretation rests solely with my own judgment.

Chapter 9

Elite and utilitarian crafts in the Aztec state

Elizabeth M. Brumfiel

For the Spanish conquistadores, the Tlatelolco market
was one of the wonders of the Aztec world. 'We were astounded
at the number of people and the quality of merchandise that
it contained, and at the good order and control that was
maintained, for we had never seen such a thing before', wrote
Bernal Díaz (1956 [1568], 215). 'All the things which are sold
there . . . are so numerous and of such different quality and
the great market place . . . was so crowded with people that
one would not have been able to see and inquire about it all
in two days.' (Díaz 1956 [1568], 217).

The variety of goods and services offered in the Tlatelolco
market was impressive. The market contained goods for the
elite wrought in gold, silver, precious stones, feathers, bone,
and shell. It contained richly embroidered and unadorned
clothing, agricultural produce, meat and eggs, fish and other
aquatic foods, salt, hides and leather goods, ceramics, wooden
containers, obsidian knives and swords, metal axes, lumber,
bricks, stone, lime, firewood, charcoal, pine torches, *chiles*,
paper, cochineal and other dyes, paints, cacao, slaves, bees'
honey, maguey honey, maguey sugar and wine, medicinal
herbs, prepared medicines, and prepared food and beverages.
There were also barbers, street porters, workmen and master
craftsmen in the market, awaiting employment (Anonymous
Conqueror 1917 [1556]. 65–67; Cortés 1970 [1519–26],
62; Díaz 1956 [1568], 215–17).

The larger number of people participating in the Aztec
market system and the range of goods and services offered
seem to validate the adaptationist argument: that highly integrated political units owe their existence to their ability to
sustain complex, efficient economies. However, a closer
examination of the Aztec economy suggests that its pattern
of development is not that which would be expected given an
adaptationist perspective.

In the adaptationist perspective, political integration
should be accompanied by increases in the efficiency, stability,
and/or capacity of the economic system. Since adaptationist
approaches emphasize the biological well-being of human
populations, efficiency in the production and distribution of
basic necessities is considered more consequential than
efficiency in the production and distribution of sumptuary
goods or art. But in the case of the Aztecs, political integration
seems not to have been accompanied by dramatic improvements in subsistence goods production. In hinterland communities surrounding the Aztec capital, part-time specialization in subsistence goods manufacture combined with food
production for household use characterized production both
before and during the period of Aztec dominance. Political
integration was accompanied by a dramatic growth in full-time
specialization within Tenochtitlan, the Aztec capital, but
much of this was devoted to the production of prestige goods
for elite consumption, not basic necessities.

The persistence of part-time specialization in subsistence

goods production and the rapid expansion of full-time specialization in prestige goods production in the Aztec state are the
focus on this paper. After a brief summary of Aztec political
history, and a review of the ethnohistorical and archaeological
evidence of economic changes accompanying Aztec political
development, discussion turns to the relationship of the
division of labor and prestige goods production to the processes
of Aztec political development.

Aztec political history

Understanding Aztec economic history requires at least
a brief acquaintance with Aztec political history. There are
two reasons for this. First of all, the factors of production
were embedded in political institutions. In particular, land and
labor were tied to political statuses: lordship, citizenship,
conqueror, etc. (Carrasco 1978). Political claims on the factors
of production limited the ability of the Aztec economy to
respond to purely economic variables such as supply and
demand. Second, to the extent that the Aztec rulers played
managerial roles in the Aztec economy, they shaped the
economy to serve their own interests. Sometimes it was in
their interests to promote economic efficiency, but sometimes
it was not. Then as now, economic efficiency could be sacrificed to more pressing political problems and objectives. In
short, Aztec production and exchange occurred within a
broader political context, and this context requires some
understanding.

The years AD 1250–1560 cover three phases of political
development in central Mexico: the pre-Aztec period (1250–
1430), the Aztec period (1430–1520), and the early colonial
period (1520–1560). In the pre-Aztec period, political integration on the regional level was lacking. It was a time of endemic
warfare among small city-states. During the Aztec period,
political integration was achieved within the Valley of Mexico,
and imperial conquests extended Aztec dominance over much
of Mesoamerica. In the early colonial period, Mexico was ruled
by Spain. Central Mexico experienced some dramatic changes
in ecology, population, and social stratification, but within
native communities, there was a degree of continuity in the
organization of production and exchange.

In both the pre-Aztec and Aztec periods, the small city-
state was the most basic political unit (Sanders 1956, 1968;
Soustelle 1961; Gibson 1964, 1971). The city-states contained
populations of from 5000 to 50,000 people, and they covered
areas of from 80 to 200 km² (Sanders 1968, 99; Sanders,
Parsons and Santley 1979, 151–52; Hicks 1982a, 231–32).
Each city-state was governed by a paramount (*tlatoani*) who
ruled by virtue of his membership in the local royal lineage. He
was assisted by a group of nobles that included his own
children and the descendants of past rulers, his vassal lords
(*tetecutin*) and the descendants of past vassal lords (Carrasco
1971, 351–54). This elite stratum constituted under 10 per
cent of the regional population (Cook and Borah 1963, 243).

Support for the elite was organized in a highly decentralized fashion. The ruler was supported by the tribute and labor
of 'free' commoners, but he also received produce and labor
from commoners attached to his patrimonial estates. Vassal
lords and a few lower-ranking nobles also held patrimonial
estates by which they were supported (Carrasco 1976, 1978).
These estates supplied nobles with foodstuffs, cloth, domestic
service, and an array of other goods (Guzmán 1938; Carrasco
1977; Hicks 1982a, 238–41). Lower-ranking nobles who held
no estates lived as dependents in the households of their higher-
ranking relatives (Carrasco 1976, 22–23).

Commoners were food producers and craftsmen. Some
resided in proximity to the ruler's palace in the central town
of the city-state; others lived in surrounding villages and hamlets (Sanders, Parsons and Santley 1979, 153; Hicks 1982a,
231–32). Commoners were organized in corporate groups
(*calpulli* or *tlaxilacalli*) sharing joint liability for tribute goods
and service and supplying contingents of soldiers in time of
war. In return for their services to the elite, the *calpulli* or
tlaxilacalli was granted land which it distributed in small plots
to its members to provide for their subsistence (Carrasco 1978,
30; Hicks n.d.a).

Prior to Aztec state formation in 1430, the city-states of
central Mexico were embroiled in ceaseless political struggles.
Warfare between city-states was endemic, and internal political
competition was intense. Much of the violence centered upon
struggles of succession to determine who would control the
patrimonies of the noble houses and who would rule the city-
states (Brumfiel 1983, 268–70). But by 1430, the rulers of
three city-states within the Valley of Mexico (Tenochtitlan,
Texcoco, and Tlacopan) had been able to forge a military
alliance, to conquer almost all the city-states within the Valley
of Mexico, and to begin a series of far-flung expansionary
conquests. When the Spaniards arrived less than a century later,
this Triple Alliance dominated much of Mesoamerica (see
Davies 1973).

What is known as the Aztec state was a system of vertical
control set up by the rulers of Tenochtitlan, Texcoco, and
Tlacopan to deal with the administration of city-states subordinate to them. Normally, the Triple Alliance rulers established direct bureaucratic control over conquered peoples
solely for the purpose of tribute collection. Defeated paramounts were relied upon to use their traditional authority and
the existing governmental apparatus to maintain order within
their domains. In areas at some distance from the Valley of
Mexico, defeated paramounts enjoyed considerable autonomy
(Gibson 1971, 389–92); within the Valley of Mexico, the
judicial and political autonomy of subordinate rulers was more
thoroughly compromised (Hodge 1984; Offner 1983, 87–120).
The term 'Aztec state' also refers to the system of internal
political control that increased the power of Triple Alliance
rulers when dealing with their own subjects (see Rounds 1979).
As will become evident, the distribution of prestige goods by
Triple Alliance rulers played a key role in achieving this heightened control over both subjects and defeated paramounts.

Although the Aztec state was, technically speaking, a
triumvirate, the ruler of Tenochtitlan became the *primus inter*

pares, dominating the rulers of Texcoco and Tlacopan (Gibson 1971, 383–89). The city of Tenochtitlan with a population of 200,000 was by far the largest city in the Valley of Mexico, five or six times larger than Texcoco, the second largest city in the Valley (Sanders, Parsons, and Santley 1979, 154). In the discussion that follows, this *de facto* dominance is recognized by referring to the ruler of Tenochtitlan as 'the Aztec ruler' and to the city, itself, as '*the* Aztec capital'.

The Aztecs were conquered by the Spaniards in 1521. In the subsequent half century, central Mexico experienced some dramatic changes. The native population declined to one quarter or less of its prehispanic level (Cook and Borah 1960). Patterns of tribute liability and payment changed, particularly for the native nobility and certain classes of craftsmen who had been exempt under native rule (Gibson 1964, 197–200). Some regions experienced rapid ecological deterioration resulting in altered resources and industries (Melville 1983). Even so, in some regions and in some aspects of life, prehispanic patterns persisted (Charlton 1972, 1–9; Parsons et al. 1982, 61–62; Kellogg 1983). Tenochtitlan–Mexico City continued to be the center of regional control; the small city-states came to serve as units of colonial administration (Gibson 1964, 34).

Specialization in the colonial era

The early colonial period produced the *Matrícula de Huexotzinco*, a document containing highly detailed information on patterns of specialization in central Mexico. Although this information dates to forty years after conquest and comes from an area that lay outside the Aztec sphere of conquest, it can be used to construct a model of specialization against which the archaeological evidence from earlier periods can be compared. As we shall see, the archaeological evidence suggests a pattern of specialization in Aztec hinterland communities that does not differ greatly from that recorded for colonial Huexotzinco. The *Matrícula* has been published by Prem (1974). Carrasco (1974) and Dyckerhoff and Prem (1976) discuss the patterns of specialization which it documents.

The *Matrícula de Huexotzinco* is a census of twenty-four communities in the province of Huexotzinco dating to 1560 (Prem 1974, see Fig. 9.1). The census lists 800 individuals, mostly male heads of households, identified by name and grouped according to civil status and residential ward. Some individuals are further identified by profession, their specialties indicated by native glyphs sometimes glossed in written Nahuatl (Carrasco 1974). There are 1597 specialists; they constitute 20% of the population (Dyckerhoff and Prem 1976, 165). The distribution of specialists by community is recorded in Fig. 9.2. The distribution conforms in some ways to adaptionist expectations, but in other ways it does not.

In keeping with adaptationist expectations, many specialists were engaged in the extraction or production of subsistence goods: mats, sandals, pottery vessels, baskets, wild game, pine resin, mineral lime, pine torches, and fish.[1] These account for 42% of all recorded specialists. The construction trades, i.e., wood working and stone cutting, account for 27% of all

specialists. The production of elite goods such as painted manuscripts, feathered adornments, smoking tubes and flower arrangements accounts for just 9% of specialists. The provision of services to the church accounts for 13% of the specialists, and the provision of services to the general population accounts for another 6%. Four per cent were employed in Spanish enterprises.

Also in keeping with adaptationist expectations, the geographic distribution of some specialists follows the distribution of natural resources. For example, over 80% of the specialists engaged in forest-based industries such as wood working, hunting, pine resin extracting, and pine torch cutting are concentrated in just three communities, those located on the northern edge of the province with access to the high wooded slopes of Itztaccihuatl. Numerous mat makers lived in the towns of San Luis Coyotzinco and San Bartolomé Tocuillan, near the lowland marshes north of Huexotzinco (Dyckerhoff and Prem 1976, 166).

On the other hand, the prevalence of part-time specialization is not in keeping with adaptationist expectations; economic efficiency is better served by full-time specialization. Nevertheless, a summary of the Huexotzinco census by colonial authorities states that only 377 individuals in the entire province (less than 5% of the total population earned a living

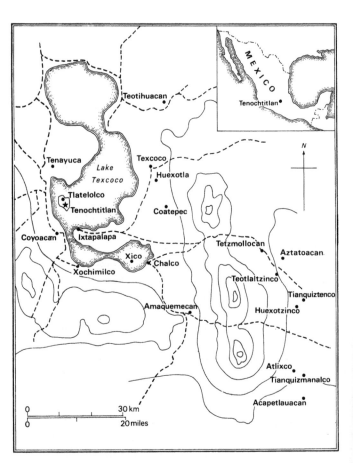

Fig. 9.1. Highland central Mexico, showing the Valley of Mexico and the province of Huexotzinco

Fig. 9.2. The distribution of specialists by community, province of Huexotzinco, 1560 (data from Prem 1974).

Communities	Married male heads of households, commoners	Married male heads of households, nobles	Wood workers	Mat makers	Stone cutters	Sandal makers	Potters	Doctors	Basket makers	Hunters	Pine resin extractors	Painters/scribes	Lime burners	Feather workers	Tobacco tube makers	Flower workers	Pine torch cutters	Fishermen	Total
San Juan Huexotzinco	390	275	1	1	4	—	—	1	4	—	—	2	1	1	2	3	—	1	21
Santiago Xaltepetlapan	491	100	5	—	9	11	5	1	11	—	—	4	1	—	1	2	—	—	50
Santa María Almoyahuacan/ San Pablo Ocotepec	606	147	—	—	30	6	3	5	—	—	—	7	—	3	2	1	—	—	57
San Simón Tlanicontlan	228	96	9	3	9	—	3	3	—	—	—	2	—	—	—	4	—	—	33
San Sebastián Tlayacaque	104	36	1	—	1	—	—	2	1	—	—	—	1	—	—	1	—	—	7
San Francisco Tianquiztenco	194	147	4	6	6	—	—	—	—	—	—	—	5	—	2	—	—	—	23
Santa María Acxotlan	411	46	—	—	3	—	10	3	—	—	1	—	—	—	1	—	—	—	18
San Bartolomé Tocuillan	261	29	4	42	2	5	—	—	2	—	—	5	—	—	—	6	—	5	71
San Luis Coyotzinco	839	74	7	29	9	18	9	1	9	—	—	—	1	—	5	2	—	2	91
San Esteban Tepetzinco	200	87	4	—	—	10	—	5	4	5	1	9	1	—	2	4	—	—	45
San Antonio Tlatenco	96	23	1	—	2	2	—	1	—	—	—	—	—	—	—	—	—	—	6
San Nicolás Cecalacoayan	299	67	5	—	8	8	3	—	2	3	—	1	2	—	—	1	—	—	33
San Lorenzo Chiauhtzinco	263	44	13	11	7	—	—	1	1	2	—	3	2	—	1	1	—	—	42
San Agustín Atzompan	253	41	19	—	2	5	—	2	4	—	—	—	—	7	—	1	—	—	40
Santa María Tetzmollocan/ San Salvador	1241	46	82	17	12	9	31	17	4	28	39	7	—	21	3	—	12	1	283
San Felipe Teotlaltzinco	476	64	45	11	9	9	12	1	2	3	11	3	5	—	—	—	11	—	122
San Gregorio Aztatoacan	900	24	60	53	14	13	11	14	6	6	—	1	7	4	10	—	—	7	205
San Pedro Atlixco	111	} 46	4	—	2	—	—	—	1	—	—	1	3	—	—	—	—	—	11
San Martín Tianquizmanalco	71	}	4	—	3	—	2	—	—	—	—	—	—	—	—	—	—	—	9
Santa María Acapetlauacan	802	—	12	3	12	—	2	9	8	5	—	1	9	—	1	—	—	3	65
Total	8266	1392	280	176	144	96	91	66	59	52	52	45	37	36	30	26	23	19	1232

(The nobles figure 46 is bracketed together across San Pedro Atlixco and San Martín Tianquizmanalco.)

from their crafts and held no land (Scholes and Adams 1958, 89); another 389 individuals are identified as non-landholding professional merchants). Presumably, the remaining specialists combined their specialties with subsistence agriculture (Dyckerhoff and Prem 1976, 165).

In addition, the distribution of many specialists does not adhere to adaptationist expectations. The proportion of specialists in non-extractive activities is not regularly greater in market towns (Huexotzinco and San Salvador) than in non-market towns. This could indicate that the services of some specialists were contracted for outside the marketplace with the number of specialists closely paralleling the level of demand as determined by community size. Apparently, this was the case for native doctors (*tlama*) whose distribution roughly parallels community size ($r^2 = .58$). However, in most cases, the distribution of specialists does *not* parallel community size; instead their distribution across communities is uneven and lumpy. For example, 23% of all flower workers are concentrated in San Bartolomé Tocuillan, and 20% of all manuscript painters are residents of San Esteban Tepetzinco; both towns contain less than 3% of the provincial population. This lumpy distribution of specialists between communities also characterizes the patterning of specialization within communities. Let me explain.

The census groups commoner heads of households in units of twenty, usually by residential ward (*barrio* or *calpulli*). The units of twenty often contain several different types of specialists; more importantly, a single specialty is often represented by several adjacent individuals. This is not always true; 22% of all specialists occur as the sole representative of their specialty in the unit of twenty where they are listed. But 51% of all specialists occur in groups of two or five adjacent individuals in the unit of twenty commoners, 20% of all specialists occur in groups of six to eleven adjacent individuals, and 6% of all specialists occur in groups of fifteen to twenty adjacent individuals in the unit of twenty commoners. The lumpy distribution of specialists both within and across communities is probably a consequence of two variables: the way in which specialists were recruited and the part-time character of most specialization.

According to Durán (1967 [1581] II, 477), fathers were required to teach their trades to their sons so that all the different types of specialties would always be present within a domain. With specialization occurring on a part-time basis, sons would have inherited both agricultural land and a trade from their father. But the agricultural land would have imposed residential immobility on the sons. Their need to maintain access to their agricultural land would have kept brothers together in their native ward where they would all practice the same specialty. The brothers may even have cooperated as a single unit of production; there is some archaeological evidence for a multi-household unit of craft production during the Aztec era in central Mexico (Mason 1980, 180; Spence 1985, 11).

Specialization was coupled with market exchange. As noted above, there were two market towns within the province of Huexotzinco. They were part of a system of markets facilitating exchange at the local and regional levels within central Mexico and beyond (Durán 1971 [1570], 213–19; Motolinía 1950 [ca. 1536–43], 59; Paso y Troncoso 1979, 11, 18, 23, 31, 34, 37, 59, 62, 85, 250, 288, 311). The tax records of the mid sixteenth-century Coyoacan market in the Valley of Mexico record the array of goods handled by the market system during the Early Colonial period (Berdan 1975, 371–83; Anderson, Berdan, and Lockhart 1976, 138–49). These records list forty-two different products, most of which were subsistence goods: lumber, mats, sandals, pottery vessels, medicine, baskets, meat, hides, pine torches, fish, brooms, spindles, warping frames, tumplines, maguey-fiber shirts, chia, lake scum (a food), mineral lime, obsidian blades, salt, grinding stones and metal tools, of which the last five probably came from outside the community. Some of the products sold might be considered elite goods: a bark-clay concoction (which was chewed), candles, bells, embroidered cloth, tobacco products, and cacao, the last two of which were probably from outside the community. Extensive overlap between the products sold in Coyoacan market and the products produced by Huexotzinco's specialists is suggestive of the importance of the market as an outlet for rural specialization.

In addition, specialization articulated with non-market institutions of exchange. This is indicated by the very fact that the Huexotzinco census records the occupational specialties of individuals. Specialists were identified so that they could pay a special form of tribute to local rulers, providing specialized goods and services in place of the more common tribute in food, firewood, agricultural and domestic labor (Hicks 1982a, 241–42). In return, specialists benefited from one or more forms of patronage from local rulers. In the most basic form of patronage, specialists were awarded agricultural lands so they could sustain themselves through subsistence agriculture (Carrasco 1978, 34–36). This was a form of staple finance so decentralized it hardly qualifies as finance! In prosperous Xochimilco, 20 km south of Tenochtitlan–Mexico City, some specialists (carpenters, masons, wood-cutters, fishermen, feather workers, and sandal makers) are said to have their fields cultivated for them by non-specialist commoners (Carta de los Caciques 1870 [1563], 196). The allocation of labor for such a purpose may be considered a second form of decentralized staple finance. Also in Xochimilco, administrative and ritual personnel and certain craft specialists (carpenters, stonecutters, and 'other craftsmen') were feasted twice annually by their local ruler, at which times they were also given shares of tribute cloth that their ruler received from his non-specialist commoners (Carrasco 1977, 237, 248). This cloth may have freed the specialists from subsistence agriculture by enabling them to purchase food in the marketplace (Carrasco 1977, 234). This would qualify as wealth finance.

In summary, the evidence from the *Matrícula de Huexotzinco* and other documents suggests that during the early colonial period rural populations were served by a variety of specialists, most of whom were engaged in the production of subsistence goods circulated to the general population through market exchange. Some prestige goods were also produced in rural areas. The tribute system provided a second mechanism of distribution, moving the products of commoner specialists to local elites. Although this system for the most part conforms to adaptationist expectations, it fails to meet those expectations in two ways: in the part-time status of specialists and in their inefficient spatial distribution. The inefficient spatial distribution is probably one of the inefficiencies adhering to part-time specialization.

This pattern of specialization seems to have characterized the prehispanic era also. At least, this model drawn from colonial documents is compatible with the available archaeological evidence.

Specialization in the prehispanic era

The prevalence of part-time specialization in central Mexico both before and after its integration under Aztec rule is indicated by several bodies of archaeological data. Intensive, systematic surface collection at Huexotla, a community of regional importance during the thirteenth and fourteenth centuries, yielded tools and waste materials indicative of several extractive or manufacturing industries: felsite blades used in the extraction of maguey fibers, heavy scrapers and jars used in the extraction of maguey syrup, projectile points for deer hunting, small fired clay balls used as blowgun projectiles in hunting birds and rabbits, large and small spindle whorls for spinning maguey and cotton thread, obsidian cores from obsidian blade production, waste flakes from the production of projectile points and scrapers, ceramic molds for clay spindle whorls, figurines, and urn adornments and so on. At Huexotla, these tools and waste products were either ubiquitous, indicating productive activity common to all households (i.e., non-specialized industries), or they occurred in very light concentrations indicative of part-time specialization. They were never found in large, dense concentrations that would suggest full-time specialization by large numbers of people (Brumfiel 1980, 462, 475). A detailed investigation of the distribution of chipped stone debris at Xico in the southern Valley of Mexico yielded similar results (Brumfiel 1986).

Part-time specialization is also apparent in the obsidian workshops examined by Spence at Late Postclassic Teotihuacan:

> Although the obsidian cover on most of these sites is heavier than usual, none have the abundant debris that would be expected with full-time specialization . . . Also, 60 per cent of a sample of fine blades from the workshops show use, the same sort of patterned wear that appears commonly on Aztec blades from non-workshop sites. This wear was probably produced by everyday household and agricultural activities, and offers further evidence that obsidian working occupied only a fraction of the time of the workshop site occupants [Spence 1985, 7].

Spence (1985, 11–12) was also able to delineate changes in the volume and intensity of the obsidian industry over time. Comparing the density of debris and the workshop area for the pre-Aztec era with that of the period of Aztec dominance, Spence found indications of a 30–60% increase in workshop output, just matching the growth of the local population. Little of the increase in output was produced by intensification of production within existing workshops (indicated by greater densities of obsidian debris). Most of the increased output was produced by an increase in the number of part-time specialists rather than the movement of part-time specialists into full-time specialization. Thus, even under conditions of expanded demand and production, the pattern of part-time specialization was maintained.

A regional division of labor based on environmental variation is indicated by differences in tool type frequencies at Huexotla and Xico. Both sites were occupied during the pre-Aztec era and during the era of Aztec dominance, but they lie in different environmental zones. Huexotla is located at the foot of the thin-soiled, sometimes dry piedmont in the eastern Valley of Mexico. Xico is located on the moist, deep alluvial soils of the Chalco lake-bed which was reclaimed during the twelfth through fifteenth centuries for *chinampa* (raised field) agriculture (Parsons et al. 1982). Tool frequencies for the two sites are recorded in Figs. 9.3 and 9.4; some differences in the two sites are obvious. Felsite blades, heavy scrapers, and large spindle whorls, all associated with the exploitation of the maguey cactus, are common at Huexotla but virtually absent at Xico. Maguey is a plant well suited to the drier conditions of piedmont agriculture (Sanders 1965, 32, 45). Unifacially utilized prismatic blades are four times more common at Huexotla than Xico, probably reflecting Huexotla's greater proximity to the wooded slopes of the Sierra de Nevada hence the greater use of blades to shape wooden agricultural implements (the people of Xico probably purchased their wooden implements instead of making them). Notched sherds, probably used to weight nets for snaring aquatic fowl, are present at lakebed Xico but absent at landlocked Huexotla.

Certain materials in the Huexotla and Xico collections supply evidence of the procurement of non-local goods through regional exchange. These products include obsidian, grinding stones, salt (indicated by the fabric-marked ceramics used to package it), mineral lime, cotton (indicated by small spindle whorls), and small amounts of jade and shell. Such products are associated with pottery from the pre-Aztec period as well as wares from the period of Aztec dominance, suggesting that systems of regional exchange operated prior to the political integration of the region as well as afterwards. However, some non-local products (especially salt and green obsidian) are more frequent in the later contexts indicating that regional exchange did intensify once political integration had been achieved.

Political integration was also accompanied by changes in local production. At Huexotla, tool frequencies indicate an

	Early Aztec		Late Aztec	
Agricultural implements:				
Felsite blades (for extracting maguey fibers)	16	(4.4)	157	(5.7)
Heavy scrapers (for extracting maguey syrup)	4	(1.1)	137	(4.9)
Thick-walled vessels (for extracting maguey syrup)	261	(73)	3,114	(112)
Unifacially retouched prismatic blades				
(for making agricultural implements)	266	(74)	4,098	(148)
Hunting implements:				
Projectile points (arrow and javelin tips)	8	(2.2)	52	(1.9)
Fired clay balls (blowgun projectiles)	6	(1.7)	34	(1.2)
Spinning implements:				
Large spindle whorls (for maguey fiber)	11	(3.1)	44	(1.6)
Small spindle whorls (for cotton fiber)	10	(2.8)	37	(1.3)
Imported goods:				
Fabric-marked sherds (salt containers)	30	(8.4)	792	(26)
Large spindle whorls (non-local types)	3	(0.84)	21	(0.76)
Large-spindle whorls (local types)	8	(2.2)	19	(0.33)
Green obsidian (from Pachuca)	2,419g	(156g)	21,385g	(771g)
Grey obsidian (various sources)	561g	(417g)	3,882g	(140g)

(*Note*: figures in parentheses are frequencies per 1000 rim sherds.)

Fig. 9.3. Distribution of artifacts at Huexotla by time period.

	Early Aztec		Late Aztec	
Agricultural implements:				
Felsite blades (for extracting maguey fibers)	0	–	0	–
Heavy scrapers (for extracting maguey syrup)	0	–	0	–
Unifacially retouched prismatic blades				
(for making agricultural implements)	101	(20)	74	(33)
Hunting implements:				
Projectile points (arrow and javelin tips)	13	(2.6)	11	(4.9)
Fired clay balls (blowgun projectiles)	11	(2.2)	3	(1.3)
Notched sherds (net weights)	2	(0.4)	1	(0.4)
Spinning implements:				
Large spindle whorls (for maguey fiber)	1	(0.2)	0	–
Small spindle whorls (for cotton fiber)	5	(1.0)	1	(0.4)
Imported goods:				
Fabric-marked sherds (salt containers)	372	(73)	407	(181)
Green obsidian (from Pachuca)	224g	(47g)	251g	(117g)
Grey obsidian (various sources)	603g	(127g)	247g	(115g)

(*Note*: figures in parentheses are frequencies per 1000 rim sherds.)

Fig. 9.4. Distribution of artifacts at Xico by time period.

intensification in the production of foodstuffs (maize and maguey syrup) accompanied by a decline in cloth production and possibly hunting (Brumfiel 1980, 465). At Xico, tool frequencies suggest an intensification of maize production along with a decrease in chipped stone tool making and possibly the production of cloth (Brumfiel 1986). I suspect that these changes in production were stimulated not only by an increasingly complex and efficient regional division of labor but also by commoners' using the market system to acquire what they needed for their tribute payments (Brumfiel 1980, n.d., Hicks n.d.b). Some tribute goods collected by the Aztec ruler and distributed to members of his court were used by the elite to purchase subsistence goods in the market place (Calnek 1978a, 101–2). This was particularly true of cloth and cacao which served as media of exchange. Hinterland commoners selling subsistence goods in the marketplace in exchange for cloth and cacao were able to acquire the quantities they needed for tribute payment. Cloth and cacao would be paid in to the capital as tribute and flow out again in payment for food. In such a system, regional exchange intensified but the regional division of labor did not.

In summary, the Valley of Mexico enjoyed a high degree of economic efficiency during both the pre-Aztec and Aztec periods. Within communities, there was a degree of specialization in the production of subsistence goods. However, specialization occurred on a part-time basis, an established pattern that the political integration of central Mexico during the Aztec period did little to alter. Between communities, differences in environment and resources were exploited by differences in subsistence goods production with some local products circulating to the regional population. Under Aztec rule, the volume of regional exchange increased significantly. However, taxation was probably as potent a stimulus to regional exchange as the efficiency conferred by a more complex division of regional labor. Taxation in cloth and cacao may have stimulated the production of food for sale in the urban markets. As such, it would have facilitated the Aztec system of state finance without enhancing the efficiency of regional economic production.

Specialization in the Aztec capital

Tenochtitlan was a huge urban center containing 150,000 to 200,000 people. On the basis of the size and density of sixteenth-century house plots within the city, Calnek (1972, 114) has argued for the existence of 'an exceptionally high level of occupational specialization, and a nearly total dependency of the urban population . . . on external support areas for subsistence.' Calnek's position is widely accepted, and it implies a striking difference in the frequency of full-time specialization in the hinterland and in the Aztec capital.

Foremost among the non-food producing residents of Tenochtitlan were the political elite of the Aztec state. According to Cortés (1970 [1519–26], 26), over 600 lords and nobles, each with his personal servants, converged on

Montezuma's palace each morning and remained there until nightfall. In addition, the palace was attended by *telpochtlatoque* and *calpixque,* officials in charge of the urban population and it housed a resident staff of tribute stewards, craftsmen, entertainers, domestics, a palace guard, and numerous wives and children (Durán 1971 [1570], 82, 201; Díaz 1956 [1568], 210–11). All those in attendance at the palace and the priests who attended the approximately eighty temples that lay within the walled central precinct of Tenochtitlan (Cortés 1970 [1519–26], 64; Sahagún 1950–69 [1577], Bk. 2, Appen. 2) were fed daily from the palace kitchen using provisions and labor supplied by the imperial tribute system (Cortés 1970 [1519–26], 68; Díaz 1956 [1568], 210–11; Sahagún 1950–69 [1577], Bk. 8, Ch. 13, Par. 10; Zorita 1963 [1566–70], 182).

Many of those who attended Montezuma's court maintained their own households outside of the palace; these required additional means of support. The highest ranking members of the court, who were either the native rulers of hinterland communities or the vassal lords of rulers, were supported by the produce and labor of their own patrimonial estates. The foodstuffs, cloth, and domestic service from these estates freed them from dependence upon state finance at least insofar as subsistence was concerned.

Lower-ranking nobles and commoners were supported by the redistribution of imperial tribute goods. Grants from the stores of tribute were awarded whenever a warrior, merchant, or craftsman had performed a service of particular distinction for the state (Berdan 1975, 126–29), and grants were also made at regular intervals, according to a schedule of tribute collection and ritual activity (Broda 1976, 41–42). The grants typically contained loads of food staples, cotton, cacao, and cloth; jewels and feathered insignia were included in the grants made to nobles. As mentioned earlier, it may be that some of these items (particularly the cacao and cloth) were not intended for direct consumption; they were used in the marketplace to purchase subsistence goods that were not supplied by the grants.

The size of the elite establishment supported by imperial tributes is not known. Calnek (1978a, 100) estimates that one-quarter to one-third of the population of Tenochtitlan could have been supported by the redistribution of the foodstuffs from the imperial tribute. Parsons' (1976b, 250) estimate runs closer to one-half of the populace. In addition to this, a sizeable number of people must have been supported by the exchange of non-food tribute wealth for foodstuffs in the urban market. It may well be that the majority of people living in Tenochtitlan could accurately have been described as *'gente de guerra, . . . que no entendían en otra cosa sin en servirle [a Montezuma] en los usos militares'* ('people of war, who knew nothing else but serving Montezuma in military functions,' Paso y Troncoso 1979 [1580], 196). If so, their contribution to the regional division of labor would have depended upon how much of the tribute coming from outside the Valley of Mexico circulated to the general population. It has been proposed that their contribution was substantial, with significant quantities of tribute placed in general circulation (Brumfiel 1980, 467); however, this view has been disputed by Sanders (1980, 474) and Clark (n.d., 26) and is probably incorrect.

Several investigators have proposed that, in addition to the elite establishment, Tenochtitlan held substantial numbers of full-time specialists in utilitarian crafts (Sanders, Parsons, and Santley 1979, 180; Parsons et al. 1982, 384; Hassig 1982, 44). According to this model, the efficiency of the regional economy was enhanced by a division of labor between agricultural producers in the hinterland and full-time utilitarian craft specialists in the capital. Some division along these lines certainly must have occurred, but its importance is debatable. What we know of the occupational structure of Tenochtitlan argues against heavy urban involvement in utilitarian craft production. According to a list compiled by Monzón (1949, 50–51), the people of Tenochtitlan were metalsmiths, flower workers, feather workers, lapadaries, makers of rabbit-hair embroidered cloth, merchants, fishermen, mat makers, makers of the medicinal oil *uxitl*, pulque makers, tavern keepers, water carriers, curers and diviners (also see Rojas 1983). Though quantitative data are lacking, it should be noted that elite crafts and service industries are well represented in this list, and extractive industries and utilitarian crafts much less so. Hicks (n.d.b) has emphasized the importance of prestige goods production in Tenochtitlan's economy, and there is considerable documentary and archaeological evidence to justify such an emphasis.

The native histories document Tenochtitlan's rapid emergence as a center of elite craft production. The pre-imperial Aztecs of the fourteenth and early fifteenth centuries are depicted as a population of lacustrine hunters and fishermen, who, as allies of the powerful Azcapotzalco, relied upon the spoils of war as a secondary source of income (Alva Ixtlilxochitl 1975–77 [1600–40], I, 312, 315; Tovar 1975 [1583–87], 41). Only a narrow range of precious goods were procured for the city by long-distance traders (just three types of feathers), suggesting that the volume of elite goods in the urban market was low and that few elite craftsmen dwelt within the city (Sahagún 1950–69 [1577], Bk. 9, Ch. 1). Although the Aztecs had improved their status by 1420, they are still said to have drafted carpenters, masons, and other specialists from outside the city to construct their homes, temples, and palaces (Alva Ixtlilxochitl 1975–77 [1600–40], I, 347). However, just ten years later, the Aztecs, now the dominant political power within the Valley of Mexico, are credited with sending specialists from their own city to add luster to the court of an allied ruler (Alva Ixtlilxochitl 1975–77 [1600–40], II, 84).

Pieces of Aztec sculpture recovered from modern Mexico City (ancient Tenochtitlan) also indicate the rapid development of elite craft production in the Aztec capital. The monumental sculptures of Tenochtitlan form a stylistic grouping distinguished by their large size, complex iconography, fine design and craftsmanship (Kubler 1943; Nicholson 1971; Pasztory 1983, 141). The style coalesces during the mid-fifteenth century, shortly after Aztec regional dominance was established, and it comes to an end less than a century later with Spanish conquest. Despite its short duration, the number of pieces belonging to this style is 'prodigious' (Nicholson and Keber 1983, 26), and stylistic development within the tradition was rapid (Pasztory 1983, 143). This indicates that, for at least one of the elite crafts, Tenochtitlan had become a center of artistic creation with artists engaged in the continual refinement of expression and the production of works in quantity.

It may soon be possible to trace the development of many other elite crafts in Tenochtitlan with great precision. The recent excavation of the Aztec Templo Mayor in Mexico City has resulted in the opening of more than eighty offertory caches, each containing a variety of natural objects and craft goods, some imported in finished form but many the work of local specialists (Matos 1982). When these materials are fully analyzed and placed in a chronological sequence, they should reveal the pace of development and the pattern of elaboration of elite crafts. The reports now available already make it clear that, from construction stage IIIa onward, the offerings at the Templo Mayor were richer than any found at temples outside the Aztec capital (Batres 1904; Noguera 1935; Espejo 1945). This suggests that under Aztec patronage elite craft production reached new heights of development. Both quantitatively and qualitatively, elite craft production kept pace with the growth of Aztec political power.

The dynamic character of elite craft production in the Aztec capital offers a sharp contrast to the more static utilitarian industries located in hinterland communities. This contrast poses two questions requiring further discussion. Why *was* utilitarian craft production in the hinterland so static, i.e., why were the benefits of full-time specialization not exploited more aggressively? Why *was* elite craft production in the Aztec capital so dynamic, i.e., what was the source of the heightened demand for the elite goods produced by urban specialists? It is to these questions that I now turn.

Hinterland specialization and the Aztec state
The low frequency of full-time specialization in the Aztec hinterland is remarkable. Ecological diversity and population density ought to have made full-time specialization profitable; the apparent reluctance of hinterland peoples to engage in full-time specialization seems to violate the canons of economic rationality. However, it may be possible to account for this behavior by referring to structural imperfections of the market system, imperfections that raised the costs and lowered the returns to full-time specialization. Given the structure of the Aztec market system, part-time specialization in utilitarian craft production may have yielded the maximum returns.

Smith (1976, 333–38) has argued that meddling by political functionaries is the most frequent cause of market imperfections in the economies of agrarian states. Polities often impose inflexible prices, taxes, and trade restrictions upon market exchange, and their restrictions frequently create imperfections that discourage rural producers from market participation. Similar arguments have been offered by Eisenstadt (1963, 151–52), Wallerstein (1974, 15), Carrasco (1978, 63–64), Feinman (1980), Appel (1982, 25–28), and Wolf (1982, 84), all of whom observe that commerce is as likely to be stifled as promoted by the evolution of centralized, integrated political systems.

There was considerable political intervention in local markets prior to Aztec dominance. Markets were taxed and regulated by local rulers (Hicks 1981, 3–4), and local rulers attempted to monopolize all the market activity within their domains by blocking the development of intermediate level market centers on the peripheries of their territories (Hicks 1982b). Under Aztec rule, marketing competition was encouraged, but market activity continued to be taxed (at the rate of 20%, Durán 1967 [1581] II, 264), and in Tenochtitlan, at least, market exchange occurred under set (but not necessarily unchanging) prices (Sahagún 1950–69 [1577] Bk. 9, Ch. 5). These activities may have continued to affect exchange adversely. But while taxation and fixed prices raise the cost of market participation, they are costs borne by full-time and part-time specialists alike. For this reason, political intervention cannot account for the prevalent pattern of part-time specialization.

Hicks (n.d.b) has cited a second factor hampering the development of full-time specialization: the availability of 'a steady, reliable supply of basic food staples and other necessities' for the support of non-food producing specialists. Hicks points out that the existence of reliable food surpluses in central Mexico is highly problematic:

> Central Mexico has, on the whole, an excellent agricultural environment, but there is nonetheless considerable variation from year to year . . . Frosts, floods, droughts, locust plagues, and unseasonal snowfalls have all had adverse effects on crops. In the century between 1525 and 1625, Gibson [1964, 452–59] records 23 years in which adverse conditions seriously affected crop yields [Hicks n.d.b.].

Hicks suggests that the size of commoners' subsistence plots was barely adequate for subsistence in a below-average year; in many years there would have been little surplus for market sale. Thus, states Hicks (n.d.b), it would have been risky to rely heavily on small-scale producers as suppliers of food.

But, of course, small-scale producers were the primary market for the utilitarian goods produced by hinterland specialists. To exploit this market and yet survive, these specialists would have needed access to sources of food that could sustain them when harvests were light and marketed food surpluses disappeared. Part-time specialization combined with subsistence agriculture would have been one means by which the producers of utilitarian goods coped with periodic shortages of marketed food.

Hicks (n.d.b) also points out that marketed food supplies were stable when marketing occurred in conjunction with the tribute system; coercion could extract surpluses when market prices could not. But whenever food entered the market as a consequence of the tribute system, it was exchanged for exotic or highly crafted goods. Which is to say, specialists who entered the market system offering goods and services to the elite faced a more secure demand for their products and might ultimately demand food in return for their services while specialists who offered goods and services to rural food-producers faced the fluctuating demand as peasants cut consumption to deal with poor harvests (Wolf 1966, 16–17). Full-time specialization was less risky for those who produced elite goods; it was more problematic for the makers of utilitarian products.

Elite goods and the Aztec state

Tenochtitlan's emergence as a center of elite craft production was quite rapid, roughly paralleling the city's rise as a center of political power. And just as the political integration of central Mexico under the Aztecs reached heights not equaled since the Classic era nearly a millennium earlier, so elite craft production in central Mexico increased in both quantity and quality until it surpassed all but the finest products of Classic Teotihuacan. What accounts for the dynamic character of elite craft production in Aztec Mexico? Was it simply a reflection of the concentration of wealth and power in Tenochtitlan, an epiphenomenon of economic and political events but with little influence upon those events? Or was the growth of elite craft production structurally related to the process of political integration, constituting a necessary part of that process? Before answering these questions, it is necessary to consider why elite craft goods were in demand in central Mexico.

Almost entirely, elite craft products were articles of dress and personal adornment: richly embroidered capes and loin cloths, earrings, lip plugs, and nose plugs of obsidian, rock crystal, amber, and gold, necklaces of gold and precious stones, pendants of gem-studded gold or turquoise mosaics, arm bands, leg bands, sandals, feather and gold ornaments for the hair, adornments for the back, and special items of military attire (feathered body suits and shields). These elements of dress all served as important markers of social identity (Hunt 1977, 159; Anawalt 1980). They distinguished nobles from commoners, rulers from vassal lords, and one deity from another. They could also work transformations of status: when humans assumed the attire of gods, they became divine (Pasztory 1983, 217).

Because elite craft products marked social status, their exchange was an appropriate means of validating status and sociopolitical relationships. Changes in social identity associated with the life cycle or succession to political office were recognized and validated by gifts of precious goods (Alva

Ixtlilxochitl 1975–77 [1600–40], I, 352; Durán 1967, [1581], II, 51, 64–65). Military alliances were proposed and periodically reaffirmed by reciprocal exchanges of precious goods, an apt way of indicating the mutual acceptance of each party's political ambitions (Alva Ixtlilxochitl 1975–77 [1600–40], I, 372, 375). The mutual acceptance of hierarchial relationships was expressed in asymmetrical exchanges of precious goods (Alva Ixtlilxochitl 1975–77 [1600–40], I, 348, 357; Durán 1967 [1581], II, 69). And to signal (or provoke) hostility as a prelude to war, an enemy's status could be impugned by substituting common goods for elite craft products or women's clothing for warrior's attire in situations of conventionalized exchange (Durán 1967 [1581], II, 92).

As markers of social status and items of exchange, elite craft products also acquired importance as a type of political capital (Appel 1978; 1982, 31–33; Blanton and Feinman 1984, Hicks 1981, n.d.b). A gift of elite craft products was a highly satisfactory way of rewarding clients, attracting allies, and soliciting favors from one's superiors. Such gifts could be used in negotiating highly instrumental political transactions with precious goods offered as a reward for services rendered (Alva Ixtlilxochitl 1975–77 [1600–40], I, 334, 348, 371; II, 84). Only in these instrumental contexts were gifts of 'material worth' (i.e., tribute-producing lands) appropriate substitutes for the more 'symbolic' elite craft goods (Alva Ixtlilxochitl 1975–77 [1600–40], I, 339, 344, 354, 425; II, 36, 44, 48).

Fig 9.5 summarizes fifty-four cases of gift-giving in central Mexico prior to Aztec dominance. It demonstrates that elite craft goods were exchanged in a large number of situations, some symbolic and some transactional, all focused upon expressing and manipulating the configuration of socio-political relationships.[2]

Affirming, monitoring, and manipulating sociopolitical relationships were very common activities during the era of autonomous city-states that preceded Aztec dominance. It was an era of political instability and competition, rift with shifting coalitions and conspiracy, internal struggle and external warfare. Since elite craft goods provided the idiom for expressing and modifying these relationships, it is likely that a strong and steady desire for precious goods existed prior to Aztec dominance (Appel 1978, 1982, 31–33; Hicks 1981, 1983). If the production of elite craft goods was low relative to the later Aztec period, it was probably because of inelasticities in the supply of raw materials, not in the desire for the finished products.

Prior to Aztec dominance, it was difficult to obtain the raw materials from which elite craft goods were made. Brilliantly colored feathers, amber, turquoise and jadite, gold and other metals, ocelot skins, marine shells, and cotton for richly embroidered textiles were all products of the tropical lowlands. Their procurement was complicated by several factors. One was the distance and danger involved in moving goods from the lowlands to the highlands. Mesoamerica was without draft animals and wheeled vehicles so all overland transport was by human carrier and the costs were relatively

high (Hassig 1985, 122–26). In addition, the slow-moving caravans of merchants loaded with precious goods offered tempting targets for banditry (Durán 1967 [1581], II, 107, 155, 163, 178, 185, 357, 383, 436), which raised the cost of precious raw materials still further and lessened the appeal of mercantile enterprise (Sahagún 1950–69 [1577], Bk. 4, Ch. 12). Finally there may have been a problem in finding highland products for which there was a demand in lowland markets (Berdan 1975, 305; Hicks 1981).

However, Aztec imperial expansion increased the supply of precious raw materials. They entered Tenochtitlan in great quantity as items of tribute (Barlow 1949), supplying the attached specialists employed in the ruler's palace (Durán 1967 [1581], II, 341; Sahagún 1950–69 [1577], Bk. 8, Ch. 14; Bk. 6, Ch. 19). Imperial expansion may also have enlarged the supply of precious raw materials obtained through trade. Transport costs were reduced (Hassig 1985, 125–26), and the Aztec rulers made provincial rulers responsible for the safety of the highland merchants trading in their domains. In at least one case, the Aztecs decreed that a market, well stocked with precious goods, be established for the convenience of highland merchants (Durán 1967 [1581], II, 62). In addition, the balance of trade between the Aztec heartland and its tropical trading partners may have been improved by the threat of force: when Tehuantepec's ruler slaughtered the Valley of Mexico merchants trading in his domain to express his disgust with their 'worthless highland goods', he was severely punished by the Aztec army (Durán 1967 [1581], II, 357–62). The raw materials obtained by merchants supplied the independent specialists who produced elite craft goods for market sale (Berdan 1975, 270; Calnek 1978a, 103; Hassig 1982, 43).

Thus, the expansion of elite craft production in Tenochtitlan could be regarded, in part, as a simple consequence of Aztec imperialism. Imperial expansion increased the supply of exotic raw materials to elite craftsmen in the Valley of Mexico and made it possible for them to expand their production in order to meet the existing demand for elite craft goods. However, it should not be assumed that the structure of demand for elite craft goods remained unchanged as the Aztec state consolidated its power. Given the importance of elite goods in constructing and communicating social status, hierarchy, and alliance, we should anticipate that Aztec dominance was accompanied by some major changes in the structure of demand. These changes did occur. There was a tremendous increase in the level of gift-giving as the Aztec rulers instituted a system of centralized patronage to consolidate their power and as the entire noble stratum of Aztec society became caught up in a politically innocuous system of competitive wealth display. As much as the changes in the accessibility of precious raw materials already noted, these changes in the structure of demand account for the dynamic character of elite craft production in Aztec Mexico. First, we can examine the patronage system of the Aztec state.

In the era preceding Aztec dominance, intense political

	Food	Elite craft goods	Tribute lands	Grants of unspecified content
I. Distributions by rulers or potential rulers				
1. In ritual contexts				
a. Declarations of war.		1		
b. Ritual occasions in other domain.		2		
c. Ritual occasions in own domain.				
Number of cases: 3				
2. Expressions of status etiquette (noblesse oblige)				
a. Hospitality to a foreign ruler or his emissaries.				2
b. Demonstrations of royal pleasure.	1	1		2
c. Patron of virtue.		1		1
d. Patron of the arts.				
e. Patron of ritual.				
f. Patron of the nobility.				
g. Patron of the poor.				
h. Restitutions for own misconduct.				
Number of cases: 7				
3. In instrumental contexts				
a. To ask a favor of another ruler.		2		1
b. To negotiate or confirm military alliances with other rulers.		6		2
c. Promised rewards to allied rulers for aid to be given in war.			1	1
d. Rewards to allied rulers for aid given in war or public works.		1	2	3 / 5
e. Rewards for valor in war.		1	2	
f. Rewards for a specific service to the state.			5	3
g. Promised rewards for an explicit service desired by the ruler.		2	2	1
h. Wages for continuing service.				
i. To mollify dynastic competitors.				
Number of cases: 36				
II. Gifts by non-rulers				
1. In ritual context				
a. Ritual occasions of local rulers.		1		
b. Ritual occasions in other domains.				
c. Ritual occasions of other private citizens.				
d. Own ritual occasions.				
Number of cases: 1				
2. Expressions of status etiquette (fealty and citizenship)				
a. Hospitality to a ruler or his emissaries.		4		
b. Signal of submission.				
c. Signal of congratulation.				
d. Patron of ritual.				
Number of cases: 4				
3. In instrumental contexts				
a. To ask a favor of a ruler.		2		
b. To win pardon for misconduct.		1		
c. To prevent raiding.				
Number of cases: 3				

Fig. 9.5. Gifts and distributions prior to Aztec dominance. Because a single case can include both food and craft goods or craft goods and tribute lands, the number of grants listed by product sometimes exceeds the number of cases analyzed.

competition had generated web-like systems of alliance and patronage. These alliance networks, cutting across the boundaries of kin groups and local city-states, constituted a major barrier to the emergence of any strong, highly centralized regional polity. It was only after these systems had been shattered by the intensification of warfare (resulting in the death or exile of most of the high-ranking participants) that political integration on the regional level could occur (Brumfiel 1983, 268–73).

The Aztecs and their allies emerged from these wars in control of almost all of the Valley of Mexico. From then on, a major goal of Aztec policy was preventing the reemergence of alliance networks among the regional nobility that might challenge their power. This was accomplished by organizing a centralized system of political patronage that distributed three types of favors: the rule of hinterland city-states, tribute-producing agricultural lands, and elite craft products (for distribution of tribute lands and craft goods, see Fig. 9.6; for Aztec control over succession in hinterland city-states see Alva Ixtlilxochitl 1975–77 [1600–40], II, 89, 190–92; Anales de Cuauhtitlan 1945 [1570], 20; Paso y Troncoso 1979 [1579]; 52; Zorita 1963 [1566–70], 266). The patronage system was an effective means of restructuring the pre-Aztec system of political alliance. Vertical ties between patrons and clients were maintained while horizontal alliances were discouraged. Patronage systems are structurally suited to discouraging the growth of horizontal alliances for they are composed of dyadic ties that place clients in opposition to each other as competitors for the patron's favor (Paine 1974, 24–28; Graziano 1975, 10–12; Eckstein 1977, 88). Schneider (1977, 23) observes that 'often the intent of constructing a clientele is to defuse organized opposition'. At times, this can be more important than the actual resources extracted from clients. For the Aztecs, the resources extracted from clients were considerable (labor for public works and wars of conquest), but preventing the emergence of organized opposition to the state was probably of equal importance.

Initially, the emphasis was upon restoring the ruling offices of hinterland city-states to compliant members of the local ruling lineages and distributing tribute lands to lower-ranking nobles who distinguished themselves in battle (Alva Ixtlilxochitl 1975–77 [1600–40], I, 379–80; II, 89; Anales de Cuauhtitlan 1945 [1570], 50; Durán 1967 [1581], II, 82–83, 98, 113, 130, 151). But after the 1458 conquest of Coixtlahuaca brought a large tribute in lowland products to the Aztec ruler, elite craft items began to overshadow tribute lands as the reward most frequently distributed. For the purposes of maintaining centralized power, elite craft goods had several advantages over tribute-producing lands.

First, craft goods implied continuing dependence upon the state. The Aztec ruler Itzcoatl is said to have argued against the restoration of local rulers on the grounds that it would be better to have them dependent upon the gifts and honors that the state would bestow only when their acts and good service merited it (Alva Ixtlilxochitl 1975–77 [1600–40],

II, 88). The same argument would dictate a preference for precious goods over tribute lands in distributions by the state, if precious goods were available in sufficient quantity.

Second, because craft goods could bear symbols, they were more serviceable in communicating state ideology (Townsend 1979). The Aztecs set forth an ideology linking prestige to achievement in warfare and achievement in warfare with service to the gods (Erdheim 1973; Conrad and Demarest 1984). At first, verbal symbols were used to convey this ideology. After the Aztec victory over Coyoacan in 1428, distinguished warriors were awarded tribute lands and noble titles that endowed their achievements with cosmological significance.[3] But during the reign of Montezuma I (1440–68), achievement in warfare was marked by costume. Montezuma instituted a series of sumptuary laws limiting many items of dress to warriors of distinction (Durán 1967 [1581], II, 236–38). Of particular interest is the way in which traditional markers or ascriptive status were redefined by the state as markers of military achievement:

> . . . He who does not dare to go to war,
> Even though he be the king's son . . . will have to wear
>   the clothing of the common man . . .
> He will not wear cotton garments,
> He will not wear feathers, he will not receive flowers,
> Like the great lords . . .
> He will be held in contempt as a man of low rank
> [Durán 1964 (1581), 142].

In addition, Montezuma introduced the first large-scale sacrifices of war captives, using their immolation as the centerpiece of ceremonial pageantry that supplied the context in which precious goods were distributed and displayed (Durán 1967 [1581], II, 172–75, 192–95, 309–10). Thus the link of prestige to warfare and warfare to religious duty was completed.

The new prestige system enhanced the unity of the state. As Calnek (1978b) and Rounds (1979) have observed, it created a community of interest uniting the Aztec rulers and the traditional powerholders who were subject to them. In addition, it probably reduced competition over the inheritance of positions at the heads of noble houses (*teccalli*). These positions were relatively few in number, and much competition and alliance building in the pre-Aztec era had been due to the efforts of potential heirs to secure such positions. But the new system of prestige could admit as many qualified individuals as existed: it is said that when Montezuma declared a perpetual state of war between the Aztecs and their adversaries in Tlaxcala and Puebla, 'all were very glad, seeing that now their sons and kinsmen would have the opportunity to exert themselves and win honor and renown' (Durán 1967 [1581], II, 237–38). Individuals did not have to form competitive coalitions to capture this type of status; it did not generate the politically dangerous horizontal alliances that might have threatened Aztec hegemony.

A final advantage of elite craft goods as favors dispensed

	Food	Elite craft goods	Tribute lands	Grants of unspecified content
I. Distributions by rulers or potential rulers				
1. In ritual contexts				
a. Declarations of war.		3		
b. Ritual occasions in other domain.	1	15		
c. Ritual occasions in own domain.		21		
Number of cases: 40				
2. Expressions of status etiquette (noblesse oblige)				
a. Hospitality to a foreign ruler or his emissaries.		16		
b. Demonstrations of royal pleasure.		11		
c. Patron of virtue.	1	8		
d. Patron of the arts.		1		
e. Patron of ritual.		4		
f. Patron of the nobility.		1		
g. Patron of the poor.	5	8		
h. Restitutions for own misconduct.		2		
Number of cases: 52				
3. In instrumental contexts				
a. To ask a favor of another ruler.	1	8		
b. To negotiate or confirm military alliances with other rulers.		9		
c. Promised rewards to allied rulers for aid to be given in war.				2
d. Rewards to allied rulers for aid given in war or public works.		7	2	
e. Rewards for valor in war.		24	8	
f. Rewards for a specific service to the state.	7	17	2	3
g. Promised rewards for an explicit service desired by the ruler.				
h. Wages for continuing service.	2	7		
i. To mollify dynastic competitors.			5	
Number of cases: 92				
II. Gifts by non-rulers				
1. In ritual contexts				
a. Ritual occasions of local rulers.				
b. Ritual occasions in other domains.		1		
c. Ritual occasions of other private citizens.		1		
d. Own ritual occasions.		2		
Number of cases: 4				
2. Expressions of status etiquette (fealty and citizenship)				
a. Hospitality to a ruler or his emissaries.		5		
b. Signal of submission.		26		
c. Signal of congratulation.		3		
d. Patron of ritual.	1	1		
Number of cases: 35				
3. In instrumental contexts				
a. To ask a favor of a ruler.		1		
b. To win pardon for misconduct.		2		
c. To prevent raiding.	4	4		
Number of cases: 9				

Fig. 9.6. Gifts and distributions during the period of Aztec dominance. Because a single case can include both food and craft goods or craft goods and tribute lands, the number of grants listed by product sometimes exceeds the number of cases analyzed.

by the Aztec patronage system was the strong sensory impression they made. As props and costuming for the drama of Aztec religious ritual, elite craft goods contributed to the intensity of religious experience (Aguilera 1977, 124–40). The intensity of emotion experienced during the rituals validated the claims of the Aztec state that it played a role of cosmic urgency in preserving the world order and lent sanctity to the new prestige system instituted by the state.

The Aztec state, then, became a major consumer of elite craft goods, a major locus of heightened demand. But the state was not the only consumer. The existence of considerable demand for precious goods among private citizens is implied by the fact that at the time of Spanish conquest the Tlatelolco market was well stocked with elite goods and substantial numbers of elite craftsmen in Tenochtitlan (and perhaps a few nearby communities such as Xochimilco) produced primarily for the market and only occasionally for the state (Sahagún 1950–69 [1577], Bk. 9, Ch. 20). What was the source of this private-sector demand? It is evident that the exchange of precious goods continued to mark changes in social identity that occurred during the life cycle of high ranking individuals (Hicks n.d.b, 13–14). But precious goods had also been used to negotiate political alliances, and this function should have diminished dramatically as the Aztec patronage system took effect. If not countered by other factors, the reduction in alliance building would have lowered private sector demand for elite craft goods. Changes in the economic and social spheres must have kept this from happening.

Hicks (n.d.b) has suggested that the large-scale distribution of precious goods by the Aztec ruler and his allies caused a general inflation in elite craft goods: 'The lavishness with which the Triple Alliance rulers were able to dispense gifts must have raised the general standard of high-level gift giving throughout the region.' The need for more elite craft goods to meet this higher standard of giving could have more than made up for the reduction in the frequency of political negotiation requiring gift exchange. An added possibility is that, under Aztec dominance, a new prestige system developed centered upon the display, consumption, and distribution of large quantities of elite craft goods by private citizens.

Private feasting and competitive gift-giving were integral parts of Aztec culture by the time of Spanish conquest (Moreno 1962, 104). At the feasts and gift-giving marking life crises, people 'exalted and raised themselves; they surpassed and much exceeded themselves. There was vying and competition' (Sahagún 1950–69 [1577], Bk. 4, p. 122). Prestige was also gained by assuming certain ritual responsibilities: offering slaves for sacrifices, caring for an idol in one's home, observing a fast or sponsoring a dance in honor of a particular god (Carrasco 1961). Feasting in honor of life crises and individual sponsorship of ritual activity were both widely distributed in Mesoamerica; they were not innovations introduced by the Aztec state. But the state may have encouraged the elaboration of the private feast-giving, gift-giving, status-achieving complex by making the precious goods

distributed in these observances more readily available and by raising the valuation of achieved status relative to the status of inherited positions at the heads of noble houses.

Though private feasting and ritual sponsorship developed independent of state control, the state must have welcomed their intensification. Like the state-sponsored system honoring achievement in warfare, the prestige competition based on feasting and ritual sponsorship demobilized political opposition: it did not generate horizontal alliances so dangerous to the Aztec state. In addition, it generated a sustained demand for large quantities of elite craft goods. This insured that the precious goods distributed by the state through its patronage system would not go unappreciated. It also provided buyers for the elite craft goods produced for market sale by growing numbers of urban craftsmen.

Conclusion: utilitarian and elite goods in political development

The adaptationist approach generates certain expectations about changes in production and exchange that ought to accompany political integration. First, these changes ought to involve subsistence goods. Second, political integration should improve the efficiency, stability, and/or capacity of the economic system. In areas of high environmental diversity, political integration ought to entail an increasingly complex division of labor with an expanding volume of exchange.

In the case of the Aztecs of central Mexico, these expectations are only partially fulfilled. Specialization in the production of many subsistence goods was present. But both before and after the formation of the Aztec state, such goods were most often produced by part-time specialists living in rural communities who also engaged in subsistence agriculture. The persistence of part-time specialization suggests the existence of structural impediments to specialization that the Aztec state, despite its considerable resources, did not overcome. Hicks (n.d.b) has emphasized that the absence of a secure supply of marketed goods precludes full-time specialization. He has also pointed out that fluctuating crop yields in the Valley of Mexico worked against such stability. The persistence of part-time specialization in subsistence goods production can be seen as a response to unstable market conditions brought about by annual variation in agricultural productivity.

The volume of regional exchange did expand during the period of Aztec rule. Peasant households were able to acquire more of some non-local subsistence goods such as obsidian and salt. However, much of the expansion in regional exchange seems to have consisted of rural producers marketing food to acquire products needed for tribute assessments. This did not involve the exchange of goods between specialist producers, simply the flow of tribute wealth into the center as payment of taxes and out from the center in exchange for food. Thus, it may be more proper to regard the expanded volume of regional exchange as evidence of a reorganized system of elite extraction or finance rather than a reflection of increased economic specialization and efficiency.

The most dramatic economic change occurred in the production and exchange of prestige goods. This sector of the economy experienced rapid growth. The Aztec capital, Tenochtitlan, became a center of artistic production where highly skilled, full-time craft specialists manufactured a wide array of goods for elite consumption. The expansion of prestige goods production in the capital provides a sharp contrast to the more static production of subsistence goods in smaller towns and hamlets. The adaptationalist approach does not anticipate the dynamism of the prestige goods sector of the economy and cannot account for it. In the adaptationist approach, growth in the production and exchange of prestige goods is regarded as epiphenomenal or incidental (Tourtellot and Sabloff 1972, 132; Sanders, Parsons and Santley 1979, 400–2; Sanders 1984, 277).

Schneider (1977) finds this assessment of prestige goods unfortunate. She points out that prestige goods cannot be dismissed as non-essential because the bestowal of luxuries is capable of influencing energy flows (also cf. Spencer 1982):

> Patron–client relations, established and maintained through the exchange of gifts and favors, contribute . . . to the mobilization of energy. By virtue of the obligations created by his bestowals, the patron can often claim a portion of the surplus labor of his dependents [Schneider 1977, 23].

This is particularly true in cases when states arise out of clusters of polities already organized under local hierarchies of control. What is mobilized in these cases is not simply the energy of the client, but also the dependents of the client: the effects of gift-giving are multiplied. In such cases, what the giving of luxuries does is to order relations among nobles and, thus, to direct the flow of mobilized energy.

However, the ordering of new relations and new energy flows must often be accompanied by the undermining of old relations, old alignments and flows that resist subordination to state control and threaten its dominance. As Kurtz (1978, 170; 1981, 179) points out, undermining old relations and alignments is likely to be an important process in the course of state formation; it may even be *the* important process. Sometimes this destruction involves the physical removal of participants from the political scene: by death in battle, execution, imprisonment, or exile. But sooner or later, the confrontation between the old and new will occur on a field of symbols. This is so because power is wielded by coalitions or teams, not by individuals (Bailey 1969, 25–26), and the competition to attract and hold members to the coalition will inevitably involve efforts to define for followers where duty and/or rewards of value lie. This is why the 'management of meanings' underpins political action (Cohen and Comaroff 1976, 87), and why 'control over communication' should be regarded as a political resource (Paine 1976, 80)

Highly crafted prestige goods can be encoded with symbolic messages about social status, hierarchy, and alliance

Because they convey these messages in an emotionally striking way, their argument is compelling. It is not surprising, then, that major political transformations are often accompanied by an elaboration of elite craft production. The production of art is part of the political process.

Acknowledgements

This paper was first presented at the XIth International Congress of Anthropological and Ethnological Sciences, Vancouver (1982), at a symposium organized by Tim Earle.

I am grateful to Ursula Dycherhoff, Susan Kus and Larry Steinhauer for discussing Aztec craft production with me in ways that contributed immensely to this chapter.

Notes

1. Utilitarian products are those considered necessary for the sustenance of commoner households. Gibson (1964, 355–56) provides a list of what such products were in the mid sixteenth century. Guided by his list, I have classified the specialists appearing in the *Matrícula de Huexotzinco* in the following way:
   Specialists in utilitarian products: mat makers, sandal makers, potters, basket makers, hunters, pine resin extractors, lime burners, pine torch cutters, and fishermen. Also included in the *Matrícula* but not shown in Fig. 9.2 are spinners (21; most of the spinning and weaving was done by women and would not appear in the census), dyers (11); makers of *tochomitl* (4; literally "rabbit hair" but more likely 'colored thread' cf. Sahagún 1950–69 [1577] Bk. 10, p. 77, n. 10), straw workers (2), string makers (2), net maker (1), wild honey gatherer (1).
   Construction specialists: wood workers and stone cutters. These were most commonly employed in the construction of housing for the elite (cf. Sahagún 1950–69 [1577], Bk. 10, Ch. 8). Specialists were probably not needed for the construction of commoners' houses (Zorita 1963 [1566–70] 163; Katz 1966, 47).
   Elite craft specialists: painters/scribes, feather workers, tobacco workers, flower workers. Also included in the *Matrícula* but not shown in Fig. 9.2 are metal workers (2) and paper maker (1).
   Service specialists: doctors. Also included in the *Matrícula* but not shown in Fig. 9.2 are singers for church services (189), boundary guards (20), store owners (7), catechists (6), unknown religious specialists (6).
   Employed in Spanish enterprises: field hands (44), teamsters (6), bread makers (4), tailors (3), shoe maker (1), butcher (1), wheelwright (1).

2. The cases of gift-giving documented in Alva Ixtlilxochitl (1975–77 [1600–40] and Durán (1967 [1581], II) suggest that gifts were given for three reasons in Late Postclassic Mexico: to validate ritual acts, to conform to status etiquette, and to induce others to comply with one's wishes. These functions can be sorted out by differences in the scheduling of gift-giving and the expectations of reciprocity that accompanied it. In the gift-giving that validated ritual acts, giving occurred automatically in stereotyped situations and without expectations of immediate reward. Gift-giving to conform to status etiquette also occurred without expectations of immediate reward, but giving was initiated by the giver. Instrumental gift-giving was initiated by the giver, and it carried clear expectations of reciprocity, to the extent that 'gifts' were sometimes conditional upon the completion of a specified act. Of course, these distinctions tended to blur in practice; large distributions on ritual occasions could

solidify alliances and win popular support; generous rewards to valiant soldiers could raise the prestige of the ruler; etc.

Cases of gift-giving to validate ritual acts prior to the period of Aztec dominance are Alva Ixtlilxochitl 1975–77 [1600–40], I, 352 and Durán 1967 [1581], II, 57, 64–65, 79. Cases of gift-giving to conform to status etiquette prior to the period of Aztec dominance are Alva Ixtlilxochitl 1975–77 [1600–40], I, 308, 312, 326, 365, 372, 441, 541, II, 50; Durán 1967 [1581], II, 65, 79. Cases of instrumental gift-giving prior to the period of Aztec dominance are Alva Ixtlilxochitl 1975–77 [1600–40], I, 312, 334, 336, 339, 341, 344, 345, 348, 354, 355, 357, 363, 365, 366, 368, 370, 371, 375, 405, 426, 438, 441, 536, 537, 538, 539; II, 22, 36, 44, 48, 50, 51–52, 56, 67, 71, 75, 76, 84; Durán 1967 [1581], II, 51, 69, 76–77.

Cases of gift-giving to validate ritual acts during the period of Aztec dominance are Alva Ixtlilxochitl 1975–77 [1600–40], II, 104; Durán 1967 [1581], II, 92, 125, 126, 155, 156, 172, 174–75, 248, 250, 257, 276–77, 279, 289, 290, 293, 295–97, 297–98, 302, 308–10, 311, 316, 318, 325, 327, 345, 346, 392–94, 414, 415, 416, 436, 437, 442, 443, 458, 465, 474, 476, 483. Cases of gift-giving to conform to status etiquette during the period of Aztec dominance are Alva Ixtlilxochitl 1975–77 [1600–40], I, 445, 544, 558, II, 102, 121, 129, 130, 131, 150–51, 162, 164, 172, 173, 205, 209, 212–14, 215, 217, 218, 219; Durán 1967 [1581], II, 114, 122, 129, 151, 158–59, 160, 161, 168, 170, 174, 181–82, 188, 192, 201, 203, 229, 231, 242, 253–55, 276, 285, 292, 310, 319, 321, 328, 330, 341, 346, 348, 353, 355, 361, 366, 381, 385–86, 392, 408, 409, 416, 420, 421, 422, 423, 431, 456, 457, 507, 510, 519, 521, 533–34, 535, 536, 540. Cases of instrumental gift-giving during the period of Aztec dominance are Alva Ixtlilxochitl 1975–77 [1600–40], I, 380, 449, 549, 562; II, 103, 105, 118, 134, 142, 144, 145, 149, 150, 155, 157–58, 159, 162, 166, 172, 201, 203, 209, 211, 216; Durán 1967 [1581], II, 82–83, 98, 106, 113, 121, 130, 149, 151, 165, 168, 169, 177, 178, 179–80, 195, 197, 203, 217, 224, 226, 227–28, 239, 246, 251, 264, 267, 273–74, 310, 311, 328, 330, 339, 346, 347, 349, 353, 355, 359, 361, 362, 368, 381, 384, 385, 386, 388–89, 408, 412, 416, 425, 427, 431, 433, 435, 436, 442–43, 462, 466, 483, 490, 495, 507, 511.

3. Among the titles distributed were:

Acolnahuacatl: 'He of the Twisted Water'. According to Garibay (1969, 320), this is a metaphoric name for Mictlantecuhtli, the god of the dead. 'Twisted Water' alludes to the waters of Mictlan, the underworld, twisted in seven streams. Acolnahuac was also a location within Tenochtitlan.

Cuauhquiahuacatl: 'He of the Eagle Gate.' The Eagle Gate was one of the entrances to the central civic–ceremonial precinct of Tenochtitlan (Marquina 1960, 36). Eagles were symbolic of the sun, of its life giving force, of the warm fertile spring and summer seasons, of young manhood and valiant warriors (Hunt 1977, 57–74). The Eagle Gate contained a store of weapons that could be used in defense of the heart of the city. It was also a place where captives were sacrificed on the feast day of Macuiltotec (Sahagún 1950–69, [1577], Bk. 2, p. 178).

Huitznahuacatl: 'He of the South.' The south was symbolic of the sun, its life giving force, of the warm fertile spring and summer seasons, of young manhood, of warriors, of the hummingbird, and of Huitzilopochtli, 'Hummingbird of the Left,' the patron deity of Tenochtitlan (Hunt 1977, 57–74). Huitznahuac was also a temple in the central civic–cermonial precinct of Tenochtitlan where many war captives were sacrificed during the month of Panquetzaliztli (Sahagún 1950–69 [1577], Bk. 2, p. 169).

Tezcacoacatl: 'He of the Place of the Snake Mirror'. The place of the Snake Mirror was one of the entrances to the central civic–ceremonial precinct of Tenochtitlan (Marquina 1960, 36). It contained a store of weapons for the defense of the heart of the city. War captives were sometimes sacrificed there (Sahagún 1950–69 [1577], Bk. 2, 179).

Tlillancalqui: 'He of the House of Darkness.' The House of Darkness was the bowels of the earth, home of Coatlicue, a monstrous earth goddess. In Aztec sculpture she was depicted as a huge headless/snake-headed woman with raptorial claws on her hands and feet, wearing a skirt of braided snakes and a necklace of severed human hands and sacrifical hearts. Tlillancalco was also the temple dedicated to Coatlicue in the central civic–ceremonial precinct of Tenochtitlan. It held the god images of the patron deities of defeated towns and kingdoms seized by the Aztecs in warfare. In this temple, Coatlicue was fed small breads in the shape of human hands, feet, and faces daily, and she was given a sacrifical war captive once a week (Durán 1971 [1570], 211–18).

Further study may reveal the full range of mythical, cosmological, and spatial implications in all of the honorary titles borne by distinguished warriors.

Chapter 10

Forms of finance and forms of production: the evolution of specialized livestock production in the ancient Near East

Kathleen F. Galvin

Introduction

This chapter focuses on the relationship between the development of specialization in livestock production and changes in the forms of finance in early state society. It examines broad changes in livestock production in the Near East from the first appearance of complex politico-economic organization, through the emergence and elaboration of the first states. The time span roughly covers the period from approximately 6000 BC through 1000 BC. The goal is to understand how livestock were utilized by early state systems in meeting the needs of the food producing and non-food producing segments of the population, the role of food production in state economic development and maintenance, and the conditions under which specialization in livestock production came about. Generalizations concerning the nature of livestock production are based on analysis of remains of domestic fauna recovered from excavations at urban centers.

A widely recognized adaptationist or mutual-benefit model of the rise of livestock specialization postulates an early separation and specialization of herding and farming in the arid riverine zone of the ancient Near East with exchange between the two sectors mediated by centralized political-economic organization (Service 1975; Wright 1978, 63; Lees and Bates 1974). A survey of faunal data from sites with deposits dating to the period of development of state society in Mesopotamia and the Middle Euphrates region of Syria,

however, suggests the inadequacy of this model. Rather than separation and specialization along ecological parameters, the development of livestock production was intimately linked to the development of capital- and labor-intensive irrigation agriculture on the Mesopotamian alluvium. Clear indications of specialization in livestock production are lacking until fairly late in the course of development.

An alternative approach to studying economic development is from the view point of different systems of state finance. Variations in the form of state finance are tied to different relations of production and distribution and affect the nature and degree of specialization in an economic system. For example, a system of finance associated with a form of production livestock that might seem to involve excessive cost in herd capital and feed for subsistence needs, may be quite fitting in one in which income is derived in part from production for exchange.

In this chapter I will argue that the development of specialized livestock production is tied to a change in the form of state finance from a system based on payment in staples to one based on wealth, where currency comes to replace actual goods in exchange (D'Altroy and Earle 1985) and to the economic processes which have been referred to as the 'second products revolution' (Sherratt 1981). According to this alternative model, the development of livestock production can be viewed in three phases. The first phase involves the initial domestication of animals, raised primarily for meat, their integration into a subsistence-oriented household economy and the emergence of surplus livestock production. The second phase results in the development of new breeds as well as the domestication of new species whose 'secondary products' (milk, wool, hide, traction and transport) became increasingly important in meeting the demands of early state economic systems in which staples were mobilized to provision the dependent laboring population who were themselves primarily involved in food production and major state building projects. Only later, during a third phase in the development of state economic organization do these secondary livestock products begin to reflect orientation to a market economy and demand stimulated by large-scale, long-distance exchange. Only then does specialized mobile livestock production come about.

The three phases of development are outlined as follows: (1) Mixed generalized herding and farming, the prelude; (2) Livestock on state-administered estates, first steps to specialization and (3) Livestock as a commercial enterprise, specialization in production for market exchange.

In order to document these phases in the development of livestock production, data from a number of urban centers have been examined. If some form of economic symbiosis existed between pastoralists and agriculturalists, mediated by a redistributing elite, then evidence for this exchange can be expected at urban centers. For later, historic times, government accounting documents provide an excellent source of information about state mobilization and distribution. However, this form of information is lacking for earlier times and a question exists about how representative government accounts actually are. The best available source of information concerning the organization of livestock production is the durable remains of domestic animals recovered from urban centers.

The critical link between the biological capabilities and ecological requirements of different species and the organization of a livestock-breeding economy lies in the management practices which set the parameters for survival in the herd population. Culling practices directly shape the configuration of age/sex and species mix in herds. The decision to cull reflects both the costs of land, labor and herd capital as well as the potential for income to be gained by removal. Culling practices thus reflect the emphasis in an economic system on surplus production, specialization, and exchange. In this chapter information concerning the culling practices associated with different degrees of specialization in livestock production will be used to evaluate the evidence for specialized nomadic pastoralism in the arid zone of the ancient Near East.

Livestock specialization: definition and archaeological measurement

Livestock specialization refers to the differentiation and coordination of kinds of labor and other factors in production associated with herding which forms a restricted occupational group. It reflects organizational changes bringing about the segmentation of general productive activities and the coordination of activities between these segments. The degree of specialization is indicated by the extent to which the production of certain goods is limited to a subset of the working population. The greater the degree of specialization in livestock production, the lesser the degree of involvement in production of other staple items, which are then acquired through exchange. Individuals involved in livestock production convert animal resources into food energy and other materials. In systems exhibiting a low degree of specialization in production they will be able to utilize directly what they produce, and will most probably produce a wide range of goods to meet a wide variety of needs. The ability to maximize productivity may not be an important consideration in herd management. In a highly specialized form of livestock production, on the other hand, the individual will produce a much narrower range of herd products, intending to exchange these for a wide range of subsistence products. The more herding can be considered an occupational specialization, the more likely herd management practices will reflect production for exchange, rather than subsistence. The configuration of species and age/sex profiles in faunal assemblages is expected to reflect the commitment to specialized production.[1]

The following statements reflect some of the important criteria for defining degree of specialization in livestock management practices and indicate some of the expectations for each of the developmental stages considered in this paper. In a faunal assemblage reflecting a relatively unspecialized system, well-adapted, low-cost species producing a wide variety of products will predominate. In addition, the species mix and age/sex profile of the assemblage will indicate that somewhat less effort has been made to optimize feed and labor costs and maximize productivity. In the first phase of development, age and sex profiles of herds will more closely approximate a pattern expected under natural conditions, reflecting the vagaries of environmental fluctuation as well as human demand. The expectation would be a very low degree of specialization since dairy, wool and traction capabilities of domestic species were initially weakly developed. Age category percentages would indicate that the most important product is meat with animals functioning as part of a mixed household economy.

Later, during phase 2, herd composition and age/sex profiles will indicate an elaboration in management goals reflecting increasing demand for secondary products, such as wool/hair, dairy and traction and perhaps the distinction of prime and low-grade meat. The demand for these products reflects the complementary association of herding with agriculture in the riverine zone and the need of the state to provide for the subsistence needs of the laboring population. Despite the fact that in the second stage, state economic organization becomes firmly established, the surplus-oriented form of livestock production will continue to be marked by a very generalized, multipurpose character. Since a major point of the adaptationist's argument for herding specialization focuses on the economic symbiosis of the desert/steppe and riverine ecozones, evaluation of the drought adaptability of different species is an important consideration in evaluating faunal assemblages. Under these conditions species adapted to the desert/steppe will predominate in faunal assemblages.

By contrast, in a more specialized system, such as I have proposed for phase 3, there will be a greater tendency to tailor species mix and age/sex composition to maximizing a more limited range of products. Age/sex profiles will show greater stability over time indicating greater control over natural causes of mortality and reflecting formally defined, explicit culling practices. For example, with either a prime meat or dairy specialization, cattle will be expected rather than sheep and goats, despite cattle's lower overall adaptability to the arid Near East. This is true because of the lower labor cost per head and longer lactation period in cattle and added advantage of traction/transport (see Galvin 1981 for a detailed discussion of methods).

The evolution of livestock production in the ancient Near East phase I — mixed generalized herding and farming: the prelude

In the first phase of livestock production, the initial stages of plant and animal domestication and sedentary mixed herding and farming appear in a broad, east–west arc of piedmont and well-watered upland steppe to the north of the Mesopotamian alluvium during the seventh and sixth millennia BC (Braidwood and Howe 1960; Hole, Flannery and Neeley 1969; Kenyon 1960 and 1964; Perkins 1969). Early herding and rainfall agriculture combined with the hunting and gathering of a wide variety of wild species to form a mixed economy which over time became increasingly sedentary and dependent on domesticants. Subsistence-oriented herding and farming eventually supplanted hunting and gathering almost entirely (Hole, Flannery and Neeley 1969). As this first phase of domestication became complete, livestock production provided a relatively low-cost source of protein and materials utilizing the well-watered piedmont or upland steppe for grazing. Thus, in the better-watered areas of Anatolia, the Zagros Mountains or northern Syria, an extensive form of herding is documented. Yet there is no archaeological evidence that these early herders formed separate, economically specialized sociopolitical units (Braidwood and Howe 1960; Wright n.d.).

In general, the bovids (cattle [*Bos taurus*], sheep [*Ovis aries*] and goats [*Capra hircus*]) were the most common domesticants represented in faunal assemblages from sites associated with early village farming, though pig (*Sus scorfa*) was a staple in some areas by 6500 BC. The caprines (goats and sheep) dominated in most areas, except in Anatolia, where cattle tended to be most numerous (Braidwood and Howe 1960; Hole, Flannery and Neely 1969; Mellaart 1965). A high frequency of deaths before maturity suggests that the slaughter of young for meat of good quality was an overriding concern (Oates and Oates 1976a, 85; Reed 1969; Flannery 1969, 207–18).

Important changes become apparent in the time span between 6000 BC and 5000 BC. By 5500 BC sites associated with the Samarran culture, extending in a band eastward from the Middle Euphrates region to the foothills of the Zagros mountains and from Mosul south to Baghdad, show important changes in organization. See Fig. 10.1 for site locations.

Many Samarran sites (for example Tell Malaf) are located in the heartland of mixed dry farming and extensive herding in north Syria and Iraq, yet others, in some cases large villages or small towns (Choga Mami), are found in areas where dry farming is marginal at best, or impossible (Oates and Oates 1976a, 104). In contrast to earlier Neolithic sites, Samarran sites are characterized by clear differences in architecture, burial mode and distribution of luxury goods suggesting chiefdom level organization (Redman 1978, 197; Oates and Oates 1976a, 105; Kirkbride 1974; Mellaart 1965). The broad regional distribution of architectural and ceramic stylistic elements, as well as importation of exotic raw materials also suggest widespread participation in symbolic and material exchanges (see Watson and LeBlanc 1973 for an interpretation of Halafian decorated ceramics as an indicator of chiefdomlike interaction spheres).

It is important to note that the expansion of farming and herding economies from the zone where success in both involved relatively low risk and little investment capital, into areas involving considerably more risk, long-range planning and capital investment corresponds to the time of the appearance of complex sociopolitical organization. In such a context, livestock production appears in conjunction with increasingly intensive irrigation agriculture, not as a separate specialization.

Excavation at Choga Mami attests to the presence of irrigation agriculture and herding of fully domestic sheep, goats, cattle and pigs by 5500 BC (Oates and Oates 1976a, 104). Because of the low biological capacity of sheep and goats to make use of the very arid steppe and desert found in the Mesopotamian lowlands, these areas were utilized only on a seasonal basis. But if sheep and goats require shelter and feed in the riverine ecozone for part of the year, cattle and pigs are limited to the better watered microenvironments almost entirely. The introduction of the domestic pig to the Mesopotamian plain sometime between 6000 and 5000 BC clearly indicates a focus of livestock production on the riverine zone. The same is true of cattle, whose most important utility may have been traction/transport (see Hole, Flannery and Neeley 1969, 356 for discussion of developments in Khuzistan). In terms of the archaeological evidence for sites in the desert/steppe at this time, there is no evidence of occupation by nomadic herders (see Wright n.d. for discussion of the situation in the Deh Luran area).

In summary, according to the present interpretation, the shift from mixed, dry farming and extensive herding to intensive use of riverine zones of the Mesopotamian alluvium for

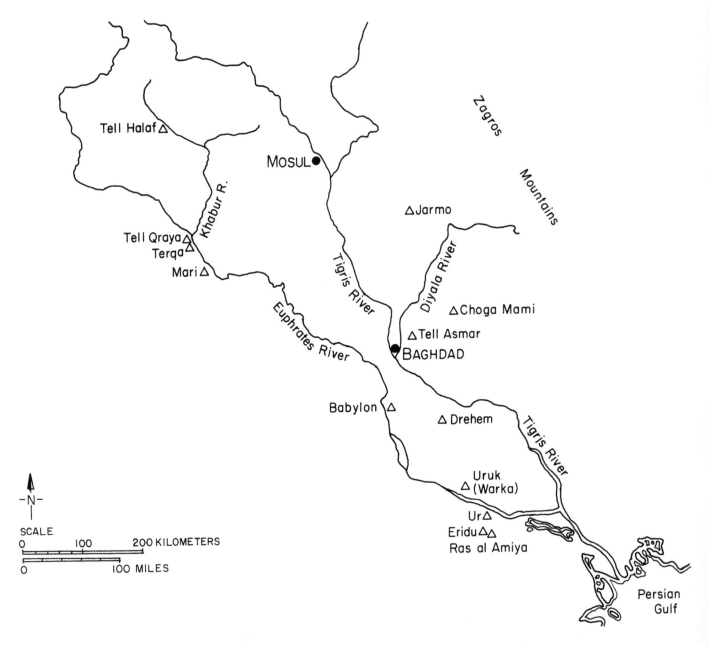

Fig. 10.1. Mesopotamia: major sites mentioned in the text

both livestock and crop production corresponded to a shift from areas where rainfall agriculture and extensive herding were possible to the arid lowlands which required the development of riverine zone resources, from agriculture requiring low to high capital investment, and from egalitarian to ranked and eventually stratified political and economic organization. The shift in plant utilization involved the development and exploitation of high yield, salt and drought adapted varieties of grain and oil/textile producing species which generally grow under conditions of irrigation (Helbaek 1964).

Phase II – livestock on state-administered estates

A second phase of development can be discerned beginning about 5000 BC and continuing through to about 1500 BC.

By 5000 BC, the settlement of the Mesopotamian alluvium was in full swing. And, by 3000 BC, large numbers of substantial villages and small urban centers dotted the plains of southern Mesopotamia, the Middle Euphrates Region and Susiana (Adams and Nissen 1972; Adams 1965; Simpson 1983). This phase is characterized by the development of state-run agricultural and crafts production primarily oriented towards local economic and political development, that is, to meet demands of the population within small city-state clusters and to acquire the raw materials and items for elite consumption through limited long-distance exchanges.

Sites of the Uruk period (ca. 3500–3100 BC) indicate building programs of a scale requiring recruitment and coordination of large labor forces as well as acquisition of large amounts of materials. The Anu Zigguart at Warka, for example, is estimated to have consumed 7500 man years of labor (Mallowan 1965). The thousands of crude bevel-rimmed bowls that dot major sites in southern Mesopotamia and the Middle Euphrates region may have been used to provide workers with rations (Johnson 1973). This suggests that the state was financing major building projects by providing employees directly with staples.

Collections of faunal remains from urban centers dating to this period are rare and published analyses even rarer. Flannery and Wright (1966, 61–63) report that at Ubaid period Eridu and Ras al Amiya (5000 through 4000 BC) sheep outnumber goats, while cattle far outnumber sheep. Not much before 4000 BC, breeds of sheep known to have good wool-bearing and milking characteristics make their appearance in Mesopotamia. If the transferral of livestock production to the Mesopotamian lowlands had involved a separation and specialization of herding and farming with some form of nomadic pastoralism developing in the steppe/desert, then if anything, a high frequency of goats or goats and sheep would be expected, not cattle. The high frequency of cattle tends to support the view that herding continued to complement farming in riverine microenvironments, and that developing the various utilities of cattle was a major consideration in live-stock management.

At the Middle Euphrates site of Tell Qraya, Uruk Period (3500–3100 BC) faunal remains from deposits of rooms and middens indicate a slightly different picture. In contrast to the far south, the steppe in this area is somewhat more amenable to seasonal grazing (see Simpson 1983 for discussion of the site and faunal analysis). Of a sample of bone (total minimal number of individuals = 48), sheep (*Ovis aries*) (43%) domi-nated over goat (*Capra hircus*) (37%), while cattle (*Bos taurus*) comprised only 10%. The species percentages at Qraya indicate much greater orientation to arid land herding, but not enough to suggest full-time nomadic pastoralism.

Further analysis of the Qraya assemblage provides additional evidence against the argument for desert/riverine economic symbiosis. Where breeds can be identified and age category percentages calculated, what emerges is an impression of a generalized, multipurpose form of herding. Age category percentages for sheep (Infant = 20%; Juvenile = 20% and Adult = 60%) and goat (Infant = 12%, Juvenile = 41% and Adult = 47%) suggest the following: 1) high percentage in the adult category indicates animals kept beyond the age appropri-ate to maximize harvesting prime meat; 2) high percentage of adult sheep can indicate production of wool and dairy produce, but breed identification provides negative evidence for this since the breed most commonly found is the rugged screw-horn, hair-type thought to have been lacking potential for both dairy and wool (Hilzheimer 1941). The high percentage of adult goats probably indicates dairy. 3) high frequency of juvenile goats and the combined percentages of infant and juvenile sheep indicate slaughter for prime meat. 4) the low frequency of cattle (mostly adult) may indicate limited use for meat or, more likely, use for dairy and traction/transport.

Over all, the assemblage reflects a system of herd management oriented to generalized, low-cost, well-adapted species producing a number of different products. There is no indication in culling pattern to suggest product specialization or concerted efforts to maximize productivity (Galvin 1980 manuscript). The species mix suggests mixed subsistence herding focusing on the riverine zone with seasonal use of the steppe/desert for grazing. The form of livestock production here in Syria appears to have been much less intensive than at Eridu at the same time, but similarly oriented to riverine resources.

By Jemdet Nasr times (3100–2900 BC) settlement pattern on the Mesopotamian plain shifted from scattered villages on water courses and small urban centers to large urban conglomerates, such as Warka. This period has been described as a time of rural abandonment, growing conflict and fortification of the main centers, but also as the time of growing economic specialization and mass production. Specialization within the state sector appears to have focused on management of food production, public works, production of elite goods and military service (Redman 1978). Somewhat like a subsistence-oriented household economy drawn large, the state economy utilized the surpluses of farming and herd-ing primarily to meet the needs of a growing administrative, crafts and manual laboring population. And, as before, the scale of state-economic activity was rather limited. Herd products, especially wool, were important in domestic textile production; while cattle provided the traction and transport functions related to expanding hydraulic agricultural opera-tions and urban development.

From the Early Dynastic I Phase (2900–2700 BC) through the Third Dynasty of Ur (ca. 2000 BC), and into the reigns of a number of regional confederations dating from about 2000 BC to the middle of the 1700s BC, government-accounting records indicate heavy state involvement in live-stock production. Representational art and faunal remains indicate that genetic changes reflecting product specialization in bovids (sheep, goats and cattle) had taken place by at least 3000 BC. From that time to about 2000 BC, the economic system made increasingly greater use of specialized breeds. During this time a number of experiments were made with domestication of other important transport animals, the equids: onager (*Equus hemionus*), donkey (*Equus asinus*) and horse (*Equus caballus*); and the camelids (*Camelus dromidarius* and *C. bactrius*).

Hilzheimer (1941), basing his observations on represen-tational art, notes in his monograph on Tell Asmar that, by about 3000 BC three breeds of sheep are identifiable, by 2000 BC, there are five. These include: a screw-horned breed (producing hair, milk and meat), a screw-horned type produc-ing wool, a zackelschaf or horizontally-turned screw-horned type known for wool, a spiral or ammon-horned type produc-ing wool as well as one with the unique fat-tail, known for its ability to produce oil. Yet, in his analysis of the faunal assem-blage from Tell Asmar (Early Dynastic to Gutian deposits roughly from 2900 to 2200 BC) counter to the impression created by analysis of representational art, Hilzheimer (1941, 33–34) found that neither the wool breed nor fat-tail breed of sheep were represented in faunal remains. The only sheep identified to the species level were of the hair breed mentioned above at Tell Qraya with limited wool and dairy characteristics.

The faunal remains from Tell Asmar may thus suggest that by 2500 BC, new improved breeds had been developed, but were as yet not in wide use. Somewhat like the world's fairs or technology shows in modern times, representational art of the third millennium BC may have reflected more the wished-for future rather than present reality of livestock production.

The faunal remains from Tell Asmar suggest management practices aimed at meeting local subsistence needs. Bone was collected during the 1932–33 excavations under the direction of Dr. Henri Frankfort both from public and private architecture. Considering all deposits, there is a large number of different species and wide variety of animal types represented. The species mix makes it quite evident that livestock production was closely integrated into the riverine farming economy. High percentages of cattle (19%) and pig (26%) reflect increased energy expenditure in terms of feed and environmental protection, that would be expected to accompany intensification, but certainly do not reflect development of specialized mobile steppe/desert herding. The high frequency of wild animals of the steppe/desert — onager (*Equus hemionus*) at 17% and gazelle (*Gazella subglotterosa*) at 9% indicate that that ecozone is still exploited primarily for hunting.

At sites on the Mesopotamian plain, some indications of a 'second products revolution' can be seen by about 2500 BC. Cattle, like sheep, show task or product specialization. Cattle are represented by three different species. The *Bos taurus* is a domestic short-horned dairy breed, *Bos indicus*, zebu cattle are present as is *Bos bubalus*, the water buffalo. These three were probably important for traction as well as meat, dairy products and hides (Epstein 1971). Goats are represented by a corkscrew-horned type producing long fine hair and probably meat and dairy products as well. When these third millennium BC breeds are compared with modern 'improved' stock they show a very low degree of specialization. But compared to what is known of breed development during the fourth millennium or earlier, these animals show a great refinement in certain products and task specialization (see Hirsch 1933).

From Early Dynastic Phase I (ca. 2900 BC) until well into the second millennium BC (ca. 1700 BC), livestock production functioned as an important component in a large-scale system of staple finance. At Ur, during the Early Dynastic Phase, texts note the parcelling out of small allotments of sheep and goats in payment for services to the state (Wright 1969). By the end of the millennium (2100 BC), some elaboration of state institutions associated with livestock production can be seen in the emergence of special livestock collection points, fattening establishments, and elaborate

codes concerning the rights and responsibilities of livestock producers. Shepherd contractors served as functionaries in state bureaucracies managing contracts with 'undershepherds,' who were directly responsible for maintaining herds of sheep and goats (Finkelstein 1968; Postgate and Payne 1975) and cattle (Gelb 1967, 64–69). According to the code of Hammurapi, which appears during the early part of the second millennium BC and probably reflects legal practices from somewhat earlier times, herding specialists were paid or fined in herd products. By the end of this phase, there are special urban centers which collected, held, and disbursed livestock.

Such a place was the site of Drehem where, according to ledger entries, an estimated 28,000 cattle and 350,000 sheep were recorded in a single year. Both the source and the destination of herds, giving the species, age and sex characteristics of animals, were recorded. Some animals came as voluntary donations from vassals and cities in confederation at that time. Others were forced levies, tax payments or booty from wars (Oates and Oates 1976b, 109–35; Buccellati 1966). While there were important changes in the degree of centralized state control during the third and early second millennium BC, livestock production continued to emphasize provisioning workers attached to state-run economic institutions.

As in the case of sites dating to earlier times, faunal data for the third and second millennium BC are far from abundant. At the site of Terqa in the Middle Euphrates region, faunal remains analyzed by the author were excavated from deposits covering the time period from about 2700 BC to approximately 1000 BC, with a gap in the data from about 1500 BC to 1200 BC (thought to be a period when the site was considerably reduced in size). These provide some evidence for the form of livestock production at that time.

The sample from deposits dating between 2000 and 1500 BC produced an MNI (Minimum Number of Individuals) of 354 animals of which 230 pertain to the Khanean Period (1750 to 1500 BC) occupation in what was then the center of town. Analysis of the Khanean faunal assemblage indicates sheep (37%) and goats (40%) were about equal, with cattle represented only by 11% and pig at a scant .003% (see Fig. 10.2). Horn cores of sheep indicate that the Ammon-horn wool breed was present, but much less common than the screw-horn, fat-tail breeds, and that the breed of goat present was the fine-hair, scimitar-horned variety common in the area today. Both breeds of sheep and goat are well adapted to the riverine zone and make seasonal use of desert/steppe areas. They are fairly low cost in feed and labor and productive of a variety of foods and materials. As a measure of specialization the Gini Coefficient was used to analyze the data. Sometimes also called the coefficient of concentration or coefficient of evenness of distribution, the Gini Coefficient has been widely used to measure phenomena of distribution in economic, ecological and geographical research (Wright 1937). In faunal analysis based on age category data, the Gini Coefficient is used to measure the relative distribution of a given population (in this case a species) among several categories. The index measures the deviation from a theoretical distribution in which all categories are of equal size. The computation of this coefficient is based on the sum of cumulated proportions arranged by size. The formula is as follows when categories are expressed as percentages:

$$G = \frac{2((\Sigma\,Cj) - 1)}{n - 1}$$

where for a population with n classes or categories, C = the sum of the cumulated proportions summed over all n categories. For a perfectly even distribution, the measure assumes the value of 1.0. As concentration of the population in only one category occurs, the coefficient decreases, ultimately approaching zero if the total population is concentrated in only a single category (Wright 1937, 183 and Heyderbrand 1973, 267–70). In terms of evaluating the coefficients, values of up to .70 or .80 indicate a slightly uneven distribution, while values of .50 or .40 indicate much greater concentration in one category.

The relationship between categories and the degree of differentiation within a population is expressed graphically by a Lorenz curve (Wallis and Roberts 1956, 257–58; Wright 1937, 181; Heyderbrand 1973, 267–70). In reading the graphs, the closer the index or coefficient is to one, the more closely the line of the plotted data will approach the diagonal.

Analysis of Gini Coefficients

Figs. 10.2 to 10.5 present the Minimal Numbers of Individuals, age breakdowns and Lorenz curves for the faunal analysis. Fig. 10.2 presents the full MNI for both Terqa and Qreya; Fig. 10.3 gives age breakdowns for the three dominant species as well as the indistinguishable *Ovis/Capra* bone; Figs. 10.4–10.6 are the Lorenz curves for the three dominant species for the Middle Phase Khanean deposits only. Gini Coefficients of .64 and .70 for Early and Middle Khanean Phase sheep indicate a rather low degree of specialization by

age category, and herd population parameters (Fig. 10.4) remained fairly stable from phase to phase. This may indicate that management practices were sufficient to offset environmental fluctuations. The high percentage of adult deaths for sheep ($\bar{x} = 46.7\%$) suggests animals kept for wool and perhaps dairy, while a mean of 39.3% juvenile deaths suggests some use for prime meat (Fig. 10.3).

Goats follow a pattern similar to sheep. With Gini Coefficients of .69 and .80 for both phases, they indicate even less specialization by age category (Fig. 10.5). Yet in contrast to sheep, goats show a greater fluctuation in age category percentages between Early and Middle Phases. The high percentage of juvenile deaths ($\bar{x} = 44\%$) indicates that a large percentage of goats were used for meat (Fig. 10.3). One interpretation

	Ovis aries (Sheep)		Capra hircus (Goat)		Bos taurus (Cattle)	
Adult	48.9	44.7	36.8	37.5	21.4	37.5
Juvenile	38.2	40.4	46.9	41.1	57.2	50.0
Infant	12.8	14.9	16.3	21.4	21.4	12.5
	Early Phase	Middle Phase	Early Phase	Middle Phase	Early Phase	Middle Phase

Fig. 10.3. Age breakdown by Minimal Number of Individuals, percentages by age category and phase

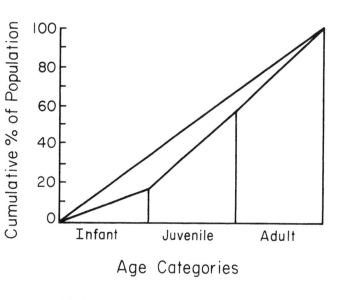

Ovis aries

Gini Coefficient = .70

Fig. 10.4. Distribution of sheep population by age category. Terqa: Khanean Middle Phase

Cultural Period	Excavation Area	Species (%)										Total M.N.I.
		Sheep	Goat	Cattle	Donkey	Camel	Deer	Gazelle	Pig	Domestic Dog	Fowl P = Present	
Medieval Islamic	Terqa ARE	33	25	17	8	8	–	–	8	–	P	12
Aramean 1st Mil. B.C.	Terqa ARE	33	17	17	17	17	–	–	–	–	P	6
Khanean 2nd Mil. B.C.	Terqa ARC & ARE	37	40	11	9	–	2	1	3	P	P	292
Late 4th Mil. B.C.	Qraya SG 2&4	43	37	11	2	–	7	–	–	P	P	46
Total M.N.I.		155	158	40	29	2	9	3	2			356

Fig. 10.2. Minimal Numbers of Individuals, percentages by period

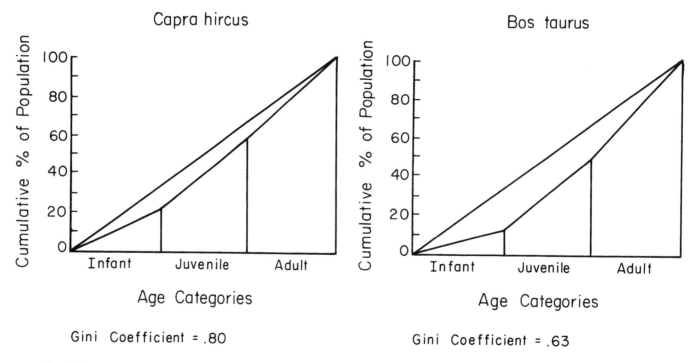

Fig. 10.5. Distribution of goat population by age category. Terqa: Khanean Middle Phase

Fig. 10.6. Distribution of cattle population by age category. Terqa: Khanean Middle Phase

of the patterning seen in goats is that there was less investment in the maintenance of goats with the effect that natural patterns of mortality were more apparent. Reports from recent drought years in Syria (1958–60) indicate goats function somewhat as a famine hedge (US Army 1965, 262).

The small, dairy short-horn breed of cattle, found in Syria today, survives better than most other breeds of cattle in the arid environment of the Middle Euphrates region. But even at that, they are almost entirely restricted to the agricultural part of the riverine zone, and on occasion require supplemental feed and shelter. Cattle have never constituted a large portion of the livestock population. Like goat, the Khanean sample of cattle did show a significant change in age category percentages between Early and Middle Phases. This change may reflect a change in economic strategy. An increase in the Middle Phase of about 16% in deaths in the adult category indicates a larger number of individuals reaching maturity and probably greater use for traction/transport or dairy. In both phases the highest percentage of individuals is in the juvenile category (Early Phase 57.2% and Middle Phase 50.0%, Fig. 10.3). This strongly suggests that cattle were used for prime meat production. The rise in the number of adult deaths during the Middle Phase may indicate a shift away from meat specialization to greater use for dairy or traction.

Overall, analysis of the faunal assemblage from Terqa indicates a diversified use of livestock with a limited degree of specialization (measured as production of prime meat, wool or hair, or dairy products for sheep and goats). There is some indication of specialization in production of prime meat in cattle, but then, the number of cattle found in faunal assemblages is never great (Fig. 10.2).

To summarize this phase of development, generally providing food and material supplies to the staple finance institutions of city states from about 3000 BC to 1000 BC, livestock species dominating in faunal assemblages were multipurpose, well adapted and integratable into riverine food production. Little evidence exists for ecological specialization and exchange in subsistence products. Each major center as well as small rural villages produced herds and grain, manufactured domestic ceramics and textiles. By about 2000 BC, there are growing signs of specialization within the state administration involved with food animals. There are some regional differences between the Middle Euphrates Region and areas farther south. In general, livestock production in the Middle Euphrates Region continued to maintain a much more subsistence orientation; while further south a higher intensity of livestock production is noted at a number of key centers. For example, livestock in vast numbers were pooled at Drehem and a number of full-time specialists, such as shepherd contractors, functioned as part of a frequently elaborate state bureaucracy. Yet, all this testifies to the scale of development of state-regulated food production, storage and disbursal, but it does not point to the intensive development of ecologically based specialization and exchange at a time when state organization is firmly taking root.

Phase III — livestock as commercial enterprise

A third phase of development of livestock production probably begins earlier but becomes clearly evident by about 1200 BC. The shift is associated with a major change in state economic organization involving a shift from staple to wealth financing. Wealth financing (D'Altroy and Earle 1985) involves the distribution of valuables and eventually true currency rather than staple products in payment to persons working for the state. The main advantage of wealth as a basis for finance is its high value to weight ratio, minimizing the costs of transportation over long distances. The emergence of a system of finance based on wealth can be expected to be associated with the elaboration of long-distance trade of wealth goods. This shift is indicated by textual sources (Jankovskaya 1969) and appears to be tied to the development of crafts production on an industrial level and large-scale inter-regional trade in finished goods.

Long-distance trade had been an important element in Near Eastern economic organization even before the Neolithic (Redman 1978; Lamberg-Karlovsky 1975). It supplied many of the building materials lacking in Southern Mesopotamia, as well as raw materials for a number of crafts, such as metallurgy and stone-tool manufacture. It also moved finished goods, clothing, jewelry, and foodstuffs, such as wine, olive oil, sesame oil. These goods were probably not shipped in quantities sufficient to meet the demand of the bulk of the working population. Instead, their exchange served primarily to link elites in different regions and to provide the material symbols of state political and religious authority (see Sasson 1967; UCLA Ebla Conference 1983).

By the beginning of the first millennium BC, the Assyrian state was actively involved in interregional trade. Gold and silver, rather than simply serving as a standard of value for converting between different kinds of food and material products, served as a form of currency. Evidence from Terqa (Buccellati and Kelly-Buccellati 1977) and from southern Mesopotamia suggests growth of regional craft specialization (Redman 1978). Jankovskaya (1969) describes the Neo-Assyrian wool trade in which wool grown in the Middle Euphrates region was exported to the Phoenician coast where it was dyed purple with an extract from a Mediterranean shellfish, woven and shipped to various parts of the empire, including the Middle Euphrates region. There is evidence of true markets by about 800 BC and in Pre-Christian Roman times. An important element in the transition from staple to wealth financing was the domestication and introduction of the camel in Near Eastern livestock production. Camels entered southern Mesopotamia, the Middle Euphrates region and western Iran by two routes perhaps as early as 3000 BC. The Bactrian camel entered along trade routes from Afghanistan, through Iran and Assyria to points south and west (Campagnoni 1978). The dromedary most likely entered from the Arabian Peninsula (Ripinsky 1983). Camels are rarely cited in texts before 1200 BC, and camel bone is not often found in sites in the south or Middle Euphrates region before this time.

The camel made possible the first true specialization in livestock production by making profitable utilization of dry steppe and desert areas for pasture. Unlike sheep, goats and cattle, camels' prime utility was not in the protein, fat and raw materials they produced, but in their use for transport. Camels, providing the means for heavy transport over long distances, ushered in an era of trade routes linking continents.

The development of specialized camel pastoralism had important effects on other aspects of livestock production. With increasing orientation to craft specialization and production for market exchange, fewer individuals were directly involved in food production than under the system of staple finance. This necessitated a reorganization in sheep/goat and cattle herding as well as development of full-time camel pastoralism.

The faunal remains from Terqa dating from the early part of the first millennium BC and into the first millennium AD (ca. AD 900) show an important change in species percentages. During the early part of the second millennium BC, goats are roughly equal to sheep, but decline sharply during the first millennium BC (from 40% to 17%). A recent livestock survey at Ashara (former center of Terqa), Syria (Galvin 1981), shows goats at about the same percentage today. On the other hand, cattle comprise about 11% in the 1700s BC, but increase to 17% by about 1000 BC. The explanation for the decline of goats and slight rise in the number of cattle may relate to the transition to wealth finance, an upswing in the economies of centers located along transcontinental trade routes and realistic possibilities for economies of scale.

Goats are the animal *par excellence* for simple subsistence livestock production. They are highly adaptable to adverse conditions, are inexpensive and generally easy to acquire, multiply rapidly and provide a wide range of products for the household economy. In dairying or meat production on a large scale, however, they are inferior to cattle. They require more labor in handling, lactate for a shorter period of time and yield a smaller carcass (French 1970). Cattle provide renewable resources, such as dairy products and calves, as well as meat and hides in larger quantities than goats for a given amount of labor in handling per head, plus traction/transport. In situations where market exchange and economies of scale are possible, cattle, despite their lower adaptability to the arid Near East, may be economically more valuable than goats. Because of breeding particularities, camels have never supplanted cattle in riverine zone and livestock production (see Sweet 1965). Finally, by about 1500 BC, the horse was beginning to appear in Mesopotamia and the Middle Euphrates region. At first appearing as very limited elite exchanges, they later had an important impact on warfare and transportation (mules, the sterile hybrid cross of horse and donkey, served as excellent heavy duty animals of traction and transport).

Conclusion

This research has examined the role of livestock production in early state economic development, focusing on the question of the timing and economic causes of herding becoming an ecologically distinct occupational specialization. In a widely recognized adaptationist or mutual-benefit model of the development of surplus food production, the early economic separation and specialization of herding figures as a key element. According to this interpretation, the emergence and elaboration of centralized political organization centers on the role of elites in mediating exchanges of products between ecologically distinct regions. In the case of the arid Near East, this is thought to have involved the use of steppe/desert for herding and river zone for agriculture.

Evidence from sites in southern Mesopotamia and neighboring arid zone riverine settlements in the Middle Euphrates region suggests that specialization and exchange of livestock and agricultural products between ecologically different regions did not play a significant role in the development of state food production until the early first millennium BC, at a time when state-level organization had been present in the Near East for at least three thousand years.

Increasing specialization in livestock production over time is clearly indicated by the faunal record. But at first this appears as breeds refined for special tasks or products. The data strongly suggest that herding formed a complementary association with irrigation agriculture. At some sites, cattle and pigs form an important component in the faunal assemblage. These species are clearly bound by their biological requirements to the better watered areas. Sheep and goat can utilize the steppe desert, but only on a seasonal basis. Seasonal utilization does not provide a sufficient basis for full-time livestock specialization.

Conceivably herding, as a full-time occupational specialization, could have emerged in riverine microenvironments not utilized by irrigation agriculture, yet species-mix and age-category percentages suggest livestock management practices aimed at generalized, mixed herding with modest productivity that would be expected under a system of staple financing, not the more narrowly defined and intensive production to be expected where full-time specialization exists with exchange.

The emphasis on maintaining a high degree of generalization in livestock production, while improving the productive characteristics of existing breeds and domestication of new species with specialized characteristics, is reflected in the configuration of faunal remains from the time roughly between 3000 and 2000 BC. This pattern of development implies a view of the course of state economic development somewhat different than that of the adaptationists.

State systems can be distinguished from non-states by the way the society responds to the potential for surplus. In state society, production is organized in a way that attempts to insure a regular surplus from a given resource base. Part of the surplus generated by food production is used to support the activities of the state administration which is involved in massive public-works projects requiring capital outlay, planning and labor, the maintenance of political relations with surrounding states and internal security. Some part of this activity results in the development of forms of production and organization which are capable of superseding the existing extractive technology. State society tends to be developmental. That is, some portion of social energy is directed towards expansion. It is likely that in some cases the monitoring of exchanges between ecologically distinct regions may have played an important role in the early development of state administration. But ecological symbiosis between the

desert/steppe and riverine zone does not appear to have been an important element in the development of the state in Mesopotamia and the Middle Euphrates Region. In fact economic exchanges based on the utilization of the arid regions for herding and riverine zone for agriculture does not appear to have been a real possibility until after approximately 3000 years of state development. Consequently, something besides specialized surplus exchange must form the basis for state development here.

The initial impetus to specialized production and exchange must be sought in a developmental sequence involving changes in the basic means of production and organization of production. Technological change is responsible for major increments in production. Beyond this, there are organizational changes that can bring productivity closer to technical capacity and bring about the development of new technology. One important focus of such organizational changes is in the system of state finance.

During phase one, the domestication of plants and animals considered here, a technological change made possible the regularized production of surplus food. Populations exploiting the potential of food production and increasing organizational complexity appear to have had a selective advantage in controlling resources over those who did not. When the shift to stratified political–economic organization occurred, the control over household production shifted from the local corporate group to centralized administrative hierarchies. Technically, the primitive self-sufficient economy lacked the potential for sustained intensification but more importantly it lacked the organizational capacity for the accumulation and deployment of capital for productive expansion. The significance of work intensification, surplus production and capital accumulation lies not in better utilization of ecological diversity (thought to permit larger and denser populations and 'needs' for coordination) but in how the state utilizes surplus to meet the ongoing needs of elites involved in systems maintenance and expansion.

One example of this developmental process in livestock production can be seen in the evolution of transport animals. The initial domestication of the equids and camelids had little impact on the economic organization of Mesopotamia, but one thousand years later they were a critical ingredient in the expansion of long-distance, overland trade. Specialized breeds of sheep have a prominent position in representational art early in the third millennium BC, but do not appear in great numbers in faunal assemblages until the end of the millennium.

Looking at the course of state development in Mesopotamia, it is necessary to consider a phase of development in which the surplus-producing system is as yet technologically and organizationally weakly developed. Under these conditions, economic specialization and separation by desert/ steppe and riverine microenvironments in food production involved greater rather than reduced risk to the economy, since without careful planning and control carrying capacity might be exceeded for short-term gain. In these situations a more generalized, internally complementary system, retaining many features of the pre-state subsistence economy would involve less risk and still provide some surplus.

Such was the system of staple finance which emerged in early state society in Mesopotamia. The profits to be gained by fine-grained specialization were at first foregone in order to develop the technical and organizational aspects of surplus production. Theoretically, gains would eventually level off as maximal capacity was reached and environmental degradation began to impinge on further expansion under the existing technology. In the long run, however, since state organization supports conditions favorable to technological development, further elaboration of technological and organizational complexity were probable.

This appears to be the case for Mesopotamia and the Middle Euphrates Region. Initially, gains were made by intensifying utilization of the rough-quality early breeds of goat, sheep, cattle and pig in combination with irrigation agriculture in the arid riverine zone. Livestock production tended to focus on species adaptable to riverine conditions and sufficiently productive to provide food and materials for workers involved in urban development projects. There was continued experimentation with breeds exhibiting biological characteristics which provided either new products or better quality and quantity of existing products. By the end of phase 2, improved breeds dominated in faunal assemblages while several new species (primarily for traction/transport) began to appear. However, the focus of much of the faunal collection on food debris limits the utility of these data in measuring the relative abundance of these species.

There is evidence that environmental degradation began to occur in Southern Mesopotamia by the end of the second millennium BC (ca. 2000 BC). It reflects the impressive level of complexity and sophistication that state society had attained. The state system utilizing the staple form of finance may have been reaching technical capacity at this time. For several hundred years, there were no marked changes in the form of state organization in either the south or in the Middle Euphrates region.

Yet by the end of the second millennium and beginning of the first millennium BC, there were signs of economic change and further expansion. By 1200 BC, the transition to wealth financing had been made. Changes can be seen in the organization of livestock production, with the first appearance of true ecologically based specialization and exchange between desert/steppe herding and riverine agriculture. The key to this was the domestication and introduction of the camel on a large scale.

Ecologically separate, specialized livestock production figures as an important element in the adaptationist model of early state economic development. The images evoked by mobile pastoralism, caravan trade and the contrast between the desert and the sown owe much of their existence to the domestication of the camel. These images have so strongly impressed the imagination of researchers seeking to understand the early phases of state economic development that it is hard to imagine the Near East without them. Yet I have argued here that such a form of livestock production appears only after at least three thousand years of pristine state economic and political formation, far too late to have contributed in any significant way to the early stages of development.

This chapter was originally presented as a paper at the symposium "Specialization and Exchange in the Development of Complex Societies: Archaeological Evidence," XI International Congress of Anthropological and Ethnological Sciences, Vancouver.

Note

1   A second way of looking at specialization is in terms of the contribution each individual makes to the final product. In a relatively unspecialized system, each individual will be involved in most if not all stages of production from acquiring the raw materials to putting the new item to use. With increasing specialization, the individual contributes to a smaller component of a final product, the utility of which will not be realizable without the work efforts of many other people.

At present, the development of livestock specialization in the ancient Near East can be examined only at a very general level. The methods of faunal analysis are still too limited to monitor the movement of animals through a number of productive stages, as would be necessary to determine the nature and extent of contribution of different specialists to a final product.

BIBLIOGRAPHY

Aberg, N. 1921. *La Civilisation Enéolithique dans la Péninsule Ibérique.* Uppsala: A.-B. Akademiska Bokhandeln.

Adams, R. E. W. 1970. Suggested Classic period occupational speciali-zation in the southern Maya lowlands, in W. R. Bullard, Jr., ed., *Monographs and Papers in Maya Archaeology.* Papers of the Peabody Museum, Harvard University. Cambridge, Massachusetts, Peabody Museum.

    Adams, R. E. W. 1977a. *Prehistoric Mesoamerica.* Boston, Little, Brown and Company.

    Adams, R. E. W. 1977b. Comments on the glyphic texts of the 'Altar vase,' in N. Hammond, ed., *Social Process in Maya Pre-history*, New York, Academic Press.

Adams, R. E. W. and Jones, R. C. 1981. Spatial patterns and regional growth among Classic Maya cities. *American Antiquity* 46 (2): 301–22.

Adams, R. McC. 1965. *Land Behind Baghdad.* Chicago: University of Chicago.

    Adams, R. McC. 1974. Anthropological perspectives on ancient trade. *Current Anthropology* 15: 239–58.

Adams, R. McC. and Nissen, H. 1972. *The Uruk Country Side.* Chicago: University of Chicago.

Adler, A. 1982. *La Mort et le Masque du Roi.* Paris, Payot.

Aguayo de Hoyos, P. 1977. Construcciones defensivas de la Edad de Cobre peninsular: el Cerro de los Castellones (Laborcillas, Granada). *Cuadernos de Prehistoria Granadina* 2: 87–104.

Aguilera, C. 1977. *El Arte Oficial Tenochca: Su significación social.* México: Universidad Nacional Autónoma de México.

Ahler, S., Muller, J. and Rabinowitz, J. 1980. Archaeological testing for the Smithland Pool, Illinois. *Southern Illinois University at Carbondale, Center for Archaeological Investigations, Research Paper 13.*

Aldenderfer, M. S. n.d. The structure of rural lithic assemblages of the Late Classic in the central Peten lakes region, Guatemala, in T. Hester and H. Shafer, eds., *Stone Tools and Maya Civiliation*, volume in preparation.

Almagro Basch, M. 1965. El poblado de Almizaraque de Herrerías (Almería). *VI. Congresso Internazionale delle Scienze Preistoriche e Protostoriche, Roma 1962* 2: 378–79.

Almagro Basch, M. and A. Arribas. 1963. El Poblado y la necropolis megalíticos de Los Millares (Santa Fe de Mondújar, Almería). *Bibliotheca Praehistorica Hispaña* 3.

Almagro Gorbea, Maria Josefa. 1965. Las tres tumbas megalíticas de Almizaraque. *Trabajos de Prehistoria* 18.

    Almagro Gorbea, Maria Josefa. 1973. El poblado y la necrópolis de El Barranquete (Almería). *Acta Arqueológica Hispánica* 6.

    Almagro Gorbea, Maria Josefa. 1976. Memoria de las excavaciones efectuadas en el yacimiento de Tarajal (Almería), *Noticiario Arqueológico Hispánico, Prehistoria* 5: 195–98.

Almagro Gorbea, Martín and O. Collado Villalba. 1981. La Loma de la Tejería: un asentamiento campaniforme en Albarracín (Teruel). *Teruel* 66: 87–102.

Almagro Gorbea, Martín and M. Fernández-Miranda, eds. 1978. *C-14 y Prehistoria de la Península Ibérica.* Madrid: Fundación Juan March.

Alva Ixtlilxochitl, F. de. 1975–77. *Obras Históricas.* E. O'Gorman, ed. 2 vols. México: Universidad Nacional Autónoma de México [orig. 1600–40].

Ammerman, A. 1979. A study of obsidian exchange in Calabria. *World Archaeology* 11: 95–110.

Anales de Cuauhtitlan. 1945. Anales de Cuauhtitlan, in P. F. Velazquez, trans., *Códice Chimalpopoca*, pp. 1–118. México: Universidad Nacional Autónoma de México. [orig. 1570].

Anawalt, P. 1980. Costume and control: Aztec sumptuary laws. *Archaeology* 33 (1): 33–43.

Andersen, Sv. Th, Aaby, B., Odgaard, B. and Vad, B. 1983. Environment and Man: Current Studies in Vegetational History at the Geological Survey of Denmark. *Journal of Danish Archaeology*, Vol. 2.

Anderson, A. J. O., Berdan, F. and Lockhart, J., trans. and eds. 1976. *Beyond the Codices: The Nahua view of colonial Mexico.* (ULCA Latin American Center, Latin American Studies Series. No. 27). Berkeley: University of California Press.

Andrews, A. P. 1983. *Maya Salt Production and Trade.* Tucson, University of Arizona Press.

Aner, E. and Kersten, K. 1970 ff. *Die Funde der älteren Bronzezeit des nordischen Kreuzes in Dänemark, Schleswig-Holstein und Niedersachen.* Band 1–7. Neumünster: Karl Wachholtz.

Anonymous Conqueror. 1917. *Narrative of Some Things of New Spain and of the Great City of Temestitlan Mexico.* M.H. Saville, trans. New York: The Cortes Society [orig. 1556].

Appel, J. 1978. The Valley of Oaxaca in the Late Postclassic: An evolutionary perspective. Paper presented at the 43rd Annual Meeting of the Society for American Archaeology, Tucson, Arizona.

Appel, J. 1982. *Political and Economic Organization in the Late Postclassic Valley of Oaxaca, Mexico: An evolutionary perspective.* Ph.D. dissertation, Department of Anthropology, Purdue University.

Ardener, E. 1968. Documentary and linguistic evidence for the rise of the trading polities between Rio del Rey and Cameroons, 1500–1650, in I. M. Lewis, ed., *History and Social Anthropology*, pp. 81–126. London: Tavistock.

Arnaud, J. M. 1971. Os povoados Neo-Eneoliticos de Farnão e Aboboreira (Ciladas, Vila Vicosa): noticia preliminar. *II. Congreso Nacional de Arqueologia, Coimbra 1970*, pp. 199–221.

Arnold, D. E. 1975. Ceramic ecology of the Ayacucho Basin, Peru. *Current Anthropology* 16: 183–205.

Arnold, D. E. 1980. Localized exchange: An ethnoarchaeological perspective, in R. E. Fry, ed., *Models and Methods in Regional Exchange*, pp. 147–50. (SAA Papers No. 1). Washington: Society for American Archaeology.

Arribas, A. 1968. Las bases económicas del Neolítico al Bronce, in M. Tarradell, ed., *Estudios de Economía Antigua de la Península Ibérica*, pp. 33–60. Barcelona: Vicens-Vives.

Arribas, A. and Molina, F. 1979. *El Poblado de 'Los Castillejos' en las Peñas de los Gitanos (Montefrío, Granada): Campaña de Excavaciones de 1971, el Corte Núm. 1.* Granada: Universidad de Granada.

Arribas, A. and Molina, F. 1982. Los Millares: neue Ausgrabungen in der Kupferzeitlichen Siedlung (1978–1981). *Madrider Mitteilungen* 23: 9–32.

Arribas, A., Molina, F., de la Torre, F., Nájera, T. and Sáez, L. 1978. El poblado de la Edad del Cobre de 'El Malagón' (Cúllar-Baza, Granada). *Cuadernos de Prehistoria Granadina* 3: 87–116.

Aston, W. G. trans. 1972. *Nihongi, Chronicles of Japan from the Earliest Times to A.D. 697.* Tokyo, Charles E. Tuttle Company, [orig. 1896].

Athens, J. S. 1977. Theory building and the study of evolutionary process in complex societies, in L. Binford, ed., *For Theory Building in Archaeology*, pp. 353–84. New York: Academic.

Avery, George 1983. *Salt, Pots, and Diets: Replication Studies of Late Prehistoric Shell-Tempered Ceramics.* Unpublished M.A. thesis, Department of Anthropology, Southern Illinois University – Carbondale.

Bailey, F. G. 1969. *Stratagems and Spoils.* New York: Schocken.

Balfet, H. 1965. Ethnographical observations in North Africa and archaeological interpretation: Pottery of the Maghreb, in F. R. Matson, ed., *Ceramics and Man*, pp. 161–77. Chicago: Aldine.

Bareis, C. and Porter, J., eds. 1984. *American Bottom Archaeology: A Summary of the FAI-270 Project Contribution to the Culture History of the Mississippi River Valley.* Urbana: University of Illinois.

Barlow, R. H. 1949. *The Extent of the Empire of the Culhua-Mexica.* (Ibero-Americana, No. 28). Berkeley: University of California Press.

Barnes, Gina L. 1983. *Yayoi-Kofun Settlement Archaeology in the Nara Basin, Japan.* Ann Arbor, University Microfilms. To be published as *Protohistoric Yamato* by the Museum of Anthropology and the Center for Japanese Studies, University of Michigan, forthcoming.

Barnes, Gina L. n.d. Jiehao, Tonghao: Peer relations in East Asia, in A. C. Renfrew and J. Cherry, eds., *Peer Polity Interaction and Socio-Political Change.* Cambridge: Cambridge University Press. [in press].

Bartram, W. 1928. *Travels Through North and South Carolina, Georgia, East & West Florida . . .* Mark Van Doren, ed., Macy-Masius. [Original ed. 1791; Dover reprint of 1928 edition, 1955]

Batres, L. 1904. *Mis Exploraciones en Huexotla Texcoco y Monumento del Gavilan.* México: I. Guerro y comp.

Bayiga, A. 1966. *L'Homme qui voit la Nuit.* Thése en Theologie, University of Strasbourg.

Beaudry, M. P. 1984. *Ceramic Production and Distribution in the Southeastern Maya Periphery.* (B.A.R. International Series 203). Oxford: B.A.R.

Becker, C. 1982. Siedlungen der Bronzezeit und der vorrömischen Eisenzeit in Dänemark. *Offa* 39.

Becker, M. J. 1973. Archaeological evidence for occupational specialization among the Classic period Maya at Tikal, Guatemala. *American Antiquity* 38 (4): 396–406.

Becker, M. J. 1983. Indications of social class differences based on the archaeological evidence for occupational specialization among the Classic Maya at Tikal, Guatemala. *Revista Española de Antropología Americana* XIII: 29–46.

Beckwith, M. W. 1932. Kepelino's traditions of Hawaii. *Bernice P. Bishop Museum Bulletin* 95.

Bender, M. M., Baerreis, D. A. and Steventon, R. L. 1981. Further light on carbon isotopes and Hopewell agriculture. *American Antiquity* 46 (2): 346–53.

Berdan, F. F. 1975. *Trade, Tribute and Market in the Aztec Empire.* Ph.D. dissertation, Anthropology Department, The University of Texas.

Berdan, F. F. 1982. *The Aztecs of Central Mexico.* New York: Holt, Rinehart, and Winston.

Berglund, B. 1969. Vegetation and Human Influence in South Scandinavia during Prehistoric Time. *Oikos* supplement 12.

Binford, L. 1964. A consideration of archaeological research design. *American Antiquity* 29: 425–41.

Bintliff, J. 1982. Settlement patterns, land tenure and social structure: a diachronic model, in C. Renfrew and S. Shennan, eds., *Ranking, Resource and Exchange: Aspects of the Archaeology of Early European Society*, pp. 106–11. Cambridge: Cambridge University Press.

Bishop, R. L. 1980. Aspects of ceramic compositional modeling, in R. E. Fry, ed., *Models and Methods in Regional Exchange*, pp. 47–65. (SAA Papers No. 1). Washington: Society for American Archaeology.

Bishop, R. L. and Rands, R. L. 1982. Maya Fine Paste ceramics: a compositional perspective, in J. A. Sabloff, ed., *Analyses of Fine Paste Ceramics, Excavations at Seibal, Department of Peten, Guatemala.* (Peabody Museum Memoirs, vol. 15). Cambridge, Harvard University.

Bishop, R. L., Rands, R. L. and Harbottle, G. 1979. A ceramic compositional interpretation of incense-burner trade in the Palenque area, Mexico. Brookhaven National Laboratory Report BNL-26787. New York, Upton.

Black, G. A. 1967. *The Angel Site*. Indianapolis: Indiana Historical Society.

Blakely, R. L. 1971. Comparison of the mortality profiles of Archaic, Middle Woodland, and Middle Mississippian skeletal populations. *American Journal of Physical Anthropology* 34: 43–54.

Blakeman, C. 1974. *The Late Prehistoric Ethnobotany of the Black Bottom, Pope and Massac Counties, Illinois*. Unpublished Ph.D. dissertation, Department of Anthropology, Southern Illinois University, Carbondale.

Blance, B. 1971. Die Anfänge der Metallurgie auf der Iberischen Halbinsel. *Studien zu den Anfängen der Metallurgie* 4.

Blanton, R. E. and Feinman, G. 1984. The Mesoamerican world system: A comparative perspective. *American Anthropologist* 86: 673–82.

Blanton, R. E., Kowalewski, S. A., Feinman, G. and Appel, J. 1981. *Ancient Mesoamerica: A comparison of change in three regions*. Cambridge: Cambridge University Press.

Boas, N. A. 1983. Egeløj: A Settlement from the Early Bronze Age in East Jutland. *Journal of Danish Archaeology*, Vol. 2.

Boessneck, J. and von den Driesch, A. 1980. Tierknochenfunde aus vier südspanischen Höhlen. *Studien über frühe Tierknochenfunde von der Iberischen Halbinsel* 7: 1–83.

Bohannan, P. 1958. Extra-processual events in Tiv political institutions. *American Anthropologist* 60: 1–12.

Borgen, R. 1975. The origins of the Sugawara: a history of the Haji family. *Monumenta Nipponica* 30.4: 405–22.

Bott, E. 1981. Power and Rank in the kingdom of Tonga. *Journal of Polynesian Society* 90: 7–82.

Bouzek, J. 1966. The Aegean and Central Europe. An Introduction to the Study of Cultural Interrelations, 16-1300 B.C. *Památky Archeologické* LVII. 242–276.

Bouzek, J. 1982. Relations between the Aegean and Europe during the Bronze Age – a Methodological Approach. *Archeologické Rozledy* XXXIV. 56–61. Prague.

Bouzek, J. 1985. *The Aegean, Anatolia and Europe: Cultural Interrelations in the Second Millennium B.C.* Prague: Academy of Sciences.

Bove, F. J. 1981. Trend surface analysis and the lowland Classic Maya collapse. *American Antiquity* 46 (1): 93–112.

Boye, V. 1896. *Fund af Egekister fra Bronzealderen i Danmark*. Copenhagen.

Boysen, A. and Andersen, W. S. 1983. Trappendal: Barrow and House from the Early Bronze Age. *Journal of Danish Archaeology*, Vol. 2.

Braidwood, R. and Howe, B., eds., 1960. *Prehistoric Investigation in Iraqi Kurdistan*. (Studies in Ancient Oriental Civilization no. 31). Chicago: University of Chicago Press.

Braun, D. P. n.d. Social Evolution, Prehistoric Central Midwestern U.S., 200 BC–AD 600. Draft Proposal. Ms.

Braun, D. P. and Plog, S. 1982. Evolution of 'tribal' social networks: Theory and prehistoric North American evidence. *American Antiquity* 47 (3): 504–25.

Brigham, W. T. 1899. Hawaiian feather work. *Bernice P. Bishop Museum Memoir* 1 (4).

Brigham, W. T. 1903. Additional notes on Hawaiian feather work. *Bernice P. Bishop Museum Memoir* 1 (5): 437–53.

Brigham, W. T. 1918. Additional notes on Hawaiian feather work. *Bernice P. Bishop Museum Memoir* 7 (1): 1–64.

Broadbent, N. 1983. Too many Chiefs and not enough Indians: A Peripheral View of Nordic Bronze Age Society. In *Struktur och förändring i bronsålderens samhälle*. University of Lund, Institute of Archaeology, Report Series no. 17.

Broda, J. 1976. Los estamentos en el ceremonial mexicana, in P.

Carrasco et al., eds., *Estratificación Social en la Mesoamérica Prehispánica*, pp. 37–66. México: Instituto Nacional de Antropología e Historia.

Broholm, H. C. and Hald, M. 1940. *Costumes of the Bronze Age in Denmark*. Copenhagen.

Brøste, K. and Balslev, Jørgensen. 1956. *Prehistoric Man in Denmark: A Study in Physical Anthropology. Vol. I–II. Stone Age and Bronze Age*. Copenhagen.

Brumfiel, E. M. 1980. Specialization, market exchange, and the Aztec state: A view from Huexotla. *Current Anthropology* 21: 459–78.

Brumfiel, E. M. 1982. Ethnohistoric synthesis, in J. R. Parsons, E. Brumfiel, M. H. Parsons and D. J. Wilson, *Prehispanic Settlement Patterns in the Southern Valley of Mexico: The Chalco-Xochimilco Region*, pp. 75–92. (Memoirs No. 14). Ann Arbor: The University of Michigan Museum of Anthropology.

Brumfiel, E. M. 1983. Aztec state making: Ecology, structure and the origin of the state. *American Anthropologist* 85: 261–84.

Brumfiel, E. M. 1986. The division of labor at Xico: The chipped stone industry, in B. L. Isaac, ed., *Economic Aspects Prehispanic Highland Mexico*. pp. 245–79 (Suppl. 2 of Research in Economic Anthropology). Greenwich, CT: JAI Press.

Brumfiel, E. M. n.d. Tribute allocation and the organization of rural labor in the Aztec state, in P. J. Netherly and D. A. Freidel, eds., *New Models for the Political Economy of Pre-Columbian Polities* [future publication].

Buccellati, G. 1966. *The Amorites of the Ur III Period*. Naples: Istituto Orientale de Napoli.

Buccellati, G. and Kelly-Buccellati, M. 1977. *Terao Preliminary Report No. 1*, Issue 3. Malibu: Undena.

Buck, P. H. (Te Rangi Hiroa). 1957. Clothing, in P. Buck, ed., *Arts and Crafts of Hawaii* (Section V). Honolulu, Bernice P. Bishop Museum Press.

Bureau, R. 1972. *La Religion d'Eboga*. Thèse de doctorat d'etat. Paris V.

Burgess, C. 1980. *The Age of Stonehenge*. London: Dent.

Burnham, P. 1980. *Opportunity and Constraint in a Savanna Society*. London and New York, Academic Press.

Butler, B. M. 1977. *Mississippian Settlement in the Black Bottom, Pope and Massac Counties, Illinois*. Ph.D. dissertation, Department of Anthropology, Southern Illinois University, Carbondale.

Buttler, J. J. 1963. Bronze Age Connections across the North Sea. *Palaeohistoria* 9.

Calnek, E. E. 1972. Settlement pattern and chinampa agriculture at Tenochtitlan. *American Antiquity* 37: 102–15.

Calnek, E. E. 1975. Organización de los sistemas de abastecimiento urbano de alimentos: El caso de Tenochtitlan, in J. Hardoy and R. Schaedel, eds., *Las Ciudades de América Latina y sus Areas de Influencia a Través de la Historia*, pp. 41–60. Buenos Aires: Ediciones A.I.A.P.

Calnek, E. E. 1978a. El sistema de mercado en Tenochtitlan, in P. Carrasco and J. Broda, eds., *Economía Política e Ideología en el México Prehispánico*, pp. 97–114. México: Nueva Imagen.

Calnek, E. E. 1978b. The City-State in the Basin of Mexico: Late Pre-Hispanic period, in R. P. Schaedel, J. E. Hardoy, N. S. Kinzer, eds., *Urbanization in the Americas from its Beginnings to the Present*, pp. 463–70. The Hague: Mouton.

Campagnoni, Bruno 1978. The camel: its distribution and state of domestication in the Middle East during the Third Millennium B.C. in light of finds from Shahr-i Sokhta, in R. H. Meadow and M. A. Zeder, eds., *Approaches to Faunal Analysis in the Middle East*, pp. 91–104. Cambridge: Harvard University.

Canouts, V., May, E., Lopinot, N. and Muller, J. 1984. Cultural frontiers in the Upper Cache Valley, Illinois. *Center for Archaeological Investigations, Research Paper* 16.

Carrasco, P. 1961. The civil–religious hierarchy in Mesoamerican communities: Pre-Spanish background and colonial development. *American Anthropologist* 63: 483–97.

Carrasco, P. 1971. Social organization of ancient Mexico, in G. F. Ekholm and I. Bernal, eds., *Archaeology of Northern Meso-america, Part 1*, pp. 349–75. (Handbook of Middle American Indians, Vol. 10.). Austin: University of Texas Press.

Carrasco, P. 1974. Introducción – La matrícula de Huexotzinco como fuente sociológica, in H. Prem, ed., *Matrícula de Huexotzinco*, pp. 1–16. Graz: Akademische Druck-u. Verlagsanstalt.

Carrasco, P. 1976. Los linajes nobles de México antiguo, in P. Carrasco, et al., eds., *Estratificación Social en la Mesoamérica Prehispánica*, pp. 19–36. México: Instituto Nacional de Antropología e Historia.

Carrasco, P. 1977. Los señores de Xochimilco en 1548. *Tlalocan* 7: 229–65.

Carrasco, P. 1978. La economía del México prehispánico, in P. Carrasco and J. Broda, eds., *Economía Política e Ideología en el México Prehispánico*, pp. 15–76. México: Neuva Imagen.

Carta de los Caciques. 1870. Carta de los caciques e indios naturales de Suchimilco a Su Magestad . . . (2 de Mayo de 1563), in *Colección de Documentos Inéditos . . . de Indias*, vol. 13, pp. 293–301. Madrid: José María Pérez [orig. 1563].

Chang, K. C. 1980. The Chinese Bronze Age: A modern synthesis, in W. Fong, ed., *The Great Bronze Age of China*, pp. 35–50. New York: The Metropolitan Museum of Art and Alfred A. Knopf.

Chapman, R. W. 1978. The evidence for prehistoric water control in south-east Spain. *Journal of Arid Environments* 1: 261–74.

Chapman, R. W. 1981. Archaeological theory and communal burial in prehistoric Europe, in I. Hodder et al., eds., *Pattern of the Past: Studies in Honour of David Clarke*, pp. 387–411. Cambridge: Cambridge University Press.

Chapman, R. W. 1982. Autonomy, ranking and resources in Iberian prehistory, in C. Renfrew and S. Shennan, eds., *Ranking, Resource and Exchange: Aspects of the Archaeology of Early European Society*, pp. 46–51. Cambridge: Cambridge University Press.

Charlton, T. H. 1972. *Post-Conquest Developments in the Teotihuacan Valley, Mexico. Part 1: Excavations.* (Report No. 5). Iowa City: Office of State Archaeologist.

Chayonov, A. V. [Tschajanow] 1923. *Die Lehre von der baeuerlichen Wirtschaft: Versuch einer Theorie der Familienwirtschaft in Landbau.* Berlin: Verlagsbuchhandlung Paul Parvey.

Chayonov, A. V. 1966. *The Theory of Peasant Economy.* Homewood, Illinois: The American Economic Association. [orig. 1925.].

Childe, V. G. 1957. *The Dawn of European Civilization.* London: Routledge and Kegan Paul.

Chilver, E. M. and Kaberry, P. 1967. The Kingdom of Kom, in D. Forde and P. Kaberry, eds., *West African kingdoms in the 19th century.* Oxford, Oxford University Press for the International African Institute.

Cieza de Léon, Pedro de. 1862. La crónica del Perú. *Biblioteca de Autores Españoles* 26: 349–458. Madrid; Ediciones Atlas. [orig. 1551].

Claessen, H. J. M. 1984. The internal dynamics of the early state. *Current Anthropology* 25: 365–79.

Clark, J. E. n.d. Obsidian: Notes from the primary Mesoamerican sources. MS., Department of Anthropology, The University of Michigan.

Clay, R. B. 1976. Tactics, strategy, and operations: The Mississippian system responds to its environment. *Mid-continent Journal of Archaeology* 1 (2): 138–62.

Cobb, C. n.d. Dissertation Proposal, Department of Anthropology, Southern Illinois University, Carbondale.

Cobo, B. 1956. Historia del nuevo mundo, II. *Biblioteca de Autores Españoles*, v. 92. Madrid, Ediciones Atlas [orig. 1653].

Cock, C. G. 1977. Los kurakas de los Collaguas: poder político y poder económico. *Historia y Cultura* 10: 95–118.

Coe, W. R. 1967. *Tikal: A Handbook of the Ancient Maya Ruins.* Philadelphia, University Museum.

Cohen, A. P. and J. L. Comaroff. 1976. The management of meaning: On the phenomenology of political transactions, in B. Kapferer, ed., *Transaction and Meaning*, pp. 87–107. (ASA Essays in Social Anthropology, Vol. 1). Philadelphia: Institute for the Study of Human Issues.

Cole, Fay-Cooper, et al. 1951. *Kincaid: A Prehistoric Illinois Metropolis.* Chicago: University of Chicago Press.

Coles, J. M. 1982a. Metallurgy and Bronze Age society, in *Studien zur Bronzezeit.* Festschrift für W. A. v. Brunn. Mainz.

Coles, J. M. 1982b. The Bronze Age in North-western Europe: Problems and Advances. *Advances in World Archaeology, Vol. 1.* New York: Academic.

Coles, J. M. and Harding, A. F. 1979. *The Bronze Age in Europe.* London:Methuen.

Conrad, G. W. and Demarest, A. A. 1984. *Religion and Empire.* Cambridge: Cambridge University Press.

Cook, D. C. 1979. Subsistence base and health in prehistoric Illinois Valley: Evidence from the human skeleton. *Medical Anthropology* 3: 109–24.

Cook, D. C. and Buikstra, J. E. 1979. Health and differential survival in prehistoric populations: Prenatal dental effects. *American Journal of Physical Anthropology* 51: 649–64.

Cook, J. 1784. *A Voyage to the Pacific Ocean, vol. II.* Dublin: H. Chamberlaine.

Cook, S. F. and Borah, W. 1960. *The Indian Population of Central Mexico 1531–1610.* (Ibero-Americana, No. 44). Berkeley: University of California Press.

Cook, S. F. and Borah, W. 1963. Quelle fut la stratification sociale au centre du mixique durant la première moitié du XVIe siècle? *Annales, économies, sociétés, civilisations* 18: 266–58.

Coquery-Vidrovitch, C. 1978. Research on an African mode of production, in D. Seddon, ed., *Relations of Production*, London: Frank Cass and Co.

Cortés, H. 1970. *Cartas de Relación.* México: Porrua [orig. 1519–26].

Costin, C. 1984. The organization and intensity of spinning and cloth production among the late prehispanic Huanca. Paper presented at the Annual Meeting of the Institute of Andean Studies, Berkeley.

Cremin, W. M. 1978. *Paleoethnobotany: Implications for Crab Orchard Exploitation of the Shawnee Hills, Southern Illinois.* Ph.D. Dissertation, Department of Anthropology, Southern Illinois University, Carbondale.

Crouwell, J. H. 1981. *Chariots and other means of Land Transport in Bronze Age Greece.* Altlard Pierson Series, Vol. 3. Amsterdam.

Culbert, T. P. 1977. Maya development and collapse: an economic perspective, in N. Hammond, ed., *Social Process in Maya Prehistory.* New York, Academic Press.

Cummins, T. 1984. Kinshape: design of Hawaiian feather capes. *Art History* 7: 1–20.

D'Altroy, T. 1981. *Empire growth and consolidation: the Xauxa region of Peru under the Inkas.* Doctoral dissertation, Department of Anthropology, University of California, Los Angeles.

D'Altroy, T. and Earle, T. K. 1985. State Finance, wealth finance, and storage in the Inka political economy. *Current Anthropology* 26: 187–206.

Date, Muneyasu 1963. Iseki bunpu yori mita kodai chiiki no kosatsu [Treatise on protohistoric territorialism as seen in the distribution of archaeological sites], in Kashiwara Archaeological Research Institute, ed., *Kinki Kobunka Ronko*, pp. 51–58. Tokyo, Yoshikawa Kobunkan.

Davies, E. N. 1985. The Gold of the Shaft Graves, The Transylvanian Connection. *Temple University, Aegean Symposium.*

Davies, N. 1973. *The Aztecs: A history.* Norman: University of Oklahoma Press.

Davy, D. M. 1982. *Proximity and Human Behavior: Settlement Locational Pattern Change in Prehistoric Illinois.* Ph.D. dissertation, Department of Anthropology, Southern Illinois University, Carbondale.

Deevey, Jr., E. S., Rice, D. S., Rice, P. M., Vaughan, H. H., Brenner, M. and Flannery, M. S. 1979. Mayan urbanism: impact on a tropical karst environment. *Science* 206 (4416): 298–306.

De Heusch, L. 1975. What shall we do with the drunken king? *Africa* 45 (4): 363–73.

De Maret, P. 1980. Preliminary Report. *Nyame Akuma* XVII, 10–12.

Díaz del Castillo, B. 1956. *The Discovery and Conquest of Mexico.* A. P. Maudslay, trans. New York: Noonday Press [orig. 1568].

Dickinson, O. T. P. K. 1977. *The Origins of Mycenean Civilization.* (SIMA 49). Göteborg.

Dietz, S. 1984. Kontinuität und Kulturwende in der Argolis von 2000–700. Ergebnisse der neuen schwedisch–dänischen Ausgrabungen in Asing. In *Agäischen Frühzeit.* Kleine Schriften aus dem vorgeschichtlichen Seminar, Marburg 17.

Douglas, M. 1963. *The Lele of the Kasai.* London: Oxford University Press.

Douglas, M. 1967. Primitive rationing: A study in controlled exchange, in R. Firth, ed., *Themes in Economic Anthropology* (A.S.A. Monographs 6), pp. 119–47. London: Tavistock.

Drennan, R. D. 1976. Religion and social evolution in Formative Mesoamerica, in K. V. Flannery, ed., *The Early Mesoamerican Village,* pp. 345–68. New York: Academic.

Drennan, R. D. 1984. Long-distance transport costs in prehispanic Mesoamerica. *American Anthropologist* 86: 105–12.

Drennan, R. D. and Nowack, J. A. 1984. Exchange and socio-political development in the Tehuacan Valley, in K. G. Hirth, ed., *Trade and Exchange in Early Mesoamerica,* pp. 147–56. Albuquerque: University of New Mexico Press.

Driesch, A. von den. 1972. Osteoarchäologische Untersuchungen auf der Iberischen Halbinsel. *Studien über frühe Tierknochenfunde von der Iberischen Halbinsel 3.*

Driesch, A. von den. 1973. Tierknochenfunde aus dem frühbronze-zeitlichen Gräberfeld von 'El Barranquete', Provinz Almería, Spanien. *Saügetierkundliche Mitteilungen* 21: 328–35.

Driesch, A. von den and Boessneck, J. 1981. Die Fauna von Zambujal, in E. Sangmeister and H. Schubart (1981), pp. 303–14.

Driesch, A. von den and Kokabi, M. 1977. Tierknochenfunde aus der Siedlung 'Cerro de los Castellones' bei Laborcillas/Granada. *Archäologie und Naturwissenschaften* 1: 129–43.

Driesch, A. von den and Morales, A. 1977. Los restos animales del yacimiento de Terrera Ventura (Tabernas, Almería). *Cuadernos de Prehistoria y Arqueología, Universidad Autónoma de Madrid* 4: 15–34.

Dumont, L. 1970. *Homo Hierarchicus.* London, Weidenfeld and Nicolson.

Durán, D. 1964. *The Aztecs: The history of the Indies of New Spain.* D. Heyden and F. Horcasitas, trans. New York: Orion [orig. 1581].

Durán, D. 1967. *Historia de las Indias de Nueva España e Islas de la Tierra Firme.* 2 vols., México: Porrua [orig. 1581].

Durán, D. 1971. *Book of the Gods and Rites of the Ancient Calendar.* F. Horcasitas and D. Heyden, trans. Norman: University of Oklahoma Press [orig. 1570, 1579].

Dycherhoff, U. and Prem, H. J. 1976. La estratificación social en Huexotzinco, in P. Carrasco et al., eds., *Estratificatión Social en la Mesoamérica Prehispánica,* pp. 157–77. México: Instituto Nacional de Antropología e Historia.

Earle, T. K. 1977. A reappraisal of redistribution: Complex Hawaiian chiefdoms, in T. K. Earle and J. E. Ericson, eds., *Exchange Systems in Prehistory,* pp. 213–29. New York: Academic Press.

Earle, T. K. 1978. *Economic and Social Organization of a Complex Chiefdom: The Halelea District, Kaua'i, Hawaii* (Anthropological Paper, No. 63). Ann Arbor: The University of Michigan Museum of Anthropology.

Earle, T. K. 1982. The ecology and politics of primitive valuables, in J. G. Kennedy and R. B. Edgerton, eds., *Culture and Ecology: Eclectic Perspectives,* pp. 65–83. (Special Publication, No. 15). Washington, D.C.: American Anthropological Association.

Earle, T. K. 1985a. Commodity exchange and markets in the Inca state: Recent archaeological evidence, in S. Plattner, ed., *Markets and Marketing* (S.E.A. Monographs in Economic Anthropology, No. 4), pp. 369–97. Lanham, MD: University Press of America.

Earle, T. K. 1985b. The uses of style in complex chiefdoms. Paper delivered in symposium *Anthropological Approaches to Style.* Minneapolis, Minn., January.

Earle, T. and D'Altroy, T. 1982. Storage facilities and state finance in the upper Mantaro Valley, Peru, in J. Ericson and T. Earle, eds., *Contexts for Prehistoric Exchange,* pp. 265–90. New York: Academic Press.

Earle, T. K., D'Altroy, T., Hastorf, C., Scott, C., Costin, C., Russell, G. and Sandefur, E. 1985. Preliminary report of the 1982 and 1983 field research of the Upper Mantaro Archaeological Research Project. Ms. under preparation for the Institute of Archaeology, University of California, Los Angeles.

Earle, T. K., D'Altroy, T., LeBlanc, C., Hastorf, C. and LeVine, T. 1980. Changing settlement patterns in the Upper Mantaro Valley, Peru. *Journal of New World Archaeology* 4 (1): 1–49.

Eckstein, S. 1977. *The Poverty of Revolution: The state and the urban poor in Mexico.* Princeton: Princeton University Press.

Eisenstadt, S. N. 1963. *The Political Systems of Empires: The rise and fall of the historical bureaucratic societies.* New York: The Free Press.

Ekholm, K. 1972. *Power and Prestige: The rise and fall of the Kongo kingdom.* Uppsala: Akademisk Avhandling.

Ekholm, K. 1977. External exchange and the transformation of Central African social systems, in J. Friedman and M. Rowlands, *The Evolution of Social Systems,* pp. 115–36. London: Duckworth.

Engels, F. 1972. *The Origins of the Family, Private Property and the State.* E. Reed, ed., R. Vernon, trans. New York: Pathfinder Press [orig. 1884].

Engels, F. 1975. The Origin of the Family, Private Property, and the State. In *Karl Marx and Frederick Engels, Selected Works* pp. 449–583. Moscow: Progress Publishers [Fourth Edition, original 1891].

Epstein, H. 1971. *The Origin of the Domestic Animals of Africa.* 2 vols. New York: Africana Publishing Co.

Erasmus, C. J. 1965. Monument building: Some field experiments. *Southwestern Journal of Anthropology* 21 (4): 277–301.

Erdheim, M. 1973. *Prestige und Kulturwandel: Eine Studie zum Verhältnis subjektiver und objektiver Faktoren des kulturellen Wandels zur Klassengesellschaft bei den Azteken.* Wiesbaden: Focus-Verlag.

Ericson, J. 1977. Egalitarian exchange systems in California: a preliminary view, in T. Earle and J. Ericson, eds., *Exchange Systems in Prehistory,* pp. 109–26. New York, Academic Press.

Espejo, A. 1945. Las ofrendas halladas en Tlatelolco. *Tlatelolco a Través de los Tiempos* 5: 15–29.

Evans, R. K. 1978. Early craft specialization: An example from the Balkan Chalcolithic, in C. L. Redman et al., eds., *Social Archaeology: Beyond Subsistence and Dating,* pp. 113–29. New York: Academic.

Evans-Pritchard, E. 1937. *Witchcraft, Oracles and Magic among the Azande*, Oxford, Clarendon Press.

Evans-Pritchard, E. 1948. *The Divine Kingship of the Shilluk*. London: Oxford University Press.

Feinman, G. 1980. *The Relationship between Administrative Organization and Ceramic Production in the Valley of Oaxaca*. Ph.D. dissertation, Department of Anthropology, City University of New York.

Feinman, G. 1982. Changes in the organization of ceramic production in prehispanic Oaxaca, Mexico. Paper presented at the symposium, 'Multidimensional Approaches to the Study of Ancient Ceramics,' Lhee, The Netherlands.

Ferreira, O. da V. 1966. Os artefactos pre-historicos de âmbar e sua distribuição em Portugal. *Revista de Guimarães* 76: 61–66.

Finkelstein, J. J. 1968. An Old Babylonian herding contract and Genesis 31:38f. *Journal of the American Oriental Society* 88: 30–7.

Flannery, K. V. 1968. The Olmec and the Valley of Oaxaca: A model for inter-regional interaction in Formative times, in E. P. Benson, ed., *Dumbarton Oaks Conference on the Olmec*, pp. 79–110. Washington, D.C.: Dumbarton Oaks.

Flannery, K. V. 1969. Origins and ecological effects of early domestication in Iran and the Near East, in P. J. Ucko and G. W. Dimbleby, eds., *The Domestication and Exploitation of Plants and Animals*, pp. 73–100. Chicago: Aldine.

Flannery, K. V. and Wright, H. T. 1966. Faunal remains from 'hut sounding' at Eridu, Iraq. *Sumer* 22: 61–63.

Folan, W., Kintz, E., and Fletcher, L. 1983. *Coba. A Classic Maya Metropolis*. New York, Academic Press.

Ford, R. I. 1974. Northeastern archaeology: Past and future directions. *Annual Review of Anthropology* 3: 385–413.

Fowler, M. R. 1969. The Cahokia Site, in M. L. Fowler, ed., *Explorations into Cahokia Archaeology*, pp. 1–30. Illinois Archaeological Survey, Bulletin 7.

Fowler, M. R. 1974. Cahokia: Ancient capital of the Midwest. *Addison-Wesley Module in Anthropology* 48.

Fowler, M. R. 1978. Cahokia and the American Bottom: Settlement archaeology. B. Smith, ed., *Mississippian Settlement Patterns*, pp. 455–78. New York: Academic Press.

Frank, A. G. 1969. *Latin America: Underdevelopment or Revolution?* New York: Monthly Review.

Frankenstein, S. and Rowlands, M. J. 1978. The internal structure and regional context of Early Iron Age society in South-Western Germany. *Bulletin of the Institute of Archaeology* 15: 73–112.

Frankfort, H. 1948. *Kingship and the Gods*. Chicago, Oriental Institute.

Freidel, D. A. 1981. The political economics of residential dispersion among the Lowland Maya, in W. Ashmore, ed., *Lowland Maya Settlement Patterns* (School of American Research Advanced Seminar Series) pp. 371–82. Albuquerque, University of New Mexico Press.

Freidel, D. A. 1986. Terminal Classic Lowland Maya: successes, failures, and aftermaths, in J. A. Sabloff and E. W. Andrews V, eds., *Late Lowland Maya Civilization: Classic to Postclassic* (School of American Research Advanced Seminar Series). Albuquerque, University of New Mexico Press.

French, M. H. 1970. *Observations on the Goat*. (Studies no 80). Rome: Food and Agriculture Organization of the United Nations.

Fried, M. H. 1960. On the evolution of social stratification and the state, in S. Diamond, ed., *Culture in History*, pp. 713–31. New York: Columbia University Press.

Fried, M. H. 1967. *The Evolution of Political Society: An Essay in Political Anthropology*. New York: Random House.

Friedman, J. 1975. Tribes, states, and transformations, in M. Bloch, ed., *Marxist Analyses and Social Anthropology* (Association of Social Anthropology Studies, No. 2), pp. 161–202. New York: Wiley.

Friedman, J. and Rowlands, M. J. 1978. Notes toward an epigenetic model of the evolution of 'civilisation,' in J. Friedman and M. J. Rowlands, eds., *The Evolution of Social Systems*, pp. 201–76. Pittsburgh: University of Pittsburgh Press.

Fry, R. E. 1979. The economics of pottery at Tikal, Guatemala: models of exchange for serving vessels. *American Antiquity* 44 (3): 494–512.

Fry, R. E. 1980. Models of exchange for major shape classes of Lowland Maya pottery, in R. E. Fry, ed., *Models and Methods in Regional Exchange*, pp. 3–18. (SAA Papers No. 1). Washington: Society for American Archaeology.

Fry, R. E. 1981. Pottery production–distribution systems in the southern Maya Lowlands, in H. Howard and E. L. Morris, eds., *Production and Distribution: A Ceramic Viewpoint*. Oxford, BAR International Series 120.

Fry, R. E. and Cox, S. 1974. The structure of ceramic exchange at Tikal, Guatemala. *World Archaeology* 6 (2): 209–25.

Gall, P. L. and Saxe, A. A. 1977. The ecological evolution of culture: The state as predator in succession theory, in T. K. Earle and J. E. Ericson, eds., *Exchange Systems in Prehistory*, pp. 255–68. New York: Academic.

Galvin, K. F. 1980. The Ashara, Syria Livestock Survey. Unpublished field journals.

Galvin, K. F. 1981. *Early State Economic Organization and the Role of Specialized Pastoralism*. Ann Arbor: University Microfilms.

Gamble, C. 1982. Leadership and 'surplus' production, in C. Renfrew and S. Shennan, eds., *Ranking, Resources and Exchange: Aspects of the Archaeology of Early European Society*, pp. 100–05. Cambridge: Cambridge University Press.

García Sánchez, M. and Spahni, J. C. 1959. Sepulcros megalíticos de la region de Gorafe (Granada). *Archivo de Prehistoria Levantina* 8: 43–113.

Garcilaso de la Vega (Suarez de Figeroa, G.) 1962. *The Florida of the Inca*. J. G. and J. J. Varner, trans. (third printing). Austin: University of Texas Press. [orig. 1605].

Garibay K., A. 1969. Vocabulario, in Bernardino de Sahagun, *Historia General de las Cosas de Nueva España*, A. Garibay, ed., vol. 4, pp. 319–73. México: Porrua.

Geiger, F. 1973. El sureste español y los problemas de la aridez. *Revista de Geografía* 7: 166–209.

Gelb, I. J. 1967. The growth of a herd of cattle in ten years. *Journal of Cuneiform Studies*. 21: 64–69.

Gentleman of Elvas 1866. Discovery of Florida, in B. Smith, trans., *Narratives of the Career of Hernando de Soto . . .*, pp. 5–228. [reprint 1968, Gainesville, Florida: Palmetto Books]. [orig. 1557].

Geschiere, P. 1981. *Village Communities and the State*. London, Routledge Kegan Paul.

Gibbons, E. 1964. *Stalking the Blue-Eyed Scallop*. New York: David McKay Company.

Gibson, C. 1964. *The Aztecs under Spanish Rule*. Stanford: Stanford University Press.

Gibson, C. 1971. Structure of the Aztec empire, in G. F. Ekholm and I. Bernal, eds., *Archaeology of Northern Mesoamerica Part 1*, pp. 376–94. (Handbook of Middle American Indians, Vol. 10.) Austin: University of Texas Press.

Gilman, A. 1975. The later prehistory of Tangier, Morocco. *American School of Prehistoric Research, Bulletin* 29.

Gilman, A. 1976. Bronze Age dynamics in southeast Spain. *Dialectical Anthropology* 1: 307–19.

Gilman, A. 1981. The development of social stratification in Bronze Age Europe. *Current Anthropology* 22. 1–23.

Gilman, A. in press. The Iberian Peninsula, 6000–1500 B.C., in R. W. Ehrich, ed., *Chronologies in Old World Archaeology*, 2nd ed. Chicago: University of Chicago Press.

Gilman, A. and Thornes, J. B. 1984. *Land-Use and Prehistory in South-East Spain*. London: George Allen & Unwin.

Gimbutas, M. 1965. *Bronze Age Cultures in Central and Eastern Europe*. The Hague: Mouton.

Goldman, I. 1970. *Ancient Polynesian Society*. Chicago: University of Chicago Press.

Goldmann, K. 1980/81. Die mitteleuropäische Schwertenentwicklung und die chronologie der Bronzezeit Europas. *Acta praehistorica et archaeologica 11/12*.

Gonçalves, V. 1980. Cerro do castelo de Santa Justa (Alcoutim), excavações de 1979: extractos do caderno de campo. *Clio-Revista do Centro de Historia da Universidade de Lisboa* 2: 133–39.

González Gómez, C., López González, J. de D. and Domingo García, M. 1981. University of Granada radiocarbon dates I. *Radiocarbon* 24: 217–21.

Goody, J. 1971. *Technology, Tradition and the State in West Africa*. London: Oxford University Press.

Gräslund, B. 1980. Climatic Fluctuations in the Early Subboreal Period: A Preliminary Discussion. *Striae*.

Graziano, L. 1975. *A Conceptual Framework for the Study of Clientelism*. (Western Societies Program Occasional Paper No. 2.) Ithaca, New York: Cornell University Center for International Studies.

Green, T. J. and Munson, C. A. 1978. Mississippian settlement patterns in southwestern Indiana, in B. Smith, ed., *Mississippian Settlement Patterns*, pp. 293–330. New York: Academic Press.

Greenberg, J. H. 1966. *The Languages of Africa*. The Hague, Mouton.

Greenland, D. J. 1975. Bringing the Green Revolution to the shifting cultivator. *Science* 190: 841–44.

Guaman Poma de Ayala, F. 1936. *Nueva Corónica y Buen Gobierno*. Paris: Institut d'Ethnologie. [orig. 1613].

Guzmán, E. 1938. Un manuscrito de la colección Boturini que trata de los antiguos señores de Teotihuacán. *Ethnos* 3: 89–103.

Hachmann, R. 1957. *Die frühe Bronzezeit im westlichen Ostseegebiet und ihre mittel- und südosteuropäischen Beziehungen*. Atlas der Urgeschichte 6. Hamburg.

Hagstrum, M. 1984. The technology of ceramic production of Huanca and Inka wares from the Yanamarca Valley, Peru. *Ceramic Notes* 3 [in press].

Halstead, P. and O'Shea, J. 1982. A friend in need is a friend indeed: Social storage and the origins of social ranking, in C. Renfrew and S. Shennan, eds., *Ranking, Resource and Exchange*, pp. 92–99. Cambridge: Cambridge University Press.

Hammond, N. 1973. Models for Maya trade, in C. Renfrew, ed., *The Explanation of Culture Change*, pp. 601–07. Pittsburgh: University of Pittsburgh Press.

Hammond, N. 1975. *Lubaantun, A Classic Maya Realm*. (Peabody Museum Monographs, no. 2.) Cambridge: Harvard University.

Hammond, N. 1982. *Ancient Maya Civilization*. New Brunswick, New Jersey, Rutgers University Press.

Hammond, N., Harbottle, G. and Gazard, T. 1976. Neutron activation and statistical analysis of Maya ceramics and clays from Lubaantun, Belize. *Archaeometry* 18 (2): 147–68.

Hankey, V. and Warren, P. 1974. The Absolute Chronology of the Aegean Late Bronze Age. *Bulletin of the Institute of Classical Studies* 21: 142–52.

Hänsel, B. 1977. Zur historischen Bedeutung der Theisszone im das 16. Jahrhundert. In *Jahresbericht des Institut für Vorgeschichte der Universität Frankfurt a. M.* Munich.

Hänsel, B. 1982. Südosteuropa zwischen 1600 und 1000 v. Chr, in *Südosteuropa zwischen 1600 und 1000 v. Chr.* Berlin.

Harding, A. F. 1983. The Bronze Age in Central and Eastern Europe: Advances and Prospects. *Advances in World Archaeology* 2: 1–50.

Harding, A. F. 1984. *The Myceneans and Europe*. New York: Academic Press.

Harding, H. and Hughes-Brock, H. 1974. Amber in the Mycenean World. *Annual of British School of Archaeology at Athens* 69: 145–72.

Harris, M. 1979. *Cultural Materialism*. New York, Random House.

Harrison, P. D. and Turner II, B. L., eds. 1978. *Pre-Hispanic Maya Agriculture*. Albuquerque: University of New Mexico Press.

Harrison, R. J. 1974. A reconsideration of the Iberian background to Beaker metallurgy. *Palaeohistoria* 16: 63–105.

Harrison, R. J. 1977. The Bell Beaker cultures of Spain and Portugal. *American School of Prehistoric Research, Bulletin* 35.

Harrison, R. J. 1980. *The Beaker Folk: Copper Age Archaeology in Western Europe*. London: Thames & Hudson.

Harrison, R. J. 1984. Nuevas bases para el estudio de la paleo-economía de la Edad del Bronce en el norte de España. *Scripta Praehistorica Francisco Jorda Oblata*, pp. 287–315.

Harrison, R. J., Bübner, T., and Hibbs, V. A. 1976. The Beaker pottery from El Acebuchal, Carmona (Prov. Sevilla). *Madrider Mitteilungen* 17: 79–141.

Harrison, R. J. and Gilman, A. 1977. Trade in the second and third millennia B.C. between the Maghreb and Iberia, in V. Markotic, ed., *Ancient Europe and the Mediterranean: Studies in Honour of Hugh Hencken*, pp. 90–104. Warminster, Wilts: Aris & Charles.

Haselgrove, C. 1982. Wealth, prestige, and power: The dynamics of late iron age political centralisation in south-east England, in C. Renfrew and S. Shennan, eds., *Ranking, Resource and Exchange*, pp. 79–88. Cambridge: Cambridge University Press.

Hassig, R. 1982. Tenochtitlan: the economic and political reorganization of an urban system. *Comparative Urban Research* 9: 39–49.

Hassig, R. 1985. *Trade, Tribute and Transportation: The Sixteenth-Century Political Economy of the Valley of Mexico*. Norman: University of Oklahoma Press.

Hastorf, C. 1983. *Prehistoric Agricultural Intensification and Political Development in the Jauja Region of Central Peru*. Ph.D. dissertation, Department of Anthropology, University of California, Los Angeles.

Hatch, J. W. and Wiley, P. P. 1974. Stature and status in Dallas society. *Tennessee Archaeologist* 30: 108–31.

Haviland, W. A. 1970. Guatemala and Mesoamerican urbanism. *World Archaeology* 2 (1): 186–97.

Haviland, W. A. 1974. Occupational specialization at Tikal, Guatemala: stoneworking—monument carving. *American Antiquity* 39 (3): 494–96.

Haviland, W. A. 1981. Dower houses and minor centers at Tikal, Guatemala: An investigation into the identification of valid units in settlement hierarchies, in W. Ashmore, ed., *Lowland Maya Settlement Patterns* (School of American Research Advanced Seminar Series) pp. 89–117. Albuquerque, University of New Mexico Press.

Hawkes, Chr. 1977. Zur Wessex-Kultur. *Jahresbericht des Institut für Vorgeschichte der Universität Frankfurt a.M.* Munich.

Hedeager, L. and Kristiansen, K. 1981. Bendstrup — en fyrstegrav fra den romeske jernalder, dens sociale og historiske miljø. (Bendstrup — a Princely Grave from the Early Roman Iron Age: Its Social and Historical Context) *KUML 1981*.

Hedeager, L. and Kristiansen, K. 1985. Krig og samfund i Danmarks oldtid. *Den jyske historiker*.

Helbaek, H. 1964. Early Hassunan vegetation at es-Sawwan near Samarra. *Sumer* 20: 45–48.

Helck, W. 1977. Agypten und die Agäis im 16. Jahrhundert v. Chr. *Jahresbericht des Institut für Vorgeschichte der Universität Frankfurt a.M.* Munich.

Helms, M. 1981. Precious metals and politics: style and ideology in the Intermediate Area and Peru. *Journal of Latin American Lore* 7: 215–37.

Heyderbrand, W. V. 1973. *Hospital Bureaucracy.* New York: Dunellen.

Hicks, F. 1981. Merchant Barrios and the Balance of Trade in Pre-hispanic Mesoamerica. Paper presented at the 80th Annual Meeting of the American Anthropological Association, Los Angeles, California.

Hicks, F. 1982a. Texcoco in the early 16th century: The state, the city and the *calpolli. American Ethnologist* 9: 320–49.

Hicks, F. 1982b. Acolman and Tepechpan: Tribute and Market in the Aztec heartland. Paper presented at the 44th International Congress of Americanists, Manchester, England.

Hicks, F. n.d.a. The political and economic organization of pre-hispanic central Mexico, in R. Spores, ed., *Colonial Ethnohistory.* (Handbook of Middle American Indians, Supplement) Austin: University of Texas Press [in press].

Hicks, F. n.d.b. First steps toward a market-integrated economy in Aztec Mexico, in H. J. M. Claessen, ed., *Early State Dynamics.* Leiden: E. J. Brill [in press].

Hill, J. (ed.). 1977. *Explanation of Prehistoric Change.* Albuquerque: University of New Mexico Press.

Hilzheimer, M. 1941. *Animal Remains from Tell Asmar.* (Studies in Ancient Civilization No. 20). Chicago: Oriental Institute of Chicago.

Hirano, Kunio 1962. Taika zendai no shakai kozo [Pre-Taika social organization]. *Iwanami Koza Nihon Rekishi 2: Kodai* 2: 81–122. Tokyo, Iwanami Shoten.

Hirano, Kunio 1983. *Be* entry in *Kodansha Encyclopedia of Japan.* Tokyo, Kodansha.

Hirsch, S. 1933. *Sheep and Goats in Palestine.* Tel Aviv: Palestine Economic Society.

Hirth, K. G. 1984. Trade and Society in Late Formative Morelos, in K. G. Hirth, ed., *Trade and Exchange in Early Mesoamerica,* pp. 125–46. Albuquerque: University of New Mexico Press.

Hitchins, P. 1978. Technical studies on materials from Yayoi period Japan: their role in archaeological interpretation. *Asian Perspectives 1976* 19.1: 156–71.

Hodder, I. R. 1974. Regression analysis of some trade and marketing patterns. *World Archaeology* 6 (1): 172–89.

Hodder, I. R. 1980. Trade and exchange: Definitions, identification and function. In R. E. Fry, ed., Models and Methods in Regional Exchange, pp. 151–55. (SAA Papers No. 1). Washington: Society for American Archaeology.

Hodder, I. R. (ed.) 1982. *Symbolic and Structural Archaeology.* Cambridge: Cambridge University Press.

Hodder, I. R. and Orton, C. R. 1976. *Spatial Analysis in Archaeology.* Cambridge, Cambridge University Press.

Hodge, M. G. 1984. *Aztec City-States.* (Memoirs, No. 18). Ann Arbor: The University of Michigan Museum of Anthropology.

Hodges, R. 1982. The evolution of gateway communities: Their socio-economic implications, in C. Renfrew and S. Shennan, eds., *Ranking, Resource and Exchange: Aspects of the Archaeology of Early European Society.* Pp. 117–23. Cambridge: Cambridge University Press.

Hole, F. 1966. Investigating the origins of Mesopotamian civilization. *Science* 153: 605–11.

Hole, F., Flannery, K. V. and Neeley, J. A. 1969. *The Prehistory and Human Ecology of the Deh Luran Plain.* (Memoir No. 1). Ann Arbor: University of Michigan Museum of Anthropology.

Holste, F. 1953. *Die Bronzezeit in Südund Westdeutschland.* Handbuch der Urgeschichte Deutschlands 1. Berlin.

Hopf, M. 1981. Pflänziche Reste aus Zambujal, in E. Sangmeister and H. Schubart (1981), pp. 315–40.

Hopf, M. and Muñoz, A. M. 1974. Neolitische Pflanzenreste aus der Höhle Los Murcielagos bei Zuheros (Prov. Córdoba). *Madrider Mitteilungen* 15: 9–27.

Hopf, M. and Pellicer Catalán, M. 1970. Neolithische Getreidefunde in der Höhle von Nerja. *Madrider Mitteilungen* 11: 18–34.

Hopkins, D. 1984. Agrarian reform and the diversification of small-holdings: An Andean case study. Paper presented at the 83rd Annual Meeting of the American Anthropological Association, Denver, Colorado.

Horton, R. 1971. Stateless societies in the history of West Africa, in J. R. Ajayi and M. Crowder, eds., *History of West Africa, Volume I.* London: Longmans.

Howe, E. 1983. Metals provenientes del alto Mantaro: un analisis preliminar. Report submitted to the Instituto Nacional de Cultura, Lima.

Hunt, E. 1977. *The Transformation of the Hummingbird: Cultural Roots of a Zinacantecan Mythical Poem.* Ithaca: Cornell University Press.

Hunt, T. F. 1911. *The Cereals in America.* New York: Grange Judd Co.

Hurault, J. 1962. *La Structure Sociale des Bamileke.* Paris, Mouton.

Hüttel, H. G. 1977. Altbronzezeitliche Pferdetrensen. *Jahresbericht des Institut für Vorgeschichte der Universität Frankfurt a.M.* Munich.

Hüttel, H. G. 1982. Zur Abkunft des danubischen Pferd-Wagen. Komplexes der Altbronzezeit. In *Südosteuropa zwischen 1600 und 1000 v. Chr.*

Inoue, M. 1970. *Taika Kaishin* [The Taika Reforms]. Tokyo: Kobundo Shobo.

Isbell, W. 1978. Environmental perturbations and the origin of the Andean state. In C. L. Redman et al., eds., *Social Archeology: Beyond Subsistence and Dating,* pp. 303–13. New York: Academic Press.

Jacob-Friesen, G. 1970. Skjerne und Egemose, Wagenteile südlicher Provenienz in Skandinavischen Funden. *Acta Archaeologica* XL. Copenhagen.

Jacobs, J. 1969. *The Economy of Cities.* New York: Random House.

Jacobs, J. 1984. *Cities and the Wealth of Nations: Principles of economic life.* New York: Random House.

Jankovskaya, N. 1969. Some problems of the economy of the Assyrian Empire, in I. M. Diakonov, ed., *Ancient Mesopotamia.* Moscow: Nauka.

Jensen, J. 1982. *The Prehistory of Denmark.* Methuen.

Jensen, J. 1984. Kedelvognen fra Skallerup. *Nationalmuseets Arbejdsmark:* 138–47.

Jidaibetsu Kokugo Daijiten [Great Dictionary of Japanese by Chronological Period]. 1968. Tokyo: Jodaigo jiten henshu iinkai.

Jodin, A. 1959. Nouveaux documents sur la civilisation du vase campaniforme au Maroc. *XVI. Congrès Préhistorique de France, Monaco,* pp. 675–87.

Johansen, Ø. 1981. *Metallfunnene i Østnorsk bronsealder.* Kultur-tilknytning og forutsetninger for en marginalekspansion. (English Summary). Universitets Oldsaksamlings Skrifter, Ny Rekke nr. 4. Oslo.

Johansen, Ø. 1981. Bronsealderproblemer – en teori om melleim-haadler-virksomhed, in *Varia 9.* Oslo: Universitets Oldsaksamling.

Johnson, A., and Earle, T. n.d. *The Evolution of the Human Society.* Palo Alto: Stanford University Press [in press].

Johnson, G. A. 1973. *Local Exchange and Early State Development in Southwestern Iran* (Anthropological Papers, No. 51). Ann Arbor: The University of Michigan Museum of Anthropology.

Johnson, G. A. 1978. Information sources and the development of decision-making organizations, in C. Redman et al., *Social*

Archaeology. New York, Academic Press.

Jørgensen, Bender, L., Munksgård, E. and Nielsen, K-H. 1982. Melhøj-fundet. En hidtil upåagtet parallel til Skrydstrupfundet. (Melhøj – an unheeded Parallel to the Skrydstrup Find). *Aarbøger for Nordisk Oldkyndighed og Historie.*

Junghans, S., Sangmeister, E. and Schröder, M. 1960. Metallanalysen kupferzeitlicher und frühbronzezeitlicher Bodenfunde aus Europa. *Studien zu den Anfängen der Metallurgie* 1.

Junghans, S., Sangmeister, E. and Schröder, M. 1968–1974. Kupfer und Bronze in der frühen Metallzeit Europas. *Studien zu den Anfängen der Metallurgie* 2.

Kalb, P. 1981. Zur relativen Chronologie portugiesischer Megalithgräber. *Madrider Mitteilungen* 23: 55–77.

Kamada, M. 1984. Oken to bemin sei [Kingly authority and the *be* system]. *Koza Nihon Rekishi I: Genshi, Kodai* 1: 233–68.

Kanaseki, H., and Sahara, M. 1978. The Yayoi period. *Asian Perspectives 1976* 19.1: 15–26.

Kashiwara 1983. *Kashiwara-shi Soga Iseki* [Soga Site, Kashiwara City]. Nara, Nara Kenritsu Kashiwara Kokogaku Kenkyusho.

Katz, F. 1966. *Situación Social y Económica de los Aztecas Durante los Siglos XV y XVI.* México: Universidad Nacional Autónoma de México, Instituto de Investigaciones Históricas.

Kellogg, S. 1983. The Cultural Survival of Indians in Central Mexico, 1521–1600: A reinterpretation. Paper presented at the Southwestern Social Science meetings/Southwestern Historical Association meetings, Houston, Texas.

Kenyon, K., 1960 and 1964. *Excavations at Jericho.* Vols. 1 and 2. Jerusalem: British School of Archaeology.

Kidder Jr., J. E. 1966. *Japan Before Buddhism.* London, Thames and Hudson; New York, Frederick A. Praeger.

Kiley, Cornelius J. 1973. State and dynasty in archaic Yamato. *Journal of Asian Studies* 23.1: 25–49.

Kiley, Cornelius J. 1977. *Uji* and *kabane* in ancient Japan. *Monumenta Nipponica* 32: 365–76.

Kiley, Cornelius J. 1983. Uji entry in the *Kodansha Encyclopedia of Japan.* Tokyo, Kodansha.

King, J. 1784. *A Voyage to the Pacific Ocean,* Vol. III. Dublin, H. Chamberlaine.

Kirch, P. 1982. Advances in Polynesian prehistory: three decades in review, in F. Wendorf and A. E. Close, eds., *Advances in World Archaeology,* vol. 1, pp. 51–97. New York, Academic Press.

Kirkbride, D. 1974. Umm Dabaghiyah: a trading outpost? *Iraq* 36: 85–92.

Kitano, K. 1976. *Kawachi Nonaka Kofun no Kenkyu* [Investigations of the Nonaka Tomb in Kawachi]. Kyoto, Rinsen Shoten.

Kleinberg, Jill 1970. *The Organization and Functions of the be in Pre-Taika Japan.* Unpublished M.A. Thesis, Center for Japanese Studies, University of Michigan.

Kneberg, M. 1959. Engraved shell gorgets and their associations. *Tennessee Archaeologist* 15 (1): 1–39.

Kodansha Encyclopedia of Japan (in English). 1983. Tokyo, Kodansha.

Kohl, P. 1975. The archaeology of trade. *Dialectical Anthropology* 1: 43–50.

Kohl, P. 1978. The balance of trade in Southwestern Asia in the mid-third millennium B.C. *Current Anthropology* 19: 463–92.

Kokushi Daijiten [Great Encyclopedia of National History]. 1979. Tokyo, Yoshikawa Kobunkan.

Kottak, C. P. 1972. Ecological variables in the origin and evolution of African states: the Buganda example. *Comparative Studies in Society and History* 14: 351–80.

Kristiansen, K. 1980. Besiedlung, Wirtschaftsstrategie in der Bronzezeit Dänemarks. *Praehistorische Zeitschrift* 55. Band, Heft 1, 1–37.

Kristiansen, K. 1981. Economic models for Bronze Age Scandinavia – Towards an integrated approach, in A. Sheridan and G. Bailey, eds., *Economic Archaeology: Towards an integration of ecological and social approaches,* pp. 239–303. (International Series 96.) Oxford: British Archaeological Reports.

Kristiansen, K. 1982. The formation of tribal systems in later European prehistory: Northern Europe, 4000–500 B.C., in C. Renfrew, M. J. Rowlands, B. A. Segraves, eds., *Theory and Explanation in Archaeology,* pp. 241–80. New York: Academic.

Kristiansen, K. 1984a. Ideology and Material Culture – an Archaeological Perspective, in M. Spriggs, ed., in *Marxist Perspectives in Archaeology,* pp. 72–100. Cambridge: Cambridge University Press.

Kristiansen, K. 1984b. Krieger und Häuptlinge in der Bronzezeit Dänemarks. Ein Beitrag zur Geschichte des bronzezeitlichen Schwertes. *Jahrbuch des Römisch–Germanischen Zentralmuseums* 31.

Kristiansen, K. in press. Center and Periphery in Bronze Age Scandinavia. Manuscript.

Kubach, W. 1977. Zum Beginn der bronzezeitlichen Hügelgräberkultur in Süddeutschland. *Jahresbericht des Institut für Vorgeschichte der Universität Frankfurt a.M.* Munich.

Kubler, G. 1943. The cycle of life and death in metropolitan Aztec sculpture. *Gazette des Beaux Arts* 23: 257–68.

Kurtz, D. V. 1978. The legitimation of the Aztec state, in H. J. M. Claessen and P. Skalnik, eds., *The Early State,* pp. 169–89. The Hague: Mouton.

Kurtz, D. V. 1981. The legitimation of early inchoate states, in H. J. M. Claessen and P. Skalnik, eds., *The Study of the State,* pp. 177–200. The Hague: Mouton.

Lafferty, R. 1973. *An analysis of Prehistoric Southeastern Fortifications.* Unpublished M.A. thesis, Department of Anthropology, Southern Illinois University, Carbondale.

Lafferty, R. 1977. *The Evolution of Mississippian Settlement Patterns and Exploitative technology in the Black Bottom of Southern Illinois.* Unpublished Ph.D. dissertation, Department of Anthropology, Southern Illinois University, Carbondale.

LaLone, D. 1982. The Inka as a nonmarket economy: supply on command versus supply and demand, in J. Ericson and T. Earle, eds., *Contexts for Prehistoric Exchange,* pp. 291–316. New York, Academic Press.

Lamberg-Karlovsky, C. C. 1975. Third Millennium modes of exchange and modes of production, in C. C. Lamberg-Karlovsky and J. Sabloff, eds., *Ancient Civilization and Trade,* pp. 341–68. Albuquerque: University of New Mexico Press.

Larson, L. H. 1980. *Aboriginal Subsistence Technology on the Southeastern Coastal Plain during the Late Prehistoric Period.* Gainesville: University Presses of Florida.

Lautensach, H. 1964. *Iberische Halbinsel.* Munich: Keysersche Verlagsbuchhandlung.

Lawson, J. 1709. *A New Voyage to Carolina* . . . London. [reprint, 1966, University Microfilms, March of America Facsimile Series, Number 35].

LeBlanc, C. 1981. *Late prehistoric Huanca settlement patterns in the Yanamarca Valley, Peru.* Ph.D. dissertation, Department of Anthropology, University of California, Los Angeles.

Lechtman, H. 1976. A metallurgical survey in the Peruvian Andes. *Journal of Field Archaeology* 3: 1–42.

Lechtman, H. 1979. Issues in Andean metallurgy, in E. Benson, ed., *Pre-Columbian Metallurgy of South America.* Washington: Dumbarton Oaks.

Lechtman, H. 1984. Andean value systems and the development of prehistoric Metallurgy. *Technology and Culture* 25: 1–36.

Lees, S. H. and Bates, D. G. 1974. The origins of specialized nomadic pastoralism: a systemic model. *American Antiquity* 39: 187–93.

Leisner, G. and Leisner, V. 1943. Die Megalithgräber der iberischen

Halbinsel. I: Der Suden. *Römisch-Germanische Forschungen* 17.

Leisner, G. and Leisner, V. 1951. *Antas do Concelho de Reguengos de Monsaraz*. Lisbon: Instituto para a Alta Cultura.

Leisner, G. and Leisner, V. 1956. Die Megalithgräber der Iberischen Halbinsel: Der Westen. *Madrider Forschungen* 1 (1).

Leisner, G. and Leisner, V. 1959. Die Megalithgräber der Iberischen Halbinsel: Der Westen. *Madrider Forschungen* 1 (2).

Leisner, V. 1965. Die Megalithgräber der Iberischen Halbinsel: Der Westen. *Madrider Forschungen* 1 (3).

Lenski, G. and Lenski, J. 1978. *Human Societies: An Introduction to Macrosociology*. New York: McGraw-Hill.

Leonard, W. H. and Martin, J. H. 1963. *Cereal Crops*. New York: MacMillan and Co.

Le Page du Pratz, A. S. 1972. *The History of Louisiana* . . . Baton Rouge: Claitor Publishing Division. [Translation, orig. 1758].

LeVine, T. 1985. *Inka administration of the central Andes*. Ph.D. dissertation, Archaeology Program, University of California, Los Angeles (in preparation).

Lewis, R. B. 1974. Mississippian Exploitative Strategies: a Southeast Missouri Example. *Missouri Archaeological Society, Research Series* 11.

Littauer, M. A. and Crouwell, J. H. 1979. *Wheeled Vehicles and Ridden Animals in the Ancient Near East*. Leiden.

Loewe, M. 1980. Wooden documents from China and Japan: recent finds and their value. *Modern Asian Studies* 14.1: 159–62.

Lomborg, E. 1964. Hvilshøjkvindens hår. *SKALK* nr. 2.

Lomborg, E. 1973. *Die Flintdolche Dänemarks*. Nordiske Fortidsminder. Serie B – in quarto. Bind 1. Copenhagen.

Lopez A., F., Nieto C., R. and Cobean, R. H. 1981. La Producción de Obsidiana en la Sierra de las Navajas, Hidalgo. Paper presented at the symposium 'La Obsidiana en Mesoamérica,' Centro Regional Hidalgo, Instituto Nacional de Antropología e Historia.

Lothrop, S. K. 1938. Inka treasure as depicted by Spanish historians. *Frederick Webb Hodge Anniversary Publication Fund* 2. Los Angeles: Southwest Museum.

Lumbreras, L. 1974. *The Peoples and Cultures of Ancient Peru*, B. Meggers, trans. Washington D.C., Smithsonian.

Ma, C. 1980. The splendor of ancient Chinese bronzes, in W. Fong, ed., *The Great Bronze Age of China*, pp. 1–19. New York: The Metropolitan Museum of Art and Alfred A. Knopf.

McBryde, F. W. 1947. *Cultural and Historical Geography of Southwest Guatemala*. Washington, D.C.: Smithsonian Institution, Institute of Social Anthropology 4.

McCoy, P. C. 1977. The Mauna Kea adz quarry project: a summary of the 1975 field investigations. *Journal of Polynesian Society* 86: 223–44.

MacGaffey, W. 1970. The religious commissions of the BaKongo. *Man* NS vol V: 27–38.

Malinowski, B. 1922. *Argonauts of the Western Pacific*. London: Routledge & Kegan Paul.

Mallart Guimera, L. 1981. *Ni Dos ni Ventre*. Namterre, Laboratoire d'ethnologie.

Mallowan, M. E. L. 1965. *Early Mesopotamia and Iran*. New York: McGraw-Hill.

Malmer, M. P. 1963. *Metodproblem inom järnålderns konsthistoria*. Acta Arch. Lundensia. Series in 8°. Lund.

Malmer, M. P. 1981. *A Chronological Study of North European Rock Art*. Antikvariska Serien 32, Stockholm.

Malo, D. 1951. Hawaiian antiquities. *Bernice P. Bishop Museum Special Publication* 2 (2nd ed.). [orig. 1898].

Marcus, J. 1976. *Emblem and State in the Classic Maya Lowlands: An Epigraphic Approach to Territorial Organization*. Washington, Dumbarton Oaks.

Marcus, J. 1983a. Lowland Maya archaeology at the crossroads. *American Antiquity* 48 (3): 454–88.

Marcus, J. 1983b. On the nature of the Mesoamerican city, in, E. Z. Vogt and R. M. Leventhal, *Prehistoric Settlement Patterns: Essays in Honor of Gordon R. Willey*, Albuquerque and Cambridge, MA: University of New Mexico Press and Peabody Museum.

Marquina, I. 1960. *El Templo Mayor de México*. México: Instituto Nacional de Antropología e Historia.

Martin, A. C., Zim, H. S. and Nelson, A. L. 1951. *American Wildlife and Plants: a Guide to Wildlife Food Habits*. New York: McGraw-Hill. [Dover Reprint 1961.]

Marx, K. 1975a. The Eighteenth Brumaire of Louis Bonaparte, in *Karl Marx and Frederick Engels, Selected Works*, pp. 96–179. Moscow: Progress Publishers. [orig. 1852].

Marx, K. 1975b. Wages, Price and Profit, in *Karl Marx and Frederick Engels, Selected Works*, pp. 185–226. Moscow: Progress Publishers. [orig. 1865.]

Mason, R. 1980. *Economic and Social Organization of an Aztec Provincial Center: Archaeological research at Coatlan Viejo, Morelos, Mexico*. Ph.D. dissertation, Department of Anthropology, The University of Texas at Austin.

Matheny, R. T. 1976. Maya lowland hydraulic systems. *Science*, 193: 639–46.

Mathers, C. 1984. Beyond the grave: the context and wider implications of mortuary practice in south-eastern Spain, in T. F. C. Blagg, et al., eds., *Papers in Iberian Archaeology*, pp. 13–46. Oxford: BAR International Series 193.

Matos Moctezuma, E., ed. 1982. *El Templo Mayor: Excavaciones y estudios*. México: Instituto Nacional de Antropología e Historia.

Meigs, P. 1966. Geography of coastal deserts. *Arid Zone Research* 28.

Meillassoux, C. 1960. Essai d'interpretation du phénomène économique dans les sociétés traditionelles d'autosubsistence. *Cahiers d'Études Africaines* 4.

Meillassoux, C. 1971. Introduction, in C. Meillassoux, ed., *The Development of Indigenous Trade and Markets in West Africa*, pp. 49–86. London: Oxford University Press.

Meillassoux, C. 1981. *Maidens, Meal and Money Capitalism and the Domestic Economy*. Cambridge, Cambridge University Press.

Mellaart, J. 1965. *Earliest Civilizations of the Near East*. New York: McGraw-Hill.

Melville, E. 1983. *The Pastoral Economy and Environmental Degradation in Highland Central Mexico, 1530–1600*. Ph.D. dissertation, Department of Anthropology, The University of Michigan.

Mergelina, C. de. 1942. La estación arqueológica de Montefrío (Granada). I: Los dólmenes. *Boletin de Arte y Arqueología, Universidad de Valladolid* 8: 33–106.

Merquior, J. 1979. *The Veil and the Mask: Essays in Culture and Ideology*. London, Routledge & Kegan Paul.

Miaffo, D. 1977. *Rôle sociale de l'Autopsie publique traditionelle chez les Bamileke* Memoire de DES. Departement de Sociologie, Université de Yaoundé, Cameroun. Mimeo.

Millon, R. 1973. *Urbanization at Teotihuacan, Mexico: The Teotihuacan Map*. Austin: University of Texas Press.

Milner, G. R. 1982. *Measuring Prehistoric Levels of Health: a Study of Mississippian Period skeletal Remains from the American Bottom, Illinois*. Ph.D. dissertation, Department of Anthropology, Northwestern University.

Milner, G. R. 1983. *The Turner and DeMange Sites*. (Assisted by J. A. Williams). American Bottom Archaeology. FAI-270 Site Reports. Urbana: For the Illinois Department of Transportation by the University of Illinois Press.

Milner, G. R. 1984a. *The Julien Site*. (Assisted by J. A. Williams) American Bottom Archaeology. FAI-270 Site Reports. Urbana:

For the Illinois Department of Transportation by the University of Illinois Press.

Milner, G. R. 1984b. Social and Temporal Implications of Variation among American Bottom Mississippian Cemeteries. *American Antiquity* 49 (3): 468–89.

Moholy-Nagy, H. 1975. Obsidian at Tikal, Guatemala. *Actas del XLI Congreso Internacional Americanistas, Mexico* 1: 511–18.

Moholy-Nagy, H., Asaro, F. and Stross, F. 1984. Tikal obsidian: sources and typology. *American Antiquity* 49 (1): 104–17.

Monzón, A. 1949. *El Capulli en la Organización Social de los Tenochca.* (Publicaciones del Instituto de Historia, Ira. ser., num. 14). México: Universidad Nacional Autónoma de México.

Moore, S. F. 1958. *Power and Property in Inka Peru.* New York, Columbia University Press.

Moreno, M. M. 1962. *La Organización Política y Social de Los Aztecas.* México: Instituto Nacional de Antropología e Historia.

Morgan, W. N. 1980. *Prehistoric Architecture in the Eastern United States.* Cambridge: MIT Press.

Morris, C. 1967. *Storage in Tawantisuyu.* Ph.D. dissertation, Department of Anthropology, University of Chicago.

Morris, C. 1974. Reconstructing patterns of non-agricultural production in the Inka economy, in C. Moore, ed., *The Reconstruction of Complex Societies,* pp. 49–68. Cambridge, MA. American School of Oriental Research.

Morúa, M. 1946. *Historica y Genealogía Real de Los Reyes Inka,* C. Bayle, ed. Madrid: Comsejo Superior de Investigaciones Científices, Instituto Santo Toribio de Mongrovejo. [orig. 1590].

Motolinía (Benavente), T. de. 1950. *History of the Indians of New Spain.* E. A. Foster, trans. (Documents and Narratives Concerning the Discovery and Conquest of Latin America, N.S., 4.) Berkeley: The Cortes Society [orig. ca. 1536–43].

Muller, J. 1966. *An Experimental Theory of Stylistic Analysis.* Ph.D. dissertation, Department of Anthropology, Harvard University.

Muller, J. 1976. Mississippian population and organization: Kincaid locality research, 1970–1975. MS. on file, Revised version in press with Illinois Archaeological Survey, Bulletin.

Muller, J. 1977. Individual variation in art styles, in J. N. Hill and J. Gunn, eds., *The Individual in Prehistory: Studies of Variability in Style in Prehistoric Technologies,* pp. 23–39. New York: Academic Press.

Muller, J. 1978a. The Kincaid system: Mississippian settlement in the environs of a large site, in B. Smith, ed., *Mississippian Settlement Patterns,* pp. 269–92. New York: Academic Press.

Muller, J. 1978b. The Southeast, in J. D. Jennings, ed., *Ancient native Americans,* pp. 280–325. San Francisco: W. H. Freeman.

Muller, J. 1979a. Structural studies of art styles, in J. M. Cordwell, ed., *The Visual Arts: Plastic and Graphic,* pp. 139–211. The Hague: Mouton.

Muller, J. 1979b. From the ridiculous to the sublime: Small sites in complex systems. Paper given at the 75th Annual Meeting, American Anthropological Association, Cincinnati.

Muller, J. 1983. The Southeast, in J. Jennings, ed., *Ancient North Americans,* pp. 373–419. San Francisco: W. H. Freeman.

Muller, J. 1984a. Mississippian Specialization and Salt. *American Antiquity* 49 (3): 489–501.

Muller, J. 1984b. Review of *Pre-Columbian Shell Engravings from the Craig Mound at Spiro Oklahoma* by P. Phillips and J. Brown. *American Antiquity* 49 (3): 669–70.

Muller, J. 1984c. Serpents and dancers: Art of the Mud Glyph Cave. MS. on file, Department of Anthropology, University of Tennessee.

Muller, J. and Stephens, J. E. n.d. Mississippian sociocultural adaptation. Ms.

Müller-Karpe, H. 1977. Zur altbronzezeitlichen Geschichte Europas.

Jahresbericht des Institut für Vorgeschichte der Universität Frankfurt a.M., Munich.

Müller-Karpe, H. 1980. *Handbuch der Vorgeschichte, Band IV, 1–3 Bronzezeit.* Munich: C. H. Bech.

Munksgård, E. 1974. *Oldtidsdragter.* Copenhagen.

Muñoz Amilibia, A. M. 1982. Poblado eneolítico del tip 'Los Millares' en Murcia, Espana. *XVI. Congreso Nacional de Arqueología, Murcia-Cartagena. Programa y Ponencias.* pp. 71–75.

Murra, J. V. 1960. Rite and crop in the Inca state, in S. Diamond, ed., *Culture in History,* pp. 393–407. New York: Columbia University Press.

Murra, J. V. 1962. Cloth and its functions in the Inka state. *American Anthropologist* 64: 710–28.

Murra, J. V. 1972. El control vertical de un máximo de pisas ecológicos en la economía de las sociedades andinas, in J. Murra, ed., *Visita de la Provincia de León de Huánuco, Tomo* 2, pp. 427–76. Huanuco, Peru, University of Hermilio Valdizan.

Murra, J. V. 1980. *The Economic Organization of the Inca State.* Greenwich CT: JAI Press [orig. 1956].

Murra, J. V. 1982. Public talk to the Department of Anthropology, University of California, Los Angeles, January.

Murra, J., and Morris, C. 1976. Dynastic oral tradition, administrative records and archaeology in the Andes. *World Archaeology* 7: 270–78.

Myer, W. E. 1928. Indian trails of the Southeast, in *Forty-second Annual Report of the Bureau of American Ethnology,* pp. 727–857. Washington: Government Printing Office.

Mylomas, G. 1972. *Ho taphikos kyklos B ton Mykinon.* 2 vols. Athens.

Nara Kyoiku Iinkai 1961. *Sakurai Chausuyama Kofun* [The Chausuyama Tomb, Sakurai]. Nara-ken Shiseki Meisho Tennen Kinenbutsu Chosa Hokoku, Vol. 19. Nara: Nara Kyoiku Iinkai.

Nelson, F. W. in press. Obsidian exchange networks in the Maya Lowlands, in T. H. Charlton, ed., *Models for Production and Exchange in Mesoamerica.* Provo, University of Utah Press.

Nelson, F. W., Sidrys, R. and Holmes, R. D. 1978. Trace element analysis by X-ray fluorescence of obsidian artifacts from Guatemala and Belize, in G. R. Willey, ed., *Excavations at Seibel, Department of Peten, Guatemala. Artifacts.* (Memoirs no. 14). Cambridge, MA: Peabody Museum.

Nicholson, H. B. 1971. Major sculpture in pre-Hispanic central Mexico, in G. Ekholm and I. Bernal, eds., *Archaeology of Northern Mesoamerica, Part 1,* pp. 92–134. (Handbook of Middle American Indians, Vol. 10.) Austin: University of Texas Press.

Nicholson, H. B. and Keber, E. 1983. *Art of Aztec Mexico: Treasures of Tenochtitlan.* Washington: National Gallery of Art.

Nicolaisen, J. 1962. Afrikanske Smede (African Smiths). *KUML.*

Nielsen, F. O. and Nielsen, P. O. in press. Middle and Late Neolithic Houses at Limesgård, Bornholm: A Preliminary Report. To appear in *Journal of Danish Archaeology,* vol. 4.

Nihon Rekishi Daijiten [Great Encyclopedia of Japanese History]. 1959. Tokyo, Kawade Shobo Shinsha.

Noguera, E. 1935. La Cerámica de Tenayuca y las excavaciones estratigráficas, in *Tenayuca,* pp. 141–201. México: Departamento de Monumentos Artísticos Arqueológicas e Históricas.

Nuñez Cabeça de Vaca, A. 1871. *Relation of Alvar Nuñez Cabeça de Vaca.* B. Smith, trans., New York. [Facsimile reprint of translation, March of America Facsimile Series, 9, Xerox]. [orig. 1542].

Oates, J. and Oates, D. 1976a. *The Rise of Civilization.* Oxford: Phaidon.

Oates, J. and Oates, D. 1976b. Early irrigation agriculture in Mesopotamia, in G. de G. Sieveking, I. H. Longworth and K. E.

Wilson, eds., *Problems in Economic and Social Archaeology*, pp. 109–35. London: G. Duckworth.

Offner, J. A. 1983. *Law and Politics in Aztec Texcoco*. Cambridge: Cambridge University Press.

Okita, M. 1980. Kofun jidai shukogyo no ichirei [One example of Kofun period crafts], in Kokubu Naoichi Hakase Koki Kinen Ronshu Hensan Iinkai ed., *Nihon Minzoku Bunka to Sono Shuhen: Kokohen*. Shimonoseki, Yamaguchi-ken, Shin Nihon Kyoiku Zusho Kabushiki Gaisha.

Oldeberg, A. 1942–43. *Metallteknik under förhistorisk tid I–II*. Lund.

Oldeberg, A. 1974. *Dei ältere Metallzeit in Schweden*. Stockholm.

Osaka Bunkazai Senta 1977. *Osaka-fu Bunkazai Bumpuzu* [Distribution maps of cultural properties in Osaka Prefecture]. Osaka, Osaka Bunkazai Senta.

Ostuka, H. and Kobayashi, S. eds., 1982. *Kofun Jiten* [Dictionary of Mounded Tombs]. Tokyo, Tokyodo.

Ota, A. 1955. *Nihon Jodai Shakai Soshiki no Kenkyu* [Research on the social structure of ancient Japan]. Tokyo, Homitsu Shobo.

Ottenjahn, H. 1969. *Die nordischen Vollgriffsschwerten der älteren und mittleren Bronzezeit*. Römisch–Germanischen Forschungen 30. Berlin: de Gruyter.

Paço, A. do, and Sangmeister, E. 1956. Vila Nova de São Pedro, eine befestigte Siedlung der Kupferzeit in Portugal. *Germania* 34: 211–30.

Page, J. S. 1959. *Estimator's General Construction Man-hour Manual*. Houston: Gulf Publishing Co.

Paine, R. 1974. *Second Thoughts About Barth's 'Models'*. (Occasional Paper No. 32). London: Royal Anthropological Institute.

Paine, R. 1976. Two modes of exchange and mediation, in B. Kapferer, ed., *Transaction and Meaning*, pp. 63–86 (ASA Essays in Social Anthropology. Vol. 1). Philadelphia: Institute for the Study of Human Issues.

Palerm, A. 1973. *Obras Hidráulicas Prehispánicas en el Sistema Lacustre del Valle de Mexico*. México: Instituto Nacional de Antropología e Historia.

Parsons, J. 1976a. *Prehispanic settlement patterns in the Upper Mantaro, Peru: a preliminary report of the 1975 field season*. Unpublished ms. submitted to the Instituto Nacional de Cultura, Lima and to the National Science Foundation, Washington, D.C.

Parsons, J. 1976b. The role of chinampa agriculture in the food supply of Aztec Tenochtitlan, in C. Cleland, ed., *Culture and Continuity*, pp. 233–62. New York: Academic Press.

Parsons, J. R., Brumfiel, E., Parsons, M. H. and Wilson, D. J. 1982. *Late Prehispanic Settlement Patterns in the Southern Valley of Mexico: The Chalco-Xochimilco Region*. (Memoirs, No. 14). Ann Arbor: The University of Michigan Musuem of Anthropology.

Parsons, J. and Hastings, C. 1977. *Prehispanic settlement patterns in the Upper Mantaro, Peru: a progress report for the 1976 field season*. Unpublished ms. submitted to the Instituto Nacional de Cultura, Lima and to the National Science Foundation, Washington, D.C.

Parsons, L. A. and Price, B. J. 1971. Mesoamerican Trade and its role in the emergence of civilization, in R. F. Heizer and J. A. Graham, eds., *Observations on the Emergence of Civilization in Mesoamerica* (Contributions to the University of California Archaeological Research Facility, no. 11), pp. 169–95. Berkeley.

Paso y Troncoso, F. del, ed. 1979. *Relaciones Geográficas de México*. México: Editorial Cosmos [orig. 1580].

Pasztory, E. 1983. *Aztec Art*. New York: Harry N. Adams.

Peebles, C. 1971. Moundville and surrounding sites: Some structural considerations for mortuary practices II. *Memoirs of the Society for American Archaeology* 25: 68–91.

Peebles, C. and Kus, S. M. 1977. Some archaeological correlates of ranked societies. *American Antiquity* 42: 421–48.

Perkins, D. 1969. Fauna of Çatal Hüyük. *Science* 164 (3876): 177–79.

Philippi, D. L. 1969. (trans.) *Kojiki*. Tokyo, University of Tokyo Press.

Phillips, P. and Brown, J. A. 1975. *Pre-Columbian Shell Engravings from the Craig Mound at Spiro, Oklahoma*. Cambridge: Peabody Museum.

Pielou, E. C. 1977. *Mathematical Ecology*. New York: John Wiley & Sons.

Piggott, S. 1983. *The Earliest Wheeled Transport: From the Atlantic Coast to the Caspian Sea*. London: Thames and Hudson.

Piña Chan, R. 1978. Commerce in the Yucatan peninsula: the Conquest and Colonial period, in T. A. Lee, Jr. and C. Navarrete, eds., *Mesoamerican Communication Routes and Cultural Contacts*. (Papers of the New World Archaeological Foundation, no. 40). Provo Utah: Brigham Young University.

Pingel, V. 1982. Zum Schatzfund vom Valcitran in Nordwestbulgarien. In *Südosteuropa zwischen 1600 und 1000 v. Chr*. Prähist. Arch. in Südosteuropa Band 1.

Plog, S. and Braun, D. P. 1984. Some issues in the archaeology of 'tribal' social systems. *American Antiquity* 49 (3): 619–25.

Polanyi, K. 1944. *The Great Transformation: The political and economic origins of our time*. New York: Rinehart.

Postgate, J. N. and Payne, S. 1975. Some Old Babylonian shepherds and their flocks. *Journal of Semitic Studies* 20: 1–21.

Powell, T. G. E. 1963. Some implications of Chariotry, in *Culture and Environment*. Essays in Honour of Sir Cyril Fox. London.

Prem, H. J., ed. 1974. *Matrícula de Huexotzinco*. Graz: Akademische Druck-u. Verlagsanstalt.

Price, B. J. 1977. Shifts in production and organization: A cluster-interaction model. *Current Anthropology* 18: 209–33.

Price, B. J. 1979. Turning state's evidence: Problems in the theory of state formation, in M. B. Leons and F. Rothstein, eds., *New Directions in Political Economy*, pp. 269–306. Westport, CT: Greenwood.

Primas, M. 1977. Zur Informationsausbreitung im südlichen Mitteleuropa. *Jahresbericht des Institut für Vorgeschichte der Universität Frankfurt a.M.*, Munich.

Rands, R. L. 1967. Ceramic technology and trade in the Palenque region, Mexico, in C. L. Riley and W. W. Taylor, eds., pp. 137–51. *American Historical Anthropology*. Carbondale, Southern Illinois University Press.

Rands, R. L. and Bishop, R. L. 1980. Resource procurement zones and patterns of ceramic exchange in the Palenque region, Mexico, in R. E. Fry, ed., *Models and Methods in Regional Exchange*, pp. 19–46. (SAA Papers No. 1). Washington: Society for American Archaeology.

Randsborg, K. 1967. 'Aegean' bronzes in a grave in Jutland. *Acta Arch*. 38: 1–27.

Randsborg, K. 1974. Social Stratification in Early Bronze Age Denmark – a Study in the Regulation of Cultural Systems. *Prähistorische Zeitschrift* 49: 38–61.

Rathje, W. L. 1971. The origin and development of lowland Classic Maya civilization. *American Antiquity* 36: 275–85.

Rathje, W. L. 1972. Praise the gods and pass the metates: A hypothesis of the development of lowland rainforest civilization in Middle America, in M. P. Leone, ed., *Contemporary Archaeology*, pp. 365–92. Carbondale: Illinois University Press.

Rathje, W. L. 1973. Classic Maya development and denouement: A research design, in T. P. Culbert, ed., *The Classic Maya Collapse*, pp. 405–54. (School of American Research Advanced Seminar Series). Albuquerque, University of New Mexico Press.

Rathje, W. L., Gregory, D. A. and Wiseman, F. M. 1978. Trade models and archaeological problems: Classic Maya examples, in T. A. Lee, Jr. and C. Navarrete, eds., *Mesoamerican Communication Routes and Cultural Contacts*. (Papers of the New World Archaeological Foundation, no. 40). Provo, Utah, Brigham Young University.

Redman, C. L. 1978. *The Rise of Civilization: From Early Farmers to Urban Society in the Ancient Near East*. San Francisco: W. H. Freeman.

Reed, C. 1969. A review of the archaeological evidence on animal domestication in the prehistoric Near East, in R. Braidwood and B. Howe, eds., *Prehistoric Investigation in Iraqi Kurdistan*, pp. 119–45. Chicago: University of Chicago.

Reina, R. E. and Hill, R. M., II. 1978. *The Traditional Pottery of Guatemala*. Austin, University of Texas Press.

Renfrew, C. 1969. Trade and culture process in European prehistory. *Current Anthropology* 10: 151–60.

Renfrew, C. 1972. *The Emergence of Civilization: The Cyclades and the Aegean in the third millennium B.C.* London: Methuen.

Renfrew, C. 1973. *Before Civilization*. New York: Knopf.

Renfrew, C. 1975. Trade as action at a distance: Questions of integration and communication, in J. A. Sabloff and C. C. Lamberg-Karlovsky, eds., *Ancient Civilization and Trade*, pp. 3–59. Albuquerque: University of New Mexico Press.

Renfrew, C. 1976. Megaliths, territories, and populations. *Dissertationes Archaeologicae Gandenses* 16: 198–220.

Renfrew, C. 1977. Alternative models for exchange and spatial distribution, in T. Earle and J. Ericson, eds., *Exchange Systems in Prehistory*, pp. 71–90. New York: Academic Press.

Rice, D. S. 1976. *The Historical Ecology of Lakes Yaxha and Sacnab, El Peten, Guatemala*. Ph.D. dissertation, Pennsylvania State University, State College.

Rice, D. S. 1986. The Peten Postclassic: a settlement perspective in J. A. Sabloff and E. W. Andrews V, eds., *Late Lowland Maya Civilization: Classic to Postclassic* (School of American Research Advances Seminar Series). Albuquerque, University of New Mexico Press.

Rice, D. S. and Rice, P. M. 1980. The northeast Peten revisited. *American Antiquity* 45 (3): 432–54.

Rice, D. S. and Rice, P. M. 1982. The Central Peten Historical Ecology Project. Final summary report, 1979, 1980, and 1981 seasons. Ms., files of the authors.

Rice, D. S. and Rice, P. M. 1984. Lessons from the Maya. *Latin American Research Review* 19 (3): 7–34.

Rice, P. M. 1981. Evolution of specialized pottery production: A trial model. *Current Anthropology* 22 (3): 219–40.

Rice, P. M. 1984. Obsidian procurement in the central Peten lakes region, Guatemala. *Journal of Field Archaeology* 11 (2): 181–94.

Rice, P. M. 1986a. Maya pottery techniques and technology. *Ceramics and Civilization* 1, American Ceramic Society.

Rice, P. M. 1986b. The Peten Postclassic: perspectives from the central Peten lakes, in J. A. Sabloff and E. W. Andrews V, eds., *Late Lowland Maya Civilization: Classic to Postclassic* (School of American Research Advanced Seminar Series). Albuquerque, University of New Mexico Press.

Rice, P. M., Michel, H. V., Asaro, F. and Stross, F. 1985. Provenience analysis of obsidian from the central Peten lake region, Guatemala. *American Antiquity* 50: 591–604.

Ripinsky, M. 1983. Camel ancestry and domestication in Egypt and the Sahara. *Archaeology* 36 (5): 21–27.

Ritzenthaler, R. and P. 1962. *Cameroons Village, an ethnography of the Bafut*. (Publications in Anthropology, 8). Milwaukee: Milwaukee Public Museum.

Robicsek, F. and Hales, R. 1981. *The Maya Book of the Dead. The Ceramic Codex*. Charlottesville, University of Virginia Museum.

Rojas, J. de. 1983. Los compradores en el mercado de Tenochtitlan. *Revista Español de Antropología Americana* XIII: 95–108.

Rounds, J. 1979. Lineage, class, and power in the Aztec state. *American Ethnologist* 6: 73–86.

Rowe, J. 1946. Inka culture at the time of the Spanish conquest. *Bureau of American Ethnology Bulletin* 143 (2): 183–330.

Rowlands, M. J. 1971. The archaeological interpretation of prehistoric metalworking. *World Archaeology* 3: 210–24.

Rowlands, M. J. 1979. Local and long distance trade and incipient state formation on the Bamenda Plateau in the late 19th century. *Paideuma* 25: 1–19.

Rowlands, M. J. 1980. Kinship, alliance and exchange in the European Bronze Age, in J. Barrett and R. Bradley, eds., *Settlement and Society in the British Later Bronze Age* (BAR British Series 83), pp. 15–55. Oxford: British Archaeological Reports.

Rowlands, M. J. 1984. Conceptualizing the European Bronze and Early Iron Age, in John Bintliff, ed., *European Social Evolution – Archaeological Perspectives*. University of Bradford.

Rowlands, M. J. 1985. Notes on the material symbolism of grass-fields palaces. *Paideuma* 31: 20–32.

Russell, G. and Hastorf, C. 1984. Stone Tools as a Measure of Agricultural Change in the Andes. Paper delivered at the 49th Annual Meeting of the Society for American Archaeology, Portland.

Sahagún, B. de. 1950–69. *Florentine Codex: General History of the Things of New Spain*. A. Anderson and C. Dibble, trans. 12 vols. Santa Fe: School of American Research [orig. 1577].

Sahlins, M. D. 1958. *Social Stratification in Polynesia*. (American Ethnological Society, Monograph 29). Seattle: University of Washington Press.

Sahlins, M. D. 1972. *Stone Age Economics*. Chicago: Aldine.

Sahlins, M. D. 1982. The apotheosis of Captain Cook, in M. Izard and P. Smith, eds., *Between Belief and Transgression*. Chicago, University of Chicago Press.

Saitta, D. J. 1983. On the evolution of 'tribal' social networks. *American Antiquity* 48 (4): 820–24.

Sakamoto, T. et al. eds., 1965. *Nihon Shoki Jo, Ka*. Volumes 1, 2. Tokyo, Iwanami Shoten.

Sanders, W. T. 1956. The Central Mexican symbiotic region, in G. R. Willey, ed., *Prehistoric Settlement Patterns in the New World*, pp. 115–27. (Viking Fund Publications in Anthropology, No. 23). New York: Wenner-Gren Foundation for Anthropological Research.

Sanders, W. T. 1965. *The Cultural Ecology of the Teotihuacan Valley*. Mimeographed, Department of Sociology and Anthropology. The Pennsylvania State University.

Sanders, W. T. 1968. Hydraulic agriculture, economic symbiosis and the evolution of states in central Mexico, in B. J. Meggers, ed., *Anthropological Archeology in the Americas*, pp. 88–107. Washington, D.C.: Anthropological Society of Washington.

Sanders, W. T. 1980. Comment, on Brumfiel's 'Specialization, market exchange, and the Aztec State: A view from Huexotla.' *Current Anthropology* 21: 474.

Sanders, W. T. 1984. Formative exchange systems: Comments, in K. G. Hirth, ed., *Trade and Exchange in Early Mesoamerica*, pp. 275–79. Albuquerque: University of New Mexico Press.

Sanders, W. T., Parsons, J. R. and Santley, R. S. 1979. *The Basin of Mexico: Ecological Processes in the Evolution of a Civilization*. New York: Academic Press.

Sanders, W. T. and Price, B. J. 1968. *Mesoamerica: The evolution of a civilization*. New York: Random House.

Sangmeister, E. 1976. Das Verhältniss der Glockenbecherkultur zu den einheimischen Kulturen der Iberischen Halbinsel, in J. N. Lanting and J. D. van der Waals, eds., *Glockenbecher Symposium Oberried 1974*, pp. 423–36. Bussum: Fibula-van Dishoeck.

Sangmeister, E. and Schubart, H. 1981. Zambujal: die Grabungen 1964 bis 1973. *Madrider Beiträge* 5 (1).

Santley, R. S. 1984. Obsidian exchange, economic stratification, and the evolution of complex society in the Basin of Mexico, in K. G. Hirth, ed., *Trade and Exchange in Early Mesoamerica*, pp. 43–86. Albuquerque: University of New Mexico Press.

Sasson, J. M. 1967. *Northmost Syria: a Survey of its Institutions Before Fall of Mari.* Ann Arbor: University of Michigan.

Savory, H. N. 1968. *Spain and Portugal: The Prehistory of the Iberian Peninsula.* London: Thames & Hudson.

Savory, H. N. 1972. The cultural sequence of Vila Nova de S. Pedro: a study of the section cut through the innermost rampart of the Chalcolithic castro in 1959. *Madrider Mitteilungen* 13: 21–37.

Schaedel, R. 1978. Early state of the Inkas, in H. Claessen and P. Skalnik, eds., *The Early State*, pp. 289–320. The Hague, Mouton.

Schauer, P. 1972. Frühe Griffzeugen Schwerten. *Jahrbuch des Römisch–Germanischen Zentralmuseums, Mainz.* pp. 39–44.

Schauer, P. 1972. Frühe Griffzeugen Schwerten. *Jahrbuch des Römisch–Germanischen Zentralmuseums, Mainz.* p. 39–44.

Schauer, P. 1984. Spuren minoisch–mykenischen Einflusses im atlantischen Westeuropa. *Jahrbuch des Römisch–Germanischen Zentralmuseums* 31.

Schneider, J. 1977. Was there a pre-capitalist world system? *Peasant Studies* 6: 20–29.

Scholes, F. V. and Adams, E. B., eds. 1958. *Sobre el Modo de Tributar los Indios de Nueva España a Su Magestad – 1561–1564.* (Documentos para la Historia del México Colonial, No. 5). México, Porrua [orig. 1561–64].

Schousbo, P.O. 1983. A Neolithic Vehicle from Klosterlund, Central Jutland. *Journal of Danish Archaeology*, vol. 2.

Schüle, W. 1967. Feldbewässerung in Alt-Europa. *Madrider Mitteilungen* 8: 79–99.

Schüle, W. 1980. *Orce und Galera: zwei Siedlungen aus dem 3. bis 1. Jahrtausend v. Chr. im Sudosten der Iberischen Halbinsel.* Mainz an Rhein: Verlag Philipp von Zabern.

Seeman, M. F. 1979. Feasting with the dead: Ohio Hopewell charnel house ritual as a context for redistribution, in D. S. Brose and N. Greber, eds., *Hopewell Archaeology: the Chillicothe Conference*, pp. 39–46. Kent, Ohio: Kent University Press.

Senda, M. 1980. Territorial possession in ancient Japan: The real and the perceived, in the Association of Japanese Geographers ed., *Geography of Japan.* Tokyo, Teikoku Shoin.

Service, E. R. 1958. *A Profile of Primitive Culture.* New York: Harper and Row.

Service, E. R. 1962. *Primitive Social Organization.* New York: Random House.

Service, E. R. 1975. *Origins of the State and Civilization.* New York: Norton.

Shafer, H. J. and Hester, T. R. 1983. Ancient Maya chert workshops in northern Belize, Central America. *American Antiquity* 48 (3): 519–43.

Shennan, Stephen. 1982a. Exchange and ranking: The role of amber in the earlier bronze age of Europe, in C. Renfrew and S. Shennan, eds., *Ranking, Resource and Exchange: Aspects of the Archaeology of Early European Society.* Pp. 33–45. Cambridge: Cambridge University Press.

Shennan, Stephen. 1982b. Ideology, change and the European early bronze age, in I. Hodder, ed., *Symbolic and Structural Archaeology*, pp. 155–61. Cambridge: Cambridge University Press.

Shennan, Susan. 1982. From minimal to moderate ranking, in C. Renfrew and S. Shennan, eds., *Ranking, Resource and Exchange: Aspects of the Archaeology of Early European Society*, pp. 27–32. Cambridge: Cambridge University Press.

Sherratt, A. 1976. Resources, technology and trade: An essay in early European metallurgy, in G. Sieveking, I. J. Longworth and K. E. Wilson, eds., *Problems in Economic and Social Archaeology*, pp. 557–81: London: Duckworth.

Sherratt, A. 1981. Plough and pastoralism: aspects of the second products revolution, in I. Hodder, G. Isaac and N. Hammond, eds., *Studies in Honor of David Clarke*, pp. 261–305. Cambridge: University Press.

Sherratt, A. 1983. The secondary exploitation of animals in the Old World. *World Archaeology* 15: 90–104.

Sidrys, R. 1976. Classic Maya obsidian trade. *American Antiquity* 41 (4): 449–64.

Sidrys, R. 1977. Mass-distance measures for the Maya obsidian trade, in T. Earle and J. Ericson, eds., *Exchange Systems in Prehistory*, pp. 91–107. New York: Academic Press.

Silva, C. T. da. 1971. O povoado pre-historico da Rotura: notas sobre a ceramica. *II. Congreso Nacional de Arqueologia, Coimbra 1970*, pp. 175–92.

Simonsen, J. 1983. A Late Neolithic House Site at Tastum, North-western Jutland. *Journal of Danish Archaeology*, vol. 2.

Simpson, K. 1983. *Settlement Patterns on the Margins of Mesopotamia: Stability and Change along the Middle Euphrates, Syria.* Ann Arbor: University Microfilms.

Siret, H. and Siret, L. 1887. *Les Premiers Ages du Metal dans le Sud-Est de l'Espagne.* Antwerp.

Siret, L. 1948. El tell de Almizaraque y sus problemas. *Cuadernos de Prehistoria Primitiva* 2: 117–24.

Smith, B. D. 1974. Middle Mississippian Exploitation of Animal Populations: a Predictive Model. *American Antiquity* 74: 274–91.

Smith, B. D., ed. 1978a. *Mississippian Settlement Patterns.* New York: Academic Press.

Smith, B. D. 1978b. Variation in Mississippian Settlement Patterns, in B. Smith, ed., *Mississippian Settlement Patterns*, pp. 479–503. New York: Academic Press.

Smith, C. A. 1976. Exchange systems and the spatial distribution of elites: The organization of stratification of agrarian societies, in C. A. Smith, ed., *Regional Analysis: Volume II, Social Systems*, pp. 309–74. New York: Academic Press.

Smith, J. R. 1950. *Tree Crops: A Permanent Agriculture.* New York: Devin-Adair Co.

Snodgrass, A. 1975. Mycenae, Northern Europe and radiocarbon dates. *Archaelogia Atlantica*, 1: 33–48.

Soustelle, J. 1961. *Daily Life of the Aztecs.* P. O'Brien, trans. Stanford: Stanford University Press.

Spence, M. W. 1985. Specialized production in rural Aztec society: Obsidian workshops of the Teotihuacan Valley, in W. J. Folan, ed., *Contributions to the Archaeology and Ethnohistory of Greater Mesoamerica*, pp. 76–125. Carbondale: Southern Illinois University Press.

Spencer, C. S. 1982. *The Cuicatlan Cañada and Monte Alban: A study of Primary State Formation.* New York: Academic Press.

Spindler, K. 1976. Die neolithische Parede-Gruppe in Mittelportual. *Madrider Mitteilungen* 17: 21–75.

Spindler, K. 1981. Cova da Moura. *Madrider Beiträge* 7.

Spindler, K. and Gallay, G. 1973. Die Tholos von Pai Mogo/Portugal. *Madrider Mitteilungen* 13: 38–108.

Sprockhoff, E. 1940. Altbronzezeitliches aus Neidersachsen, in *Studien zur Vor- und Frühgeschichte Carl Schuckhardt zum achtzigsten Geburtstag Dargebracht*, pp. 24–47. Berlin: de Gruyter

Stavenhagen, R. 1968. Seven fallacies about Latin America, in J. Petras and M. Zeitlin, eds., *Latin America: Reform or Revolution?* pp. 14–31. Greenwich, CT: Fawcett.

Steward, J. 1955. *Theory of Culture Change.* Urbana: University of Illinois Press.

Stoltman, J. B. 1978. Lithic artifacts from a complex society. The chipped stone tools from Becan, Campeche, Mexico. *Occasional Paper* 2: 1–30. New Orleans, Middle American Research Institute.

Stross, F. H., Hester, T. R., Heizer, R. F. and Jack, R. N. 1976. Chemical and archaeological studies of Mesoamerican obsidians, in R. E. Taylor, ed., *Advances in Obsidian Glass Studies, Archaeological and Geochemical Perspectives*, pp. 240–58. Park Ridge, NJ: Noyes Press.

Stross, F. H., Sheets, P., Asaro, F. and Michel, H. 1983. Precise characterization of Guatemalan obsidian sources, and source determination of artifacts from Quirigua. *American Antiquity* 48 (2): 323–46.

Struwe, K. W. 1971. *Die Bronzezeit Periode I–III*. Neumünster: Karl Wachholtz.

Swanton, J. R. 1928. Social Organization and Social Usages of the Indians of the Creek Confederacy, in *Forty-second Annual Report of the Bureau of American Ethnology*, pp. 23–472. Washington: Government Printing Office.

Swanton, J. R. 1946. The Indians of the Southeastern United States. *Bureau of American Ethnology, Bulletin* 137. Washington: Government Printing Office.

Sweet, L. 1965. Camel raiding of the North Arabian Bedouin: a mechanism of ecological adaptation. *American Anthropologist* 67: 1132–50.

Tanabe, S. 1966. *Suemura Koyoshigun I* [Ancient Kiln Sites of Suemura I]. Kyoto, Heian Gakuen Kokogaku Kurabu.

Tanabe, S. 1981. *Sueki Taikei* [Encyclopedia of Sue Ware]. Tokyo, Kadokawa Shoten.

Tardits, C. 1980. *Le Royaume Bamoum*. Paris, Librarie Armand Colin.

Tarradell Mateu, M. 1955. Ausgrabungen von Gar Cahal (Schwarze Höhle) in Spanisch Marokko. *Germani* 33: 13–23.

Taylor, W. 1972. *The Myceneans*. London: Thames & Hudson (4th impression).

Teramura, M. 1966. *Kodai Tamazukuri no Kenkyu* [Research on ancient bead-making]. Kokugakuin Daigaku Kokogaku Kenkyu Hokoku 3. Tokyo, Yoshikawa Kobunkan.

Teramura, M. 1980. *Kodai Tamazukuri Keiseishi no Kenkyu* [Research on the history of the bead-making industry]. Tokyo, Yoshikawa Kobunkan.

Terray, E. 1974. Long distance trade and the formation of the state. *Economy and Society*, 4.

Thompson, J. E. S. 1964. Trade relations between the Maya highlands and lowlands. *Estudios de Cultura Maya* 4: 13–49.

Thrane, H. 1962. Hjulgraven fra Storehøj ved Tobøl i Ribe amt (The wheel grave from Storehøj near Tobbøl, Ribe County). *KUML* pp. 80–113.

Thrane, H. 1977. Über Verbindungen zwischen Odergebiet in der Bronzezeit, besonders in Per. IV. *PAN Oddzial we Wroclawiu – Komisja Nauk Hamanistyc-zhych. Sekoja Archaeologiczna*.

Tilly, C. 1975. Food supply and public order in modern Europe, in C. Tilly, ed., *The Formation of National States in Western Europe*, pp. 380–455. Princeton: Princeton University Press.

Tosi, M. 1984. The notion of craft specialization and its representation in the archaeological record of early states in the Turanian basin, in M. Spriggs, ed., *Marxist Perspectives in Archaeology*, pp. 22–52. Cambridge: Cambridge University Press.

Tourtellot, G. 1978. Getting what comes unnaturally: on the energetics of Maya trade, in R. Sidrys, ed., *Papers on the Economy and Architecture of the Ancient Maya* (Monograph no. 8, Institute of Archaeology). Los Angeles, University of California.

Tourtellot, G. and Sabloff, J. A. 1972. Exchange systems among the ancient Maya. *American Antiquity* 37: 126–35.

Tovar, J. de. 1975. Códice Ramirez, in M. Orozco y Berra, ed., *Crónica Mexicana-Códice Ramirez*, pp. 9–92. México: Porrua [orig. 1583–87].

Townsend, R. F. 1979. *State and Cosmos in the Art of Tenochtitlan*. Washington: Dumbarton Oaks.

Trigger, B. 1974. The archaeology of government. *World Archaeology* 6: 95–106.

Tsunoda, R. and Goodrich, L. C. 1951. *Japan in the Chinese Dynastic Histories*. South Pasadena, P.D. and Ione Perkins.

Turney-High, H. H. 1949. *Primitive War: Its Practice and Concepts*. Columbia SC: University of South Carolina Press.

UCLA Ebla Conference 1983. Unpublished conference held at the University of California, G. B. Buccellati coordinator.

Uerpmann, H. P. 1979. Informe sobre los restos faunísticos del corte no. 1., in A. Arribas and F. Molina, eds., *El Poblado de 'Los Castillejos' en las Peñas de los Gitanos (Montefrío, Granada: Campaña de Excavaciones de 1971, el Corte Núm. 1*, pp. 153–68. Granada: Universidad de Granada.

US Army 1965. *U.S. Army Handbook for Syria*. Washington D.C.: Special Operations Research.

Vancouver, G. 1798. *A Voyage of Discovery to the North Pacific and Round the World*, Vol. 1. London: G. G. and J. Robinson.

Vander Leest, B. J. 1980. *The Ramey Field, Cahokia Surface Collection: A Functional Analysis of Spatial Structure*. Ph.D. dissertation, Department of Anthropology, The University of Wisconsin-Milwaukee.

Van der Leeuw, S. 1977. Towards a study of the economics of pottery making, in B. L. van Beek, R. W. Brandt and W. Greunman-van Waateringe, eds., *Ex Horreo, Cingyla* IV, pp. 68–76. Amsterdam: Albert Egges van Giffen Instituto de Pre- and Protohistory.

Vansina, J. 1984. Western Bantu Expansion. *Journal of African History* 25: 129–45.

Vargo, L. 1979. The *bemin* system in early Japan, in Nish and Dunn eds., *European Studies on Japan*. Tenterden, Kent, Paul Norbury Public.

Vilá Valentí, J. 1961. La lucha contra la sequía en el sureste de España. *Estudios Geográficos* 22: 25–44.

Vladar, J. 1973. Osteuropäische und Mediterrane Einflüsse in Gebiet der Slowakei während der Bronzezeit. *Slowenska Arch.* 21: 253–357.

Vulpe, A. 1977. Kritische Anmerkungen zu den karpatenlandischen Kulturerzeugnissen der Altbronzezeit. *Jahresbericht des Institut für Vorgeschichte der Universität Frankfurt a.M.*, Munich.

Wada, S. 1976. Kinai no iegata sekkan [House-shaped stone coffins of the Kinai region]. *Shirin* 59.3: 1–59.

Wada, S. 1983. Kofun jidai no sekko to sono gijutsu [Stone-working and its technology in the Kofun period]. *Hokuriku no Kokogaku* 26: 501–34.

Wada, S. in press. Political interpretations of stone coffin production in protohistoric Japan, in R. Pearson, et al, eds., *Windows on the Japanese Past: studies in archaeology*. Ann Arbor, Center for Japanese Studies.

Walker, M. 1977. The persistence of Upper Palaeolithic tool-kits into the early southeast Spanish Neolithic, in R. V. S. Wright, ed., *Stone Tools as Cultural Markers: Change, Evolution and Complexity*, pp. 354–79. Canberra: Australian Institute of Aboriginal Studies.

Walker, M. 1981. Climate, economy and culture change: the S. E. Spanish Copper Age, in J. García-Barcena and F. Sánchez-Martínez, eds., *Miscelánea, Union Internacional de Ciencias Prehistóricas, X. Congreso, México, D.F., Octubre 19–24, 1981*, pp. 171–97.

Wallerstein, I. 1974. *The Modern World-System: Capitalist Agriculture and the Origins of the European World Economy in the Sixteenth Century*. New York: Academic Press.

Wallis, W. and Roberts, H. V. 1956. *Statistics*. New York: Free Press.

Walthall, J. A. 1981. Galena and aboriginal trade in Eastern North America. *Illinois State Museum, Scientific Papers*, Vol. XVII.

Wanscher, O. 1980. *Sella Curules. The Folding Stool, an Ancient Symbol of Dignity*. Copenhagen.

Warnier, J. P. 1975. *Precolonial Mankon: the Development of a Cameroon Chiefdom in its Regional Setting.* Ph.D. dissertation, University of Pennsylvania, Philadelphia.

Warnier, J. P. 1983. *Sociologie du Bamenda pre-colonial.* Thèse de doctorat d'état, Université de Paris X.

Watson, P. J. and LeBlanc, S. 1973. Excavation and analysis of Halafian materials from southeast Turkey. Paper presented at the 72nd Annual Meeting of the American Anthropological Association, New Orleans.

Webb, M. C. 1973. The Peten Maya decline viewed in the perspective of state formation, in T. P. Culbert, ed., *The Classic Maya Collapse* (School of American Research Advanced Seminar Series), pp. 367–404. Albuquerque, University of New Mexico Press.

Webb, M. C. 1975. The flag follows trade: An essay in the necessary interaction of military and commercial factors in state formation, in J. A. Sabloff and C. C. Lamberg-Karlovsky, eds., *Ancient Civilization and Trade*, pp. 155–209. Albuquerque: University of New Mexico Press.

Wells, P. S. 1980. *Culture Contact and Culture Change: Early Iron Age Central Europe and the Mediterranean World.* Cambridge, Cambridge University Press.

Wheatley, P. 1971. *The Pivot of the Four Quarters.* Chicago: Aldine.

Wheatley, P. 1975. Satyanrta in Suvarnadvysa from reciprocity to redistribution in ancient Southeast Asia, in J. A. Sabloff and C. C. Lamberg-Karlovsky, eds., *Ancient Civilization and Trade*, pp. 227–83. Albuquerque: University of New Mexico Press.

Whittle, E. H. and Arnaud, J. M. 1975. Thermoluminescent dating of Neolithic and Chalcolithic pottery from sites in central Portugal. *Archaeometry* 17: 2–24.

Wilk, R. R. and Rathje, W. L. 1982. Household archaeology, in R. R. Wilk and W. L. Rathje, Archaeology of the household: Building a prehistory of domestic life. *American Behavioral Scientist* 25 (6): 617–39.

Willey, G. R. and Shimkin, D. B. 1973. The Maya Collapse: A summary view, in T. P. Culbert, eds., *The Classic Maya Collapse* (School of American Research Advanced Seminar Series), pp. 457–501. Albuquerque: University of New Mexico Press.

Wittfogel, K. 1957. *Oriental Despotism.* New Haven: Yale University Press.

Wolf, E. R. 1966. *Peasants.* Englewood Cliffs, NJ: Prentice-Hall.

Wolf, E. R. 1982. *Europe and the People Without History.* Berkeley: University of California Press.

Wright, H. T. 1969. *The Administration of Rural Production in an Early Mesopotamian Town* (Anthropological Papers, no. 38). Ann Arbor: The University of Michigan Museum of Anthropology.

Wright, H. T. 1972. A consideration of interregional exchange in Greater Mesopotamia: 4000–3000 B.C., in E. N. Wilmsen, ed., *Social Exchange and Interaction* (Anthropological Papers, no. 46), pp. 95–105. Ann Arbor: The University of Michigan Museum of Anthropology.

Wright, H. T. 1978. Towards an explanation of the origins of the state, in E. R. Service and R. Cohen, eds. *Origins of the State*, pp. 49–68. Philadelphia: Institute for the Study of Human Issues.

Wright, H. T. n.d. *The Susiana Hinterland during the Era of Primary State Formation.*

Wright, H. T. and Johnson, G. A. 1975. Population, exchange, and early state formation in Southwestern Iran. *American Anthropologist* 77: 267–89.

Wright, J. K. 1937. Some measures of distribution. *Annals of the Association of American Geographers* XXVII, No. 4: 197–211.

Yerkes, R. W. 1983. Microwear, microdrills, and Mississippian craft specialization. *American Antiquity* 48: 499–518.

Young, M. 1966. The divine kingship of the Jukun. *Africa* 36, 2: 135–52.

Zaccagnini, C. 1977. Pferde und Streitwagen in Zuzi, Bemerkungen zur Technologie. *Jahresbericht des Institut für Vorgeschichte der Universität Frankfurt a.M.*, Munich.

Zeitlin, R. N. 1979. *Prehistorical Long-Distance Exchange on the Southern Isthmus of Tehuantepec, Mexico.* Ph.D. dissertation, Department of Anthropology, Yale University.

Zeitlin, R. N. 1982. Toward a more comprehensive model of interregional commodity production. *American Antiquity* 42 (2): 260–75.

Zorita, A. de. 1963. *Life and Labor in Ancient Mexico.* B. Keen, trans. New Brunswick: Rutgers University Press [orig. 1566–70].

AUTHORS INDEX

SUBJECT INDEX

For EU product safety concerns, contact us at Calle de José Abascal, 56–1°,
28003 Madrid, Spain or eugpsr@cambridge.org.

www.ingramcontent.com/pod-product-compliance
Ingram Content Group UK Ltd.
Pitfield, Milton Keynes, MK11 3LW, UK
UKHW030905150625
459647UK00025B/2880